A WOMAN, A MAN, A NATION

Understanding Latin America demands dialogue, deep exploration, and frank discussion of key topics. Founded by Lyman L. Johnson in 1992 and edited since 2013 by Kris Lane, the Diálogos Series focuses on innovative scholarship in Latin American history and related fields. The series, the most successful of its type, includes specialist works accessible to a wide readership and a variety of thematic titles, all ideally suited for classroom adoption by university and college teachers.

Also available in the Diálogos Series:

*Staging Frontiers: The Creole Circus and the Making of Popular Culture,
    1810–1910* by William Garrett Acree Jr.
The Origins of Macho: Men and Masculinity in Colonial Mexico
    by Sonya Lipsett-Rivera
Mexico in the Time of Cholera by Donald Fithian Stevens
*Mexico City, 1808: Power, Sovereignty, and Silver in an Age of War and
    Revolution* by John Tutino
*Tides of Revolution: Information, Insurgencies, and the Crisis of Colonial Rule
    in Venezuela* by Cristina Soriano
Murder in Mérida, 1792: Violence, Factions, and the Law by Mark W. Lentz
Nuns Navigating the Spanish Empire by Sarah E. Owens
Sons of the Mexican Revolution: Miguel Alemán and His Generation
    by Ryan M. Alexander
The Pursuit of Ruins: Archaeology, History, and the Making of Modern Mexico
    by Christina Bueno
Creating Charismatic Bonds in Argentina: Letters to Juan and Eva Perón
    by Donna J. Guy

For additional titles in the Diálogos Series, please visit unmpress.com.

Jeffrey M. Shumway

A WOMAN · A MAN · A NATION

Mariquita Sánchez, Juan Manuel de Rosas,
and the Beginnings of Argentina

University of New Mexico Press Albuquerque

CONTENTS

ILLUSTRATIONS

ACKNOWLEDGMENTS

Books travel long and windy roads. While I am responsible for this manuscript's shortcomings, I express gratitude to many who have helped along the way. As always, I am indebted to Donna Guy for her years of mentoring, friendship, and encouragement, and for being a model scholar. Thank you, Donna, for your constant support, and for all you and Gary have done and continue to do for me and so many others.

At the University of New Mexico Press, I thank Clark Whitehorn, Lyman Johnson, and Kris Lane, as well as their staff, their patient copyeditors, and to the anonymous readers of the manuscript for their useful comments and advice. Asunción Lavrin, Susan Socolow, and Anne Twinam have also been sources of inspiration and encouragement. At Brigham Young University, many thanks are in order to Kendall Brown for his friendship, advice, and mentoring over many years, and for his expertise with images. Thanks also to Ignacio García, Shawn Miller, Evan Ward, and Richard Kimball for their support and encouragement, and to Matt Mason for connecting me with some parallels to US history. Chris Hodson also gave me a number of ideas that made their way into this book. Jeff Turley and Mac Wilson in BYU's Spanish department endured periodic e-mails asking for translation clarification. Our librarians Mark Grover and Matthew Hill also helped by acquiring useful materials. Dean Ben Ogles and history-department chairs Don Harreld and Shawn Miller supported me with timely leaves. I also could not have done this without Steven Wheelright, Phillip McArthur, James Tueller, and Ana Ka'anga's help in providing generous office space during a writing sabbatical at BYU-Hawaii. Parts of this book were presented at the Río de la Plata Seminar at William and Mary. Thanks to Fabricio Prado and the seminar participants for their helpful comments. Thanks also to Steven Hyland and other members of the Rocky Mountain Council for Latin American Studies, who over the years have also provided useful commentary at various stages of this project.

In Argentina, I could not have done this without the helpful staff at the Archivo General de la Nación (AGN) in Buenos Aires, as well as the staff at the Archivo Histórico de la Provincia de Buenos Aires, "Ricardo Levene" (AHPBA), in La Plata. The lovely images in this book are thanks to the staff of the Museo Histórico Nacional; to the staff at the Museo Nacional de Bellas Artes; to the staff of the Archivo General de la Nación; and to Marcela Fugardo of the Museo, Biblioteca y Archivo Histórico Municipal Dr. Horacio Beccar Varela.

Many thanks to Gabriel Di Meglio for his helpful suggestions for the manuscript, as well as to Ximena Espeche. María Sáenz Quesada very generously let me have access to her copies of primary-source materials then unavailable to researchers. Her work on Mariquita was also an inspiration. Dora Barrancos, Noemí Girbal-Blacha, Marta Goldberg, Silvia Mallo, José Luis Moreno, Noemí Goldman, and the late Jorge Gelman also offered support over my years traveling to Argentina. A special thanks to Daniel Gatica for being an encyclopedia of Argentine history. And to Ximena Martinez de Bishop and her parents, Susana Magdalena Gos and Rubén Morresi, many thanks for periodic help with translations and tracking down documents (and for hospitality in Patagonia). I am grateful to Guillermo Palombo, José María, and Juan Manuel Soaje Pinto for help with knowledge and sources about Mariquita Sánchez and Juan Manuel de Rosas. Fabián Alonso and Ana Laura Montani have also been extremely helpful.

My gratitude goes out to Osvaldo Barreneche for his years of friendship and scholarly example. Thanks to Osvaldo and his wife, María Celeste, and their children for their hospitality and for being a source of inspiration and knowledge of all things Argentine. As always, I am grateful to the Gatica, Madariaga, and Darias families for opening their homes and their hearts during my visits to Argentina.

Many students have helped in one way or another over the years. Sydney Sohler, Jorge Morales, Jenna Heywood, and T. J. Beal were especially helpful in the final stages. Thanks also to David Bates, Cole and Brady Witbeck, Matthew Harris, Joseph Kline, Shelby Abbott, Robert Christensen, Moose Bingham, James Greene, Tim Greenwood, Jared Hughes, Spencer McGhie, Mason Moody, Taylor Cozzens, Christopher Dabel, Leandro Soria, Samuel Dearden, Federico Rodriguez, Nathan Wertz, and Kevin Dickey, and to my students in my Latin American history courses.

I am grateful for the mentors of my more remote past, who patiently helped set me on the path of research and writing—Adele Johnson, Anne Ng, Alan Awaya, Suzanne Tanner, and Kathy Jacques (who first encouraged me in Spanish), among others at Kahuku High and Intermediate School. Paul Spickard, Lance Chase, Ken Baldridge, Greg Gubler, Joseph Spurrier, and Ken Wagner at BYU-Hawaii were also key in my development.

My family has also been a pillar of support. My parents, Eric and Carolyn, have always encouraged me, as have my siblings and my mother-in-law, Louine Shields. Nicolas Shumway is a wonderful uncle but also a model academic and generous friend, along with Robert Mayott. And to my children, Spencer (and Alexandra), Rick, Mikelle, Trevor, Aaron, Sarah, and Timothy, thanks for being a constant inspiration to me. And to my wife, Kathy, who has been with me on this journey every step of the way, thank you forever for your love and support.

A WOMAN, A MAN, A NATION

Mariquita and Juan Manuel

Mariquita Sánchez de Mendeville loved the city of Buenos Aires, which is precisely why it was so hard for her to leave it. In some ways, Mariquita felt like Buenos Aires was her city. In 1810 as a young newlywed, she and her husband, Martín, had helped Buenos Aires break free from the Spanish Empire and start down the path of independence and nation building in what would later become the nation of Argentina. But now twenty-seven years later, in 1837, life in Buenos Aires had become so oppressive that Mariquita felt compelled to leave. To make matters worse, one of her childhood friends was to blame for it all. Well, at least her one-time friend, Juan Manuel de Rosas.

Juan Manuel de Rosas first became governor of Buenos Aires in 1829, assuming office after years of instability and chronic civil wars in which previous governments failed repeatedly to establish legitimate authority.[1] Rosas excelled at implementing order and forging (or forcing) consensus, and by 1837 he was one of the most powerful leaders in South America. However, Juan Manuel's version of order, and his methods of imposing it, alienated his old friend Mariquita Sánchez to the point that she asked government authorities for her passport so she could sail across the river to Uruguay. When Governor Rosas got wind of her request, he took offense that such a close family friend was leaving the country. It was especially sensitive because Juan Manuel knew that Mariquita was leaving because of *him*. He sent Mariquita her passport, along with a note: "Why are your leaving, Mariquita?" Her response was short and to the point: "Because I'm scared of you, Juan Manuel."[2] Thus Mariquita departed into an exile that would last much of the next fifteen years, until 1852, when Juan Manuel was overthrown and exiled to England for the last twenty-five years of his life.

The lives of Mariquita Sánchez and Juan Manuel de Rosas corresponded with the major events and processes that shaped the beginnings of the Argentine nation, many of which also shaped Latin America and the Atlantic World in the nineteenth century. Mariquita and Juan Manuel lived during much of what scholars have called the "Age of Revolution." Between 1750 and 1850, fierce imperial competition combined with Enlightenment and revolutionary ideals to dismantle European empires in the Western Hemisphere and produce a host of republics in their place.[3] Argentina was one of those republics, a country that emerged only gradually and amid great conflict. Mariquita and Juan Manuel's home city and province of Buenos Aires played a pivotal and controversial role in the emergence of the Argentine nation, which would finally become a unified country in 1862.[4]

The narrative that follows takes a dual biographical approach in which the lives of Mariquita and Juan Manuel will serve as the guiding threads through the euphoric but also troubled beginnings of Argentina's national history. Those threads are spun from letters, diaries, memoirs, newspapers, literature, and official correspondence, among other sources. While the threads of Mariquita's and Juan Manuel's lives may be the most visible, their strands will be joined by other bright and bold figures whose lives contributed to the rich tapestry of early Argentine history, including local residents, visitors, invaders, diplomats, and merchants who passed through Buenos Aires—a bustling hub of the South Atlantic World.

This book is not, and cannot be, a full biography of Mariquita and Juan Manuel. Instead, it takes an approach that places Mariquita's life alongside Juan Manuel's and then examines what comes into focus—what issues and events touched both of them. Examined alone, either life would produce a different result. Therefore, in this dual biographical approach, certain topics receive more attention while other worthy topics suffer. Despite some drawbacks, examining Mariquita's and Juan Manuel's lives together produces a fascinating and instructive perspective on the beginnings of Argentina, as well as on the larger historical contexts of their time. Along the way, certain larger themes emerge more clearly than others. Mariquita's story is in part the story of the role of women in the republic, which for Mariquita and many of her cohorts was a topic of utmost importance. Mariquita was a prominent actor in the political and cultural milieu of Buenos Aires, who, while fiercely patriotic, also embraced innovative ideas from foreign cultures. She surely is a forerunner to feminist movements that emerged in Argentina after her death.[5] And while

Juan Manuel was by no means an advocate of increasing women's rights, he was nevertheless surrounded by powerful women, including his mother, his wife, his daughter, and of course, Mariquita Sánchez. These women, among others, exerted enormous influence in their own right, both on Juan Manuel and on Buenos Aires society.

Friends and observers sometimes compared Mariquita to the famed Parisian Madame de Stael, who shaped public opinion and politics through her influential salon. Indeed, as Mariquita hosted her own salon in Buenos Aires, she saw herself as part of a larger community of progressive thinkers in the Atlantic World, thinkers who, as Claude Miliscent wrote in his St. Domingue newspaper in 1792, believed that "the true philosopher was a cosmopolitan, the friend of all men from whatever country." Like Miliscent and other like-minded thinkers in Europe and the Americas, Mariquita felt linked to a common humanity not bound by artificial national borders.[6]

Looking at Mariquita and Juan Manuel together also leads to the examination of the storied role of the Spanish American strong men, known traditionally as *caudillos*, who came to power after most of Spain's American colonies had achieved independence in the 1810s and 1820s. Most Spanish American countries failed to establish stable republics after independence, and authoritarian leaders stepped into the void.[7] For example, Rosas's time in power roughly follows the career of Antonio López de Santa Anna of Mexico, who was in and out of the presidency numerous times between 1833 and 1855, during which time Mexico suffered various foreign interventions and lost more than half of its territory in a war with the United States of America. Like Rosas, Santa Anna was a large landowner with a strong base of support in his home region.[8] But Spanish American caudillos also had a type of parallel further north as well. American diplomats who knew Juan Manuel de Rosas compared him to perhaps the closest thing the United States had to a caudillo president—Andrew Jackson, who, like Rosas, also took office in 1829. Just as Rosas did, Andrew Jackson made his name fighting indigenous tribes and foreigners. Both pushed frontier expansion, and Rosas and Jackson also became icons of a kind of frontier masculinity.[9] Rosas and Jackson, for some observers, are also symbols of popular democracy. Consistent with the magnitude of their careers and legacy, Rosas and Jackson have inspired generations of historians who continue to debate the merits and demerits of these iconic leaders.[10]

The image of the caudillo has gone through extensive revision in recent years, particularly in Argentina. The view of Juan Manuel de Rosas as a quasi-omnipotent caudillo on horseback who ran his country like one of his large estates has given way to a more complex figure—that of a leader who worked frequently within old and new social and governmental structures.[11] Without excusing his numerous excesses, the image of Rosas that emerges in the pages that follow is one of nuance. Juan Manuel de Rosas navigated complex cultural and political worlds and attempted to create consensus where previous administrations could not. In Buenos Aires, city and province, he worked frequently within established social and political parameters to build support among popular and elite classes, as well as with indigenous tribes, while at the same time establishing pacts and confederations among various provinces. His emphasis on gaining popular support showed that he recognized the power of popular groups, and of popular opinion, in the Río de la Plata region and beyond.[12] In fact, it could be said that Juan Manuel and Mariquita each contributed in their own ways to the shaping of public opinion, a process that became more important and pronounced as the nineteenth century progressed.[13]

Nuances aside, Juan Manuel de Rosas was part of a hemispheric context where various societies and leaders opted for authoritarian solutions to the challenges of nation building, whether it was Santa Anna in Mexico, Dr. Francia in Paraguay, or Simón Bolívar in Venezuela, among others.[14] Speaking of Simón Bolívar, he appears periodically in this narrative as a kind of hemispheric touchstone of revolutionary activity. Bolívar was a key player in the liberation movements against Spain, and a number of prominent Argentines served under his command at one time or another. In addition, Bolívar's political and intellectual experiences expose key problems and issues that were relevant not only to his sphere of action, but also to the rest of the Americas down to the Río de la Plata region. And finally, Bolívar was a keen observer of hemispheric events, including in Argentina. In short, Bolívar's occasional appearances in these pages is a reminder that, although Buenos Aires lies at the end of the world from some perspectives, it was nevertheless well connected to people, places, and processes across the hemisphere and beyond.[15]

The role of foreign influence in shaping Argentine society—and challenging its sovereignty—is another issue that frequently comes into focus when examining Mariquita and Juan Manuel together. Mariquita's and Juan Manuel's lives were both buffeted and enriched by foreign influences, as was the development and identity of their emerging nation. Rosas, as a provincial and national leader, had pragmatic political and economic concerns as he interacted with foreign powers, and many times politics and economics were inseparably linked. Mariquita, meanwhile, admired and embraced foreign ideas and cultures. Her second husband, the Frenchman Jean Baptiste de Mendeville, became the French consul in Buenos Aires in 1828, which pulled Mariquita directly into the world of international relations. As it happened, Argentine-French relations were turbulent during much of Governor Rosas's rule, in part because of intense international competition for influence in Argentina. Decades before the European "scramble for Africa" in the late nineteenth century, there was a type of European scramble for Latin America after Spain lost its American colonies to independence. Mexico lost the most—ceding half of its territory to the United States after the Mexican-American War in 1848. Argentina lost some territory as well when, in 1833, Great Britain occupied the Malvinas Islands (Falklands to them) in the South Atlantic, which belonged to Argentina (and to Spain in the colonial era). While such territorial conquest was not the norm, England and other major European powers, along with the USA, sought to gain wealth, power, and cultural influence in Argentina throughout the nineteenth century.[16] In Argentina, foreign intervention and foreign culture were welcomed by some and shunned by others, sometimes depending on the political expediency of the moment. As will be seen, Mariquita and Juan Manuel were caught in the cross hairs of all of these processes, many times on opposite sides.

Sometimes Mariquita's and Juan Manuel's stories touch on an event or an issue that in turn illuminates networks of relationships that extend beyond Argentina into the Atlantic World. History does not happen neatly within the borders of kingdoms, empires, or nations. Transnational forces were frequently at work in shaping Argentina. To mention just one brief example, Mariquita's first husband, Martín Thompson, traveled as an envoy of Buenos Aires to the United States of America in 1816 to seek support for Argentina's independence movement, leaving Mariquita and their children for four long years. Understanding the impact of Martín's mission on his country, and on his and Mariquita's family, calls for a discussion of the high-stakes games of international politics, and the enormous pressures they exerted on individuals and nations during Spanish America's quest for independence. While this and other examples might at times seem like tangents, they can also be viewed as stories that light up hemispheric and global connections and networks that

intersected in Mariquita's and Juan Manuel's lives, and in the life of the fledgling Argentine nation.

The vortex of forces swirling around Latin American independence and
early nation building also highlights the uncertainties, or the contingencies,
of history. Looking back from the twenty-first century, it might be easy to
connect the dots and see a logical, and maybe even an inevitable, development
of the Argentine nation. The lived experience of the historical actors, however, was different. At every turn they faced unexpected twists and unintended
consequences of their own and others' actions. In hindsight, Juan Manuel de
Rosas's long rule may appear stable, and his power assured. However, when
Mariquita Sánchez left for exile to Uruguay in 1837, she was confident that
Rosas would soon be overthrown, and that she would return quickly to her
lovely home in Buenos Aires. Governor Rosas, meanwhile, far from enjoying
a sense of stability and security, felt threatened constantly from every quarter.
To understand how Mariquita and Juan Manuel experienced their history is,
in part, to understand the uncertainties of developing events.[17]

The narrative approach taken in this book will be attentive to this contin-
gent nature of history, letting events unfold as the historical actors experienced
them. At times, the text includes historical background designed to provide
readers with a foundation to understand decisions that Mariquita and Juan
Manuel make, sometimes in future chapters. Occasionally I will point out the
purpose of these background sections, although I try to keep this limited.
Similarly, I do not provide the reader with a detailed rubric on how to interpret
the lives of Mariquita and Juan Manuel, preferring instead to allow readers
to interpret from the narrative. Readers may find it helpful to first read the
glossary of terms located at the back of the book, which is designed to provide
useful context for the narrative (see p. 267).

Before moving forward, it is useful to understand that Mariquita Sánchez
and many of her friends embraced the ideas of Romanticism that spread across
much of the Western world in the early 1800s.[18] Romanticism was a lifestyle
choice that emphasized emotion and passion, and its adherents relished the
highs and lows of life and, significantly, captured many of their thoughts in
writing, whether in poems or in personal correspondence. In her middle-age
years, Mariquita became close with one of her son's friends, Esteban Echeverría, who traveled to Europe in the early 1830s and became enamored by
the Romantic Movement, which he helped bring back to the Río de la Plata

region. Esteban Echeverría, Mariquita Sánchez, and their fellow *porteño* Romantics were joined by others from Buenos Aires to Bogotá and beyond. Thus, if Mariquita's words sometimes seem overly dramatic, it is a reminder of her membership in a community of Romantics that spanned the Atlantic World and included the likes of Victor Hugo, who happened to be one of Mariquita's favorite authors.

Also before continuing, a note on usage of names is important. I will often use first names, Mariquita and Juan Manuel, to refer to our two main protagonists in part because I hope to bring the reader as close to the subjects as possible. Moreover, Mariquita had various names and nicknames throughout her life. She also had a number of surnames, including that of her father (Sánchez), her first husband (Thompson), and her second husband (Mendeville). And while she is referred to at times by those surnames, she is commonly known in Argentine history, distinguishingly and endearingly, as Mariquita—including in the last two biographies of her, written by María Sáenz Quesada and Graciela Batticuore. Therefore, to remain consistent with usage in Argentina, I will usually refer to her as Mariquita.

I will attempt to present roughly the same amount of material on Mariquita and Juan Manuel, although source availability creates certain ebbs and flows between them. There is also an imbalance in what historians have written on Mariquita and Juan Manuel. Both have sparked discussion among historians, but scholars have written much more about Juan Manuel, and his legacy is much more controversial. Indeed, Juan Manuel de Rosas is one of the most polemical figures in Argentine history.[19] The last major biography of him in English was John Lynch's 1982 masterpiece, *Argentine Dictator* (republished in an abridged edition in 2001).[20] What follows here is a new approach to Juan Manuel de Rosas based on fresh looks at old primary and secondary sources, and also based on recent research from Argentina and elsewhere.

Regarding Mariquita, little has been published on her in English.[21] With a few exceptions, when she does appear in English, it is frequently from her account of the 1806 English invasion of Buenos Aires. In Spanish, she has received consistent, though not voluminous, attention from scholars since the early twentieth century, although her legacy does not spark the controversy of her friend Juan Manuel. Mariquita's role in nineteenth-century Argentine society, including the role of women in general, is a significant theme of her story. Her multifaceted identities of patriotic *porteña* who nevertheless embraced foreign ideas and was married to a French consul also offer a variety of possible interpretations of her significance in Argentine history.[22]

The parallel lives of Mariquita and Juan Manuel also allow for an examination of many of the divisions that plagued Argentine society in the nineteenth century and continue to influence the country today. They both reflect, in their own ways, views from their time regarding issues of race, class, gender, and political ideology. And in some ways, they both could fit into the competing lines of historical thought in Argentine society, namely the ideological divides between the liberals and conservatives in their various incarnations. Juan Manuel fits prominently in these debates, and Mariquita could be inserted into them as well. However, the narrative that follows will show that Mariquita and Juan Manuel do not always fit neatly into these or other categories that historians have imposed on them over the last many decades.[23]

The various chapters of the book follow the basic chronology of Mariquita's and Juan Manuel's lives, with some exceptions made for thematic unity. Chapters 1 and 2 cover what life was like for them growing up during the late colonial period (including why Juan Manuel changed the spelling of his last name). Chapter 3 covers the monumental English invasions of 1806 and 1807, in which both Mariquita and Juan Manuel participated. Chapter 4 examines Buenos Aires in the global context of revolutions, with a highlight on Mariquita's literary salon that she hosted in her home from the early 1800s to the 1830s. Chapters 5, 6, and 7 speak of the struggle to form an independent country, including the enormous international pressures exerted on Argentina and on Mariquita's family in particular. These chapters also touch on the struggle to organize the Argentine nation, the independence wars, and early nation building. Chapters 8, 9, 10, and 11 cover Juan Manuel's rise to power and the attempts to dislodge him (something Mariquita wished for dearly), including major foreign interventions. Chapter 12 deals with Juan Manuel's fall from power, his exile in England, Mariquita's return to Buenos Aires, and Argentina's continuing struggle toward unification. The epilogue examines briefly how Mariquita and Juan Manuel have lived on in the history, culture, and imagination of Argentina up to the modern day.

It is not my intention with this book to instruct Argentines in their own history. I will be gratified if Argentines find some use for it, but this book is intended largely for a non-Argentine audience who have had little exposure to Mariquita Sánchez or to the recent scholarship on Juan Manuel de Rosas.

Nor is it my purpose to exalt or condemn Mariquita or Juan Manuel. I hope to understand them on their own terms, as much as is possible. If Mariquita and Juan Manuel were somehow able to read these pages today, my hope is that they would recognize at least part of themselves in the narrative.[24] In the end, I hope the reader will feel a bit closer to Mariquita and Juan Manuel, two friends torn apart by the struggles of Argentina's beginnings.

The Colonial Background: On the Fringe of an Empire, at the End of the World

The history of Mariquita and Juan Manuel's Buenos Aires was part of a long history of the expansion of Spain's New World Empire, the expansion of Europe, and the rise of global empires.[25] After Columbus established the Spaniards in the Caribbean, other Spanish explorers and conquerors set out in search of wealth, and for a water passage through the new continents. In 1516, Juan de Solís found what he called the Mar Dulce (Sweet Sea or Freshwater Sea) near modern-day Uruguay, not knowing it was in reality a massive estuary of the Paraná and Uruguay river systems, whose headwaters came from as far north as Paraguay and Brazil. Captain Solís did not get far. He was soon killed by warriors of the Charrúa tribe. A few years later, Sebastian Cabot sailed hundreds of miles up the Mar Dulce river system, reaching modern-day Paraguay. There, to Cabot's delight, he found Natives who possessed objects made of silver, inspiring him to give the river a new name, the Río de la Plata (River of Silver or River Plate), a name that reflected his hope that the river was a gateway to riches.[26]

Second Time's the Charm: The Two Foundings of Buenos Aires, 1536 and 1580

Encouraged by positive reports about the "River of Silver" region, Spanish settlers led by Pedro de Mendoza founded a settlement at the mouth of the Río de la Plata in 1536, which they called "Santa María del Buen Aire" (Saint Mary of the Good Air). As with Captain Solís twenty years before, however, the Spaniards soon faced stiff resistance from indigenous peoples defending their homelands. This time, warriors from the Querandí tribe besieged and attacked the settlement before it could take root, reducing its European inhabitants to starvation and cannibalism.[27] The Spaniards abandoned the town and moved upriver, more than eight hundred miles, where they founded the city of Asunción in 1537. Over the next forty years, the Spaniards gradually pushed southward, founding cities as they went. In 1580, Juan de Garay led a second founding of Buenos Aires. For good measure, and perhaps in hopes of more divine protection this time around, Garay added a new component to the city's original name. It was now officially called the "Ciudad de la Santísima Trinidad y Puerto de Santa María del Buen Aire" (City of the Holy Trinity and Port of Saint Mary of the Good Air). From then on, the city would be known simply as Buenos Aires, and its inhabitants were called *porteños* (people from the port city of Buenos Aires and its surrounding region). Three hundred settlers officially founded Buenos Aires with Juan de Garay in 1580. By 1620 there were one thousand inhabitants in Buenos Aires. In the early 1700s, the population had increased to roughly fifteen thousand, and by 1806 it stood at nearly forty thousand.[28]

Many of Juan Manuel de Rosas's ancestors came to Buenos Aires during the late 1600s and early 1700s, largely from the northern regions of Spain, such as Burgos and Cantabria.[29] Some of Mariquita's ancestors on her mother's side came out of Spain's northwestern region of Galicia, an area of Spain originally settled by Celtic tribes centuries earlier, complete with bagpipes and all. Each region of Spain had its own culture and identity, and in some parts, even their own language. Catalans from Barcelona, Basques from northern Spain, Galicians from the Northwest, and others all brought their regional identities with them to the New World and would frequently join religious groups and militia units based on their regional Spanish identity.

Conquerors and colonizers of Argentina also brought African slaves with them. Over the course of the colonial period, tens of thousands of Africans were brought forcibly to the Río de la Plata's shores. By 1800, roughly 25 percent of Buenos Aires had full or partial African ancestry. Porteños of all races used a variety of racial terminologies when it came to African-descended peoples. The terms *negro* ("black" in Spanish) and *moreno* usually denoted pure African blood (and likely slave status), while *mulato* and *pardo* referred to African-descended peoples of mixed ancestry.[30] Visitors to Buenos Aires or Montevideo could not help but notice slaves and free blacks working as skilled laborers and artisans, or serving as soldiers in the local militias. African-descended populations in Buenos Aires and beyond also developed vibrant social and

MAP 1.1. Map of the Argentine Confederation in the Era of Rosas, circa 1840. Courtesy of Think Spatial, Geography Department, Brigham Young University.

cultural organizations that helped support their various communities (sometimes called "nations").[31] Few Indians lived in the city of Buenos Aires—less than 1 percent. Many of the indigenous tribes of the Pampas vigorously defended their homelands in a struggle with Hispanic settlers and government officials that lasted into the twentieth century and continues today.[32]

European settlers engaged in agriculture, cattle raising, cottage industries, and smuggling. The fertile Pampas provided rich land for a variety of crops, as well as for large herds of wild cattle, which the settlers periodically rounded up and slaughtered for their hides and tallow. As the city grew, porteños sought out commercial opportunities wherever they could find them—both legal and illegal. Spanish regulations mandated that all trade from Buenos Aires and its surrounding hinterlands go to Upper Peru (modern-day Bolivia), then over the Andes mountains to Lima, up to Panama, then to Cuba, and finally to Spain. The return route for merchandise was supposed to be the same. All this was part of a complex royal administration through which the monarchs of Spain tried to balance the various interest groups of the kingdom, from noble to merchant to peasant. Monopoly was the Spanish crown's way of giving everyone the protection they needed and the things they deserved, based on their social class.[33] The inefficiencies of the monopoly system were obvious to porteños who lived in a port facing the Atlantic Ocean, and thus smuggling was an integral part of the porteño economy from the earliest years of the city's history. Even royal officials could turn a blind eye to foreign merchant ships docking in Buenos Aires for "repairs" but leaving with a new cargo of hides.[34]

Buenos Aires was also a key component of Spain's imperial defense system. It was the bottom link in a chain of cities that extended north to Asunción and into Upper Peru, and finally to Lima, the capital of the Viceroyalty of Peru. This line was meant in part to keep the Portuguese from encroaching on Spanish territory from their base in Brazil.[35] Spanish and Portuguese soldiers and settlers struggled over lands to the east of Asunción, where Jesuit missionaries built prosperous missions among the indigenous Guaraní tribes.[36] Further south, just across the river from Buenos Aires, Spain and Portugal also fought for control of the Banda Oriental, the fertile "eastern bank" of the Río de la Plata and Uruguay Rivers (modern-day Uruguay). From the sixteenth to the early nineteenth century, the *orientales* (easterners) would live alternately under Spanish or Portuguese rule depending on who had the upper hand at the moment.[37] In addition to Portuguese threats, English ships prowled the coasts south of Buenos Aires, seeing it as "res nullius," or land without an owner, and thus open to whoever could lay claim to it. In 1578, for instance, Sir Francis Drake of England sailed by the Río de la Plata, then continued south to the Strait of Magellan, a voyage that raised Spanish fears over English intentions in South America. Over the next many years, English freebooters as well as scientific explorers traveled through the region as well. To Spanish eyes, the eastern and southern flank of their empire seemed under steady threat.

These and other incursions convinced Spanish reformers that something needed to be done about the empire's vulnerable edges. To help administer its New World territories, the Spanish crown had long before created viceroyalties (vice-kingships) in Mexico City and in Lima, Peru, each governed by a viceroy (vice-king) who represented royal authority in the Americas. But Lima, which had authority over Buenos Aires, was simply too far away to effectively meet the challenges along the frontiers in the Río de la Plata region, not to mention Patagonia, the name given to the southern end of the continent after Magellan's crew sailed through in 1520. So crown officials decided, in 1776, to split the viceroyalty of Peru and make Buenos Aires the capital of a new jurisdiction: the Viceroyalty of the Río de la Plata.

This was part of a series of changes in the empire known as the Bourbon Reforms, named for the governing royal family of Spain in the eighteenth century. The reforms aimed to strengthen and streamline the empire with modern political, economic, and social policies.[38] Reformers also solidified the boundaries of their empire by signing the Treaty of Madrid with Portugal in 1750, but Spain and Portugal would continue to fight over the Eastern Shore of the Río de la Plata into the early 1800s—conflicts that would have direct impact on the lives of Mariquita and Juan Manuel. In short, the Bourbon Reforms sought to protect, populate, and develop the edges of the Spanish Empire. Making Buenos Aires the capital of a new viceroyalty fit right into Spain's plans.

Beginning in 1776, Buenos Aires governed a massive territory that included most of modern-day Bolivia, Paraguay, Argentina, and Uruguay. Buenos Aires's new status made it equal to the great urban and administrative centers of Mexico City, Lima, and Bogotá. Because Upper Peru (modern-day Bolivia) now belonged to Buenos Aires, after 1776 the riches of Upper Peru's fabulous silver mines, instead of going to Lima, now headed southeast to Buenos Aires on their way to Europe, stimulating various parts of the economy as they went. Spanish reformers hoped the new viceroyalty, infused with new wealth, would invigorate the region's development and protect the Spanish Empire's southern frontier against threats from Portugal and other European powers.[39] Crown policies did indeed promote economic growth, as seen in part by the intense demand for slaves. Seventy thousand Africans arrived in the Río de la Plata region between 1770 and 1812.[40]

To defend the Spanish Empire also meant to populate it. In 1778, for example, an expedition left Buenos Aires to found a settlement called Carmen de Patagones at the mouth of the Río Negro, some six hundred miles south of Buenos Aires on the Atlantic coast. While the settlement was meant in part to deter European encroachment, local tribes proved to be a more immediate threat.[41] Indigenous groups in the Río de la Plata region had resisted Spanish advances since the early 1500s, killing a number of early explorers and settlers, including Captain Juan Solís and Buenos Aires founder Juan de Garay. Native resistance persisted throughout the colonial period and into the nineteenth century. Nevertheless, alliances were sometimes forged between Spaniards and Indians along the frontiers. "Friendly Indians," as they were called, frequented frontier outposts and taverns where they developed relations—trading and otherwise—with Hispanic settlers. Soon, a growing mestizo (mixed-race) population emerged.

While some tribes agreed to negotiate and trade, others defended their homelands with skill and determination. The indigenous tribes of the Pampas had their own complex internal dynamics as new tribes moved in and displaced or absorbed older ones. This was especially true when groups of Mapuche Indians—also called Araucanians—came from Chile, over the Andes, and into the Pampas region in the eighteenth and nineteenth centuries. They brought their language with them, and their skills as fighters, as well as the ability to organize powerful tribal confederations.[42] Masters of the horse and lance, the indigenous peoples were formidable opponents to Hispanic settlers.

Conflicts between Natives and Hispanic settlers were common along the frontier. The government in Buenos Aires built lines of forts and manned them with soldiers, but the area controlled by Buenos Aires did not extend much beyond the port city. Indigenous tribes often raided within a few miles of Buenos Aires itself, making off with cattle, horses, and human captives, particularly women. For Spaniards, the image of the white woman captured by Natives was a powerful metaphor of the struggle between what they saw as Hispanic civilization against Native barbarism. At the taverns and in the village markets, news about the latest raid and kidnapping were common topics. Like their counterparts in North America, settlers who pushed further into the frontier ran a greater risk of being attacked by indigenous groups defending their lands.

No one knew that better than Clemente López de Osornio, a talented militia commander and ambitious estanciero (rancher) from Buenos Aires.[43] Since the 1760s, Clemente had pushed his ranching activities into the Indian frontier, to lands more than a hundred miles southeast of Buenos Aires along the Salado River, near to where it empties into the Río de la Plata (see map 1.1 on p. 11). Clemente's military and ranching careers shaped him into a seasoned and successful Indian fighter. However, his choice to run cattle in Indian-controlled territory put him in chronic danger. One day in 1783 a band of indigenous warriors got the better of him and his son, killing both of them and leaving their bodies strewn on the Pampas. Clemente would never know his grandson, Juan Manuel de Rozas, born just ten years after his death, or his grandson's neighbor, a young girl by the name of Mariquita Sánchez.

CHAPTER ONE

Growing Up in the Viceroyalty of Buenos Aires

The good news arrived at 2:00 a.m. on the morning of March 20, 1793—a son had come to Agustina Teresa López and León Ortiz de Rozas. The family's servants and slaves quickly spread the message around the neighborhood, perhaps with a bit more excitement than normal because this was the firstborn son of the family. Later that very day, León and Agustina had their new child baptized. The priest carefully recorded the event on thick paper. He included numerous details that, at first glance, might appear tedious. However, a closer look at the handwritten record reveals key beliefs and principles that ordered Hispanic society:

> In the city of The Holy Trinity, the Port of Saint Mary of Buenos Aires, on the thirtieth day of the month of March of seventeen ninety-three, I, Dr. don Pantaleón de Rivarola, chaplain of the 3rd Battalion of the Infantry Regiment . . . poured oil and chrism on Juan Manuel José Domingo . . . legitimate son of don León Ortiz de Rozas, native of this city, Lieutenant of the 5th Company of the 2nd Battalion of said regiment, and doña Agustina Teresa López, native of this city. The Godparents were Don José de Echeverría and his wife doña María Francisca Ramos; the paternal grandparents, don Domingo Ortiz de Rozas, native of Rozas of Soba Valley, in the Archbishopric of Burgos, captain of the grenadiers of the 1st Company of the said Regiment, and doña Catalina Gogihola; maternal grandparents, don Clemente López de Osornio, sergeant major of the militias of this city and doña Manuela Rubio y Gamiz.[1]

As the record showed, baby Juan Manuel possessed all the elements for the making of a charmed life. He was a legitimate child, born to a respectable military family that was linked directly to Spain by his paternal grandfather. Although his lineage was not fully elaborated, these references implied that good blood ran in his veins. The honorific title of *don* or *doña* that preceded each name also showed that the child was born into a family from the upper crust of society. The priest, Father Rivarola, was also sure to reference the respected positions held by Juan Manuel's ancestors in the Spanish Empire, many of them military in nature. The information in the baptismal record was in line with other illustrious details found elsewhere in the infant's family history. The nobility of the Ortiz de Rozas family dated back to the medieval times of Pelayo, an early hero in the fight to expel the Muslim Moors, who conquered Spain in the year 711. More recently, Juan Manuel's great uncle on his father's side had served as governor of Buenos Aires and the captain of Chile. His maternal grandfather, Clemente López de Osornio, was also an accomplished military commander in the region, from the 1750s until his death at the hands of Indians in 1783.[2]

After his baptism, baby Juan Manuel was brought back to his house three blocks north of the main plaza of Buenos Aires. Among his neighbors that welcomed him into the world were Cecilio Sánchez; his wife, Magdalena Trillo; and their six-year-old daughter, Mariquita. Cecilio was a wealthy merchant, while Juan Manuel's parents, León and Agustina, had more of a ranching background. The two families were close, especially since Cecilio had served as the new mother's guardian a few years earlier, after Agustina was left an orphan. Now Cecilio's daughter, Mariquita, would become friends with the blue-eyed baby, Juan Manuel.

León Ortiz de Rozas Protects the Empire and Marries Well

As his baptismal record showed, Juan Manuel's ancestors had a long tradition of military service, which his father, León Ortiz de Rozas, continued. As a young officer, León volunteered to join a 1785 expedition to defend the new settlement of Carmen de Patagones—more than five hundred miles south of Buenos Aires—from persistent Indian attacks. The mission, however, did not fare well. Indians defeated the Spanish forces, and León was captured. His life was spared only because the chief that captured him had a brother in Spanish custody. An embassy of Indians traveled to Buenos Aires to arrange an exchange that set León free. He came home to a hero's welcome and received a promotion for his efforts. He also returned with a more intimate knowledge of the Indians and perhaps with some personal connections to them. In short, the name of Rozas began to be known among the tribes of the Pampas.[3]

Soon after returning from captivity, León fell in love with Agustina López de Osornio, the beautiful, orphaned daughter of the slain Clemente López de Osornio (her mother died soon after her husband). Orphaned at the age of sixteen, Agustina showed great natural ability in caring for her siblings, which she did with the help of their guardian, the Spanish merchant Cecilio Sánchez. Cecilio also helped administer the family's properties, which Agustina and her siblings would later inherit. By the time she was twenty years old, the fame of her beauty had spread throughout the region. She was also very wealthy, and mature beyond her years. León Ortiz de Rozas quickly fell in love with all of these things about Agustina. Although León's family was not as wealthy as hers, Agustina was attracted to the thirty-year-old lieutenant, a hero of the Indian wars, and himself a budding rancher like her father. The two were married in 1790. Soon after their wedding, León received a new military assignment— to manage the cattle and horses that outfitted and fed the Spanish army in Buenos Aires. This was fine with Agustina, who had inherited her father's love of ranching life. When in the city, the couple stayed in what had been Agustina's parents' home, three blocks from the main plaza, the Plaza Mayor. It was a large house with rooms for renters and servants quarters.[4] Their property was large, but not quite as big as Cecilio Sánchez's home a few doors away.

Cecilio Sánchez Comes to America

While Juan Manuel's closest Spanish ancestor came to Buenos Aires two generations before him, Mariquita's father, Cecilio Sánchez, was born and raised in Spain. He was from the southern city of Granada, in the region of Spain known as Andalucía, named after the Moorish Kingdom of Al-Andaluz, which governed much of the area from 711 to 1492.[5] Cecilio was thus an *andaluz*, or Andalusian, which meant that he and his fellow andaluzes had their own identity and culture, as did Spaniards from other parts of the Iberian Peninsula, many with distinct histories, languages, and cultures. In 1771, Cecilio Sánchez de Velasco left Granada and headed to Buenos Aires.

Cecilio possessed a number of traits that prepared him for success in his new land. First of all, he was a hard worker, and secondly, he was a native of the Iberian Peninsula. He was thus a *peninsular*, a Spaniard born in Spain, a distinction that carried a number of important advantages. By the 1770s, the Spanish crown had grown increasingly suspicious of "Creole" Spaniards—Spaniards born in the New World (*criollos*). Crown officials worried that criollos were more loyal to their American homelands than to the distant metropolis of Madrid. As another part of the Bourbon Reforms—over the course of the eighteenth century—local Creoles were, little by little, excluded from important positions in the imperial bureaucracy. The privileging of peninsular Spaniards gave Cecilio an advantage. There was also a large peninsular Spaniard community in Buenos Aires that welcomed and supported him. Moreover, Spain's imperial economy included monopolistic trading policies that assured Spanish merchants and Spanish ports privileged access to American markets.[6]

Cecilio's Spanish birth and business connections made him an extremely eligible bachelor. Within a few months of his arrival, he did what many other newly arrived Spanish men did: he married a wealthy widow from Buenos Aires named Magdalena Trillo.[7] A descendant of merchants from Galicia in northwestern Spain, Magdalena's first husband built up a successful merchant business, and she inherited all his wealth on his death, including a number of properties in the city. Magdalena the Galician and Cecilio the Andalusian fell for each other and the two were married in 1771.

Cecilio's qualities and connections soon brought him success in the city's civic and business affairs. He became an official of the town council, the cabildo, which met in the town council hall (also known as the "cabildo") located in the main plaza of the city. For a time, he also administered the home for abandoned children, making sure, as he put it, that the infants were not devoured by dogs. Among his many business activities, Cecilio went into the meat business with Clemente López de Osornio, a partnership cut short by Clemente's death at the hands of Indians in 1783. When Clemente's wife died two years later, Cecilio became the guardian of Agustina López de Osornio—who would later become Juan Manuel's mother—and her siblings.

Cecilio and Magdalena were also a very pious couple. They donated money for the construction of the church of San Pedro Telmo, a few blocks south of the Plaza Mayor (the main plaza). Magdalena was a member of a prominent women's group that paid special devotion to the Virgin of La Merced. This they did in religious ceremonies throughout the year, but also in an annual festival every September 24 in honor of the Virgin, which included a procession throughout the city. Cecilio and Magdalena were also close friends with the archbishop of Buenos Aires, Father Azamor y Ramírez.[8]

When their daughter was born on All Saints Day, November 1, 1786, Cecilio and Magdalena, being the believers they were, named her María Josepha Petrona de Todos los Santos Sánchez Velazco y Trillo (María of All Saints). She became Mariquita for short.[9] She would be their only child, which meant she would have all their attention. It also meant that someday she would inherit all their wealth.

The Sánchez de Velazco family lived three blocks north of the main plaza in a large home that fronted three streets, taking up most of the block.[10] On their property they had an *aljibe*, a cistern that provided water for the neighborhood (*aljibe* being one of the thousands of Arabic words adopted by the Spaniards during centuries of Muslim rule in Spain). When Mariquita was two years old, the viceroy conducted a census, which offers a picture of the home Mariquita grew up in. It included Cecilio, the head of household (thirty-seven years old); his wife, Magdalena (thirty-three); her son from her first marriage, Fernando del Arco (thirteen); and the two-year-old Mariquita. Also part of the household were two laborers, an orphan girl, two free mulatto servants, a free black woman, and her child. Four slaves were also part of the household, a reminder of the brisk slave trade conducted in the region.[11] In 1790, Cecilio and Magdalena welcomed León and Agustina Ortiz de Rozas as neighbors when the newlyweds moved in just across the street. And when little Juan Manuel came into the world in 1793, the six-year-old neighbor, Mariquita Sánchez, would have been enthralled by the baby's piercing blue eyes.

How did each couple raise their children? Attitudes and practices relating to child-rearing are difficult to pin down for this time period. A few manuals for parents did exist (as will be discussed in the next chapter). From all appearances, the Sánchez and Rosas families seemed fairly traditional in the values they developed in their children, which included respect for parental, Church, and royal authority, and for the societal values emanating from these institutions and customs. How those values transitioned to their children is part of the story of this book.

Young Mariquita and Juan Manuel's Buenos Aires

Mariquita and Juan Manuel grew up in the same neighborhood of Buenos Aires, at least when his family was in the city. Their houses were only a few doors away and their families were well acquainted with one another. Although Mariquita was six years his senior, they grew up essentially in the same generation. Mariquita wrote a memoir about what it was like growing up in the viceroyalty. Her *Recuerdos del Buenos Aires virreinal*, although written later in her life, provides a direct window to the city. By the time Mariquita wrote this memoir, she had embraced the tenets of the Romantic Movement. Her memories were thus filtered through her heightened sensibilities of Romanticism, which may have given her more powerful and emotional ways of expressing herself. Despite this filter, her memoir serves as a useful source on life in late eighteenth-century Buenos Aires.

Buenos Aires, in Mariquita's description, was the great center of activity in the region. The viceroy and his ministers made up a kind of miniature royal court in the city. Although it was a bustling city, Mariquita remembered that the inefficient and cumbersome Spanish monopoly system created chronic shortages and high prices. Spanish ships did import a variety of things, but for Mariquita there were never enough *fine* things. Thus, the wealthy people were always itching to get more items of elite taste. She remembered that even the viceroy would come around borrowing various items when he was hosting a big event in his home. Fashion was also lacking in the city, she remembered. A few overworked tailors did business in the city, but no one dressed very well. The poor walked the city barefooted.[12]

Mariquita lived in one of the most luxurious homes in the city, and she took time in her memoir to describe the typical residences of wealthy porteños. Each house usually had a great room, used only for special occasions, with furniture made of jacaranda wood, damasks (fine woven cloth with images on both sides), and luxurious carpets from Spain. The more commonly used smaller living room might be covered in part by a rug from the province of Córdoba, a few hundred miles northwest of Buenos Aires. Religious images decorated the tables while some homes even boasted parrots and other caged birds. Wealthy families used silver plates and utensils while other families used pewter. Hot chocolate, coffee, and toast were a typical breakfast. Lunch would be between one and three o'clock, while dinner would be as late as 10:00

or 11:00 p.m. The diet of well-to-do porteños was a mixture of Spanish and French food, most of which was cooked by slaves. And if you wanted the best sugar in town, it had to come from Havana, Cuba.[13]

Buenos Aires had only one hotel—Los Tres Reyes (The Three Kings), just north of the fort on Santo Cristo Street. A few restaurants and bakeries dotted the streets, and one of Mariquita's favorites was a French bakery about five blocks from her home, famous for its exquisite coffee and pastries. Porteños also gathered at other cafes to play billiards and chat. Wealthy families could also order in to eat. A certain Monsieur Ramón had a catering business that brought cooking equipment and servants into porteño homes to serve a fine dinner. Monsieur Ramón was also famous for training slaves to be cooks. For a fee, he would turn a slave into a fine chef after two years of courses.[14]

Products from other provinces enriched life in Buenos Aires. Mariquita praised the fine linens from Córdoba and Corrientes, and cloth and tapestries from Mendoza. Mariquita was especially fond of the wine from Mendoza and San Juan Provinces, as well as their olives, nuts, and plums, and she found the raisins particularly exquisite. Beef was also plentiful and cheap, so much so that many times only the most succulent portions would be eaten—such as the tongue. However, the low price for beef, she noted, did not bode well for the gauchos of the countryside, who might have lived better if meat prices were higher. Mariquita called the gauchos "the most reviled" of all the classes of people in the country.[15]

RELIGION

Mariquita spent a good portion of her memoirs describing the religious life in Buenos Aires. The very name of the city, Ciudad de la Santísima Trinidad y Puerto de Santa María del Buen Ayre (City of the Holy Trinity and Port of Saint Maria of the Good Air), showed that Buenos Aires was a Catholic city. In Mariquita's youth in the 1790s, the city boasted seven parishes, four monasteries, two convents, and an archbishopric. There was an office for the Inquisition in Buenos Aires, but Mariquita did not remember it ever having the occasion to burn anyone. The Inquisition did examine all books that came into the city. No book could go on sale until approved by the Holy Office. The Church was also behind much of the education in the city, and the San Carlos School was run by priests and it taught many of the elite children.[16]

Good Catholics were expected to attend Mass frequently, although porteño women (porteñas—see glossary) seemed to be, to Mariquita's eyes, more zealous than porteño men (porteños). Pious women would attend Mass, perhaps sitting on the floor on a small carpet carried by a slave or servant. Mariquita remembered one priest who spoke with such power and eloquence that women sometimes fainted while listening to his sermons. Another priest asked a female parishioner: "Where was God before the Creation?" She answered without hesitation: "He was cutting wood to burn those who wanted to know the answer to that question."[17]

Although women may have attended Mass more than their male cohorts, men were nevertheless involved in many pious and charitable works. The wealthy men of the city formed a brotherhood that donated money and other services, including raising funds to support the women's hospital. These same men also worked with condemned prisoners, taking them to see confessors before their execution, providing them with good food for their last meals, and accompanying them to the hangman's noose when it was time to meet their fate.[18]

For Mariquita, the highlight of the religious calendar in Buenos Aires, like elsewhere in the Catholic world, was the Holy Week of Easter. It was a time of remembrance, penance, and fasting. Various religious processions occurred throughout the week. In the old days, some zealous believers went on a "procession of blood" in memory of the crucifixion of Jesus Christ, lacerating their own flesh with metal and glass as they marched. The highlight of Holy Thursday was a grand gala where everyone dressed up in their finest attire. Holy Friday, however, was a day of dread. Processions commemorated Jesus's descent from the cross and his burial in the tomb. At twelve noon on Holy Saturday, porteños throughout the city burned effigies of Judas, the betrayer of Jesus. Families also began preparing their big Easter feast, which they started to eat as soon as the clock struck midnight. After eating, porteños attended Easter Mass at 3:00 or 4:00 a.m., which would celebrate Christ's resurrection. Then the most important processions of the week would commence. One procession with an elaborately decorated float representing the resurrected Christ would leave the Merced Church, two blocks north of the Plaza Mayor, while at the same time a procession of the Virgin would leave the church of Santo Domingo, three blocks south of the plaza. The two processions then wound their way through the streets until they both reached the Plaza Mayor, where they saluted each other before returning to their churches.[19]

Mariquita herself was a woman of faith, although not an orthodox believer. Some references in her letters indicate that she did not believe in a literal interpretation of the bible. On one occasion in her diary, Mariquita referred to the biblical story of the tower of Babel as a lie.[20] Despite her skepticism, many of her letters contain references to divinity and petitions for heavenly aid. She also owned a prayer book, *God Is the Love Most Pure*, by German Christian mystic Karl Eckartshausen. The book provided her with comfort in times of trial. Eckartshausen's teachings also bolstered Mariquita's sense of universal brotherhood. In "Supplication on behalf of all my men, my brothers," Eckartshausen pleads to the heavens that "the spirit of harmony and peace reign among men, and may they love each other as brothers, as children of the same father."[21] Mariquita tried to live these ideals.

EDUCATION AND CHILD-REARING

While Mariquita grew up in a very robust religious environment in Buenos Aires, educational culture, in her estimation, was sorely lacking. First of all, the methods of education were quite severe. "When parents sent their children to school, they gave instructions to treat their kids harshly rather than with kindness." One school, known for meting out daily whippings, had the motto: "Learning comes with a little blood."[22] Mariquita remembered some dialogues she overheard between students and teachers that illustrated the nexus of education and violence. "You don't know your lesson? Six lashes and get back to studying it. You still don't know it? Twelve lashings!" One particular teacher, a Señor Salcedo, took his students to watch a public execution, then whipped them afterward so they would never forget what they saw. Education was also based on social class. Poor girls learned skills like mending and sewing that would prepare them for work in domestic service. Upper-class girls were taught to sing and play music. Reading was not a high priority.[23]

Mariquita was fortunate that she was able to attend a school run by doña Francisca López. Mariquita's parents also helped teach her to read and write, as did many merchants who wanted their daughters to help in the family business. And as an only child, Mariquita's education received even more emphasis.[24] Mariquita also had access to her family's library.[25] As she grew older, Mariquita would read everything she could get her hands on.

Race in the Viceroyalty. Mariquita's memoirs also make frequent reference to the role of blacks and mulattoes in Buenos Aires. Mariquita and Juan Manuel grew up surrounded by black servants as well as slaves. As mentioned earlier, by 1800, 25 percent of Buenos Aires was either black or of mixed black ancestry. Blacks and mulattoes served in the local militias and worked as skilled artisans in workshops throughout the city. They were also street vendors and laundresses who washed clothes in the nearby river. People of color also found work as chefs, and even as musicians in the city orchestra.[26] The Sánchez and Rozas families both owned black and mulatto slaves and servants. The carriage and wagon drivers of the Rozas family were of African descent.[27] And while there was often the appearance of peaceful and good relations between masters, slaves, and servants, tension, mistrust, and mistreatment were never far below the surface.

Mariquita related a story that captured elements of white porteños' views of race. The child of a wealthy porteño family passed away. At nearly the same time, a young slave boy from the household died as well. In preparation for burials, the family dressed their son as Saint Michael and had the slave boy dressed as the devil. According to Mariquita, the slave mother "cried and begged, but being a slave, in the end she had to shut up." Fortunately for the grieving mother, when Church authorities got word of the costumed corpses, they intervened and ensured that the little slave boy was given a proper Christian burial.[28]

Juan Manuel in the City and Countryside

Juan Manuel also experienced a strict upbringing, but unlike Mariquita, he did not leave a memoir of his childhood days. Many of the glimpses we have into the Ortiz de Rozas family come from the writings of León and Agustina's grandson, Lucio Mansilla, who recorded a number of family stories and traditions as well as memories of his own time spent in the Rozas household.[29] While Mariquita was an only child, Juan Manuel was one of Agustina's twenty children, although only ten lived to adulthood. He was the second child and oldest son. According to family tradition, Agustina nursed her children herself, contrary to the common practice of using wet nurses. Agustina's milk was reportedly so abundant that sometimes she would help nurse her friends' children. María Gonzáles de Lavalle, for example, would sometimes bring her son Juan to Agustina, who suckled him.[30] The two mothers could not have known that the babies Juan Manuel de Rozas and Juan Lavalle would grow up to be mortal political enemies.

The Ortiz de Rozas family was traditional in many ways, although not in all. They upheld the customary ideals of Hispanic family life, namely, respect for Church authority and for the authority of parents. But while Mariquita's family followed what many considered the more traditional patriarchal family structure where the husband took the lead, Juan Manuel's did not. Ideals about family life expressed in laws, preached from pulpits, and honored by tradition were frequently different from what families experienced in real life. Each couple, each family, negotiated the meanings of what it meant to be a husband or wife, a mother or daughter, a father or son.

And so it was with León Ortiz de Rozas and Agustina Clemente Osornio, who as a couple possessed complementary personality traits. León was a very respected man in his community and had an easy-going manner. His successful military background showed that he could fight, lead, and excel. However, in Agustina, he chose a spouse with a dominant personality. Recognizing that reality, León was content to let her take the initiative in many family matters and even in some business affairs. León would preside at the dinner table, leading the family in prayers, but he left much of the family business to Agustina's active hand. When not engaged in ranching activities, León liked to pass the time reading, perhaps composing some poems, and playing cards with close friends.[31]

Agustina, meanwhile, ran a large part of the household and took the lead in raising the children. Some would say that Agustina inherited her personality from her father, Clemente, the tough militia commander and rugged frontiersman. According to her grandson Lucio Mansilla, Agustina "was born to command and to control, and she did command and control."[32] Another biographer wrote that Agustina had "that confidence of those born to live without equivocation." She never worried about making a mistake, and she possessed the natural "gift of authority" that led her to believe in her own infallibility.[33] At the same time, Lucio Mansilla emphasized that his grandfather "was not docile or weak," nor did his wife "lead him by the nose." What might have looked like weakness to some, Lucio Mansilla explained, was really León's love for Agustina. His love was "mixed with confidence" in his wife, who was "diligent, active, energetic, hard-working, organized, thrifty, economical, charitable, as

FIGURE I.I Agustina López de Osornio de Ortiz de Rozas, Juan Manuel's strong-willed mother, by Carlos Enrique Pellegrini. Courtesy of the Museo Nacional de Bellas Artes, Buenos Aires.

well as imperious." A saying among her children put it: "If my mother had vices, then I want to be like her, faults and all!"[34]

Agustina was also heavily involved in charitable works, for she believed it was the duty of the wealthy to care for the poor, just as Catholic doctrine taught. Every Friday she would hitch up the large family carriage, and with Francisco, her tall mulatto driver, she would travel through different neighborhoods distributing goods to needy families. Agustina would sometimes even bring sick people into her home and either nurse them back to health or care for them until they passed away.[35]

Another well-known family story captures Agustina's bravery and independence. One night, at about 2:00 a.m., Agustina heard noises on the rooftop of her house. Believing the noise came from thieves, she sprang into action. Instead of waking her husband, she ordered a servant to be sure to close his door so as to not disturb his slumber. Agustina then grabbed a metal rod, climbed the stairs, and chased off two intruders who had scaled the outer walls into the roof and were trying to climb down into the inner courtyard of the house. Agustina went back to bed, and only the next morning did León and the rest of the household find out what happened.[36]

While Agustina and León had a home in the city not far from Mariquita's, they also spent at least a few months of each year on their ranch deep in the countryside. Toward the end of November or in early December, the Ortiz de

Rozas family left the city to spend most of the summer at Rincón de López, the ranch they renamed in honor of Agustina's slain father. At the crack of dawn, the Rozas caravan would leave the city and head southeast. León, Agustina, and the kids traveled in the family *galera* (carriage), driven by their mulatto servant, Pancho. The galera was the best way to travel in comfort across the Pampas. Its high wheels handled the roughest roads with ease and also kept it from bogging down in the mud holes that dotted the route.[37] Behind the family came the slaves and servants hauling the luggage in the much less comfortable *carretas*, the large, two-wheeled carts used for long-range transportation. Armed guards—including some Indians and mestizos—escorted the whole group, a reminder to all that they were traveling into territory still under nominal Indian control. The family convoy plodded on, amid the whistles and whips of the drivers, toward what looked like an endless horizon. When they arrived at the military outpost in Chascomús, about eighty miles from Buenos Aires, it meant their journey was almost over. Finally, after three or four days of travel, the Rozas family would arrive at the Rincón de López ranch.[38]

While the ranch house might have been empty when the Rozas family was absent, the surrounding lands were not. Dozens of families lived on the Rozas lands, and the arrival of the owner (the *patrón*) was always big news, prompting residents to gather to greet the family. Upon arrival, León might oversee some of the unloading, but he would soon make his way into the house to start a card game of *trucos* with his friends who came to meet him. Agustina, on the other hand, would immediately get on her horse and begin putting the ranch in order. As she went about her business, Agustina would at times engage her husband in some edgy humor. León was apparently from a less illustrious family than his wife, and she sometimes would not let him forget it. "And you, who are you?" she would quip when angered by something León had done. "You are nothing but an ennobled adventurer . . . while I descend from the Dukes of Normandy . . . and if you hassle me anymore, I'll show you that I'm a relative of the Virgin Mary."[39]

But León could assert himself, even if by the looks of things Agustina ran the show. One morning during one of their summers at the ranch, León approached his wife and asked her to go with him to one of their favorite old haunts on the property. "Do you know something, Agustina? It's been years since we've visited the orchard. Would you like to go see it?" Agustina accepted the invitation, and the two left the ranch compound and headed toward the mouth of the Salado River. Upon arriving at the orchard, the couple sat down on a stone bench, and León posed a question. "Isn't it true that I love you dearly?" Taking this as an openly aired, and thus indecent, proposition from her husband, and being the proper and prudent woman that she was, she rebuffed him. "Rozas, why do you show me such disrespect?" León quickly assured her he had no such intentions. Then, pulling out some cords from a pouch, he said. "Do you see these? They are to show you that the man is the man, and that if I allow you to run things it is not out of weakness, but it is only because of the immense love I have for you, and because I know you are loyal." He then grabbed her and softly, almost symbolically, whipped her a few times with the cords. Agustina did not resist or speak. After he was finished, they left the orchard and never spoke of the incident again. When they returned to the ranch house later that day, Agustina went on with business as usual.[40]

No one was more excited to get to Rincón de López than young Juan Manuel. There, with his horse, the vast plains lay before him. It was here, according to one biographer, that Juan Manuel began to "absorb the pampa." As a young boy he mastered the skills of the ranch hands (*peones de campo*) that lived and worked on the lands that made up the estancia. On any given day Juan Manuel would spend time chasing down and capturing wild cattle and ostriches using some bolas, the snaring sling of the Pampa Indians.[41] Or he might be breaking horses or driving and branding cattle. And because most of these activities took place on horseback, Juan Manuel became an expert rider and learned to perform the feats of agility on horseback required by life on the plains. This meant he could ride at a gallop anywhere on the Pampa and avoid quagmires and elude the rodent holes that could send horse and rider to terrible falls. It was on the Pampa that the young Rozas also came to know intimately the ways of the gaucho. Gauchos were ranch hands, similar in many ways to the cowboys of the American West.[42] They lived along the cattle and Indian frontiers, and many of them were mestizos and mulattoes, evidence of the prevalence of the African population in the Río de la Plata. They could live independently, eating from the bounties of the Pampa and trading hides and ostrich feathers, among other items. They might also settle down and attach themselves to a certain landowner as a ranch hand. Gauchos were known for their stubbornness and independence, and for their willingness to fight to defend their masculine honor. To gravely insult a gaucho was to invite a fight, and perhaps even a duel to the death. Duels elsewhere in the hemisphere could involve pistols (like Alexander Hamilton's with Aaron Burr in 1804), but gauchos dueled with knives, which they always kept with them.[43] Young Juan Manuel surely knew men with scarred faces and blinded eyes, and he perhaps witnessed a few knife fights himself. Juan Manuel also saw evidence of the gauchos' hunting skills, going after the deer or ostriches of the Pampas, or the fierce pumas, which the gauchos could hunt with lances or, for the stouter of heart, with a rolled-up poncho on one fist and their trusty knife in the other. The gauchos' abilities with the tools of their trade—knives, horses, lances—also translated well to the battlefield. With a bit of training, a group of gauchos could make a fearsome cavalry unit. Juan Manuel frequently ate and worked among the gauchos on his family estate, learning their ways and their speech.

While at the Rincón de López, Juan Manuel also came to know many of the Indian tribes of the Pampas. He was raised on the stories of how his grandfather Clemente and his uncle Andrés met their fate at the hands of Indians. Other stories abounded in the porteño community of Indian raids and killings, of captivity and daring rescues. Juan Manuel also came to understand that there were many white captives held by the Indians all over the Pampas. At the same time, Juan Manuel knew there were many "friendly" Indians as well. Friendly tribes came frequently to Rincón de López to trade cattle hides, or perhaps ostrich feathers, or the skins of the puma, guanaco, and fox. León always kept on hand what the Natives desired most in return: tobacco, yerba mate, alcohol, and beads. The Indians camped in their leather tents, where they would drink mare's milk and eat horsemeat or other fare from the abundant Pampa. As he did with the gauchos, Juan Manuel mingled with these friendly Indians, became friends with many of them, and began establishing personal connections of his own. He even began learning their language. As Juan Manuel walked among the Indians, he heard words and phrases that surely captured a young boy's imagination. *Lighen* (silver); *linco che* (army of soldiers); *lihue* (the spirit of life); and *vachi lihue opongelay* (in this life there is nothing that brings satisfaction).[44]

The Education of Juan Manuel

León and Agustina knew there was more to learning than what the Pampas could teach. Between eight and thirteen years of age, Juan Manuel attended a school taught by Francisco Xavier de Angerich, a prominent medical doctor and educator in Buenos Aires. Besides schoolwork, Agustina took a special interest in teaching her children to work, and not just on the ranch. Like many parents of the time, Agustina thought storekeeping was a good place to start, so she arranged a job for her son Gervasio in a nearby shop. One day, after the workers finished a meal, the owner asked Gervasio to wash the dishes. The boy demurred. "I didn't come here for this," he said. Such menial labor, in his mind, violated his social status. The storekeeper sent him home, adding that he would be speaking to his mother about the matter. Gervasio, knowing his mother, probably knew what was coming as he hurried home. The owner soon showed up at the Rozas home and told Agustina about the unwashed dishes. Summoning Gervasio, Agustina grabbed him by the ear and pulled him down in front of the visitor. "Kneel down and ask the pardon of this gentleman!" she commanded. Gervasio did, and after receiving assurance that the storekeeper had indeed forgiven the young offender, Agustina ordered Gervasio to "get back to work" where his boss would "make a man out of" him.[45]

Agustina also wanted Juan Manuel to learn the lessons of storekeeping. Like his brother, Juan refused to do menial labor. But when Agustina tried to force Juan Manuel to conform, he, unlike his brother, stubbornly refused. As punishment, his mother grabbed him by his ear and locked him in a room, saying, "There you'll stay, with nothing but bread and water, until you learn to obey me!" After spending one night in the room, Juan Manuel decided enough was enough. The next night, while all were asleep, he forced the lock, left a short note, and fled with nothing but the shirt on his back. In the morning, all his parents found was an empty room and Juan Manuel's note: "I leave all that is not mine. Juan Manuel de Rosas." His message was clear: No one was going to force him to do what he did not want to do. Nor did he need anything from anyone. He could make his own way in life. To punctuate his statement, from that note on, Juan Manuel changed the spelling of his last name from Rozas to Rosas, with an "s" instead of a "z" in the middle. Forever after, he would be known as Juan Manuel de Rosas.[46] Biographer Manuel Galvez may have gotten some of it right when he said that Juan Manuel de Rosas "came out like his mother."[47] Or it could be said that he came out like his grandfather Clemente.

When Juan Manuel left that night, he headed for the home of his cousins, the Anchorena family, where he found clothes and a job. Juan Manuel proved to be a hard worker, a quick learner, and an adept administrator. He soon mended relations with his parents, and by the time he was eighteen years old, he was running much of their properties by himself.[48]

The Atlantic World in Mariquita and Juan Manuel's World, circa 1793

As Mariquita and Juan Manuel passed the days of their youth according to the rhythms of the city and countryside, life in and around Buenos Aires was influenced by events and ideas from the rest of the Americas and across the Atlantic World. During their childhoods, the world was convulsed by revolution. The American Revolution showed that colonies could sever ties with their mother country and build new nations based on principles of liberty. The American revolutionaries made bold political and social statements about freedom and equality, but the actual result was a moderate revolution that still excluded large numbers of white and nonwhite voters and allowed slavery to continue.[49]

The French Revolution, on the other hand, shook the Atlantic World to its core. For a few tumultuous years, the French Revolution offered a more radical and violent form of revolution, and at a fast pace. This was especially the case after the Jacobin faction steered the revolution down a path of extremism and terror after 1792. While slavery continued in the United States after independence, the radicals in Paris boldly abolished slavery in 1794. French revolutionaries also declared that all men could vote, regardless of their wealth and status, something that took decades to come about in the United States of America. In the Jacobin way of thinking, anyone who opposed the French Revolution was deemed an enemy of the state and would suffer the terror of the state.

The Argentine priest Gaspar Juárez was in Europe in 1792 and 1793 just as the French Revolution took its radical turn. His letters to his friends back in the Viceroyalty of the Río de la Plata reveal the chaos and fear of the time. The French Revolution, he wrote, had thrown all European cities into a state of confusion. Even Italy trembled because they feared that the French revolutionaries would come to Rome itself and cover it in "fire and blood." Even more worrisome, France was about to declare war on Spain, threatening to bring its revolutionary madness to Madrid and who knew where else. The casualties of the revolution were grave, the priest continued, not only in people killed, but also in the customs and institutions it destroyed. Based on his observations, Father Juárez believed that the Revolution was shattering religious and political authority. Marriage was no longer sacred in France, and all religious holidays were abolished. The idea of monarchy itself was under siege. "At any moment we are expecting to hear news of the beheading of the King [of France] and his Queen." Juárez concluded, "All is horror," and if God does not intervene with his all-powerful hand, "everything will go from bad to worse."[50]

Just a few weeks before Juan Manuel de Rozas was born, news arrived in Buenos Aires that confirmed Father Juárez's worst fears: the revolutionaries in Paris had beheaded King Louis XVI, and France had declared war on Spain. The day before Juan Manuel's birth, on March 29, perhaps even as Agustina was feeling her first pangs of labor, Viceroy Arredondo of Buenos Aires issued a decree designed to stop the spread of French influence. Anyone who had dealt with French ships, he decreed, would be put to death and have their possessions confiscated. In addition, he ordered everyone to keep a watchful eye on French citizens in the viceroyalty. Moreover, he continued, "no one should introduce books, letters, or other seditious or inappropriate writings" of French origin. Nor should any resident in any way support "French ideas" or spread news about the recent events in France, under the pain of death and confiscation of property. A few months later, viceregal officials seized a French ship, the *El Dragón*, when it arrived in Montevideo. On board, customs officials found a trove of prohibited books by Enlightenment authors such as Rousseau and Voltaire.[51] The French Revolution's *Rights of Man* or Olympe de Gouge's *Declaration of the Rights of Women and the Female Citizen*—and especially the latest Jacobin literature—would not be welcome in Buenos Aires. The infant Juan Manuel was oblivious to these perceived threats. The problem was that others, including Mariquita Sánchez, were growing more and more interested in revolutionary ideas, including the right to be free.

CHAPTER TWO

Marriage

In July of 1801, fourteen-year-old Mariquita Sánchez was very concerned about her freedom. In this case, it was the right to make a choice about the most important subject of all: true love. Her parents, Cecilio and Magdalena, were trying to force her to marry a man they had chosen for her. Mariquita, however, loved someone else, and she stubbornly resisted her parents' wishes. When Mariquita and her suitor asked for permission to marry, her parents absolutely refused. Neither side gave in. And so the struggle went on, month after month, then year after year. Finally, after three years of drama, Mariquita could stand it no longer. On Tuesday, July 10, 1804, Mariquita wrote a letter to the viceroy, telling him that for the last three years she had used all kinds of "gentle strategies," with love and moderation, to get permission from her parents to marry, first from her father, and then after he died, from her mother. However, Mariquita wrote, "all has been in vain and each day she grows more inflexible." Mariquita declared that it was now time for her to defend her "rights" in the name of her "love, salvation, and reputation."[1]

New ideas, French and otherwise, inevitably made their way into Buenos Aires in the 1790s and afterward, and Mariquita Sánchez eagerly sought them out. But Mariquita did not have to depend on foreign ideas when it came to rebelling against her parents in the name of love. She and her suitor could make their own choices about love. Moreover, Catholic doctrine also prized freedom when it came to choosing a marriage partner. Her younger friend Juan Manuel de Rozas also needed no help rebelling against parental authority, as he had his own battle with his powerful mother, Agustina, over his decision to marry. Both Mariquita and Juan Manuel faced opposition to their plans for marriages, and they both showed their courage and resourcefulness to achieve their desires.

FIGURE 2.1 Anonymous miniature portrait of Mariquita Sánchez. Courtesy of Museo Histórico Nacional, Buenos Aires.

FIGURE 2.2 Martín Thompson, Mariquita's husband, a naval officer and a diplomat. He died in 1819 while returning from a diplomatic mission to the US. Courtesy of the Archivo General de la Nación, Buenos Aires.

Rebellious Love

By the time Mariquita turned fourteen years old, Cecilio and Magdalena had already chosen her husband. His name was Diego del Arco, a peninsular Spaniard and respectable merchant who was much older than Mariquita. This was a fine choice, a traditional choice, and it followed the familiar pattern of a peninsular Spaniard marrying a wealthy porteña. But Mariquita had already set her eyes on someone else: her blond and blue-eyed second cousin on her mother's side, Martín Jacobo de Thompson. Thompson was an odd name for Buenos Aires at the time, and he might have been an odd choice for a good Catholic girl like Mariquita. Odd because the name Thompson implied English ethnicity, which in turn raised the specter of possible Protestant heritage, and Protestantism was still heresy in the Spanish America of 1800.

Mariquita's suitor, Martín Thompson, was born a Catholic, but his father, William Thompson, was not. How Martín's father became a Catholic merits some telling because it reveals the abiding interest in religious purity in the Hispanic culture of the era. William Paul Thompson (Guillermo Pablo Thompson in the Spanish sources) was an English merchant who moved to the Spanish port of Cádiz in the late 1740s. Before he left England, Thompson converted to Catholicism. He ended up in Buenos Aires in 1751, where he set himself up as a merchant and began looking for a wife. Marriages between Catholics and Protestants were forbidden, and Thompson's red face, foreign accent, and British surname raised concern. To quiet any suspicion, William Thompson put a file together to prove his Catholic identity, including a letter from the priest who baptized him in England. Thompson was allowed to marry, and after his first wife died, he married Tiburcia López. Together they had one child, Martín Jacobo, in 1777.[2]

While William Thompson confronted one of the biggest pillars of the Spanish Empire—that of religious conformity—his son Martín's choice of profession highlighted another major concern—that of racial purity. Martín decided at a young age that he wanted to be an officer in the Royal Spanish Navy. For such a prestigious position, the Spanish crown only accepted candidates of proven loyalty and honor, and a key component of honor was pure Spanish blood. Law required prospective officers to prove their "purity of blood," an idea dating back to the Middle Ages when Spaniards tried to keep themselves from intermixing with non-Christians of other races, such as Jews and Muslims.

Thousands of Jews lived in Iberia dating back to Spain's days as a Roman province and before. Then in 711, Muslims invaders from North Africa (the Moors) conquered the Iberian Peninsula, beginning what would be more than seven hundred years of Muslim rule in much of Spain. Spaniards began a slow process of "reconquest" of the Iberian Peninsula in the mid-700s. It was during these early stages of the Reconquest (as it came to be known) that some of Juan Manuel de Rozas's ancestors achieved their noble status. Queen Isabella and King Ferdinand conquered the last Muslim kingdom in Granada in 1492. That same year, the Spanish monarchs gave the Jews in Spain an ultimatum: convert to Christianity or be expelled. Many Jews converted, while others were deported. Similar persecution was heaped upon the remaining Muslims. Even after these victories and persecutions, Spaniards still harbored deep fears that vestiges of Jewish and Muslim blood survived in their population, and that some of the "new converts" to Christianity were still practicing their heretical religion in secret.[3] The Spanish crown, through the Inquisition and other means, sought to root out such practices and protect its definition of pure Christian blood and pure Christian religion.

More than a thousand years after the wars of reconquest against the Moors began, Spanish military officers still were required to prove that they were free of inferior blood. Thus, in 1796, the nineteen-year-old Martín Thompson presented to his superiors an extensive document, including pages and pages of genealogy, proving his pure blood and heritage. Various witnesses confirmed that Martín was indeed the legitimate son of his parents, and that all of his relatives were honorable "old Christians" who had lived and died as true believers. Witnesses were also asked if Martín's family had any trace of "new converts, Indians, Moors, mulattoes, mestizos, or any other race that would cause infamy," and if "their aforementioned ancestors were known to be of pure blood going back four generations."[4] In short, Martín's lengthy document made his case. Tellingly, his father's Protestant background was largely ignored, which showed that there was more than a little ceremony and symbolism in the process.

The point was that Martín Thompson was clearly trusted as a good and loyal subject with the correct religious and racial makeup. He received his commission as a naval officer, which, together with his blond hair and blue eyes, made Martín quite a figure in porteño society. It was more than enough to catch the eye of his younger cousin on his mother's side, Mariquita Sánchez. The two had ample opportunity to meet and fall in love through routine family interactions, and it was socially acceptable for second cousins to marry, as wealthy porteño families sought literally to keep wealth in the family.[5]

By July of 1801, Martín had proposed marriage and Mariquita accepted. Martín later recounted what happened next. "I asked permission of her parents, with the hope of gaining their approval for our marriage." He saw no reason for them to refuse. Even less did he think that Cecilio and Magdalena would "make themselves masters of their daughter's free will." But her parents did end up doing just that. Cecilio and Magdalena refused Martín's request, then forbade him from ever coming to their home again. Legally, Mariquita's parents had the right to act this way, for by law minors needed parental permission to marry (twenty-three and twenty-five years old for women and men respectively).

This was part of the Hispanic tradition of patriarchal power—*patria potestad* in Spanish—which dated back to Roman times and beyond. In the Roman-

Hispanic sense, patriarchy was the legal power and authority the father wielded over his wife and children.[6] Over time this traditional concept was bolstered and strengthened by various legal codes, such as laws about child custody and disciplining children, and parents having influence over who their children married, at least while they were minors.[7] A recent royal decree from Spain in the 1770s, known as the Royal Pragmatic on Marriage, gave parents even more power to oppose marriages to "unequal" partners. The definition of "unequal" was left ambiguous, but parents invoked it especially regarding racial inequality (the old "purity of blood" idea), and also for perceived inequalities in a variety of other areas.[8] Cecilio and Magdalena were happy to invoke all the legal and cultural power they could to withhold their permission, and no amount of pleading could change their minds.

Cecilio was not content to stop there. He used his powerful political connections to get Martín transferred, first across the river to Montevideo, then across the Atlantic to Spain.[9] But Cecilio was still not finished. He next sought to purge Mariquita's heart of her love for Martín. Cecilio sent her for a time to the Casa de Ejercicios, a house of spiritual retreat similar to a convent, which provided a secluded and protected environment for women seeking a haven from worldly concerns or threats. It was also a place where embattled parents like Cecilio and Magdalena could send wayward and rebellious daughters, in hopes that introspection and spiritual meditation would help them see the error of their ways.[10]

Mariquita withstood all of her parents' intrigues and stratagems. She relied on her own strong will, but she also had support from the clergy. The Catholic Church's official stance was that free will should be paramount in marriage, and no one should be forced into the holy sacrament of marriage. The archbishop of Buenos Aires and close friend of Cecilio and Magdalena, Father Azamor y Ramírez, penned a powerful treatise in favor of the right of couples to marry the mate of their choice. He even argued that Samson's marriage to Delilah, as told in the Old Testament, was just and good because it was a free choice. The archbishop died before Mariquita and Martín's conflict with her parents, but Mariquita's confessor, Father Cayetano Rodríguez, was a known supporter of couples in their situation.[11] Perhaps with Father Cayetano's help, Mariquita managed to send a note to Martín in Spain asking him to return home to fulfill his promise of marriage, which he promptly did.

Cecilio Sánchez passed away in 1802. And while Mariquita mourned, she and Martín hoped his death would finally open the way for them to marry. Martín renewed his pleas with Mariquita's mother, Magdalena. At times she appeared to be softening, but then, as Martín recounted, "within a few moments she would change her mind again." And because Mariquita was just seventeen years of age, she was still five years away from being able to make her own decisions about marriage independently of her mother.

Five years was too long to wait. In the face of Magdalena's intransigence, Mariquita and Martín decided to pursue their case in court. Although parents could refuse permission, the law also allowed children to challenge their parents' opposition in court. Parental opposition was supposed to be "rational," which meant it was based on legitimate reasons. Parents pressured, cajoled, and persuaded, and maybe even got boyfriends shipped across the sea, as Cecilio did with Martín. If parents and children could not come to a consensus, the children had the right to take the case to court. The judge overseeing these *disenso* (dissent) cases would gather evidence, listen to witnesses, and then decide whether to uphold the parents' objections as "rational" or to overrule them as "irrational" and grant the minor children the right to marry.[12]

In early July of 1804, Martín began gathering evidence to make his case to the judge. He contacted a friend, a scribe, who was authorized to record legal oaths and declarations. Martín asked his friend to visit Magdalena's home and give her one last chance to agree to the wedding. When the scribe showed up at her door on the morning of Friday, July 6, Magdalena knew exactly what it meant: Mariquita and Martín were going to take her to court. Magdalena told the scribe that she would consult with her lawyer, and that a letter expressing her position on the matter would be forthcoming later that day. Magdalena was going to fight.

Martín showed up in court on Saturday, July 7, with documents and letters ready to initiate a case. And so, the disenso (dissent) case of Mariquita and Martín against her mother began. Over the next few days, mother, daughter, and fiancé would all submit various letters of testimony to the court. Martín began by writing a letter recounting the couple's three-year odyssey of love, suffering, and separation. Finding it "intolerable to keep enduring these disruptions," Martín submitted himself "to the integrity of Your Excellency," asking the judge to empower Mariquita to marry without her mother's permission. That "Excellency" was the viceroy of Río de la Plata himself, the Marquis de Sobremonte. A revision of the Royal Pragmatic on Marriage just the year

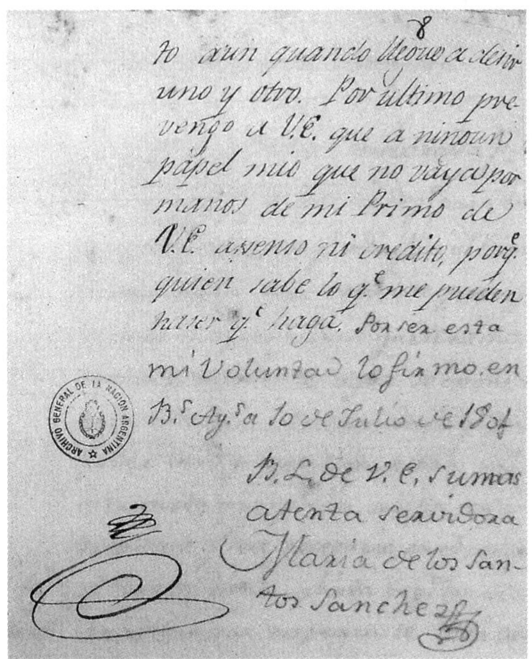

FIGURE 2.3 Last page from one of Mariquita's letters in her and Martín Thompson's disenso case against her mother. Visible is Mariquita's warning to the court against accepting any documents unless they are from her suitor, Martín. Her signature at the bottom is in her own handwriting. Courtesy of the Archivo General de la Nación, Buenos Aires.

before placed the viceroy in charge of hearing the disenso cases of prominent citizens. Because Mariquita was from an influential family, and because of Martín's position in the Royal Navy, the case fell under Viceroy Sobremonte's jurisdiction.

On July 10, Mariquita wrote a letter telling Viceroy Sobremonte that it was time for her to defend her rights. She also asked the viceroy to place her in a kind of safe house, away from her mother, which he did. Mariquita feared that the "tears of a mother" might convince her to reject Martín. She also feared that her mother might try some trick to derail their case. With that in mind, Mariquita warned the viceroy not to accept any document supposedly written by herself (Mariquita) unless it came directly from Martín, because "who knows who might try to do what" with her. She signed the letter, "This being my will I so declare in Buenos Aires, the 10th of July 1804."[13]

The court was also aware that nefarious tactics could be employed in such cases, and the judge was not going to accept letters without verification either. Over the years royal officials witnessed all kinds of trickery and coercion— forged letters from parents, boyfriends deceiving girlfriends into signing letters, and more.[14] Verifying validity of letters was done in person when possible. So on the morning of July 12, a court notary visited Mariquita in her safe house. The notary asked her if the letters the court had received were truly written by her, and if they expressed her free will on the matter. To swear in the affirmative, Mariquita put her thumb, pointer, and middle fingers together to symbolize the Holy Trinity; then she made the sign of the cross by touching her forehead, her chest, and then her right and left shoulders in smooth succession. She then swore to tell the truth: the letters of July 10 and 11 "were true" and "the signature found at the bottom of each of them, which says *María de los Santos Sánchez*," was made by her hand.[15] Satisfied that Mariquita's free will was to marry Martín, Viceroy Sobremonte turned his attention to Mariquita's mother. The viceroy gave her two days to either grant permission to her daughter or "present the cause or reason she has to deny her permission." Magdalena complied with an exhaustive list of complaints and justifications.

She of course wanted Mariquita to marry someday, but it was not this day because her dead husband had opposed it, and because Thompson was too close of a cousin, and furthermore she did not approve of his military career, which did not prepare him to run the family businesses, and their marriage would thus be a scandalous and ruinous affair, and even though she might accept Thompson if he were the last man on earth, there were other eligible suitors vying for Mariquita's hand, and under the circumstances no prudent magistrate would force a mother to concede when her young and gullible daughter was being deceived by a cunning pretender, something easily recognized by those who, in the autumn of their lives, see the follies of their own youthful escapades and who can thus clearly see that Martín and Mariquita's relationship was nothing more than passion and seductive fascination, which any good and spiritual daughter would avoid by honoring the will of her parents, because if she didn't she would create eternal bitterness and scandal in the family, something that the viceroy, a good Christian father himself, would never allow because he supported good marriages and rejected bad ones.

In his and Mariquita's defense, Martín claimed that Magdalena's lengthy list of arguments was based on the "weakest of pretexts that could be imagined." Spanish law, he argued, never meant to make parents the arbiters of the free will of their children, nor did it grant parents the right to capriciously oppose marriages. Moreover, he continued, Magdalena failed to acknowledge the sacred purpose of "the holy sacrament of marriage." Martín was insulted by her attacks on his education and character, especially because his reputation was respected by all who knew him. Magdalena's case, he concluded, was nothing more than a "shot in the dark" that deserved only his "Excellency's disdain."[16]

Viceroy Sobremonte took all the evidence into consideration, and on Friday, July 20, 1804—nearly two weeks after the case began—he issued his final judgment. Magdalena Trillo, he concluded, failed to present "just and rational evidence of any kind" that could "legally block the marriage between the midshipman don Martín Thompson and her daughter María de los Santos Sánchez y Trillo." Viceroy Sobremonte thus granted Mariquita and Martín permission to marry. The court informed Martín and Magdalena the next day.[17] Elated, Martín and Mariquita were married a few months later, on June 29, 1805, in the Church of La Merced by her confessor, Fray Cayetano Rodríguez. Her mother, Magdalena, now resigned to the marriage, served as one of the witnesses.[18]

Mariquita and Martín soon welcomed children into their family. Clementina was born in 1807, followed by Juan (1809), Magdalena (1811), Florencia (1812), and Albina (1815).[19] Mariquita, as will be seen, was always an attentive and energetic mother.

Juan Manuel and Encarnación

Mariquita Sánchez was not the only stubborn youth in her neighborhood. Juan Manuel was eleven years old when Mariquita and Martín took Magdalena to court, and he most likely heard gossip about the case around town. A few years later, in 1813, Juan Manuel clashed with his parents, with Agustina in particular, when he decided to get married. From his youth Juan Manuel had a serious and focused nature. He seemed uninterested in the carousing life, and as a young teenager he set his eye on Encarnación Ezcurra—the daughter of a prominent porteño family—with her beautiful black eyes and a strong and loyal character. During their courtship, Juan Manuel visited Encarnación frequently when he was in the city; when away in the countryside he rode the many miles to visit her as often as he could. When Juan Manuel proposed marriage to Encarnación, he was just twenty years old.[20]

Juan Manuel's mother, Agustina, immediately opposed the marriage. Her reason was simple: Juan Manuel was simply too young. To support her argument, Agustina could have pointed to the recent wedding of Captain José de San Martín, an Argentine who became a decorated commander in the Spanish army in Europe. Only a few months before, San Martín had returned to

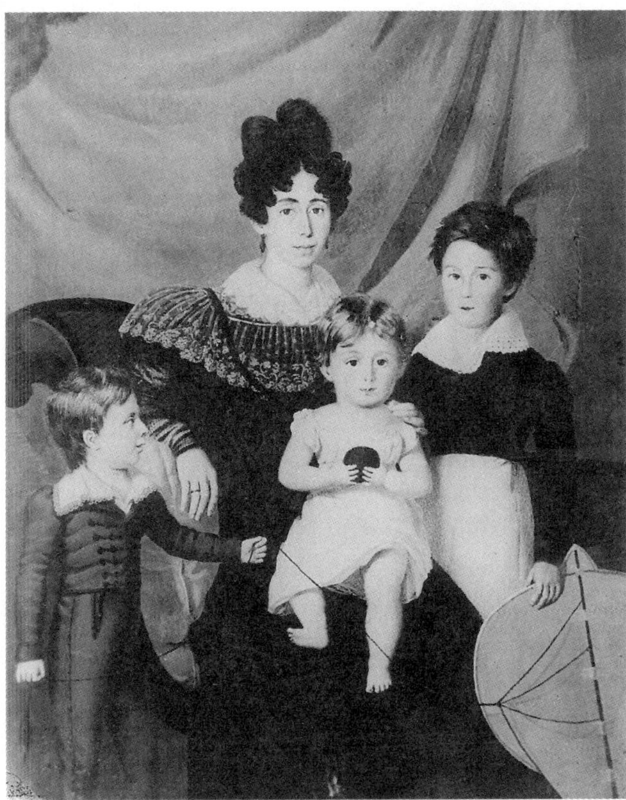

FIGURE 2.4 Portrait of María Sánchez de Thompson and her first three children: Clementina, Juan, and Magdalena. Courtesy of the Museo Histórico Nacional, Buenos Aires.

Buenos Aires and, soon thereafter, married the young porteña Remedios de la Escalada. She was fourteen and he was thirty-four. That timing was more to Agustina's liking: a man waiting to marry until he was more mature, economically secure, and ready to shoulder the responsibilities of a family. Juan Manuel disagreed. He never doubted his abilities to succeed in any endeavor, family matters included. Had he not been running large ranching operations since he was eighteen years old? Would that not give him the means to support a family? Nevertheless, Agustina persisted in her opposition.

A few years earlier, Mariquita and Martín had gone to court to get permission to marry, but only after years of struggling against parental intransigence. In their case, as with many other couples dealing with parents' opposition, going to court was usually a last resort. Before taking legal action, and risking the scandal of a public family conflict, many young people tried various strategies to convince their parents to give their consent. Couples pleaded and persuaded, and if that failed, bolder action could follow, such as running away, even attempting daring escapes by night out of second-story windows. And of course, children could cave in to parental persuasion and call off a marriage.[21]

Juan Manuel and Encarnación came up with their own ingenious strategy to convince Agustina that the marriage needed to proceed. Their plan was a simple one: to make Juan Manuel's mother, Agustina, believe that Encarnación was pregnant out of wedlock. This tactic played to the importance of honor in Hispanic society. Honor was a multifaceted concept in Buenos Aires, as it was elsewhere. One's honor could be tied to racial purity and social class. Male honor was frequently linked to the respect men felt they deserved, as men, from others in society. Insults to one's honor, whether by a peer or a social inferior, might lead to a duel. For women, the highest form of honor in Hispanic society was female sexual purity, a double standard that did not apply to men. Traditionally, honor was a concept associated with the upper classes. Honorable families consisted of wealthy men who married chaste wealthy women who would then bear legitimate children. Anything less than that, for elite families at least, would be scandalous.[22]

It was precisely the threat of scandal that Juan Manuel was counting on. Once a woman was pregnant out of wedlock, there was only one way to avoid dishonor: she had to marry the father of her unborn child.[23] Juan Manuel asked Encarnación to write him a letter saying they needed to marry as quickly as possible because she was pregnant. Encarnación agreed, wrote the letter, and Juan Manuel left it in a place where his mother was sure to find it. And find it Agustina did. She immediately rushed to see Encarnación's mother to tell her the news.[24] Needless to say, wedding plans were soon in the making. After all, Agustina wanted her grandchildren to have the same "legitimate child" reference on their baptismal record, just like Juan Manuel did twenty years earlier. Juan Manuel and Encarnación were married on March 13, 1813. Their first child, Juan Bautista, was born in 1814, followed by a daughter, María, who only lived one day after her birth in 1816. In 1817, a daughter, Manuela, was born.[25] Manuelita (Little Manuela), as she was called, would become her father's favorite child.

Attitudes toward Child-Rearing and Proper Behavior

How did porteño families raise their children at the turn of the nineteenth century? Assessing and measuring child-rearing practice during this time is difficult. The history of the family, including the history of childhood, is dynamic, with each generation challenging certain tenets of preceding generations. The Bourbon Reforms added an additional measure of change as Spanish officials sought to increase royal control over its subjects, including more government intervention into family life. One example was the Royal Pragmatic on Marriage (as seen in the court battle between Mariquita and her mother), which gave the crown authority to rule in these kinds of disputes instead of the Catholic Church.[26]

Manuals on child-rearing and child education did exist in Spain and its colonies, although it is hard to prove that Mariquita or Juan Manuel or their parents read this or that manual. Because both Mariquita and Juan Manuel started their families at relatively young ages, they and their parents were exposed to many of the same ideas regarding the proper raising of children. Agustín Ginestá's manual published in 1797, *Protector of Children*, reflects some of the latest theories of the age, many of them inspired by Enlightenment ideas.[27] Published in Spain, Ginestá's advice touched on a number of topics, including breastfeeding, how to handle fussy babies, and how to best discipline children. A mother's milk, Ginestá argued, was far superior to a hired wet nurse's, echoing a common critique of the day.[28] However, if a wet nurse was necessary, she needed to have good health and good morals since breast milk could transmit undesirable qualities. In addition, "no woman in good conscience can breast feed a child while in a violent emotional state, because of the serious consequences that have been observed." Moving to another topic, Ginestá wrote that parents should pay attention to crying babies since that is their only form of communication. However, he continued, "there are children who cry out of habit, with little or no cause. If this is the case, pay no attention to their screams." Ginestá also advised against overly harsh punishment of children. "You should reprimand them rarely, and punish them even less, and all with mildness and without showing anger." Whether in rewarding or disciplining your child, Ginestá asserted, "always let them know, as much as possible, the reason behind it, for this will benefit their health and morals."

Ginestá also believed it was fine to let children speak and ask lots of questions: "otherwise, besides retarding their learning of common knowledge, they will grow up introverted and timid."[29]

While Mariquita did not reference in her memoir or letters any manual she or her parents may have read, she was quite critical of child-raising practices of her youth during the late eighteenth century. Surely her critique was in part a commentary on her own parents' approach to child-rearing. As children emerge from infancy, Mariquita recalled, "parents begin to be more serious and to withhold their affection." Parents thought it their duty to be severe and to maintain formal relationships with their children. "It was respect mixed with fear." Children referred to their parents as "sir" and did not make eye contact with them.[30] At least in Mariquita's recollection, many of the ideas about mild-mannered parenting found in Ginestá's *Protector of Children* were not implemented fully by her parents or others.

Mariquita's critique of parental behavior continued as she discussed the question of marriage. Her own harrowing experience served as an example, and she was not alone. The parents, she wrote, had the upper hand unless couples were willing to fight back. "The father arranged everything according to his will." He might choose a husband and only "tell his wife and daughter three or four days before the wedding." Marrying for love was not much of an option. To speak about matters of the heart was a "diabolical farce" to parents, and their "poor daughters knew better than to express even the slightest opinion" on such matters. Instead of letting her choose her own husband, a "beautiful young girl" would be forced to marry a man "old enough to be her father." In those days, she continued, "it was not considered important to enjoy oneself," nor was it customary to marry the mate of one's choosing. This put daughters in a predicament. They would "suffer a thousand sorrows" agonizing over whether to fight their parents or "abandon their own desires." For that reason, Mariquita concluded, many young women chose to become nuns rather than being forced to marry a man who inspired "aversion rather than love." The very word "love" was "scandalous in the mouth of a young woman! Love was persecuted. Love was seen as a deprivation."[31]

A glance at some of the newspapers of the time also reveals discussions about proper behavior and attitudes about child-rearing. The *Telégrafo Mercantil*, a weekly newspaper in Buenos Aires, included a "Festive Satire" in many of its editions. These satires took aim at behavior the paper's editors deemed inappropriate, by contrast implying their view of appropriate behavior. Mariquita was an avid reader, and it is highly likely that both she and her parents read the *Telégrafo* frequently. On January 17, 1802, the *Telégrafo's* "Festive Satire" contained a number of references to issues related to Mariquita and her family. By that date, she and Martín had already promised themselves to one another, and the conflict with her parents had begun. The satire on January 17 referred to certain types of people and behavior as being "lovely examples," although it was obvious to readers that the editors believed such attitudes and behaviors to be inappropriate. "Cloris is in church, and her husband is at work, and the kids are in bed, while the pot on the stove is cold—a lovely example!" In the next line, "a mother quarrels with her daughter because she wants to get married, then leaves her home alone with all the freedom to roam—a lovely example!" Other questionable behaviors and attitudes were ridiculed in the lines that followed: A ten-year-old girl knew the latest dance steps but could not say her rosary. Another couplet pointed out the contradiction that many people chose not to get married in the region, yet, every day, people abandoned children at the city's foundling wheel.[32]

The editors then turned their attention to the practice of swimming in the river and the various dilemmas that accompanied public bathing. Social space in city streets, homes, and buildings could be regulated and monitored by city officials and family members. The waters of the river, however, constituted a different space more difficult to control, a space where genders and ethnicities could mix in ways that would be scandalous on land. If the practice was targeted in the newspaper, it was likely a popular pastime among the people, including members of the middle and upper classes, who would have been the main audience of the *Telégrafo*. The editors left no doubt about their views. "That women, single and married, take off their clothes, in the presence of a thousand men, to bathe [in the river]—what lovely examples! That Portia prevents her daughter from sitting too close to Gil, while she goes into the river in the arms of Blas. And finally, that in the river, as if it was a whorehouse, men, women, and children all jump in and swim together—what a beautiful example!"[33] The next week's edition included more criticism of river-bathing culture. The editors rejected those who entered the river "with whites and blacks, without shame or decorum or respect."

One line in the *Telégrafo's* "Festive Satire" of January 24 would have hit Mariquita right in the heart: "I decry he who gives his promise of marriage to

Inés, and then leaves her playing the tambourine." This was in reference to men who, like the Don Juan of fiction, promised to marry a young woman only to abandon her, many times after having sexual relations with her, thus leaving her honor in ruins. And while Martín had not abandoned Mariquita in 1802, he had promised his hand in marriage, and that promise remained unfulfilled. Further down in the satire was another critique that would have caught Mariquita's eye. The author repudiated "the ugly girl who, like the fires of hell, has cut all her hair in the English style."[34] We may not know if Mariquita wore her hair English-style in 1802. But we do know from her memoirs that during her youth, she came to admire foreign ideas and foreign fashion (see chapter 3).

While these satirical verses may have been somewhat playful and humorous, the sentiments of the *Telégrafo Mercantil* reveal tensions between certain elite groups (like the editors) and certain cultural practices (like swimming in the river) that seemed to be practiced by a cross section of porteño society. If the editors of the *Telégrafo* had their way, parents like Cecilio and Magdalena (and just a few years later, Mariquita and Juan Manuel) would raise their children to honor traditional morals, including the traditional racial and class divisions that the Spanish Empire was trying desperately to uphold.

Conclusion

Mariquita's and Juan Manuel's courtships did not follow the ideal script their parents desired for them. Their experiences demonstrate that family life rarely conformed to the norms laid out by parents, ecclesiastical and civil officials, and newspaper editors like those in the *Telégrafo Mercantil*. Rather, family life was a series of negotiations. Parents had a preponderance of power, but children exercised power as well, sometimes formally in the courts, but more often informally through determined resistance and strategic maneuvers. Love was enough to motivate Mariquita and Juan Manuel to rebel against their parents. Children had been doing that since the beginning of time. But couples did have allies, since the Catholic Church supported freedom to choose in marriage.

However, questions of freedom in the early 1800s touched on other issues besides marriage. Ideas about the political rights of individuals and peoples were also fermenting in the Río de la Plata. Some of these ideas were coming from within the Spanish Empire itself, which experienced its own version of the Enlightenment—sometimes called the Catholic Enlightenment—which emphasized innovative thinking in science, technology, and economics rather than in politics and religion.[35] And Spain's American colonies themselves contributed in their own way to the age of Enlightenment.[36] But toward the end of the eighteenth century, more and more ideas also flowed into Spain and its colonies from France, England, the United States, and elsewhere. Mariquita was friends with people like Manuel Belgrano, who traveled to Europe and absorbed elements of Enlightenment thought that he hoped would influence the Río de la Plata region.[37] And although the Spanish Inquisition prohibited many writings that promoted new freedoms, those prohibitions fueled even greater interest.[38] There were even a few people Mariquita knew in the city who hoped to break away from Spain altogether and create a new nation. Mariquita was fascinated by all of these ideas and sought them out wherever she could find them. She also sought out fine foreign merchandise, especially items brought by British merchants. Little did she know that the British were about to show her and her city another side of English civilization—a side with red coats, bagpipes, and bayonets.

CHAPTER THREE

The English Invasions

On June 28, 1806, British soldiers conquered Buenos Aires. Mariquita Sánchez de Thompson watched them march into the city as tears streamed down the faces of many onlookers. The soldiers went straight to the fort and raised the Union Jack. When the British naval captain Sir Home Popham saw the flag, his squadron anchored in the river unleashed a massive cannonade that shook the city. No one had ever heard such a powerful blast before, and it brought home the tragic reality that the city had been conquered by foreigners. And, to make matters worse, as Mariquita emphasized, these foreigners were of the worst kind: they were heretical Protestants! The very next day, however, porteños began plotting to expel the invaders, which they would do just a few weeks later. Key to the porteño victory was the local militia, which included many young boys, among them a teenager named Juan Manuel de Rosas.[1]

The English invasions of Buenos Aires emerged from a complex web of events and unexpected consequences that spanned the Atlantic World and the globe, from London to South Africa and beyond. The British believed that Spanish Americans would welcome them as liberators from Spanish tyranny. Those hopes were sorely misplaced. Instead, the invasions provided a catalyst for the growth of local identity and popular democratic elements in porteño society. At the same time, the English invasions reflected the increasing presence of foreigners, foreign ideas, and foreign products in the Río de la Plata, which would have long-standing political and cultural ramifications for Mariquita and Juan Manuel, and for the beginnings of Argentina.

Throughout much of the eighteenth century, Spain was locked in a global competition for empire with Britain and other growing powers. The Spaniards had long been taking notice of British ascendance. Prominent Spanish economists and politicians had for years argued that their empire was in need of rejuvenation. Spain, they argued, was losing ground to younger, more vigorous empires like Great Britain who based their wealth and power on trade rather than on land and gold.[2] Unfortunately for Spain, in the late eighteenth and early nineteenth century, it was almost always at war with England or France—two Atlantic superpowers of the day, which created chronic disruptions in trade and communication between Spain and its colonies.[3] After 1796, Spain and France allied together against Great Britain. The British responded by blockading Spanish ports and capturing Spanish vessels on the high seas, causing further turmoil for Spain's commerce and for its dwindling treasury.[4]

Francisco de Miranda and Home Popham:
Two Friends with a Grand Plan

Besides competition from rival imperial powers, the Spanish Empire also faced threats from homegrown revolutionaries like the wealthy Venezuelan Francisco de Miranda. A decorated Spanish army officer who loved to read Enlightenment literature, Miranda deserted the Spanish military in 1783, and while living in Europe, he laid plans to liberate Spanish America from Spain's oppressive rule. Intelligent, handsome, and charismatic, Miranda was welcomed everywhere he went as an enlightened gentleman, traveling in a trans-Atlantic community of individuals who saw themselves as belonging to an informal community called the "Republic of Letters."[5] Eventually Miranda settled down in England, married, and started a family, although he still dreamt of liberating his homeland. South America, he believed, was teetering on the edge of revolution, and all he needed to do was to give it a little push, perhaps with a bit of help from the English.

One of Miranda's friends and coconspirators in many of these plans was Sir Home Popham, an experienced and well-respected officer in the Royal Navy. Together Popham and Miranda concocted plans to liberate Venezuela, plans that attracted the British government enough to outfit Popham with a sixty-four-gun warship.[6] However, according to Popham, Prime Minister William Pitt informed him personally that England would try to use diplomatic means to persuade Spain to break its alliance with Napoleon, who was now bent on expanding the French Empire throughout Europe and beyond. Nevertheless, Pitt added, if diplomacy failed, then armed intervention would become an option.[7]

Although Miranda spent years scheming to invade South America, Home Popham was first to get the chance to fulfill their dreams. In November of 1805, Popham commanded British naval forces that attacked the Dutch Cape Colony—an ally of Napoleon—in South Africa. Soon after arriving in early January 1806, the British routed the Dutch forces. The Cape Colony now belonged to England.[8] Popham, however, itched for more. With his ships at anchor, his guns silent, and the newly conquered colony secure, Popham could not help but think of what lay just a few short weeks to the west: the cities of Montevideo and Buenos Aires, the jewels of the Spanish South Atlantic. Over the years, and especially in the preceding weeks and months, Popham had heard tantalizing reports from former residents of Montevideo and Buenos Aires. Both cities were so poorly defended that they could be captured easily. In fact, one of Popham's informants remarked, Buenos Aires's inhabitants were so oppressed by their Spanish masters that they themselves would "assist in the conquest of the place."[9]

Over the next few weeks, remarkable news arrived in South Africa that spurred Popham to action. Diplomatic efforts to break Spain's alliance with France had failed. Furthermore, recent victories by Napoleon now gave him control of nearly all of Europe, and he prohibited all European ports from trading with the British. As Popham analyzed this extraordinary series of events, he concluded one thing: he could now pursue his dream of attacking Spanish America, and he would do it in the Río de la Plata region.[10] It was not difficult for Popham to convince his superior officers to give him ships and men for his expedition. Popham argued persuasively that the well-known agricultural bounties of Montevideo and Buenos Aries could support the newly won South African colony.[11] In addition, controlling the Río de la Plata would give British merchants a much-needed outlet for their goods—goods Napoleon prohibited from continental Europe.[12] Convinced by such arguments, Popham's commander allowed him to take a squadron of ships, some artillery, and a small force of men. It was a deadly force, to be sure, but not a large one, a fact that did not bother Popham because he believed the residents of Buenos Aires and Montevideo would at least acquiesce, if not collaborate, in the overthrow of Spanish power. Popham led the naval force while the ground troops were commanded by thirty-seven-year-old Brigadier General William Carr Beresford.[13] Popham and Beresford's force left South Africa on April 14, 1806. The original plan was to attack Montevideo first, but Popham changed the target to

Buenos Aires after receiving word from a passing ship that, to Popham's great delight, a large consignment of silver had just arrived in Buenos Aires from the Spanish mines of Upper Peru.[14]

Popham's fleet arrived at the northern mouth of the Río de la Plata in late May 1806. Spanish naval forces spotted Popham's squadron and informed Viceroy Sobremonte in Buenos Aires. The viceroy assumed the sails belonged to British smugglers, who were quite common in the region. Nevertheless, Sobremonte put a few militia units on alert. On June 16, 1806, the invasion force anchored eight miles downriver from Buenos Aires. As the British disembarked, porteño observers quickly sent word that these were soldiers and not smugglers. Among the first to get the news was Martín Thompson, who now was captain of the port. Martín informed the viceroy, who was enjoying an evening at the theater. Upon hearing the news, Viceroy Sobremonte immediately left the theater and, accompanied by elite cavalry units, fled to the city of Córdoba, some four hundred miles northeast of the port.[15]

On June 26, General Beresford and his men began their advance toward Buenos Aires. The force consisted of 70 officers, 1571 men, 9 cannons, and 2 howitzer guns. The British engaged in some skirmishing with small detachments of porteño militia along the way. As the British arrived on the outskirts of Buenos Aires on June 27, city leaders decided to surrender. Thus the British marched into the city center playing their bagpipes instead of firing their muskets. Beresford headed straight for the fort, where he ran up the Union Jack. A thundering cannonade quickly followed, fired by Popham's ships anchored nearby.

One of the first things Beresford did was request reinforcements from London. His 1600 men, he knew, would not be nearly enough to hold a city of 40,000 people, especially if local residents decided to resist. He and Popham also sent letters to England announcing that Buenos Aires was now open to British merchants. Hoping to win over local residents, many of whom were resentful of Spanish economic restrictions, Beresford issued decrees opening the port of Buenos Aires to free trade. Although their mission was technically unsanctioned, Beresford and Popham were sure their victory would be well received in London. Meanwhile, Popham sent his men after the silver treasure he had heard about. His men returned a few days later, their mission accomplished, with more than one million dollars of treasure and money.[16] General Beresford and Sir Home Popham were now masters of Buenos Aires.

Porteño Fear, Fascination, and Anger

"What a night!" wrote Mariquita Sánchez de Thompson, who had a front row seat for all of these events. "It cannot be overstated," she later wrote, "how all the people the viceroy put in charge of defending the city that night were so surprised by the situation, and by the impossibility of saving the country."[17] In her recollections of the invasion, Mariquita may have been a bit more sympathetic toward the civilian and military leaders. After all, her husband was captain of the port and Viceroy Sobremonte was the one who had ruled in the couple's favor during their marriage dispute with Mariquita's mother just two year earlier. Others would say the viceroy panicked, and plans for defense were abandoned, as the British marched unmolested into Buenos Aires.

Mariquita was there watching as the 71st Highlander Regiment marched into the city with its bright uniforms, playing its military pipes.[18] During the invasion and its aftermath, Mariquita showed her willingness to mourn, but also her ability to be objective, or at least attempt to be objective, in her assessment of the English presence in Buenos Aires. At the same time, she revealed a strong proclivity for new things, both material and intellectual.

As Mariquita watched the invaders enter the city, she could not help but notice a glaring difference between the British troops and the local porteño militiamen. "I will paint a picture of these two military forces," she informed her readers. "First the militia of Buenos Aires. It must be said that our country folk are not pretty. They are robust and strong, but dark-skinned." Their uniforms, if they had any, did not match, and they looked dirty and disheveled. "Everything was more miserable and ugly. Their weapons were filthy." As the occupation proceeded, Mariquita told her friend that "if the English aren't scared off by this sight, there is no hope."[19] The British invaders, on the other hand, stunned Mariquita with their appearance and organization. The soldiers of the invading regiment (the 71st Highlanders) were "the most beautiful youths, with snow-white faces." They were the "best looking troops ever seen, in the most poetic uniforms, boots with red laces, a bit of leg showing, a short skirt, and tall hats." Furthermore, the troops looked so clean. "What a huge contrast!" she exclaimed.[20]

Although some porteños were impressed by the foreigners' appearance, most were devastated by the British occupation. Among them was Mariano Moreno, a radical young liberal who read widely in Enlightenment literature.

He admired Jean-Jacques Rousseau's *The Social Contract,* and also believed in applying Adam Smith's free-trade ideas in the Río de la Plata. In short, Mariano Moreno was exactly the kind of person that was supposed to welcome the British as liberators. At least that is what people like Francisco de Miranda and Home Popham had preached for years—that colonists would jump at the chance to rid themselves of their oppressive Spanish overlords. But instead of welcoming the invaders, Mariano Moreno wept. "I myself have cried more than anyone when at 3:00 p.m. of 27 June I saw 1560 Englishmen take control of my country and install themselves in the fortress and in the other sectors of the city."[21] The British clearly misread the situation. Porteños may not have approved of all the Spanish crown's policies, but they would not—they could not—live willingly under the Union Jack.

With the British headquartered in the Plaza Mayor, porteños struggled over how to deal with the new reality. How should they interact with the British, if at all? Were the British to be treated as legitimate or illegitimate conquerors? Were they to be welcomed, shunned, attacked?

General Beresford did what he could to gain the favor of porteño residents. He issued decrees allowing free trade and reassured business owners that their property would be protected. Beresford also tried to calm fears about growing slave unrest in the city and countryside. Apparently, some masters reported that slaves had become more restless and insubordinate after the British invasion. One rumor circulating in the capital was that slaves imported from the French Caribbean were behind the unrest. This was a particularly disturbing assertion because it conjured up images of the most radical and bloody elements of the French Revolution, the ripples of which reached American shores. At least two recent examples weighed on the porteños' minds. In 1795, French slaveholders and some of their slaves had conspired to overthrow the Spanish government in Buenos Aires.[22] Even more recently, slaves in Saint-Domingue had finally succeeded in their rebellion against France and founded the new republic of Haiti in 1804. Now, in Buenos Aires, slave owners feared that the infection of revolution had spread to the Río de la Plata.[23] General Beresford wanted to win the hearts of the porteño ruling classes, and so he issued a decree that slaves should obey their masters with "total and absolute subordination," and that they should cease "spending time idly in the streets," or else face the "severe punishment that his Excellency the British Major-General sees fit to impose."[24]

After the initial shock of the invasion, many porteños were gripped by anger—anger at the British, but anger also toward Viceroy Sobremonte for fleeing, as well as toward the professional military units for surrendering so easily. One porteño, Juan Manuel Beruti, kept a running journal during the invasions (and for much of his life). By his estimation, there were more than enough defense forces—perhaps as many as eight thousand soldiers—to turn back Beresford's men. Beruti was ashamed that leadership had failed, from the viceroy on down, allowing a small, unsupported British force to take the city virtually unopposed.[25]

One of the British occupiers, Alexander Gillespie, personally witnessed another facet of local residents' anger. A few hours after the surrender of the city, Gillespie and some fellow British officers went out for some food and refreshment in the tavern of Los Tres Reyes (The Three Kings). Gillespie recorded what happened next in his memoirs. As he and his friends sat down, they noticed a number of Spanish officers sitting at the other end of the same table. As Gillespie observed this awkward situation, his eye could not help but notice the young woman serving both groups of men. The woman was beautiful, Gillespie noted, but "on her brow sat a deep frown." When she refrained from making eye contact with her English customers, Gillespie assumed her foul mood was directed at him and his companions, perhaps, he thought, because she feared they would eat their food and leave without paying.[26]

Gillespie decided to "remove every unfavourable prejudice" against him and his companions. He first assured his host that he and his friends had only chivalrous intentions. He then asked her to explain the reasons for her obvious displeasure. She thanked Gillespie for his "honourable declaration," but instead of addressing the Englishmen, she turned angrily toward the Spanish officers. In a "loud and most impressive tone," she declared: "I wish you gentlemen had informed us sooner of your cowardly intentions to surrender Buenos Aires, for I will stake my life that had we known it, the women would have turned out unanimously, and driven back the English with stones." Gillespie recorded that her "heroic speech astounded those warriors," and "after its delivery, she resumed her natural good humor and charm."[27]

For some porteños, the distress of the invasion was soon replaced by curiosity and even admiration. Mariquita found General Beresford to be courteous and respectful. In fact, he treated the archbishop of Buenos Aires with such respect that a rumor circulated in the city that Beresford was a Catholic.[28] Some mutual friendships also developed as many English officers lived with private citizens. Alexander Gillespie was even invited once to dine in the house of a porteño military captain. After a bounteous dinner, Gillespie's hosts amused their guests "with some pretty English and Spanish airs upon the guitar, accompanied by those female voices." Dinner was at two, "and the party broke up to their siesta at four o'clock."[29]

La Reconquista of Buenos Aires

Such polite and accommodating treatment of the invaders greatly disturbed other city residents who refused to forget the dishonor and humiliation of losing their city to a band of heretical Protestants. It did not take long for porteños to begin plans to retake their city.

One of the first forms of porteño resistance was to encourage desertion. The British saw it happening before their very eyes. "The Spaniards are doing all in their power to encourage our men to desert our service, and go into the country and join their own," wrote the British captain Pococke in his journal.[30] It was not hard to convince some soldiers to exchange their arduous life of sailing in cramped vessels and fighting on far-flung shores for a life of abundance on the Pampas.

Members of the Catholic clergy took an active role in the resistance as well. In the minds of many priests, the devil himself had come to Buenos Aires, and the Catholic faith was in jeopardy.[31] Priests openly preached resistance and rebellion from church pulpits. Some Church leaders engaged in even more open resistance. Priests at the church of San Francisco permitted porteño dissidents to dig a tunnel from inside the church and then under the British barracks across the street. The plan was to place thirty-six barrels of gunpowder at the end of the tunnel and blow the British to bits. The British discovered the plot before it could be carried out.[32]

One of those greatly affected by the religion question was Santiago Liniers, a French-born naval commander in the service of Spain. While attending Mass in postoccupation Buenos Aires, Liniers sensed a lack of solemnity in the service, which he blamed on the pernicious British presence.[33] Liniers soon traveled to Montevideo where he, along with Viceroy Sobremonte and others, began recruiting soldiers and making concrete plans to expel the British. Liniers and the viceroy appointed Juan Martín de Pueyrredón to raise an army in

Buenos Aires, and soon many answered his call, including men and boys from wealthy families. Numerous slaves also volunteered to fight alongside their masters. Among the young volunteers was thirteen-year-old Juan Manuel de Rozas, who accepted a commission to serve with an artillery group. Santiago Liniers was a friend of the Rozas family, and Juan Manuel was proud to serve under his command. In addition to Creole recruits, a number of friendly Indians responded to the call for aid. Chief Loncoy, for instance, offered men and horses to help expel the British.[34] By August 1, the porteños began to muster on both sides of the river.

General Beresford, meanwhile, prepared for the pending porteño assault. The center of Buenos Aires was laid out in a perfect grid pattern, with the Plaza Mayor at its center. The plaza was a rectangle with the fort on the eastern end, next to the river, and the cabildo on the opposite side (the west end). Just to the right of the cabildo was the cathedral. Cutting the plaza in half, and parallel with the fort and the cabildo, was a covered colonnade known as the *recova*. Seen from a bird's-eye view, eight different streets emptied into the plaza, and ten buildings surrounded it. Beresford placed cannons in the fort and around the plaza, and his soldiers took up strategic positions in the cabildo and the surrounding buildings, and in the streets leading out of the city. Beresford also politely rejected Liniers's demand that the British surrender without a fight.

Liniers ordered his men into the city on August 11, 1806. In addition to the regular troops, thousands of armed civilians, and many of their slaves, joined the fight. The British began immediately to suffer heavy losses inflicted by porteño forces, including from gunmen hiding in houses and on rooftops.[35] As casualties mounted, Beresford ordered a retreat to his fortified positions in the plaza—at the cathedral, in the cabildo building, in the recova, and in the fort itself. The British would triumph or fall in the Plaza Mayor. The next morning, porteño troops and civilians continued their advance, block by block, toward the city center. Civilians again fired on the British from their windows, balconies, and rooftops. Some women took part in the fighting as well. Manuela Pedraza from Tucumán Province, for example, dressed up like a man and joined in the fray.[36]

Juan Manuel and other young boys helped maneuver cannons and carry ammunition.[37] They scurried around, gathering bullets fired by the enemy to be used in turn against them. Witnesses saw one boy remove his shirt and use it to help prepare one of the cannons for firing. When one artilleryman fell dead at his cannon, another young boy took up the firebrand, lit the fuse, and fired on British positions.[38]

The Argentine second lieutenant Francisco Gonzáles de la Peña was in the thick of the fight. He and his men, along with a few daring civilians, moved from Retiro Park eastward down San José del Correo Street, fighting the British for every inch. After eleven blocks, they made a left turn onto Cabildo Street, which emptied into the corner of the plaza next to the cabildo. Gonzáles de la Peña and his men could now see into the plaza one block away, with the fort on the opposite end. By now, the fighting was concentrated, with multiple cannons blazing in a three-block radius. All around them was a living hell of canon and musket fire.[39]

From his position on Cabildo Street, Gonzáles de la Peña aimed his four-pound cannon at a British position in the plaza and took it out. He then turned his sights on an English cannon firing from the ramparts of the fort, and knocked it out of commission. The British began to waver under the withering fire of thousands of porteños. As the enemy fell back toward the fort, Gonzáles de la Peña and his men helped secure the cabildo, then moved to the recova that spanned the middle of the plaza. From there he opened fire with his musket on the British soldiers in the plaza and on the fort's ramparts. Through the smoke and haze, Gonzáles de la Peña saw the remaining British soldiers retreat into the fort. The last to enter was none other than General Beresford himself, before the drawbridge went up. Exhausted but exuberant, Gonzáles de la Peña later calculated that he fired 187 rounds from his rifle during the battle.[40]

From inside the fort, Beresford saw the plaza fill up with an angry crowd shouting for British blood. He ran up the white flag of truce. Liniers initially granted generous terms of surrender, which would allow the British to return home. However, when news of the lenient agreement spread around the city, the people rose up in protest. Besieged by popular demands to keep the British captive, and under pressure from the town council, Liniers felt compelled to retract his initial offer. Beresford protested but was in no position to resist. He and his remaining 1400 men were now prisoners.[41]

The Cabildo Celebrates and Prepares
for Another English Invasion

After the porteño victory of August 12, the city took time to bury the dead, to celebrate, and then to get ready for another possible invasion.[42] The day after the battle, invitations were sent to the most prominent gentlemen of the city—wealthy men known as *vecinos*—to attend a *cabildo abierto*. The cabildo abierto was a kind of expanded town council, a quasi-democratic element in the Spanish political system that allowed wealthy married men of the community (the vecinos) to meet with city leaders on certain occasions to debate and vote on pressing matters.[43] One hundred persons attended the meeting the next morning.

Meanwhile, a large crowd gathered in the plaza outside the cabildo, cursing the English, but also hurling insults at Viceroy Sobremonte. The multitude was very interested in everything the cabildo was discussing. In fact, the crowd had something of their own to say to the cabildo: give Santiago Liniers, the great hero of the Reconquest, official command of all defense forces in the city. As the cabildo members deliberated, it was impossible for them to ignore the growing crowd outside. Some of the throng even entered the cabildo building itself. With the raucous crowd demanding that Santiago Liniers be elevated in command, the cabildo promised to send three of their most prominent officers to speak to the viceroy himself on this matter.[44]

Besides dealing with the boisterous crowd, porteño officials took time to express gratitude to those who helped expel the British. The young boys who fought received special attention. Santiago Liniers himself gave Juan Manuel a letter to take to his mother, commending his actions.[45] The cabildo sent a report to King Charles IV in Spain, praising the young fighters who defied enemy bullets in the "face of the death." The report also honored the young boys who died, noting that their sacrifice would be a glorious entry "in the annals of the great deeds of the Río de la Plata."[46] Poets quickly joined in the praise. The boys' courage was "without equal in the history of warfare," one writer declared. It was exhilarating to see "innumerable boys, entering the fray, pulling cannons and carrying cartridges," and shouting "Long live Spain and Charles IV! Death to England!"[47] This particular poet happened to be none other than Pantaleón Rivarola, the very priest who had baptized Juan Manuel thirteen years earlier.

The British may have lost the battle, but Santiago Liniers and others knew that England was not ready to concede the war. Indeed, the British naval squadron still prowled the river, and only a few weeks after the British defeat, Great Britain sent three thousand soldiers to the Río de la Plata, with more promised to follow. By October 29, those troops were on the Eastern Shore, across the river from Buenos Aires.

With a second British invasion imminent, porteño leaders again sought recruits in the city and countryside. The British officer Andrew Gillespie, now under house arrest in the home of a prominent cabildo member, watched it happen. "All the youths of the most respectable families hastened to enroll their names, and to submit to the laws of discipline."[48] Young boys continued in the service of the city's defenses. Juan Manuel left his position with the artillery crew and enrolled in a cavalry regiment known as the Migueletes.[49]

On February 3, 1807, the cabildo received news that the British had taken Montevideo, and that Viceroy Sobremonte had again fled before them. Everyone knew that Buenos Aires was next. In the face of this imminent threat, and with Viceroy Sobremonte again proving his incompetence, the War Council of Buenos Aires took an extraordinary measure: it removed Sobremonte as viceroy and replaced him with the wildly popular Santiago Liniers. On March 9, the newly empowered Liniers issued a passionate call to the people of Buenos Aires. Will you allow the British to come again and "profane your blessed territory?" Liniers assured them that their courage and experience would lead to success. "There is no other way before you but that of glory. Your first victory brought you admiration. May the second bring you immortality."[50]

Across the river, the British appointed General Whitelocke to lead the invasion. Normal tactics called for artillery bombardment before an invasion. However, Whitelocke and others feared for the safety of the 1400 English prisoners held in Buenos Aires, including General Beresford.[51] The British prisoners might be killed in the bombardment itself, or they could be killed by porteño forces in response to the renewed invasion. As a result of these fears, Whitelocke decided to send in troops without shelling the city first. He hoped to obtain victory with a massive show of force.[52]

And so the invasion went forward. Whitelocke ordered his attack on July 5. From the beginning, the British faced stiff resistance from the streets and rooftops. Again, the civilian population joined the fight, including as many as two thousand armed slaves.[53] Although some of Whitelocke's columns achieved

FIGURE 3.1 *The English Attack Buenos Aires and Are Repulsed* by José Cardano, engraving (1807). Courtesy of the Museo Histórico Nacional, Buenos Aires.

their objectives, overall things went badly for the British.[54] For example, Brigadier General Craufurd and his men captured the convent of Santo Domingo, just one block from the main plaza. However, porteño fighters bombarded his positions with "round shot, grape, and musketry," which forced Craufurd to abandon the top of the building and take refuge below. Before long, however, General Craufurd saw six thousand porteños with cannons coming to blow open the convent doors. He decided to surrender his troops at 4:00 p.m. Meanwhile, other British columns experienced heavy losses. Overall, the British suffered over two thousand casualties in the first day.

On the morning of July 6, Liniers sent a message to Whitelocke: if the British did not abandon the city, the safety of the 1400 British prisoners from the first invasion could not be assured. With Liniers's offer (and threat) in hand, Whitelocke pondered the numerous British losses as well as the intense opposition from the porteño population. He shared his dilemma with a fellow officer. "We have suffered much in every way . . . which seldom, under any circumstances, has been equaled." The situation even made Whitelocke begin to doubt the wisdom of Britain's whole enterprise in the Río de la Plata. "Of one thing you may be assured," he continued in his letter, "Spanish America never can be English, as the inveteracy of every class of inhabitants is beyond belief."[55] Whitelocke considered calling in his five thousand reserves but concluded that any gains would be unsustainable. He thought about a massive retreat but worried about losing more men in the process. In his mind, there were no good options.

After much excruciating thought, Whitelocke made a monumental decision: to surrender Buenos Aires *and* Montevideo. In justifying his choice, he cited his concern for the safety of the captive general, Beresford, and his fellow 1400 English prisoners. In addition, the "very hostile disposition" of the Buenos Aires population against the British, in his mind, meant that the city "was in truth not worth maintaining." As for Montevideo, in Whitelocke's estimation, it was not worth holding if the British did not control Buenos Aires. Under the treaty terms, there would be an exchange of prisoners (including Beresford's men), the British would leave Buenos Aires within ten days, and they would leave Montevideo within two months. This was all "done at the Fort of Buenos Ayres, the 7th day of July, 1807."[56]

Popular Classes, Slaves, and People of Color in the Reconquest

With the British now twice defeated, the city and the viceroyalty could take some time to savor their victories and recognize and reward all those who had participated in the triumphs. The cabildo sent more reports to the king of Spain recounting the latest heroics. One report emphasized the contributions of the people of color in the fight against the British, including Indians and free blacks, for they had fulfilled their duties with "consistency, obedience, subordination, and valor."[57]

Poets soon lent their talents to praising the victorious porteños, who came in all sizes and colors. Vicente López y Planes, Mariquita's close friend, praised the contributions of "natives, blacks, quarter-bloods, and the child of the toasted inhabitant of Ethiopia." Indeed, *all* of Buenos Aires's children helped: "the merchant, the artisan, the boy, the moreno and the pardo." Together, López continued, they formed something magnificent, a "sacred fire" that ran through all the people.[58] One anonymous ballad, written from a female perspective, linked masculinity and virtue with patriotism. For those desiring her affection, the author made it clear: cowards need not apply.

> If you want to enlist under my banner, ask the god Mars for his badge . . .
> Don't say you respect or love me, you who surrendered my homeland to the English . . .
> Don't come visit my house, you who did not enlist, who is not a warrior, who doesn't fight . . .
> For each Englishman you vanquish, I will surrender to you a discreet heart . . .
> All us women declare, from today on, that we will not look upon the face of cowards . . .
> From now on I prefer those boys who hurried to war with such dedication.
> I loved hearing them shout: Charge, fire, take it to them![59]

Many slaves also played a key role in the victory, fighting alongside their masters. The cabildo wanted to reward slaves to thank them, but also to motivate them to defend the empire again if need be. The cabildo wanted to purchase the freedom of all the slaves who fought, but the city did not have enough money. So the cabildo did the best it could. "In order to encourage slaves to do the same whenever a similar situation arises," the cabildo announced that it would purchase the freedom of any slave who was left "mutilated and unable to work." The cabildo also decided that an additional twenty-five slaves would be freed through a lottery.[60] When protests erupted over the small number of freed slaves, private donors added to the total so that, in all, 130 slaves received their freedom.[61]

Even with the additional donations, the majority of slaves who fought still remained in captivity. One of them, the slave José Artayeta, saw the contradiction. José fought bravely in *both* battles against the British, risking life and limb for his master and his master's king. And now, just because he was not maimed, and was unlucky in the lottery, he was still in bitter bondage. A few months after the invasions, Artayeta petitioned the courts for his freedom, "for the good services with which he distinguished himself in the defense of this city, from the 12 August 1806 to 5 July 1807."[62] It is not known what response he received, if any. In the end, the institution of slavery survived the British invasions intact.[63]

Although slavery continued, the English invasions did give slaves, free blacks, and mulattoes fresh hope that things might change. Inasmuch as many of the militia units were, as Mariquita pointed out, made up of the "darker" segments of society, the increased power gained by the militias during and after the English invasions signaled an increased stature for people of color.[64] By no means did this signal an end to racial and class discrimination, but it nevertheless represented an important, even if small, shift of power to people of color.

New developments in the militias also helped nourish democratic impulses. During the invasions, some militias began the practice of electing their leaders. Cornelio Saavedra, for example, was chosen by his own men to lead one of the most powerful militias in the city. In other words, a militia made up of mostly lower-class men, including many blacks and mulattoes, voted for their militia leaders. The militias, then, contributed to the emergence of a type of popular sovereignty in Buenos Aires, and people like Cornelio Saavedra and Santiago Liniers became a new type of popular hero.[65]

The invasions also helped foster inklings of a new identity in the city and the region. Local, regional, and national identities are the results of long and complex processes. By 1806, decades of official discrimination against Creoles (American-born Spaniards)—fostered by the Bourbon Reforms—had driven a wedge between locals and peninsular Spaniards, and between the city and Spain itself. The city had then passed through the cataclysmic experience of two English invasions, during which a broad spectrum of porteño society participated in intense battles at close quarters. Through it all, some porteños saw Viceroy Sobremonte, and perhaps Spain itself, as a negligent, weak, and incompetent parent. One poet openly mocked the viceroy in particular, referring to him as "that famous, valiant soldier" who went to battle "without a sword in his hand."[66] Local porteños, on the other hand, performed brilliantly. In 1807, Cornelio Saavedra, the popular (and elected) militia commander, congratulated his fellow "Americans" for their courage and loyalty. The victory over the British "reaffirmed the worth of those born in the Indies" and proved that they were not "inferior to Europeans."[67]

FIGURE 3.2 *The Reconquest of Buenos Aires* by Charles Fouqueray (1909).
The British commanding officer, General Beresford, surrenders to the Buenos Aires
militia commander, Santiago Liniers. Courtesy of the Museo Histórico Nacional,
Buenos Aires.

English Influence in Buenos Aires

Although the British soldiers were turned back, the invasions nevertheless signaled a new wave of Englishmen, and English merchandise and culture, coming to the Río de la Plata's shores. It started with the invaders themselves. Of the 1400 taken prisoner, many of them chose to stay in the Viceroyalty of Buenos Aires, a new land of opportunity. Marina Cespedes, for example, housed a few English prisoners in her home after Beresford's defeat. When it came time for them to be released, she let all of them go, except for one. He was staying because he was marrying Cespedes's daughter.[68]

The Englishmen who returned to England after the failed invasions did so with stories of the bounties found in the Río de la Plata. As the invader-turned-captive Alexander Gillespie observed, the Pampas were full of all manner of profitable crops, yet "so few availed themselves" of the opportunities. Unfortunately, "luxuriant crops rise from year to year only to perish" in the field. The land, Gillespie thought, could use some better management—English management.[69] This would be the mantra for foreigners and many locals in the Río de la Plata and in Latin America throughout the nineteenth century. As many foreigners and Spanish Americans had come to believe, Spain had hampered the political and economic growth of its colonies. New ideas and influences would be needed to help them reach their potential. The English prisoners who stayed were forerunners of a new wave of unarmed invaders who would arrive in greater numbers as merchants, bankers, ranchers, and engineers. They would endeavor to set up an informal empire, one erected with English capital rather than English cannons.[70]

Conclusion

The English invasions were a catalyst for a variety of changes in porteño society. Juan Manuel de Rosas cut his teeth as a soldier by helping repel the British invasions, the first of many future military engagements that would shape him and his nation. Although some historians claim he never fought in the second battle, Juan Manuel always maintained that he fought in both, and that he had the commendation letters to prove it.[71] Juan Martín de Pueyrredón felt that the victories changed the city in palpable ways. He sensed a transformative enthusiasm that produced a "new creation of warrior men."[72] The British politician Woodbine Parish, who knew many of the participants on both sides of the invasions, later wrote that the porteños' victory "roused the people from these slumbers, and taught them for the first time their own power, and all the weakness of the mother country."[73] Mariquita Sánchez de Thompson saw profound significance in the invasions as well. The first victory over the English, she wrote in her memoirs, "was a great lesson for this people—it was a beacon! How many things were seen and learned in such a short time?" The "progress was even greater," she added, when porteño forces triumphed over the second invasion. "This people realized what they could do, and they began to think about their own destiny."[74] In short, native and foreigner alike understood that the invasions created something new in Buenos Aires.

CHAPTER FOUR

Buenos Aires in the Age of Revolution

Carriages pulled up to the splendid mansion and deposited their well-dressed passengers while other guests arrived by foot. Once inside, all kinds of fun began. The great room was large enough to accommodate more than two dozen couples dancing a waltz. While some guests danced, others watched in delight as a chemist performed entertaining experiments. Still others listened intently as a French visitor spoke of his friendship with Benjamin Constant, the prominent French intellectual who was also a consort to Madame de Stael, one of the most famous women of Paris. Local residents were especially delighted by the curious and exquisite objects on display, such as porcelain figures, mechanical clocks, and other wonders. At the end of the evening, the guests would be favored with a sumptuous dinner in the French style.[1]

Such might have been the scene in Mariquita Sánchez's literary salon, or *tertulia*, in the 1810s and 1820s, as described by historian Vicente Fidel López, who knew Mariquita in his youth. His father, Vicente López y Planes, was Mariquita's close friend and a frequent attendee of her salon. After Mariquita married Martín Thompson in 1804, she hosted a popular tertulia in her home where she tried to emulate the Parisian salons she had heard so much about. And she longed to experience French salons herself, if she could ever manage a trip to Paris. Mariquita hosted tertulias in her home for much of her life, but the principal period of her tertulia activities came between 1810 and the early 1830s, with its zenith coming perhaps in the 1820s. The discussion below reflects the impact of her salon over these years.

In Mariquita's magnificent home, her guests enjoyed music and dance, but they also engaged in conversations about the latest developments in politics and culture in the Río de la Plata and the wider world. After 1806, many of those conversations included the astonishing political developments of the time, such as the English invasions, and Napoleon's invasion of Spain in 1808, when he made his brother Joseph the king of Spain, thus throwing Buenos Aires and the rest of the Spanish Empire into a deep crisis of authority.[2] By May of 1810, with Joseph Bonaparte still on the Spanish throne, revolutionaries in Buenos Aires saw an opportunity to establish an autonomous government and perhaps even an independent nation. Mariquita, Martín, and many of their friends were major proponents of autonomy and, later, outright independence. They believed they were building a new society that would need a government, a constitution, and innovative institutions to join the family of modern nations emerging in the Americas and Europe. Indeed, Mariquita Sánchez saw herself as part of a larger trans-Atlantic community who, as Claude Miliscent wrote in his Saint-Domingue newspaper in 1792, believed that "the true philosopher was a cosmopolitan, the friend of all men from whatever country."[3]

But not everyone was eager to embrace so much change. Royalists remained loyal to the deposed Spanish king while more conservative residents of the viceroyalty questioned the more radical reforms proposed by revolutionaries in Buenos Aires. The Rozas family was somewhere in between the revolutionaries and royalists. Though not opposed to autonomy and independence, they were critical of the factions and disorder that began to emerge after Napoleon's invasion of Spain in 1808, and after Buenos Aires established an autonomous government in May of 1810. Juan Manuel was in his midteens at this time, and while many of his contemporaries rushed headlong into the growing rebellion against Spain, he remained focused on developing his growing cattle business, getting married, and starting his family.

Mariquita, France, and the Salons of Paris

Mariquita, on the other hand, was fascinated by the idea of change, and that frequently meant that she was attracted to ideas and innovations emerging from other countries. It was no secret that Mariquita liked foreign things. While she and her fellow porteños did not want to be conquered or liberated by foreigners—the English learned that the hard way in 1806—Mariquita and many of her friends nevertheless eagerly embraced other aspects of foreign influence. After all, the mother country of Spain—battered, invaded, and blockaded by foreign powers—seemed to be, in Mariquita's eyes at least, in obvious decline. For her, Spain's political troubles cast a shadow on Hispanic ideas, institutions, and cultural practices. Thus she, along with others, believed that an infusion of culture from some leading countries of the world would benefit porteño society. And while Mariquita admired many nations, it was France that captured her imagination the most, and it was the salons of Paris that she tried to emulate in her home in Buenos Aires. Indeed, some of Mariquita's contemporaries came to see and even refer to her as an Argentine version of prominent Parisian socialites like Germaine de Stael and Lady Recamier. In many ways, Mariquita's attraction to France was mirrored throughout the hemisphere, from Buenos Aires to Bogotá to Boston. France's place in Mariquita's and others' imagination makes France, and French influence, worth more than just a passing reference.

By 1810, Mariquita had become enamored by France and its brilliant capital, Paris, which, by the latter half of the eighteenth century, was heralded by many as the capital of the modern world. Other cities like London, Vienna, and New York had their charms, to be sure, but Paris came to be seen by scholars and intellectuals, especially in the West, as the best place to get all things *at once*. Paris's list of attractions was magnificent: the greatest museum in the world, the Louvre; spectacular architecture like the cathedral of Notre Dame; amazing ballet, opera, and theater; exquisite gardens and palaces; antique bookshops; great universities; dozens of daily newspapers; and perhaps best of all, French food. By 1799, the French poet Louis-Sebastien Mercier could declare with confidence that Paris "eternally rivets the gaze of the entire world."[4]

One of the great jewels of Parisian society was its influential literary salons. French salons began in the mid-1600s as a space for elite women to display their literary talents. The goal of many salons was to produce a harmonious environment that would promote enlightened conversation and help reconcile opposing views. To do so, the female host needed to master the art of inviting the right mix of guests and help shape the conversation. While salons initially focused on literature, music, and other arts, by the late eighteenth century, Parisian salons had also begun to discuss politics. By hosting and guiding salons, female *salonnières* helped create a space where citizens shared their opinions on a variety of matters, a space that allowed the growth of a new kind of authority that emerged from within Parisian society rather than from the government.[5]

Spain and its colonies had similar traditions of social gatherings, known as tertulias, although they were usually led by men. By the late eighteenth century, many tertulias in Spanish America were, like their Parisian counterparts, becoming more political. In Bogotá, for example, Antonio Nariño led an important group, known as the tertulia Eutropélica (later known as the tertulia del Buen Gusto) in the 1790s. His group discussed current views on a variety of subjects, and Nariño also lent out books to a wide variety of people from his sizeable personal library. However, when Nariño chose to translate and publish copies of the French Revolution's *The Rights of Man*, he was arrested and the translations were burned.[6] Similar groups met in Lima and other major cities throughout Spanish America in the late 1790s and early 1800s, including Mariquita Sánchez's tertulia in Buenos Aires.[7] For her and many across the Americas and Europe, Parisian salons were the most deserving of emulation.

The British, for example, saw great value in Parisian salons. The famous letter-writing Lord Chesterfield sent his son to France in the mid-eighteenth century to learn a "gentleman-like manner" in Parisian salons. The female hosts of the French salons were the key to their utility. "Our English women are not near so well informed and cultivated as the French," he informed his son. And because women "generally give the *tone* to the conversation," Lord Chesterfield concluded, French salons were superior to their British counterparts.[8] The wealthy New Englander Anne Bingham also went to Paris for almost a year in the early 1790s. Her goal was to learn the culture of the salons so that she could emulate them in her sumptuous new home in Philadelphia.[9]

Perhaps the most famous of Paris's salonnières of the late eighteenth and early nineteenth century was the wealthy and talented Germaine de Stael. Madame de Stael, as she was also called, became a model for many women in Paris, but also elsewhere, including for Mariquita Sánchez in Buenos Aires. Madame de Stael invited into her salon the leading thinkers on a variety of subjects and disciplines, including politics. She herself favored a constitutional monarchy, which brought her into conflict with Napoleon Bonaparte soon after he came to power in 1799. Napoleon did his best to put Madame de Stael in her place, telling her that the best women had the most babies. When she continued discussing politics in her salon, Napoleon exiled her to Switzerland. When she petitioned Napoleon to return, he refused because she would "make trouble." Napoleon's solution for Germaine was simple: he told her that "women should knit." Later, when Napoleon himself was in exile, he explained why Madame de Stael was so "very dangerous." It was because "she gathered together in her salon . . . all the partisans, republicans, and royalists. She put them in each other's presence; she united them all against me. She attacked me from all sides." From Napoleon's perspective, "her salon was fatal."[10] From a man who understood power came a recognition of the power a woman could wield from a salon in her home.

In the Salon of Mariquita Sánchez de Thompson

Mariquita read and heard about Germaine de Stael, and while it was difficult to match the opulence of Parisian salons, Mariquita did her best to emulate them in her tertulia in Buenos Aires.[11] And like Madame de Stael, Mariquita would come into conflict with a powerful dictator—her friend Juan Manuel—whose policies would eventually push her into exile.

Mariquita learned of Parisian salons through word of mouth as well as from literature that flowed into Buenos Aires from Europe, especially in the 1810s and 1820s. Mariquita also knew how to speak and read French, and she was well versed in the works of many French writers. It is highly likely that Mariquita read some of Madame de Stael's publications. Mariquita also heard about salons from friends who visited France and returned home with news of the latest trends in Paris. Foreign visitors also frequented Buenos Aires, and Mariquita welcomed many of them into her home, where they would share their own experiences of life in Paris and elsewhere.

The British soldier Andrew Gillespie attended tertulias after arriving in Buenos Aires as part of the English invasions in 1806. He may well have attended one in Mariquita's home since she associated with the British officers during the British occupation.[12] Salon activity in Buenos Aires intensified after 1808, when Napoleon took control of Spain and the port of Buenos Aires became more open to foreign travelers and the exchange of ideas (discussed below). Over the next many years, increasing numbers of foreigners took up long-term residence in the city as well. One of them, the Englishman William Parish Robertson, loved attending tertulias in the city. He mentioned eleven of them by name, and he would sometimes go tertulia hopping, moving from one to the next in the same night. For Robertson, the active social life put the city on par with other places he had lived. Buenos Aires was "not easily to be rivaled in the best times of any country with which I am acquainted." Robertson assured his friends he was not exaggerating. "Some of my readers may fancy I am here painting the society of Buenos Ayres *couleur de rose*; but those who have best known it at the time of which I speak, will readily recognize the truthfulness of my picture."[13]

Mariquita and her husband, Martín, were very much part of that vibrant society. After her mother died in 1812, Mariquita inherited all of her parents' assets, which included substantial financial reserves as well as various properties, including the magnificent home near the main plaza. Such a large space was one of the main components of a successful tertulia, for it allowed for a variety of entertainment and social possibilities. One later visitor, Mariquita Nin, offered a detailed description of Mariquita's mansion. "The house of Mariquita Thompson is the biggest in the city," Nin wrote. "As you enter, you see a paved garden patio with a fountain" with exotic plants and a marble cistern. The great room was magnificent, with an *estrado* in one corner, and a harp and piano in another. Three large oval windows, stretching from floor to ceiling, made it so that "light falls in rays from above." By the time Nin saw it, Mariquita had apparently sold off some of its previous furnishings. "If it is so beautiful now, I can only imagine that it was even more so then—better, richer, more sumptuous." Nin also heard that one of the men who built the house was trained in Paris, but she concluded it did not really matter. "If this is French, English, or Spanish, it doesn't matter: it is astonishingly gorgeous."[14]

Mariquita's salon was attended by the most prominent political and cultural figures of the day. True to the example of the Parisian salons of the era, Mariquita invited a mixture of guests. One of them was Bernardo de Monteagudo, a brilliant young lawyer from the northwestern province of Tucumán. Some porteños held Monteagudo in contempt because he was of darker complexion, and also because he was quite radical in his political views. Despite these attributes that might have excluded him elsewhere, Mariquita welcomed Monteagudo into her home and the two became close friends. Young poets also attended, sharing their verses, all of which, in the words of Vicente Fidel López, made her salon "a true academy of progress and culture."[15]

William Parrish Robertson, cited above, reserved special praise for Mariquita's tertulia. He remembered that "conversation, music, dancing, high spirits, good humour, were the happily combined ingredients which gave a relish to the whole."[16] Robertson also commented on Mariquita's skill in adapting the environment of her salon to her various guests. Mariquita "played the parts of the easy English countess, the vivacious and witty French marquise, the elegant, graceful porteña patrician, in such wise that each country might have claimed her for its own, so happy an art had she of identifying herself for the time being, with the nation to which her friends or visitors belonged."[17]

Mariquita thus possessed one of the ideal qualities of a classic salonnière: she made everyone feel comfortable, thus facilitating conversation and the exchange of knowledge and ideas.

The Spanish Empire on the Rocks, Again

By May of 1810, the conversations in the salons of Buenos Aires surely included the deep crisis of the Spanish Empire: perpetual warfare with powerful enemies; new ideas about colonial rights; revolutionary activities of upstart revolutionaries like Francisco de Miranda and others.

Near perpetual warfare with England and France over the previous twenty years took a terrible toll on Spanish power. Although many believed the empire would weather the current storm, as it had survived others in the past, those that looked closely saw ample cause for concern. Many Spanish and Spanish American thinkers and merchants concluded on their own that the colonies' relationship with Spain was outdated, and that Spain was also lagging behind the younger and more vigorous empires like Great Britain.[18] Although the Spanish crown was reluctant to fully embrace Adam Smith's idea of free trade, Spain did make trade freer in the late eighteenth century.[19] Meanwhile, Spanish American colonists pushed for even greater freedom to trade. This included the Rozas family and other ranchers in the Río de la Plata who would benefit from a free-trade system where they could sell their hides and salted beef to all comers in a free-market economy. In fact, the porteño lawyer Mariano Moreno (who cried when he witnessed the English invasions) sent a petition to the Spanish crown in 1809, making a powerful argument for free trade on behalf of the great ranchers of Buenos Aires.[20]

Other Spanish Americans throughout the empire, however, were proposing bigger changes than just economic reforms. As seen in the previous chapter, homegrown revolutionaries like Francisco de Miranda were openly campaigning in London and elsewhere for liberating missions against Spain's New World colonies.[21] In 1805, another young Venezuelan embarked on a mission to free South America from Spain. That year, while visiting Rome, Simón Bolívar swore an oath to liberate his homeland from Spanish tyranny. As the young Simón Bolívar gazed over the city, he had an epiphany in which he saw Rome's significance in world history. He recorded his thoughts later that evening. Although Bolívar was impressed by Rome's grandeur, overall he found

Rome's legacy lacking. Roman history produced great leaders, but for every great figure like Cincinnatus, there were a hundred like Caligula. Bolívar could think and write in these terms because he, like many other educated men of his times, knew all about Roman history. Cincinnatus, Bolívar knew, had on two separate occasions in the sixth century BCE left his plough and his farm and agreed to be the dictator of Rome when the city was threatened by a foreign invasion. After the danger passed, Cincinnatus immediately relinquished his authority and returned to his farm. Caligula, meanwhile, was a tyrannical and depraved emperor who ruled Rome from 37 to 41 CE. Young Bolívar also likely understood that certain contemporary figures were judged in light of heroes and villains from classical Greece and Rome. By the early 1800s, for example, George Washington was already being labeled as the American Cincinnatus, who left his farm to become a general and a president before returning to his plantation.[22]

Besides producing a long list of lamentable leaders—from Bolívar's perspective—Rome failed to solve the great problem of human freedom, and it was here that he saw the destiny of America, and perhaps his own destiny, come into focus. The mystery of man's freedom, Bolívar wrote, "would only be made clear in the New World." He finished his oath with a flourish that placed himself at the center of his epic review of world history: "I swear before you, I swear by the God of my fathers, I swear on their graves, I swear by my Country that I will not rest body or soul until I have broken the chains binding us to the will of Spanish might!"[23] Although the oath would not become known to others for many years, it nevertheless marked an important beginning of Bolívar's revolutionary career.[24] Upon his return to the Americas, Bolívar began seeking a resolution to the "great question of man set free."

Napoleon's Invasion of Iberia

The world may never have heard of Simón Bolívar were it not for Napoleon Bonaparte, who invaded the Iberian Peninsula in 1807 and 1808, thus throwing Portugal's and Spain's New World colonies into a confused crisis of authority. Napoleon invaded Iberia in 1807 to stop Portugal from trading with England. Although Spain was allied with Napoleon, in 1808 he decided to conquer Spain as well. Napoleon occupied Madrid, then pushed steadily south toward Seville. He arrested the Spanish king, Charles IV, and his son (and heir), Ferdinand VII.

Napoleon then crowned his own brother, Joseph Bonaparte, the King of Spain. Almost immediately, anti-French rebellions flared up throughout Spain, and many cities established their own governments, or juntas, instead of submitting to Joseph Bonaparte. A new government, the Junta Central, claimed to act in the name of the deposed king, although its members had to flee southward to escape advancing French armies.

When news of Napoleon's conquest of Madrid reached the New World, colonial officials and colonists from Mexico City to Buenos Aires debated what to do next. Viceroys in the New World believed that they continued to rule in the king's name, even if it was a deposed king. However, many Spanish American colonists believed that, in such a crisis, political authority devolved back to city councils—the cabildos—who would administer their own affairs until the king of Spain returned to the throne. Proponents of this line of thought were careful to emphasize that this would be a temporary autonomous government, *not* an independent one, which would only rule until the return of the king. Meanwhile, the rupture created by Napoleon allowed other ideas to emerge more powerfully into the debates of how to reestablish legitimacy and authority, including ideas about popular sovereignty espoused by Enlightenment thinkers.[25] Unfortunately for the cities, Spain's viceroys in the New World interpreted any move toward autonomy as an act of open rebellion that deserved a full military retaliation. When the city of Quito established such an autonomous government in 1809, for instance, the viceroy of Lima sent two thousand soldiers to crush it.[26]

The idea of an autonomous government was also discussed in Buenos Aires, especially in early 1810. Ships docking in Buenos Aires brought news that Napoleon now controlled Seville and most of Andalucía (the southern region of Spain). What remained of the "Regency" government of Spain was hanging by a thread, headquartered in the fortified port city of Cádiz on a peninsula in southwestern Spain, one of the last holdouts against the French. With Napoleon firmly entrenched on Spanish soil, it was clear that Ferdinand VII was not coming back any time soon. With this in mind, leaders of the autonomy movement in Buenos Aires set in motion a plan that had been months in the making.

The May Revolution of 1810 in Buenos Aires

The first step was to remove Viceroy Cisneros from power. On May 17, Cornelio Saavedra (another hero of the English invasions), a powerful militia commander and a strong proponent of autonomy, declared the viceroy's authority defunct. When the viceroy protested, Saavedra answered boldly: "Do you think, Sir, that Spain is made up of only Cádiz?" Buenos Aires and the rest of the provinces, Saavedra continued, did not want to suffer under French rule. Thus, we have "resolved to reassume our rights and protect ourselves."[27] The government of Spain was defunct, and Saavedra and the other militia officers demanded the meeting of a cabildo abierto to decide whether to keep the viceroy or to form an autonomous government.

On May 21, ornate invitations were sent to Martín Thompson and 450 other vecinos (wealthy married men) in and around the city to attend a cabildo abierto at 9:00 a.m. the following day. However, only about 250 vecinos showed up the next morning. As it turned out, many of them were scared to show their faces. Proautonomy soldiers were stationed in key locations throughout the city, which intimidated many royalist vecinos to skip the meeting. Despite the intimidation, many royalists did attend the cabildo abierto that day. Arguments were lively. A prominent clergyman, Bishop Lué, argued at length that Spain was the only power with the right to rule in the Americas. Another conservative member of the cabildo reminded the delegates that Viceroy Cisneros governed *all* of the viceroyalty, not just Buenos Aires. How could Buenos Aires, therefore, depose the viceroy without the consent of his subjects in the other provinces? The patriotic lawyer Juan José Paso responded that Buenos Aires was the "older sister" of the other provinces, and her sister provinces would soon be called to participate in the government. Cornelio Saavedra defended the position of the autonomists, arguing that in the present crisis authority reverted to the people, and that the authority of the people rested in the town councils (the cabildos).[28]

On May 22, the cabildo voted to create an autonomous government—a junta—that would govern the Viceroyalty of Buenos Aires until Ferdinand VII returned to the Spanish throne. As a compromise with the royalists, however, the cabildo chose the ex-viceroy, Cisneros, as the leader of the new junta, with Manuel Belgrano and Cornelio Saavedra as the other members. The compromise was short lived, however, for as soon as news got out that the old viceroy was heading the new junta, a vociferous public opposition immediately emerged in the city. Manuel Belgrano and Cornelio Saavedra withdrew quickly from the junta. For two days the patriots lobbied and gathered signatures to call for a new vote. Soldiers in the city also made known to all the will of the militias: they wanted a new, "patriotic" junta *without* any peninsular Spaniards.

It was raining on the morning of May 25 as Martín Thompson made his way to the cabildo for the next round of negotiations and voting. As the meeting commenced, a small crowd of people gathered in the plaza. Some pounded on the walls of the building, shouting that "the people want to know what's going on!" One royalist cabildo member, noticing it was just a small crowd outside, asked ironically, "Where are 'the people'"?[29] The answer offered him was that "the people" were all at lunch, but that they would come back at a moment's notice if summoned. The vote was finally called and a new junta was elected, with Cornelio Saavedra as its president. That night, Saavedra and his fellow junta members knelt in front of a crucifix and swore loyalty to Ferdinand VII.[30] A patriotic fervor in the capital, with significant plebeian elements, helped shape the autonomy debate and the new government that emerged from it.

The May Revolution of Buenos Aires joined other autonomist and insurgent movements throughout the Spanish Empire. Venezuela had declared autonomy just a few weeks before the porteños had. Then in September of 1810, much of Mexico was engulfed in a bloody struggle between royalist forces and insurgents led by Father Miguel Hidalgo. Only two days after the uprising in Mexico, Chile declared its own government that pledged to rule autonomously until Ferdinand VII returned. A few months later, in July of 1811, Francisco de Miranda, Simón Bolívar, and other Venezuelan patriots executed the boldest move yet: they declared outright independence, raising the flag of the Republic of Venezuela, complete with its own constitution.

Meanwhile, the junta of Buenos Aires set about reforming certain elements of porteño society. The junta's secretary, Mariano Moreno, wanted revolutionary change, and he wanted it quickly. Moreno believed education could help transform a society. He translated portions of Rousseau's *The Social Contract* and wanted to make it required reading for elementary-school children. Moreno also pushed for the founding of a public library, which the junta did in June. At the library's inaugural speech, Moreno argued that ever since the English invasions military concerns had made porteños forget about cultivating the arts and sciences. The new governing junta needed to intervene to prevent "the ferocity of a barbarous people" from taking over. The government, Moreno concluded, would have to build society, "creating everything" from the ground up.[31] But not everyone agreed that the government should remake society, or remake it so quickly. Cornelio Saavedra, for instance, preferred a more moderate approach to change, and thus the first factions of the May Revolution were born—the moderate Saavedristas in opposition to the more radical Morenistas.[32]

One of the junta's first items of business was to create a newspaper to speak for the new government. Mariquita Sánchez de Thompson and Juan Manuel de Rosas, both devoted readers, were likely excited about the new publication and likely read the inaugural edition of *La Gazeta de Buenos Ayres* on June 7, 1810. In the opening article, the junta secretary, Mariano Moreno, emphasized that junta members were representatives of the people. Those that turn a deaf ear to the needs of the people, Secretary Moreno wrote, could bring about, in the end, "a disastrous dissolution that engulfs the whole community in irreparable harm." The newspaper promised to cover domestic and international events and employ the ideas of "enlightened men who sustain and direct the patriotism and loyalty that has so heroically been displayed." The people should be assured, Moreno concluded, that the junta has no other goal except to "ensure the happiness of these provinces."[33]

It was easy for the junta to declare a goal of happiness for all, but to ensure that happiness, a number of questions needed to be answered. How would political power be wielded and shared among the provinces? What was the long-term solution to the current political crisis? Was the return of Ferdinand VII the eventual solution, or would it be independence? And if it was independence, would the Río de la Plata be an independent republic or an independent monarchy? To address those and other questions, the junta invited each province to send delegates to Buenos Aires to participate in the new government, called the Junta Grande.

From the beginning, however, many regions of the viceroyalty resisted Buenos Aires's claims to authority. One obstacle to unity was the sheer size and diversity of the viceregal territory Buenos Aires now claimed to govern on its own. Its territory extended from the highlands of the Andes in what is now Bolivia to the jungles of Paraguay to the Indian-controlled areas of Patagonia on the southern end of the continent. This was more than three times the size of mainland England, and twice the size of the United States of America when it became independent in 1776. Complicating matters further, the major cities of the viceroyalty had been settled in the early to mid-1500s, which meant that by 1810 those cities had more than 250 years of colonial history—more than enough time for powerful regional identities to develop. By comparison, most of England's North American colonies experienced less than 150 years of colonial status before becoming independent. These challenges of distance and of regional identities complicated attempts to govern the viceroyalty. For the ruling classes of Upper Peru (modern-day Bolivia) and Paraguay, the move to autonomy was brash and dangerous. Across the river in Montevideo, royalists also labeled the junta of Buenos Aires as traitorous.

Thus, in the early weeks and months after the May Revolution, porteño society was gripped by fear of royalist reaction both within the city and from other provinces. The junta responded with various measures to secure the revolution in Buenos Aires and beyond. First, they needed to raise money. When the junta solicited funds from porteño residents to support the armies sent to unify the various provinces, Mariquita and Martín, along with others, responded. On August 9, *La Gazeta* recognized those who contributed. "D. Martín Thompson, captain of the port, has paid six ounces of gold, three for himself, and three remaining on behalf of his wife, Doña María de los Santos Sánchez."[34]

In the same edition, *La Gazeta* announced other measures to protect the revolution. A "patriotic militia" made up purely of volunteers was created to help maintain the peace in the city. City officials also published instructions to municipal officials, detailing how they should secure their neighborhoods: they needed to take a census of all residents, including their country of origin and profession, and do a detailed inventory of weapons, paying particular attention to those who possessed sabers, machetes, pistols, rifles, or shotguns. Patrols should make regular rounds each night, and anyone who engaged in suspicious behavior would be thrown into prison (for men) or taken to the Casa de Ejercicios (for women).[35] The government also required oaths of loyalty from all public officials.[36]

Another major threat to Buenos Aires's authority came from the royalist stronghold of Córdoba Province. The junta of Buenos Aires tried to reassure royalists of its loyalty to Spain. "The capital has solemnly sworn fealty to its beloved monarch," the *Gazeta* declared on August 16, "and it challenges the world to find any act that compromises the purity of that loyalty."[37] Such declarations, however, did little to appease the anger of royalist officials. None other than Santiago Liniers, the great hero of the English invasions, raised a royalist army in the city of Córdoba to resist the junta. When Buenos Aires sent its army to confront the royalists, Liniers's forces withered, and soon he was in chains. But the junta proceeded carefully in this matter because Liniers still had popular support in Buenos Aires for his heroism against the British. The editors of *La Gazeta de Buenos Ayres* therefore took it upon themselves to undermine the ex-viceroy's popularity. On August 16, *La Gazeta* announced Liniers's capture and called it "just punishment" for a man who now sought to exterminate the very people who "by the blood of its children produced [Liniers's] crown of glory." To further destroy Liniers's credibility, the *Gazeta*'s editors offered a re-formulation of recent history: the triumph against the British was *not* the work of Liniers. Instead, the victory was won by *the people* of Buenos Aires. Proof of this conclusion was simple, the *Gazeta* concluded, for as soon as Liniers lost the support of the people, all of his actions were full of "mistakes, crimes, cowardice, and infamy."[38] On August 26, 1810, Santiago Liniers was executed.

Porteño armies then marched north to Upper Peru, and in November of 1810 they defeated a royalist army at the Battle of Suipacha. More victories followed in the months ahead, some commanded by Mariquita's friend Manuel Belgrano. Buenos Aires also found an ally across the river on the Eastern Shore. The promise of self-government sparked the passions of many orientales ("easterners" living on the Eastern Shore of the Uruguay River), including José Gervasio Artigas, a cavalry officer with a large popular following, especially among the rural gaucho population. Artigas decided to support Buenos Aires, and soon he was laying siege to the royalist stronghold of Montevideo with an army of his gaucho supporters.[39] These initial triumphs created an environment of optimism in the Río de la Plata. That optimism soon faded, however, as royalist forces regrouped and repelled rebel armies. Soon it became clear that Upper Peru as well as Paraguay were going to remain independent of Buenos Aires. Meanwhile, factional disputes in Buenos Aires weakened the government. In 1811, the Primera Junta was replaced by a new government known as the "First Triumvirate."

One of the brightest stars of the new regime was Bernardino Rivadavia. As secretary of the Triumvirate, Rivadavia pushed through reforms that increased free trade and abolished the slave trade. He also founded a museum of natural history, increased the number of secondary schools, and founded a national archive. The new Triumvirate also moved to promote certain freedoms deemed highly desirable by reformers, such as the freedom of the press.[40] It was a popular idea in the city, and in November of 1811, for example, Martín Thompson was among a group of fifty men who suggested that the cabildo create a nine-member "Junta for the Protection of Freedom of the Press."[41]

But while Bernardino Rivadavia and the Triumvirate achieved many successes, they also provoked further factionalism. Rivadavia and other members of the First Triumvirate concentrated more authority in the province of Buenos Aires by granting porteño delegates more power at the expense of delegates from other provinces. The Triumvirate also claimed the right to appoint key government officials in other provinces.[42] Thus, many from the interior provinces accused Rivadavia and the Triumvirate of promoting porteño centralism, or "porteñismo" as some came to call it, which referred to the overbearing power Buenos Aires wielded over the rest of the viceroyalty.[43]

Further divisions grew out of radical ideals held by some revolutionary leaders, ideals that threatened to destabilize traditional society. The revolutionary-army commander, Juan José Castelli, for example, was well known for his denunciations of the Catholic Church. He also addressed everyone he spoke to as "citizen." On both counts Castelli looked and sounded like a Jacobin from the radical days of the French Revolution, and he even earned the nickname "Robespierre" of the Río de la Plata. Bernardo de Monteagudo was another young firebrand who alienated traditional elites from the government in Buenos Aires. He was a regular in Mariquita's tertulia, as well as a frequent contributor to *La Gazeta de Buenos Ayres*. In December of 1811, for instance, Monteagudo published an article in *La Gazeta* that criticized the clergy, whom he called "the apostles of despotism."[44] Monteagudo also expressed radical notions of liberty for all. "You know that he who robs one man of his freedom is no less a tyrant than one who usurps the rights of a whole nation" because, he concluded, "All men are equally free."[45] Such statements might have been fine among certain crowds in Buenos Aires, but in more traditional sectors of the viceroyalty like Upper Peru, where the majority of elites depended on forced labor and tribute, such sentiments proved too threatening to the social order. If Buenos Aires was bringing radical social revolution, many elites of Upper Peru and elsewhere wanted no part of it.

Mariquita and Martín continued to offer material support to the revolutionary cause. On May 30, 1812, Mariquita was among a group of women who donated money to help purchase rifles for the cause. *La Gazeta* recorded their donations and placed their names just below a short "Patriotic Article." The article praised the women for their loyalty. It also outlined one vision of the role of women in the revolutionary process. Although short, the article captured what many men and women saw as the proper sphere of female action. "The cause of humanity," the article began, should be of interest to all women, from mothers to daughters to wives. The female role, however, had its strengths and limitations. Because women were destined "by nature and by laws to live a withdrawn and sedentary life," they were unable to "display their patriotism with the splendor of battlefield heroes." But despite those limits, the article continued, women embraced the great responsibilities placed on them to nurture all aspects of society, including public officials, the economy, domestic order, and the public good. But by paying for these rifles, these women now had a more martial outlet for their patriotism, albeit an outlet more "suitable to their makeup." By so doing, the anonymous author declared, these women would one day have the right to declare proudly to their families: "I put the weapon in the hands of that courageous soul who assured his glory, and our liberty." The author also asked that the names of the women be engraved on the rifles so that someday a soldier in need would find additional inspiration by seeing the name of a woman he was defending.[46] Some thought it was written by Bernardo de Monteagudo. However, evidence suggests that Mariquita herself may have written the tract.[47]

Mariquita and her friends' donations of weapons to the revolution signaled a shift in porteño society toward outright independence. Whereas in the early months after the May Revolution, the *Gazeta* proclaimed loyalty to Ferdinand VII, by late 1811 the newspaper had changed its tune. In June 1812 the *Gazeta* published a number of articles sympathetic to complete independence. One article suggested that the colonies should help Ferdinand VII in his struggle against the tyrant Napoleon, who still occupied most of Spain. America will help, the *Gazeta* proclaimed, and when Spain is finally free of domestic and foreign tyranny, "she will be recognized by independent American states."[48]

The *Gazeta* also published reports and commentary from other parts of the Atlantic World related to the struggle against Spain. In June of 1812, for example, *La Gazeta* featured a copy of Venezuela's declaration of independence. Venezuela had won the race, the editors declared, but the rest of America would soon follow. A "new era" had arrived, and the American provinces "will no longer be colonial factories destined to favor a small corner of Europe." No longer will a lion be subject to an ant. "South Americans, the time has come . . . to assure your future happiness."[49] The *Gazeta* also published a British article about the progress of the rebellion in Mexico, and later reproduced an editorial from a Philadelphia newspaper arguing that Spanish America was indeed ready for true independence, despite arguments to the contrary.[50] These articles from across the Atlantic World gave *porteño* readers a sense that they were involved in a revolutionary process that captured global interest from Philadelphia to London and beyond.

While the editorial from the Philadelphia paper proclaimed the promise of the May Revolution, it also revealed some of the limits of that revolution, limits that would exclude people of color. The editorial listed the main arguments against independence, then refuted them one by one. One of the main arguments leveled by royalists and others against Spanish American independence was that the blacks and mulattoes would be a "terrible stumbling block," and that rivalries among the castes of colored people would derail any attempt to establish new nations. The author of the editorial refuted these arguments but did not refute the assumptions that supported them. First of all, the Philadelphia editorial argued, blacks were not as numerous as critics of the American revolutions claimed (except in a few places like Cuba, Puerto Rico, Caracas, and Lima). There were numerous free mulattoes and pardos to be sure, but according to the editorial, these groups identified more with whites. "The pardos seek acceptance by whites—they desire to assimilate—and within two or three generations they are intertwined by blood and by common interests, such that they form one caste with the whites." Thus, the article concluded, "the influence of the blacks is nullified, and their physical power and morals do not pose any threat, if preventative measures are implemented."[51] Although the "preventative measures" were not explained in detail, it is clear that the author of the editorial (and perhaps the editors of the *Gazeta* who republished it) proposed revolutionary *political* changes, but changes that would not unduly alter the racial prejudices embedded in most societies in the hemisphere.

Besides questions of race, newspapers of the day also debated the role of women in society—a subject close to Mariquita's heart. The editors of the new weekly paper, *El Grito del Sud*, took up the subject of women in a number of their early editions. "A young woman asked me recently," one editorial began, "if among the imprescriptible rights for men could also be found rights no less imprescriptible for women." The young woman continued her line of questioning. "I suppose that the enlightenment of our sex is less advantageous than that of the opposite sex, and I also suppose that there is a right to condemn women to live forever in darkness and ignorance, without developing their talents." For her, "three hundred years of slavery and darkness was enough to exalt American men, to cry against the fierce despotism of their age-old oppressors, but the unfortunate women will have to remain silent as they see no measures taken to improve their education." In this and the following issues, editors of *El Grito del Sud* explored one aspect of women's rights that surely would have caught Mariquita's eye: the freedom of women to choose the mate of their choice. The editors criticized parents who forced their children to marry against their will, as had been seen in two recent cases. "Who is to blame if those marriages turn out badly?" the editors asked. "How could parents be the authors of the eternal torment of their children in such cases?"[52]

Tertulias, General José de San Martín, and the Revolution

Mariquita's tertulia was brilliant during these tumultuous and euphoric times when debates raged over types of governments and the social extent of revolution. As one historian later put it, Mariquita's salon was more than just "smiles and trivialities, ephemeral gallantry, or fashion criticism."[53] Politics was also a part of her tertulia. William Parrish Robertson remembered his favorite three tertulia hosts: "Doña Ana Riglos, Doña Melchora Sarratea, and Doña Mariquita Thompson were the heads of the three distinct parties, which I can scarcely call political, but which I may designate as public." And while Robertson admired all three of these women, he held Mariquita in particularly high esteem.[54]

In Mariquita's salon, Robertson continued, "public events were discussed good humouredly" and "almost philosophically." Besides the local attendees, Mariquita's home was visited constantly by "both English and French naval commanders, consuls-general and other foreign envoys and diplomatists." The prominence of the guests, and the level of conversation, made Mariquita's salon a valuable source of news and information. In fact, Robertson argued, foreign diplomats visiting her home "got much better acquainted with all the *on dits* (rumors) of the day than at the government palace." Foreign diplomats would also use Mariquita's salon to disseminate their own views and opinions because that information, they were sure, "would reach the proper quarter." Overall,

Robertson perceived that Mariquita wielded influence in the city similar to that of Lord Palmerston, an influential English politician of the era. "And sure I am that Lord Palmerston, with all his acknowledged tact, with all his splendid talent, and with all his *savoir faire*, never swayed the affairs of Downing street with more success and brilliancy than did Doña Mariquita exercise her female diplomacy in her splendid mansion."[55]

In March of 1812, a new face appeared in the tertulias of Buenos Aires. It was José de San Martín, a decorated army commander just returned from the wars against Napoleon in Spain. San Martín was born in the Río de la Plata in 1785 but moved to Spain in his youth, where he eventually distinguished himself in combat. When he heard of the May Revolution in Buenos Aires, he decided to return to his homeland and do what he could to achieve independence. He arrived in Buenos Aires on an English ship in March of 1812. A bit awkward socially, San Martín attended tertulias, which helped him integrate into porteño society. He soon fell in love with and married a prominent young porteña, fourteen-year-old Remedios de Escalada, twenty years his junior. Soon after arriving in Buenos Aires, San Martín also helped form a Masonic lodge, known as the Lautaro Lodge, many of whose members were in high government positions.[56] From behind the scenes, the Lautaro Lodge sought to consolidate the May Revolution and expel the Spaniards from the whole continent.[57] When popular sentiment turned against the First Triumvirate, in large part because it concentrated too much power in Buenos Aires, San Martín and his fellow lodge members overthrew the government in September of 1812 in the name of "protecting the liberty of the people."[58]

San Martín also engaged in the vociferous debates of the time, both in salons as well as in secret Masonic meetings. Foremost on everyone's mind was the ongoing crisis with Spain. There were two possible solutions: to await Napoleon's defeat and the return of Ferdinand VII, or to declare independence—either as a republic or as a constitutional monarchy. San Martín was not afraid to share his view that a monarchy was the best solution for the Río de la Plata.[59] Although this was an unpopular idea in many circles, San Martín was not alone in his sentiment, especially because many believed that Spain might willingly grant its colonies independence if they were governed by a monarch, especially if that monarch came from the Spanish royal family. Manuel Belgrano had already sent letters to Princess Carlota of Portugal, the sister of Ferdinand VII, asking her to be the queen of an independent kingdom in the Río de la Plata. San Martín and Belgrano thought monarchies had the potential to unite a people more effectively, while democratic republics were prone to factional conflicts. And even though Bernardino Rivadavia was theoretically opposed to the idea of a monarchy, he himself would soon be sent to Europe to search for a possible royal candidate to rule in Buenos Aires.[60]

Surely many of these debates came up in the tertulias of Buenos Aires. San Martín attended Mariquita's tertulia, where he was known for his dancing. San Martín was likely in attendance at a special tertulia Mariquita hosted on October 15, 1812, just a few days after he helped overthrow the junta. On that night, the ladies showed up wearing their finest jewelry to parade their wealth and refinement, but also to show their patriotism by donating those very jewels to the war effort. Some of those funds may have helped finance San Martín's first victory a few months later at the Battle of San Lorenzo, about two hundred miles northwest of Buenos Aires. Not long after his victory at San Lorenzo, San Martín moved to the city of Mendoza, east of Buenos Aires, at the foot of the Andes mountains. There, San Martín began to build an army that he envisioned would liberate Spanish America from Spanish power once and for all.[61]

A National Anthem

Mariquita's salon also played a role in the creation of a national anthem in 1813. After the string of military victories in the North, the government leaders felt that the revolution had progressed enough to commission a national anthem. Two anthems had been considered months earlier, but the political, military, and cultural landscape had changed such that a new song was deemed necessary to reflect new realities and budding identities. Porteño armies had experienced larger and more intense battles, and porteños felt increased bitterness toward Spain, who seemed bent on destroying its American colonies. The government in Buenos Aires wanted the new anthem to reflect these changes. A number of Mariquita's friends were candidates to produce the new anthem. Blas Parera, a Basque pianist, was a noted composer who taught piano lessons in Mariquita's home. Mariquita was also close friends with a number of poets, including her old confessor, Fray Cayetano Rodríguez, as well as Vicente López y Planes, both of whom submitted works for consideration.

In the end, Vicente López y Planes's poem took the prize and became the new "Patriotic March," with music coming from Blas Parera. In later years,

FIGURE 4.1 *The National Hymn in the Sala of Mrs. Mariquita Sánchez de Thompson* by Pedro Subercaseaux (1910). Courtesy of the Museo Histórico Nacional, Buenos Aires.

many in Mariquita's family, along with others, would claim that the national anthem was first performed in her home, with Mariquita accompanying on the harp or singing.[62] While there is dispute surrounding that particular claim, what is true is that Mariquita's tertulia was a gathering place frequented by the creators of the anthem, and her salon was a place where revolutionary ideas, and new political and cultural identities, were discussed and shaped. The government officially accepted the national anthem in early May 1813.

Perhaps someone frustrated with the political influence of Mariquita's salon produced a flyer that criticized women's involvement in politics. Published in 1813, the flyer's title was "Memorandum on the need to restrain the excessive and harmful freedom of speech of women." It was downright shameful and scandalous, the pamphlet began, the way a good number of prominent women were "freely expressing themselves in matters of political affairs." Biblical and religious history showed the dangers of such women. "Remember Eve, Delilah, and that one of [King] David's," the author continued. The list of pernicious women continued. "They say that Anne Boleyn caused the Catholic Church's exit from England, and Malinche helped 'the bandit' Cortéz" conquer Mexico.[63] If Mariquita did happen to see this little publication, she likely would have taken it as a compliment.

The Rozas Family and the May Revolution

Juan Manuel de Rosas was seventeen years old when the May Revolution of 1810 began, but he was too busy learning the cattle business to spend much time with politics. Juan Manuel was adamant that he would make his own way, without any help from his parents, later recalling that he succeeded purely from his own "industriousness" and "honor."[64] He also married Encarnación Ezcurra in 1813. Soon thereafter, Juan Manuel started a meat-salting business with two partners. They exported jerked beef to Brazil and Cuba where it was used to feed slaves.[65] Juan Manuel could have chosen a military career. After all, he had fought in the English invasions, and other porteños of his class and age were taking up arms in the cause of independence. But not all of them did. Juan Manuel's choice was to stay home and grow his business interests instead of joining the national army, although he stayed active in local military affairs, especially, as will be seen below, along the Indian frontier.

Juan Manuel's father, León Ortiz de Rozas, was not among the most vociferous supporters of the May Revolution. The Rozases were friends with Santiago Liniers, and his execution in 1810 surely affected the way they saw developing events. Nevertheless, in June of 1812, León was among a group of men who donated money to supply rifles for the local armory. This was part of the great "cause of the fatherland" and the defense of the "sacred rights of América." In a note to the *Gazeta* that proclaimed this donation, the group asked the Supreme Director to engrave their names on their rifles: so that "if circumstances require it, and your excellency orders it, we will remember the oath we swore of preferring death over the humiliation and enslavement of the fatherland." Also on that list of donors who pledged to defend the government to the death was Mariquita's husband, Martín.[66]

The Rozas family was not against the idea of independence, but they were concerned by the divisions, disorder, and factionalism that emerged in the former viceroyalty after 1810. The same day Juan Manuel and Encarnación were married in 1813, for instance, newspapers in Buenos Aires announced the passage of the new legislation by the General Assembly meeting that year. Among the new decrees was a Free Womb Law that declared, from then on, that children of slaves would be free. Another law included a declaration of equality for Indians. A statement from the assembly finished the article: "The patriotism of an American is equality: nature recognizes this truth, and it will be written with our blood across the earth so that tyrants respect it and so that the people will always remember the origin of their happiness."[67]

Juan Manuel might have supported these ideas in theory, but he questioned their utility if their application threatened law and order. He believed things had been calmer before the May Revolution, but that was more a reflection on the problem of disorder and factionalism than a longing for a return of the colonial regime. He would later write that "Neither my parents, nor I, nor my brothers or sisters, were against the cause of American independence."[68]

Conclusion

In May of 1810, the cabildo of Buenos Aires voted to create an autonomous government that would rule, ostensibly, until the return of Ferdinand VII to the Spanish throne. Although most porteños expressed support for Ferdinand VII's return initially, their attitudes began to change soon thereafter. Mariquita's salon—a place where women had a chance to influence politics and culture on a more equal footing with men—played a role in these developments.[69] Mariquita took inspiration from the French salons that had become a model of civility and culture for many around the world. Politics were also part of her salon, even if they were not its main focus. The influence of salons like Mariquita's was heightened by the chronic political instability of the day. Given the unstable state system, her and others' salons served as a kind of support to the fledgling government institutions by providing additional venues for discussion and elaboration of ideas and policies.[70] Influential local and foreign residents from all around the city attended Mariquita's salon and those of other prominent porteñas, where lively conversations helped shape developments, attitudes, and identities in the earliest stages of what would become the Argentine republic.

The lyrics of López y Planes's "Patriotic March" dispelled any myth that the porteño government was hoping to rejoin the Spanish Empire. Instead, it boldly declared the independence of a new nation. "Hear, mortals, the sacred cry: Freedom, freedom, freedom. Hear the sound of broken chains." A "glorious new nation" is rising while the Spanish lion "lies defeated at her feet." A long middle section of the anthem decries Spain's evil behavior. The mother country spits "pestilential bile" as it raises its "bloody standard" all across the Americas. From Mexico to Quito to La Paz, the Spaniards leave paths "soaked in blood" as they devour their subjects like "wild beasts." The city of Buenos Aires, the poet continues, "puts itself in the lead of the people of the illustrious Union, while free people all over the world welcome the new nation. "To the great Argentine people, hail! May the laurels be eternal, that we knew how to win. Let us live crowned with glory or swear to die in glory."

Besides being a declaration of independence, López y Planes's lyrics laid out some of the key questions that would occupy the thoughts of Argentines for generations. Who would win, and how? Would Buenos Aires truly lead the other provinces? And if some were destined to die with glory, who then might be left to face an inglorious end? The struggles surrounding these questions were also part of the story of Argentina's beginnings.

CHAPTER FIVE

The Struggle for Independence

Martín Thompson said goodbye to Mariquita and their five children and headed to the docks. The importance of his mission weighed heavily on his mind as he and his assistant boarded the ship that would carry them on a journey of more than seven thousand miles. There were no passenger ships in 1816, so Martín, like others taking long ocean voyages, booked space on a cargo ship that outfitted a few rooms for travelers. The perils of sea travel were known to all, especially on such a long trip. Rough seas, seasickness, pitching decks, and cramped quarters with little privacy were all to be expected. And there was always the possibility of sinking to the *fondo del mar* (bottom of the sea). Travelers in many ways were at the mercy of captain and crew, not only to handle stormy seas, but also to provide enough food and water. And then there was the separation. Mariquita had her children, her servants, and slaves, but living alone with five children would not be easy, especially when Martín's mission would take months, maybe even years. Mariquita also knew that there was the possibility she might never see her husband again. According to his travel documents, Martín claimed to be traveling on personal business. In fact, he was on a secret mission to the United States of America to seek support for a new nation in the Río de la Plata, a nation that was about to officially declare itself independent from Spain.[1]

The political waters Martín was entering were sure to be turbulent as well. The Spanish American rebellions had drawn the attention of all the great Western powers, and Spain and many of its fellow monarchies in Europe wanted to exterminate revolution wherever they could. Ferdinand VII finally reclaimed the Spanish throne in 1814 and vowed to reconquer his rebellious American colonies, even if it meant inflicting death and destruction on his subjects. For precisely those reasons, agents from Buenos Aries and elsewhere throughout

Hispanic America sought aid and recognition from sympathetic powers like Great Britain and the United States. However, these countries could not afford to carelessly offend the monarchies of Europe who opposed the American revolutionaries. These treacherous political waters buffeted Mariquita's family during Martín's long odyssey in the United States. At home in Buenos Aires and its fellow provinces, swirling currents of regional discord and ideological disputes dashed hopes that a new nation could peacefully and gracefully emerge from the remnants of the Spanish Empire in the Río de la Plata.

Toward Official Independence

Martín's mission in 1816 was just the latest stage of various strategies to obtain the support and recognition of foreign powers for independence in the Río de la Plata. A few years earlier, after San Martín and his cohorts overthrew the Primera Junta government in September of 1812, the new government took on the task of winning the war against Spain and organizing a new nation. As for what kind of government the new nation would have, all options were on the table. National survival was the top priority. A republic was the most popular choice, but the idea of a monarchy also had its supporters. Many felt a monarchy would provide a more unified transition to independence, and a monarchical government might also make it easier to form alliances with the monarchies of Europe, alliances that would help ensure the survival of a new nation.

In 1813, the government of Buenos Aires called for delegates from all the provinces to meet in a General Assembly, with the hope of declaring independence and creating a national constitution. Power sharing among the provinces was again a major concern. In fact, many delegates from the other provinces wanted to meet anywhere *but* in Buenos Aires, in order to have the "appropriate freedom" instead of suffering the "abuses of power" of the porteños. Many of those same delegates also requested that the assembly use the Constitution of the United States of America as a model to see if the US version could, "with some modifications, be adaptable" to the "local political situation."[2]

Across the river in Montevideo, José Gervasio Artigas also worried about the growth of porteño power. Although Artigas initially fought on behalf of the May Revolution, by 1813 he vigorously opposed Buenos Aires's increasing influence over the rest of the region.[3] Artigas sent delegates to the Buenos Aires assembly with clear instructions to push for an equitable balance of power among the provinces, also using the United States as a model.[4] Artigas also enacted land reform, granting land to the lower classes, including free blacks, mulattoes, Indians, and poor whites. Artigas's actions and attitudes did not sit well with the government in Buenos Aires. His delegates' demands for provincial power sharing were rejected, and Artigas's ideas about social change, as seen in his land-reform decrees, were deemed too radical and destabilizing. Artigas's delegates were sent home, and soon porteño armies clashed with Artigas's forces until he was finally defeated in 1815.[5]

Despite the tensions over power sharing, the 1813 assembly managed to pass significant legislation. It purged the name of Ferdinand VII from official documents, abolished titles of nobility, ended Indian tribute payments, and decreed a Free Womb Law, which declared that from then on, all children born to slaves would be free. The assembly also agreed to foster the development of patriotic symbols and patriotic identity.[6]

The government of Buenos Aires, now called the "Directory," also faced challenges caused by Ferdinand VII's return to power. In 1814, Napoleon was finally defeated, allowing Ferdinand to ascend to the Spanish throne.[7] But instead of wooing back his American territories with benevolence, Ferdinand chose to force them back with the sword. In late 1815, Spanish armies arrived in Caracas and crushed the Venezuelan Republic, forcing Simón Bolívar to flee to Jamaica to reconsider his revolutionary plans.[8] Many in the Río de la Plata region saw the writing on the wall: Spanish armies would soon be headed to Buenos Aires. It was time for more decisive action.

The Congress of Tucumán

Threatened by Ferdinand VII's counterrevolutionary forces, Argentine leaders called for another congress to craft an official declaration of independence. As with the Assembly of 1813, provincial leaders disputed where to hold the convention. "Where do you want the Congress to be?" asked Mariquita's friend Father Cayetano in 1815. "Don't you know the very name 'porteño' is hated in the United Provinces, or Disunited Provinces of the River Plate?" Juan Manuel de Rosas's cousin, Tomás de Anchorena, a porteño delegate to the congress, also sensed a palpable aversion to Buenos Aires. "More than hate toward Buenos Aires, there was a spirit of disunion, an utter selfishness against contributing to the war [of independence] and to sustenance."[9]

Porteño leaders finally agreed to hold the congress in the city of Tucumán, 760 miles northwest of Buenos Aires. Mistrust of Buenos Aires's intentions ran high, and not all provinces sent delegates. Despite provincial resentment, some porteño delegates saw themselves as the natural leaders of the congress, and, they believed, the other provinces agreed. One report sent back to Buenos Aires read: "Even though jealousies exist between the provinces, all of them recognize the superiority of Buenos Aires for its enlightenment, its population, and its location," something other delegates demonstrated by "conceding, as they have conceded up to now, to the influence and distinction of our dele-gates."[10] Despite these perceptions by porteño delegates, resentment against Buenos Aires was strong, and it would not disappear any time soon, if ever.[11]

On July 9, 1816, the Congress of Tucumán finally issued the long-awaited statement. "We, the representatives of the United Provinces in South Amer-ica," solemnly declare that "the violent ties that bound us to the kings of Spain" are now broken.[12] Mariquita Sánchez de Thompson and Juan Manuel de Rosas surely read the news with great interest when word of the declaration reached porteño newspapers. "INDEPENDENCE" read the headline on page one of *El Censor* on July 25. The good news would be spread far and wide, the editors affirmed, and the lights at the government palace would be left on for ten days in celebration. But even as porteños celebrated this seminal event, *El Censor's* editors issued warnings of possible troubles. One came in the form of a quote from Thomas Paine, which appeared in both English and Spanish. "Notwith-standing our wisdom, there is a visible feebleness in our proceedings, which gives encouragement to dissension. . . . and if something is not done in time, it will be too late to do anything, and we shall fall into a state in which neither reconciliation nor independence will be practicable." The editors understood, as did many others, that the beginnings of the new nation would be fraught with danger. What good is it to celebrate independence, the editors asked, if the country is not secured by sound principles?[13]

A new country, the United Provinces of the Río de la Plata, now took its place among the nations of the earth. What kind of government that country would have was still up for debate. Would the delegates choose a republic or a monarchy?[14] Furthermore, what country, if any, would recognize and support the new country's existence? And in the end, would the country even survive?

Mariquita and Martín, Oceans Apart

The governing Directory understood that the survival of their new nation depended in large part on international recognition. Recognition was key to any new nation's survival, for it opened the doors to treaties and alliances that would provide legitimacy and protection. In fact, recognition was so important that, to obtain it, leaders in Buenos Aires considered creating either a republic or a constitutional monarchy, whichever one might guarantee recognition by the great powers of the world.

Since the early days of the May Revolution, governments in Buenos Aires had sent agents, such as Bernardino Rivadavia, abroad to seek material aid for the revolution. In early 1816, with official independence on the horizon, the ruling Directory turned to another prominent porteño to serve as an envoy to the United States: Mariquita's husband, Martín Thompson, a man known for his "experience, zeal, and patriotism."[15] The Directory gave Martín a letter clearly outlining the objectives of his trip and the precise steps he should follow to achieve those objectives. He was on a secret mission to obtain material aid and official recognition on behalf of the revolution in Buenos Aires. However, he was instructed clearly to first get permission from the US president, Madison, before he carried out his mission. In Martín's letters of introduction to US authorities, the government in Buenos Aires expressed "appreciation and fraternity" with their "brothers" in the US, and the hope of working together toward the "absolute emancipation of the New World." A separate letter to President James Madison spoke of the "heroic example" of the United States of America and asked Madison to "help defend" the Argentine cause.[16]

After he got permission from the American president, Martín was instructed to do a long list of things: open relations and make pacts of reciprocity and trade; buy a warship; recruit foreign mercenaries to fight in the independence wars; raise money; and open secret relations with Mexico's revolutionary government. In general, he was to entertain "any proposition that would be advantageous to the progress and support" of Buenos Aires's cause. In return for such support, Martín was authorized to offer President Madison "all kinds of advantages imaginable in favor of trade from the USA" and a promise to promote the "predominance of the North Americans over British nationals."[17] The final item in his instructions was that Martín needed to "inform his superiors in these Provinces" regarding every matter of importance.[18] The insistence on getting official permission was an indication of the delicate nature of such a mission, especially when representatives of European empires were pressuring President Madison to reject any requests for aid from Spanish American rebels.

Martín's voyage from Buenos Aires to New York took eighty-four days. The long journey left him "somewhat unwell," he reported to his superiors a few days after his arrival, but he assured them he would soon "get on track toward [his] final destination" of Washington, DC.[19] Martín arrived in the US capital on August 6 and immediately sought an audience with President Madison. His attempts were frustrated, however, for a number of reasons. He was not an official representative of a recognized country, and furthermore, he was part of a great wave of agents from across Hispanic America who, in the 1810s, flooded Washington, DC, to seek aid from the American president and other government officials. Further complicating matters, the US government could not afford to needlessly offend powers like France and Spain, who pressured Washington to refuse any aid to Spanish American rebels. To his credit, Martín did manage on two occasions to meet with a chief clerk of the State Department.[20] Martín never did get his appointment with the American president.

Despite not fulfilling the first requirement of his mission, Martín went ahead with his mission anyway. He recruited men to fight in Argentina and tried to purchase weapons. He sent a number of foreign soldiers to Buenos Aires, even promising that the porteño government would pay the passage for some of them.[21] Although Martín was in clear violation of his instructions, he rushed headlong into activity anyway. All around him, other Spanish American agents were doing the same things. The Chilean patriot José Miguel Carrera, for example, recruited a shipload of Americans to fight in Chile—even to fight against Carrera's rival, General San Martín (explained below). Meanwhile, the port of Baltimore, Maryland, became a hub to recruit American ships, along with their captains and crews, to fight in the Spanish-American revolutions, and soon these privateers were prowling the Caribbean and South Atlantic to prey on Spanish shipping and port cities.[22] One American, Thomas Taylor, even had official "licenses" issued by the government of Buenos Aires, which he distributed to these privateers. Such licenses meant that, legally, these ships were not American and thus not subject to US jurisdiction or neutrality laws.

Between 1815 and 1821, roughly three thousand privateers sailed from US ports, many of them under the banners of Buenos Aires. Thousands more foreign men fought in various Hispanic American armies.[23]

One of the most famous privateers of the day was Hipólito Bouchard, a Frenchman sailing under the flag of Buenos Aires. Not long after the declaration of independence, Bouchard set out from Buenos Aires on a world tour to harass Spanish shipping and Spanish ports. He skirmished with the Spanish forces in the Philippines, then made his way to Hawai'i where he got an audience with King Kamehameha I. During his negotiations with the Hawaiian monarch, Bouchard claimed that Kamehameha officially recognized the independence of the United Provinces of the Río de la Plata, making the Kingdom of Hawai'i the first to do so.[24] But while any recognition was welcomed, porteño leaders wanted the support of great world powers like Great Britain and the United States, and that is what Martín was trying to do in the USA.

The activities of agents like Martín Thompson in Washington enraged Spanish and Portuguese representatives in Washington, who pressured US government officials to cease any aid to Hispanic American revolutionaries. Their complaints raised concern among some US politicians who worried about getting dragged into another war with a European power. In the end, the US government cracked down on privateering and other activities of Spanish American agents. By December of 1817, US secretary of state John Quincy Adams assured the French that "immediate measures" had been taken to "repress any project" designed to provoke violence in the Spanish American provinces. Adams assured that there was nothing to fear from these "absurd" plans.[25]

The "absurd plans" mentioned by Adams may not have been in reference to Martín Thompson's actions in particular, but by early 1817 the Directory in Buenos Aires decided it was time to relieve Martín of his duties. On January 10, the Directory sent Martín a letter. "To avoid possible complications," they ordered him to immediately "cease the exercise" of his functions. The letter reprimanded Martín for violating his instructions.[26] Supreme Director Pueyrredón also wrote the American president an apology, saying that Martín's own letters showed how he "arbitrarily deviated from the line of duties he was given" and admitting that the Argentines should have "chosen someone with other gifts to carry out this duty."[27] In a short note a month later, Vicente López reiterated that Martín no longer had any authority, adding that he need not feel obligated to return and report on his mission. Therefore it was up to him if he wanted to "return here or remain in that country, or any other, in complete liberty."[28] Martín had been fired, and his government did not seem to care if he ever returned.

Martín may have been driven to disregard orders because he was so enveloped by the romantic charm of the revolution that he and Mariquita had been a part of.[29] But Martín's fading mental health was also clearly a contributing factor to his failure. While it is difficult to trace the history of Martín's mental state, he did not feel well when he left Buenos Aires in the first place, and he was ill when he arrived in New York City. The pressures of his job likely intensified his illness, while his humiliating dismissal may have been enough to push him over the edge. Sometime over the next few months, Mariquita received news that Martín was in an asylum, hopelessly insane, where he would remain for two years before Mariquita would attempt to bring him home (see chapter 7 for the rest of the story).

The Congress of Tucumán Debates Monarchy, Republics, and a Constitution

While Martín languished in an asylum in New York, back in Tucumán his compatriots sought to create a new government in their newly independent state. The task before them was a daunting one: How do you handle such a large territory after it has been cut free from the moorings that had attached it to Spain for the last three hundred years? How do you replace the legitimacy and credibility of a monarchy? The way forward was anything but clear.

Thus began to unfold in the Río de la Plata the same tensions found elsewhere in the former Spanish territories as well as in the fledgling US. Although the United States impressed all observers with its stability, by 1815 the US had already suffered through threats to its union, such as the failure of the Articles of Confederation, the threat of war with France in 1798, and Vice President Aaron Burr's conspiracy in 1806. Moreover, the British had continued treating the US as a rebellious child, boarding American ships on the high seas and "pressing" American seamen into the British navy, which led, in part, to the War of 1812. More than just a war with England, the War of 1812 had all the elements of a civil war as well.[30] If the newly independent United States of America—organized nicely along the East Coast of North America with most of its major cities connected by convenient sea routes—experienced troubles creating national unity after independence, how much more might the United Provinces of the Río de la Plata struggle to form a union?

Many of the delegates at the congress favored a republic, although some, including Manuel Belgrano, seriously considered a monarchy option.[31] Whatever the case, Belgrano and others believed that the Congress of Tucumán should write a new constitution as quickly as possible. When no document emerged from the deliberations, Belgrano warned, "The sufferings of the fatherland" will continue as long as the "majestic step is not taken that will save us and assure our survival."[32]

CENTRALIST AND FEDERALIST FACTIONS

Two key divisions began to emerge in the debates at the Congress of Tucumán, divisions between Centralists and Federalists. Centralists favored a strong central government that would promote reforms to modernize the country and attract foreign immigrants and foreign investment. This included reducing the power of the Catholic Church in the country. Federalists, on the other hand, resented the idea of a stronger central government—something they came to call "Unitarianism." Federalists favored more provincial autonomy and maintaining the primacy of the Catholic Church. The Federalists of Buenos Aires had the advantage of being in the most powerful and wealthy province, which also possessed the port that oversaw most incoming and outgoing trade. Buenos Aires, with its port and with its fertile Pampas, was the best place to be a Federalist because the province possessed everything it needed to be truly autonomous.[33]

The United Provinces and the World: The Holy Alliance and the Monarchy Option

In addition to factious politics at home, the United Provinces of the Río de La Plata faced reactionary forces across the Atlantic. Napoleon's defeat in 1815 meant that European powers could now turn their attention to other matters, including the insurrections in Spanish America. While Argentine delegates deliberated independence in Tucumán, the great monarchs of Europe allied together to preserve their monarchies against revolutionary threats found anywhere in the world. On September 26, 1815, Czar Alexander I of Russia, Emperor Francis I of Austria, and Prussian King Frederick William III all signed the Treaty of the Holy Alliance (France and Spain would add their signatures to the treaty over the next few months). As one Russian diplomat wrote, the Spanish American revolutions were "not simply a Spanish question or an American question." American rebellion was a global question that needed to be solved. Russia was even considering sending its own soldiers to help stamp out the revolution in Buenos Aires and in other rebellious regions.[34]

While Russia may have believed that the revolutions could be reversed, other alliance members were more realistic. French officials saw independence in the Río de la Plata as inevitable and thus advised Ferdinand VII to make the best of an impossible situation: concede independence in exchange for an independent monarch on a throne in Buenos Aires.[35] French intelligence reported that the Supreme Director in Buenos Aires was prepared to accept a "prince of the Spanish dynasty." But Ferdinand's negotiators needed to act quickly because, according to the French, the US was on the brink of recognizing La Plata's independence, which would start a cascade of recognitions from other countries. "If Europe does not intervene," one French official concluded, "the recognition of La Plata at the approaching session of [the US] Congress is certain."[36]

The Holy Alliance was further alarmed by news of the spectacular victories of the Argentine general San Martín in Chile. After building his army in Mendoza Province, San Martín crossed the Andes into Chile in January of 1817, and, by April of 1818, he and his Chilean allies had effectively driven the Spaniards from Chile. The way was now open to Lima, the most important Spanish stronghold on the continent.[37]

Bernardino Rivadavia was in Europe during these months, also on a mission to secure support for his new country. Rivadavia suggested to members of the Holy Alliance that an independent monarchy in the Río de la Plata could be a solution.[38] Some of Rivadavia's friends in Europe thought he was crazy for even entertaining such an idea. One of those friends was the English philosopher Jeremy Bentham, the main proponent of utilitarianism, whom Rivadavia met in London. "You wish for a king for Buenos Aires and Chile," Bentham wrote Rivadavia. "If so, much good may it do you. But how much better would you be without one?" The Spaniards, Bentham continued, had a reason for a king. "But you have not that reason—nor ever had."[39]

But the Directory in Buenos Aires did have its reasons: a monarchy in the Río de la Plata could bring official recognition of independence while making it easier to forge great-power alliances that would ensure national survival.

Together with representatives of Buenos Aires, the French helped draft a plan for an independent monarchy.[40] This French Plan was brought before the Buenos Aires congress, and on November 12, 1819, the United Provinces voted to accept it, but only if an extensive list of stipulations could be met. The impossibly long list of requirements showed that porteños were not wholeheartedly committed to the idea of a monarchy unless everyone, especially the British, supported it.[41] The situation was even more complicated because everyone knew that Ferdinand VII was, at that very moment, mustering thousands of troops in the Spanish port of Cádiz to reconquer Buenos Aires.

Conclusion

The struggle to declare independence and to decide on a type of government vexed the leaders of the former Viceroyalty of the Río de la Plata. The process also placed enormous strains on Mariquita and her family, and especially on Martín, who lost his mind in the process. Strains in society provoked the emergence of powerful factions in porteño society. Whether it was Unitarians versus Federalists, or republicans versus monarchists, these divisions undermined efforts to establish a nation unified by a constitution.

But for many in the Río de la Plata, even the remote possibility of a monarch in Buenos Aires was traitorous, regardless of who they were or who they were married to. In Buenos Aires's neighboring provinces of Santa Fe and Entre Ríos, the threat of monarchy, along with other grievances, was enough to provoke the powerful caudillos Estanislao López and Francisco Ramírez to send their armies to punish Buenos Aires for violating the spirit of freedom and independence represented by the May Revolution of 1810. Their actions would unleash a series of events in 1820, a year that would forever change the fates of Mariquita and Juan Manuel.

CHAPTER SIX

The Anarchy of 1820

In January of 1820, Juan Manuel de Rosas was right where he wanted to be: one hundred miles southeast of Buenos Aires, on the other side of the Salado River, in the middle of the Indian frontier, working his lands and increasing his herds. And he intended on staying there for a while. "I have no plans to return to the other side of the Salado this year."[1] A few months later, however, Juan Manuel was in a very different mood. In an open letter to his fellow citizens, he warned them to "be ever watchful" against anyone who was promoting disorder—the "innovators, disrupters, and enemies of authority," as he called them. Juan Manuel finished his letter with a flourish. "Eternal hatred of unrest! Long live order! Loyalty to oaths taken! Obedience to elected authorities!"[2] His pastoral dream life, it seemed, was over.

1820 proved to be a most tumultuous year for the new country in the Río de la Plata. Buenos Aires was invaded by its neighboring provinces because of old disagreements over power sharing among the provinces, as well as fear of a monarchy in the Río de la Plata. A new constitution in 1819 had also proved very contentious. Juan Manuel, by now a successful rancher, was summoned by provincial authorities to defend the capital from invasion, and from an anarchy that threatened to engulf not only his province but the whole country. Juan Manuel de Rosas left his ranch to answer the call to arms as a militia commander. He and his men were victorious in battle, and Juan Manuel helped lay the foundation for peace, thus fueling his reputation as a leader who could bring order out of chaos. 1820 was also a pivotal year for Mariquita Sánchez de Thompson, although that part of the story will have to wait until chapter 7.

The Constitution of 1819

Three years after the Conference of Tucumán declared independence in 1816, the United Provinces still did not have a constitution, and the country was still not recognized by any major international power. The congress moved to Buenos Aires in 1817 to continue its deliberations. Meanwhile, Ferdinand VII was gathering twenty thousand soldiers in the Spanish port city of Cádiz to reconquer Buenos Aires and the other rebellious provinces. To prevent or forestall that invasion, the Directory continued desperately to secure international recognition, and thus protection, for their new country, even if it meant bringing a monarch to the Río de la Plata.

Finally, in 1819, the delegates in Buenos Aires produced the long-awaited constitution. The constitution declared the Catholic Church as the official state religion, and also established a bicameral legislature. The head of the government, still called the Supreme Director, would be elected by the legislature. The constitution also declared its type of government to be one of "unity." For Deán Funes, who wrote the preamble to the constitution, the new document was a perfect mix. It did *not* represent the "fanatical" democracy of Athens, the "absolutist" government of Russia, or the "complicated federation of some states" (most likely a reference to the US). Rather, Funes concluded, the new constitution was a document that "approached perfection" by striking a middle ground between "democratic convulsion, the injustice of aristocracy, and the abuse of unlimited power."[3]

For others, however, the document was far from perfect. The central government was still way too powerful—too Unitarian. From his base across the river, José Gervasio Artigas commented that with the new constitution the Supreme Director and his allies wanted to make Buenos Aires a "new Imperial Rome, sending its proconsuls as military governors of the provinces and to despoil them of all public representations."[4] Critics of the constitution also raised concerns for what the document did *not* contain. Little reference was made to the "sovereignty of the people," which was characteristic of earlier rhetoric during the Assembly of 1813. It was also disturbing to critics that the constitution did not declare a "republic" or a "president," choosing to keep the old office of Supreme Director. With no mention of the sovereignty of the people, nor of a republic, many feared that the new constitution left the door open for a monarchy. Moreover, everyone knew that government agents were still in Europe seeking a foreign prince, and secret sessions at the congress were hotly debating the issue throughout 1819 and early 1820.

Some welcome news did arrive from Spain in January of 1820. The troops Ferdinand VII was gathering in Spain to reconquer Buenos Aires revolted against him. The revolt spread, and soon troops surrounded Ferdinand's palace in Madrid and forced him to reinstate a constitutional monarchy. Plans for the invasion of Buenos Aires were scuttled. While this news allowed the Río de la Plata to breathe a sigh of relief, it also enabled Argentines to focus on enemy factions at home in the Río de la Plata. That meant civil war.

The provinces of Santa Fe and Entre Ríos were already opposed to what they saw as Buenos Aires's overreaching authority, but the new constitution and the ongoing search for a monarch now gave them even more reason to fight. Estanislao López and Francisco Ramírez, the leaders of Santa Fe and Entre Ríos Provinces, marched their armies to Buenos Aires, and on February 1, 1820, at the Battle of Cepeda, their combined armies overwhelmed Buenos Aires's defenders. The Treaty of Pilar, signed on February 23, was supposed to bring an end to the conflict by assuring that a federative government would rule the provinces. For the time being, the United Provinces of the Río de la Plata ceased to exist, and each province was left to go its own way.[5] López and Ramírez entered the city of Buenos Aires on February 25 with an escort of gauchos and Indians. They rode into the main plaza and tied their horses up to the posts surrounding the May Pyramid. The scene of bearded men clad in ponchos and bombachas next to the May Pyramid (built as a neo-Egyptian style obelisk) was a sign for many porteños that barbarism had triumphed over civilization. But the barbarian conquerors possessed virtues as well, which the local media contrasted with the pretensions of the Unitarian porteños. The *Gazeta* noted the gaucho dress of the men, yet complimented them on their principles. These gaucho leaders were "heroes" and "models of free men." And although they were "completely lacking in civilized manners," they nevertheless carried themselves with "the confidence of republicanism, without any aristocratic airs."[6] In a letter to the cabildo of Buenos Aires, Santa Fe caudillo Estanislao López justified his invasion as one of liberation. His goal was to free Buenos Aires from its own government—the Directory—as well as from the congress, "who had bargained with the courts of Portugal, Spain, France, and England to crown a European prince in the Río de la Plata, thus opposing the will of the people who have sworn to uphold the form of a federal republic."

The invaders' actions were justified, López concluded. "Without them there is no liberty."[7]

Juan Manuel Is Summoned to Defend Buenos Aires

On his estancia miles away, a concerned Juan Manuel heard about López and Ramírez's conquest of the city. By this time Juan Manuel had built himself a reputation as a leader on the frontier. He had spent a few years managing his parents' lands, the old Rincón de López estancia where he had spent so much of his youth. By 1820, however, he had started working more on his own. There appears to have been a falling out of sorts with his parents that drove him to leave their employ. Some accounts assert that Agustina accused Juan Manuel of mismanaging their affairs, an insult he could not tolerate. Evidence of some estrangement came some months later when a friend urged Juan Manuel to write a letter to his parents, who had "demonstrated that they love you."[8] Whatever the case, Juan Manuel went into partnership in the cattle business with his cousins, and soon had enough money to purchase his own estancia. Within a few years, he became one of the richest, if not the richest, rancher in the whole region.[9] Juan Manuel de Rosas at this time was entering the physical prime of his life. One biographer described him as a "young man, blonde, of some 27 years, with a solid and splendid figure, a clean-shaven face that was exceptionally handsome. He had blue eyes, white and pink skin, a penetrating look, and long sideburns with a wide base. Everything about him exudes strength and virility."[10]

Juan Manuel attempted to modernize his estates as much as he could. He wrote detailed instructions on estate management, on topics ranging from garbage collection to managing stray dogs to trying to protect resources on his land. Numerous residents lived on his lands, many of whom lived off the resources his lands provided. If all of Juan Manuel's instructions had been put into practice, then he indeed would have been an all-powerful land baron. In reality, however, Juan Manuel had to negotiate and accommodate many traditional practices of the residents on his estates, such as allowing them to use wood and hunt game on his lands. The shortage of manpower in the region gave local residents leverage against landowners, like Juan Manuel de Rosas, who otherwise would have hoped to gain more control over the lands they owned. Many residents on his lands also worked for Rosas, and if he cracked down on their subsistence activities, they might decide to move elsewhere, taking their skills with them. Through hard work, good administration, and compromises with residents on his lands, Juan Manuel steadily increased his holdings.[11]

Juan Manuel's abilities caught the eye of government leaders in Buenos Aires, who planned to expand the cattle frontier for the benefit of the province. In September of 1819, the Directory put Rosas on a commission to advise the government on frontier security and Indian policy.[12] Juan Manuel's policy toward Indians was to negotiate with them and bring them into the workforce whenever possible, and he himself employed a number of Indians. As slavery waned in Argentina, more Indians appeared as workers on the estancias of Buenos Aires.[13] In exchange for goods and commodities, Juan Manuel expected indigenous tribes to subordinate themselves to the government of Buenos Aires.[14] If any Indian group refused to negotiate, however, he advocated war. In any case, Juan Manuel and others saw the Indian frontier as a prime arena of expansion. Once enemy tribes are pushed aside, Rosas remarked in a porteño newspaper, "Buenos Aires will see itself transformed into a republic with an emporium of material and moral riches."[15]

In January of 1820, Juan Manuel was on the south side of the Salado River— in the Indian frontier—where he could better monitor and protect the frontier from Indian attacks. Although far removed from the city, he remained connected to the world of Buenos Aires through letters from his wife, Encarnación, and from copies of the newspaper the *Gazeta de Buenos Ayres*, which he received every few days by courier. By the end of January, the news had grown even more alarming, as Juan Manuel read of how the caudillos of Santa Fe and Entre Ríos were threatening the province of Buenos Aires.

In this tense environment, the government of Buenos Aires chose Juan Manuel, without notifying him first, as the mayor of his district for the year 1820. Juan Manuel read about it in the January 19 edition of the *Gazeta*.[16] He decided to reject the appointment for a number of reasons. He expressed disappointment that the government violated protocol by not informing him first, and Juan Manuel always expected protocol to be followed, especially for government business. His main reason for rejecting the position, he maintained, was because he felt he would be unable to fully perform the duties of the office. "It would be difficult to find another vecino of this district that was harder for the inhabitants to visit than I," he wrote to the government in his letter declining the appointment. His usual residence, the estancia called Independence, was more than thirty miles from his nearest neighbor, which made it "by far the furthest removed in the district." Even in good weather it was difficult to get to, but during the rainy season when the Salado River was in flood, getting to his ranch was nearly impossible. Was it "rational" and "sensible," he asked, for the government to appoint someone who was so difficult to consult? It was also impossible for someone so isolated to maintain law and order in any district. Thus, Juan Manuel officially resigned his post on February 13, 1820 before he ever started it, a testament to his strict adherence to protocol, but also to his commitment to doing a job the right way or not doing it at all.[17]

Besides his concerns over protocol and duty, Juan Manuel was worried by the continued tension and disorder in his province. Although a peace was signed at Pilar in February, the forces of Santa Fe and Entre Ríos Provinces remained in threatening positions outside the city of Buenos Aires. In the meantime, governments in the city of Buenos Aires seemed to rise and fall every few days. What was particularly disturbing for many city leaders was the increasing mobilization of the popular classes in the city.[18]

General Gregorio Lamadrid arrived in Buenos Aires in the midst of the chaotic political climate. A veteran of the wars of independence (he fought with the forces of Belgrano and San Martín), Lamadrid now offered his services to the struggling province. He stopped first to visit family, where his uncle advised him not to overcommit himself to the current government "because it was not very stable and would probably not last much longer." Sure enough, Lamadrid witnessed the rise and fall of two governments over the next few weeks. Colonel Manuel Dorrego was eventually chosen as interim governor of Buenos Aires, having recently returned from exile in the United States.[19]

With enemy armies still on porteño soil, the newly appointed governor, Dorrego, asked the ranchers in the countryside to raise militias to come to the aid of the city and province. For Juan Manuel de Rosas, defending the province was worth fighting. He sent word around his estates that he needed able-bodied men to fight, and soon raised five hundred men. These were men loyal to Juan Manuel because he allowed them to live on his land. Some felt additional loyalty because they were fugitives from justice, and Juan Manuel, like other landowners, would sometimes harbor such individuals if they were valuable workers.[20] Juan Manuel dressed his troops in red gaucho clothing—the color of his uniform during the English invasions—and then he and his

Colorados reported to the fort in Buenos Aires, where he was placed under the command of General Gregorio Lamadrid.

Juan Manuel impressed Lamadrid from the beginning, as the veteran general recorded in his memoirs. "I had taken a liking to this young man—so diligent and resolute—who I found at my side numerous times since I was given my command." When Lamadrid prepared to march out of the city, he ran into a problem. The man that was supposed to guide him across the Pampas never arrived, and Lamadrid knew he needed a guide (a *baqueano*) to travel across the vast Pampas because they were virtually devoid of landmarks. In the midst of Lamadrid's despair, a solution appeared. "Juan Manuel de Rosas came up to me and said: you don't need a guide, General. I can lead you better than anyone they can provide." Lamadrid happily accepted Juan Manuel's offer: "The truth is, my friend, you inspire much more confidence in me than the governor." Lamadrid's admiration was further evident in the way he referred to Rosas as "patriotic," "active," and "diligent."[21]

Besides serving as a guide to his general, Juan Manuel and his men helped repel the forces of Santa Fe Province in two battles in 1820. After the Battle of San Nicolás, many victorious troops looted the city. Juan Manuel's troops— the Colorados—however, were a picture of discipline. Juan Manuel also played a key role in brokering the final peace between the Buenos Aires and Santa Fe Provinces. In the negotiations, Estanislao López explained that the cattle industry, the lifeblood of his province, had been devastated by warfare, hinting that a restitution of some cattle would go a long way in their recovery. In the discussion that followed, Juan Manuel offered to personally supply twenty-five thousand head of cattle. The peace between Santa Fe and Buenos Aires, as Santa Fe governor Estanislao López later wrote, "was guaranteed by Señor Juan Manuel de Rosas."[22]

Despite the peace with Santa Fe, the situation in Buenos Aires and the rest of the country over the next few months remained chaotic. One of Estanislao López's former allies, for example, decided to keep fighting. José Miguel Carrera was a charismatic Chilean exile from a prominent family who fought the Spaniards in the early stages of Chile's independence movement. Carrera's brothers, however, had been executed for treason by San Martín,[23] and now Carrera swore to take his revenge in whatever way he could. To bolster his power, Carrera made an alliance with the Ranquel Indian tribe, and his force menaced the territory between Buenos Aires and the Andes, threatening towns and cutting off trade and communication routes.[24] While Rosas and many of his fellow ranchers also employed Indians as ranch hands and soldiers, they nevertheless condemned Carrera as a foreigner who was stirring up Indians and disrupting a whole region.[25]

Other parts of the country were also engulfed in chaos. Civil wars raged in some provinces as local identities and loyalties smothered any budding sense of national unity. The provinces of Tucumán and Entre Ríos, for example, declared themselves independent republics, and Portuguese forces occupied Montevideo and the rest of the Eastern Shore. General José de San Martín, who was now engaged in liberating Lima from the Spaniards, heard all the news with disgust. For him, the root of the problem was too much Federalism—too much power in the hands of regions and provinces. "The genius of evil has inspired the delirium of the Federation," he wrote. For him, the very word "Federation" was "full of death" and had brought only "ruin and devastation." San Martín feared what would eventually come as a result: the people of the Río de la Plata would get so tired of anarchy that they would eventually "seek a solution in oppression" by welcoming "the yoke of the first fortunate adventurer that presents himself." This solution, San Martín predicted, instead of "putting you on the path of your true destiny, will only prolong your uncertainty."[26]

An Englishman's Daring Ride Highlights the Troubled Provinces

Few people experienced the troubles that afflicted the region more than the daring English traveler Alexander Caldcleugh. His journey from Buenos Aires to Santiago, Chile, and back provides an eyewitness account of the anarchy and disorder that so rankled Juan Manuel de Rosas, General San Martín, and many others. Caldcleugh arrived in South America in 1819 and kept a record of his travels. In the tertulias of Buenos Aires and elsewhere, Caldcleugh gained some understanding of the local community and its history.[27]

After spending some time in Buenos Aires, Caldcleugh decided to travel to Chile for business. Such a journey would have been easy in previous years, he was told, but now the "unsettled state of the country" made the trip treacherous. Rebels and thieves plagued the route in many places, while Native tribes had pushed northward and cut off trade and communication between Buenos

Aires and Chile. Despite the dire warnings, Caldcleugh was determined to make the trip. He chose to travel by horse instead of by wagon, electing speed over comfort in case he needed to escape marauding Indians. Caldcleugh hired a guide, purchased horses, and loaded his saddlebags with yerba mate, Chinese tea, sugar, biscuits, and cigars, along with two horns of brandy. He dressed like a local as much as possible, wearing a poncho from Córdoba, wool boots, and a straw hat. "An English carving knife in my boot, and a brace of pistols on my saddle bow, completed my appearance."[28]

A few days into the journey, he and his guide received some bad news at a mail outpost: the Chilean renegade José Miguel Carrera and his band of Indians were in the area. Not knowing the exact location of Carrera's group, Caldcleugh and his guide set off, only to stumble into the Indians near the next mail stop. They turned their horses and galloped away, with indigenous warriors in hot pursuit. For two hours they spurred their mounts through hills and valleys. They finally found a hiding place and only narrowly escaped being discovered. Caldcleugh had chosen wisely in taking a horse instead of a wagon, for his speedy steed saved his life that day.[29] A few days later, Caldcleugh made it safely to the city of Mendoza, then went on to Chile, taking the same thirteen-thousand-foot mountain pass General San Martín had used a few years earlier on his way to glorious victories.

After concluding his business in Chile, Caldcleugh decided to return to Buenos Aires. Again, many of his friends in Chile warned him of the hazards of the trip. Going through the mountains in June, the beginning of winter, was a "considerable danger" in and of itself, but even worse perils awaited on the other side, where the route was "overrun by Indians and freebooters."[30] Braving freezing temperatures, mules falling to their deaths, and altitude sickness, Caldcleugh and his companions made it to the city of Mendoza in nine days—an impressive feat for a winter crossing. Caldcleugh had no time to relish his accomplishment, for he found the city of Mendoza gripped with fear. Again, it was José Miguel Carrera and his Indian army who now threatened to attack the city.

Such conditions made it difficult for Caldcleugh to hire a guide, but he finally secured the services of a trusted man named Dávila. Both men decided to take out some extra insurance for their journey—of a spiritual nature. The guide made a sacred vow that he would offer four reales to the Virgin of Lujan *if he arrived in Buenos Aires safely*. Caldcleugh followed suit. "I would have given our ladyship ten times as much with pleasure for the same success." Not wanting to appear excessive, he "made a vow to give eight reales."[31]

Leaving Mendoza, Caldcleugh and Dávila managed to avoid Carrera and his Indian allies. As they traveled through Córdoba Province, the two encountered the advance force of Estanislao López, the powerful governor of Santa Fe Province, who was now in a conflict with his old friend Francisco Ramírez. López and Ramírez had been allies a few months earlier when their combined forces defeated Buenos Aires in February of 1820. Now, however, they were sworn enemies—another indication of the chronic instability. Caldcleugh spent much of the night listening to López's soldiers boast of chilling "deeds of blood committed in combat." There was not one among them, he wrote, who "had not killed four of his fellow-creatures one way or other." The next morning, on June 25, Estanislao López invited the Englishman for a visit. Caldcleugh found him "sucking brandy and water through a tube." López cut quite a figure in the Englishman's eyes. "He was tall, fairer than usual, and apparently thirty years of age. He had the mark of a dreadful sabre cut over his right eye."[32] When the conversation turned to his enemy Ramírez, López assured Caldcleugh that he knew where Ramírez was camped and that he would soon "attack him and cut off his head." Caldcleugh later found out that López was true to his word.[33]

The rest of Caldcleugh's trip was relatively uneventful. On June 30, one month after leaving Chile, he "had at length the great pleasure of again entering Buenos Ayres." As Caldcleugh delivered the letters he brought from Chile, news of his arrival spread among the merchant community. From everyone's mouth came the same questions: How did they survive such a journey? What route had he taken? Caldcleugh booked passage on an American ship leaving the next day to Rio de Janeiro. If anyone asked how he spent his last night in Buenos Aires, he provided an answer: after dinner, he went to a tertulia, "where I danced until very late."[34]

Caldcleugh kept a journal of his experiences and used them to write a two-volume narrative of his travels. Reflecting on his time in the Río de la Plata, Caldcleugh lamented the "acrid and violent" relations between provinces even though they spoke "the same language" and struggled "in the same sacred cause of liberty." The conflicts not only hurt the cultural fabric of the nation but also the economy.[35] Although Caldcleugh spent some months among the Argentines and met many of their leaders, he could not discover a comprehensive explanation for the conflicts between the provinces. In his words, despite getting "deep in the politics of these petty states," he could "never learn the cause of this grand dispute, which drew forth so many forces." He doubted that the Argentines themselves knew the reasons for their disunion.[36]

Caldcleugh, nevertheless, offered a few theories to explain the perpetual conflicts. The excessive power of Buenos Aires, he believed, was part of the reason. Many in the interior blamed Buenos Aires's policies for damaging the economies of the interior provinces. Caldcleugh recorded some of the complaints he heard. "What right has [Buenos Aires] to put on any tax which shall indirectly affect other states? What right has she to place herself at the head, and consider herself superior to the rest?" At the same time, Caldcleugh was "equally certain" that many of the advantages of independence "must also be in fairness attributed to" Buenos Aires.[37]

Alexander Caldcleugh's ride there and back again between Buenos Aires and Santiago exposed the factional nature of society in the United Provinces in and around the year 1820. The disruptions of those times roused Juan Manuel de Rosas to action to defend law and order in his province.

Juan Manuel Returns and Speaks on Anarchy and Politics

In September of 1820, Juan Manuel was called back to action as the province again teetered on the edge of civil war. The provincial governor, now General Martín Rodríguez, had been chased from the capital because he was seen by many as being too Unitarian and too connected to the recent monarchist intrigues in the Constitutional Congress. On October 1, 1820, a group of soldiers revolted, occupied the central plaza, and forced Governor Rodríguez to flee. Rodríguez's crime, according to the insurgents, was that he belonged "to that destroyed faction of the congress and the Directory, the enemy of the liberty of the people and of the patriots."[38]

Governor Rodríguez requested help, and Juan Manuel again answered the call. On October 5, 1820, Juan Manuel's men entered the city and helped defeat the rebels.[39] His soldiers stood guard over the businesses, many of them foreign-owned, to protect them from looters. The discipline of Rosas's troops made a lasting impression. "You cannot imagine," one observer remarked, "the enthusiasm with which the foreigners speak of the Colorados. They all say they've never seen anything like it, since they feared getting looted no matter what side won."[40] Martín Rodríguez was restored to the governorship and granted extra powers by the legislature to deal with the rebels, a practice dating back to ancient Rome where extraordinary powers were given to leaders in times of crisis.[41] The governor also promoted Juan Manuel to the rank of colonel in the militia in recognition of his service. His appointment and skill as a militia commander made him a key part of the institutional workings of the porteño government from then on.

Others rewarded Juan Manuel with praise in song and verse. Poets began lauding him as a man of order and stability. The aging Fray Cayetano, Mariquita's old confessor, composed a sonnet in honor of the young commander and his Colorados regiment. "Record it forever in your hearts, the memory and grandeur of Rosas, who declares to all that order is restored; you will be preserved: the law is your enterprise; and lovely liberty your emblem."[42] Father Cayetano and others hoped that Rosas had helped to stem the tide of instability and violence in the country—for the past few months had brought invasions of Buenos Aires from neighboring provinces, the dissolution of the national government, civil war in other provinces, the declaration of independence by various provinces, and the resurgence of Indian violence, including that led by José Miguel Carrera.

How was the twenty-seven-year-old Juan Manuel de Rosas affected by the events of 1820? Did these events change the way he saw his city, his province, and the world? Traumatic and violent personal experiences influenced other prominent leaders toward more conservative views. Two examples include José de San Martín, whose close friend was killed by a mob in Spain, and Lucas Alamán in Mexico, who lived through the violence in his home town of Guanajuato in 1810.[43] For Juan Manuel, it is plausible that the events of 1819 and 1820 greatly influenced his thinking about what kind of authority was needed in porteño and national politics. Juan Manuel was already predisposed to enforcing his own order on things, whether as a young man or as an emerging rancher, and the political turmoil of 1820 likely intensified his already meticulous and authoritarian nature.

Soon after he helped subdue the uprising of October 1, Juan Manuel composed two documents. One was a memorandum sent to the government, and the other a "manifesto" addressed to the public. These are the first major statements made by Rosas on political matters. Taken together, they provide a window into how Juan Manuel processed the events of 1820, and they offer one of the earliest glimpses into his views on law and order. Perhaps even more significantly, these statements show how Juan Manuel perceived his role in society moving forward.

In his memorandum to the government, Rosas wrote that in early 1820 a "concussion" of anarchy engulfed the province. The "explosion" was so powerful that, in Rosas's view, it "overshadowed and buried the great work" of the May Revolution of 1810. "We should not forget that we still have a revolution on our hands," he continued. Conspiring men driven by resentment and revenge had infected the province, and some were even "seducing savages into becoming their instruments" (likely referring to Carrera). Peace was needed to resurrect civilization and to cure the wounds caused by "previous mistakes and ill-laid plans." Public institutions needed to be strengthened while "ignoble passions" needed to be curbed. Rosas proposed the appointment of a military commander, endowed with extra authority, to take charge of the area. Such a leader should be given wide-ranging power to restore "respect and security" and to impose the ultimate punishment of death when called for. Extraordinary authority was justified because of the "current state of disorder" in the province and the licentiousness of its inhabitants.[44]

In his open letter to the public, Juan Manuel presented himself as a model of law and order, even as he suffered through the same chaos as his fellow citizens. His "spirit had grown weary" of the repeated acts of anarchy and "the dissolution of all the bonds that tied citizens to authority." In the preceding months, Rosas continued, he personally witnessed the destruction of public security, and decided to act "in a way that superseded" his "unknown destiny." His successes, he noted, created a new reputation for him. He found it remarkable how much he was "recognized as a symbol of order" in the province. Although his soldiers contributed to the victories, Rosas's leadership kept them from looting as others did. "We came to save, not to destroy." Such was the influence of his "just, severe, and religious example"! The landowners and residents that Rosas and his Colorados encountered "were all impeccable witnesses" that he and his soldiers "respected the rights of all men."

Other military commanders expressed similar sentiments with Juan Manuel, which he in turn shared with his readers. "How long will we wander from resolution to resolution? For how long will crime be tolerated with impunity? When will the day come when oaths are seen as something sacred? When will the laws be respected?" All the tears of sadness and all the horrors should have been lesson enough. Rosas had conferred with other commanders and summarized their feelings: "Obedience, loyalty, and firmness are our watchwords." Speaking of himself, Rosas declared that he was a "religious observer" of oaths. "I have fulfilled them and made sure they were fulfilled."

Rosas was pleased that the provincial government was again functioning, and he hoped that the province had learned its lessons. "May the blood that was shed serve to restore the good that has been carried away by excessive passions." The fatherland pleaded for unity, for without unity, "there is no fatherland," and "without union all is a disgrace—all is death and misery." Juan Manuel blamed the anarchy on those he called "the innovators." To them, and to the entire province, Rosas declared: "Eternal hatred of unrest! Long live order! Loyalty to oaths taken! Obedience to the authorities!" Rosas ended his letter by assuring the public: "All my satisfaction comes from having tried to be virtuous" and from "serving the place where I was born, and the province to which I belong."[45] The anarchy of 1820 was indisputable. However, the manner in which Rosas recounts the events and his role in them clearly indicates his belief in the need for a stronger government, and his view of himself as a present and future power broker in the region.

Like Rosas, other members of porteño society despised innovators. Certain members of the Catholic clergy were especially opposed. For Father Paula de Castañeda, the dangerous innovators were a certain brand of intellectual who sought to bring the Enlightenment to Buenos Aires. His solution was simple: burn the offensive writings. "Let them make a bonfire in the middle of the square, and let Voltaire and his seventy volumes fall into it, for they have no use for us, then let Jean-Jacques [Rousseau] together with Volney, Paine, the one who quotes and as many muddled books which have changed your judgment continue burning." Father Castañeda then called for true reform. "Let Buenos Aires reform itself by sacrificing official holidays, turning coffee shops into schools, and cards into notebooks and paper. If we seriously set out to heal ourselves, we will be cured within the next decade."[46]

Conclusion

As the new year of 1820 dawned, the May Revolution in the United Provinces faced a myriad of threats: the Holy Alliance considered armed intervention, twenty thousand Spanish soldiers were mustering in Cádiz to reconquer Buenos

Aires, interprovincial civil war raged, and the factionalism within Buenos Aires left the province hopelessly divided.

Foreign and local observers alike witnessed the problems. Alexander Caldcleugh observed that "the frequent unhappy revolutions of the year 1820" greatly damaged the city. The city's residents had in previous years been greatly attached to the "social happiness" of the theater and other cultural arts. However, the tumult of 1820 eroded cultural life in the city. Caldcleugh noticed a decline in the number of active tertulias, and those that did operate were of poorer quality than in previous months. The political factions also infected elite families such that "a severe blow was struck" against the social fabric of the city.[47] Manuel Beruti, still writing, summed it up well in his diary: "This year has been the most fatal and shameful year we have had in our ten years of Revolution. . . . May God grant that next year be different than this one, and that we are able to become a unified and happy people, for if we continue divided, we will be most unhappy in all things."[48]

The "shameful year" greatly disrupted Juan Manuel de Rosas's pastoral life. He received his first major experience in public action when he was called to defend his province. Juan Manuel came away with a growing reputation as a man of action and order, and with an elevated rank as a militia commander, a position that, even more than being a wealthy rancher, would open doors for him to rise in political power. Politicians and businessmen praised the discipline of Rosas's troops. Poets lauded his actions as well. One compared Rosas to the first president of the United States of America. "Washington was an honorable farmer" who "turned into a warrior" when his country called him. "He left his plough" to save his country and then, with humility, returned to his farm. "Such is the path of great men." Only in America is there "a Washington, and a Rosas."[49] According to this line of thought, George Washington was the Cincinnatus of the United States because he, like the Roman hero, left his plough for a time to save his country. Some now began to call Juan Manuel de Rosas the Cincinnatus of the Río de la Plata.[50] Had he also not left his pastoral pursuits for a short season to help save the country from anarchy and then returned to his plough after the crisis was over? And while some poets hailed their leaders in the Roman tradition, Mariquita and others took advantage of the peace Juan Manuel helped bring about. They sought to create a modern society in the schools and salons of Buenos Aires and beyond.

CHAPTER SEVEN

Mariquita and the "Happy Experience" of the 1820s

On April 12, 1823, Mariquita and ten other women joined the government minister, Bernardino Rivadavia, in the inaugural ceremony of a new organization called the Sociedad de Beneficencia (Society of Beneficence). In his inaugural speech, Rivadavia declared that the founding of the new society showed that the enemies of order lay defeated, and this new organization would produce glorious results for the country. In the new Argentina, women would take on their natural role as civilizing agents, something ignored by other civilizations who, to their detriment, kept women bound in traditional roles. During the previous weeks Mariquita had helped minister Bernardino Rivadavia choose the women who would be founding members of the new society. Mariquita signed her name on the inaugural record of the organization, but she now signed it with a new last name: she was now María S. de Mendeville.

As it was with Juan Manuel de Rosas, 1820 was a pivotal year for Mariquita but for different reasons. She married her second husband in the midst of the anarchy of that year, and together she and her new companion played a key role in the rejuvenation of porteño society, something made possible in part by the peace that Juan Manuel de Rosas helped broker between Buenos Aires and its neighboring provinces. This period, which came to be known as the "Happy Experience," was led by Bernardino Rivadavia.[1] First as secretary to the provincial governor, then as president of the country, Rivadavia exercised enormous political, economic, and cultural influence on porteño society. Juan Manuel also played a part in this era, especially in frontier and Indian policy.

Mariquita's Heart Goes On

When Martín Thompson left on his diplomatic mission to the US in 1816, he left Mariquita in a precarious position. Alone, with five children to look after, her situation became even more troubled with the news that Martín was committed to an insane asylum in New York City. Martín's assistant, Joaquín, kept Mariquita apprised of her husband's condition with periodic letters, which, in Mariquita's words, made her "suffer and cry." Martín remained in the hospital for the next two years. Martín's mission failure and his insanity were surely discomforting to Mariquita as well. She kept busy caring for her children and her properties. In March of 1819, for instance, Mariquita advertised in *La Gazeta* a fully furnished house to rent and another one for sale.[2] But even with all of her domestic and business dealings, it is not clear why she did not insist that the government bring her husband home, or why she did not bring him home herself. Perhaps Martín was too ill, or perhaps she hoped he would recover in the US. Or maybe she felt no hurry to bring back a husband who, by the looks of things, was damaged beyond repair.

Finally, in late 1819, Mariquita arranged to bring Martín home on a merchant ship. To ensure a safe return, Mariquita sent Martín's assistant detailed instructions for the voyage. "I authorize you to buy all that is needed so that Martín is well cared for." Mariquita was especially concerned about food "because merchant ships are not like warships where the food is good and abundant." Mariquita also wanted her husband to look respectable. "Be sure you don't bring him poorly dressed, but dress him well as I did when he was here. In no way do I want him treated like a weak and sickly person, but rather as my husband." Mariquita also wanted Martín protected from any ill treatment. "Be careful, Joaquin, not to let anyone take advantage of him." And if anyone mistreats him, "I will be of a good mind to kill them." And finally, she asked Joaquin to make sure Martín's hair was well groomed.[3] As much as possible, Mariquita wanted a safe and dignified return.

As Mariquita feared, the return voyage was problematic. The ship's captain, according to one passenger, was a rogue who did not provide enough food for the travelers, reducing many of them to severe hunger. Martín was undoubtedly already in poor health after two years in an asylum, and he eventually succumbed to the terrible conditions. He died aboard ship and was buried at sea on October 23, 1819. Mariquita suffered greatly upon hearing the news, claiming later that Martín never ceased to haunt her dreams.[4]

Mariquita's heart, however, was ready to move on. Martín, after all, had been gone nearly four years (he left in January of 1816), the last two of which he spent in an insane asylum. What her social life was like during those years is not clear. There is no evidence that she was unfaithful to Martín, so historians are left to speculate. William Parish Robertson remembered Mariquita as a "widow" when he met her in 1817, even though Martín was still alive in New York.[5] Robertson's recollection of dates could be a bit off, but his assessment might also show that Mariquita may have been seen and treated as a widow in practice, if not a widow in fact.

Whatever the case, suitors began making their moves in earnest once news of Martín's death arrived in the capital.[6] One of them was a young Frenchman named Jean Baptiste Washington de Mendeville, named for two great heroes of the French people—John the Baptist and George Washington. A former soldier in Napoleon's army, Mendeville had arrived in Buenos Aires in 1818 and was making a living in part by teaching music lessons.[7] Just being French was an attractive trait in a city eager to join the ranks of enlightened capitals. To his admired ethnicity, Mendeville added good looks and musical skill. In addition, some of Mariquita's close friends advised her to remarry. Father Cayetano, her old friend, confessor, and confidant, would have been especially convincing on this point, emphasizing that a woman was not meant to be alone, that her children needed a father, and that the whole family needed the protection and guidance of a paternal figure, especially during times like the anarchy of 1820. Her infatuation with the dashing young Frenchman, combined with societal pressures, proved powerful and persuasive.[8]

Mariquita accepted Mendeville's proposal, and the two were married on April 20, 1820, less than six months after Martín's death. The couple thus violated the customary nine months of mourning (known as *luto*) expected of new widows. But Mariquita was never one to follow tradition when it did not suit her. Mariquita's friends might have defended her by emphasizing that she had been separated from Martín since 1816, and that, under the circumstances, the traditional mourning period need not be observed. Mariquita's critics, however, would not forget this violation of cultural norms. Mariquita gave birth to their first child seven months after the wedding, a son named Julio, raising the possibility that the mourning period was broken in more ways than one.[9]

While Mariquita ignored certain conventions, she was very concerned with other aspects of her image. In the marriage record she listed her age at thirty years old instead of her true thirty-four years, most likely to soften the age discrepancy with her new husband who was only twenty-seven. Jean Baptiste inherited Mariquita's five children—four girls and a boy. The four girls accepted him, but Juan, the oldest, had a more difficult time. Soon after the wedding, Mariquita sent Juan to live with Jean Baptiste's sister in France. It was not long before he sent a letter back to his mother, written in French: "Ma chere Maman. Je suis fort content d'etre ici. Je me trouve comme chez moi, Je vous aime toujours bien ainsi que papa et mes soeurs." (My dear Mother. I am happy here. I still love you, and I miss papa and my sisters.)[10] Mariquita almost surely glowed with pride as she read her son's letter in a language from a place she loved and longed to visit. Mariquita and Jean Baptiste would eventually have three sons together—Julio, Carlos, and Enrique.

With Jean Baptiste at her side, Mariquita's salon began to flourish anew as Buenos Aires recovered from the months of anarchy. Jean Baptiste added luster to his wife's salon in a number of ways. By marrying a Frenchman, Mariquita came one step closer to the France she so admired. Mendeville also brought his musical talents to the table. Mariquita was already well-known for her musical abilities. One newspaper noted that "the harp plucked by María Sánchez de Mendeville elicited a sweet and moving sensation that would melt the coldest of hearts."[11] Now she was joined by her new husband, a skilled pianist. To keep up with their prominent image, Mariquita and Jean Baptiste began a series of modifications to their home, updating it with many of the latest fashions. The problem was, Jean Baptiste brought no meaningful financial resources to the marriage. Thus began a pattern of overspending that would soon cause headaches for the couple. Mariquita tried to alleviate her growing financial burdens any way she could, including requesting a pension from the government, on behalf of her children, based on Martín Thompson's military service. Soon, Mariquita would be forced to sell her beloved property in San Isidro, something she would regret for the rest of her life.[12]

Despite their financial struggles, Mariquita and Jean Baptiste were fixtures of porteño culture during the early to mid-1820s. Mariquita's brilliant salon flourished in an era that came to be known as the "Happy Experience," under the governorship of Martín Rodríguez and his exuberant secretary, Bernardino Rivadavia.[13]

Secretary Bernardino Rivadavia and the "Happy Experience"

As mentioned above, Martín Rodríguez emerged as governor of Buenos Aires Province after the anarchy of 1820. Governor Rodríguez wanted to reform porteño society using modern and enlightened practices. As he looked for capable ministers to help carry out his vision, Rodríguez chose Bernardino Rivadavia as his secretary. Rivadavia had returned recently from living a number of years in Europe where he had performed numerous tasks for the porteño government. He arrived from Europe dressed in silver buckles, silk stockings, and a fancy frock coat that partially hid his ample waistline.[14]

After spending so much time abroad, Rivadavia was full of ideas of how to transform the city and province of Buenos Aires. However, Rivadavia was also familiar with Montesquieu's argument that laws and political systems that worked in one country could not simply be replicated in another. They needed to be *adapted*. But knowing which foreign models and ideas to adapt, and how quickly to adapt them, was one of the great challenges for all the new American republics. Although Rivadavia dreamed of creating a modern nation with a powerful central government, for the time being he and Governor Rodriguez were happy to allow each province its autonomy. Instead of trying to unify the whole country, Rivadavia set out to transform the city and province of Buenos Aires. For now, at least, there would be no national constitution.

During his time in Europe, Rivadavia rubbed shoulders with many of the great minds of England and France. As mentioned above, in London Rivadavia became friends with Jeremy Bentham, who influenced him in a number of ways. One of Bentham's associates related the following story. One night Rivadavia was dining in Bentham's home, and as was the custom of many foreigners, Rivadavia spat on the carpet. "Up rose Bentham, ran into his bedroom, brought out a certain utensil, and placed it at his visitor's feet, saying, "There sir, there—spit there."[15] Besides manners, Bentham also inspired Rivadavia's politics. Bentham disapproved of monarchy, and he favored universal male suffrage, a hotly debated topic in Europe during Rivadavia's time there. In addition, Bentham advocated annual elections, a secret ballot, and equal electoral districts.[16] Rivadavia returned from Europe with these and many other ideas.

With Rivadavia's help, Governor Rodríguez's administration aimed at reforming many aspects of porteño society. One of the first things Rivadavia did was ban what he and others felt was a barbaric tradition: bullfighting.[17] More significantly, Rivadavia took out loans from British creditors. British investors salivated over investment opportunities in the Río de la Plata. One analyst in London noted that "the improved state of the Financial and Political resources of South America" now made "public funds" of those countries attractive. The analyst even compared Buenos Aires financial stocks to "the advantageous purchases that were made in the stocks of the United States of America" a few years earlier.[18] Rivadavia planned on using loans to modernize the port, construct waterlines, and develop the frontier. The largest loan, issued by the Baring Brothers firm, was for one million pounds sterling. Unfortunately, scandal followed the loan from the start. The Buenos Aires government soon defaulted, and the loan would be a source of trouble for decades.[19]

In the political realm, on August 14, 1821, Rodríguez's government issued the decree of universal male suffrage in the province of Buenos Aires. This reform was more radical than the politics of most European countries of the time, and it was a testament to Jeremy Bentham's influence on Rivadavia.[20] Secretary Rivadavia also stressed reforms in education and in the use of print media. He implemented a teaching method favored by Bentham, one in which older children called "monitors" would help tutor younger students.[21] Rivadavia also oversaw the founding of a university in Buenos Aires in 1821, and added a law school soon thereafter. Rivadavia also increased publication of newspapers and books, with the hopes of reshaping culture through literature. He commissioned a translation of James Mill's *Elements of Political Economy* in 1822, as the government began to implement Mill's ideas about reducing tariffs, among other economic policies.[22]

Governor Rodriguez and Rivadavia's government also finally achieved a goal six years in the making: international recognition by a major world power. In May of 1822, US chargé de affairs John Murray Forbes wrote Rivadavia that he had received a message from the US president regarding "the immediate recognition of the Independence of those Spanish American Provinces." Forbes was a special dinner guest a few nights later on May 25, where Rivadavia toasted the United States as a great moral influence on the world stage.

Ecclesiastical Reforms

Other reforms implemented by Rivadavia aimed to reduce the power and role of the Catholic Church in porteño society. For Rodríguez and Rivadavia, the

Catholic Church had its place, but that place was to preside over spiritual matters. The national state, Rivadavia believed, had the right and duty to preside over nonspiritual matters. Thus, as part of a broader program of ecclesiastical reforms, Rodríguez's government, with Rivadavia as a guiding force, sought to transfer duties from religious organizations to secular ones. One of Rivadavia's strategies to curb Church power was to restrict the number of religious groups that could operate in Buenos Aires Province. He also abolished the ecclesiastical tithe all residents had to pay, which had helped support various Church activities. As part of these reforms, some religious orders were removed from the city, including the Followers of the Virgin of Mercy, the organization Mariquita's mother had belonged to. Rivadavia also confiscated some Church property, including a monastery run by an order of monks known as the Recoletos. The monastery's garden became the first public cemetery in the city. No longer did the Catholic Church have a monopoly on death and burial.

Many of the clergy were understandably enraged. For Father Paula de Castañeda (who had earlier called for the burning of books by Voltaire and others), Rivadavia's reforms only proved that he wanted to follow "the French, or the English, or the devil's way."[23] Rivadavia published, in the newspapers of the time, many of the debates about the ecclesiastical reforms, demonstrating his openness to a free press, but also hoping to win over the reading public to his views. The Rivadavian reforms were popular among porteño liberals, but Father Castañeda represented a large portion of the population that was more conservative. For them, Rivadavia was too radical—too innovative.

Advances for Women: Education and La Sociedad de Beneficencia

Rivadavia's most important reforms included measures to advance the role of women in porteño society. For example, he channeled government funds into more schools for girls, for he believed that depriving women of education was "entirely opposed to their future and destiny."[24]

Rivadavia had other plans for women as well, and he turned to Mariquita Sánchez de Mendeville for help. During his time in Europe, Rivadavia became friends with some of the most celebrated female minds of the era, including one of Mariquita's idols—Madame de Stael, the salon hostess who clashed famously with Napoleon. Rivadavia was convinced that a society could not progress as long as its women were shackled by traditional practices. He was not alone in his sentiments. For years newspapers in Buenos Aires had advocated more female education and an increased role for women in society.[25] Now Rivadavia would use state power to put many of these ideas into practice.

In January of 1823, with Rivadavia's support, Governor Rodríguez issued a decree ordering the establishment of a charitable society run by women and subsidized by the state. Women had long been part of charitable organizations and even directed them, but those organizations were largely associated with the Catholic Church. In explaining the significance of the new organization, Governor Rodríguez emphasized that in the past the role of women had been too vague, which in turn created "obstacles to the progress of civilization." In some ways, he continued, those obstacles were worse than wars and factionalism because women's problems were less visible and thus harder to overcome. "It is, therefore, eminently useful and just to accord serious attention to the education of women, to the improvement of her customs," which would in turn help to "create laws that establish her rights and duties and assure the happiness women deserve."[26]

Over the next few weeks, Rivadavia and a government-appointed commission considered the names of several women to be founding members of the new institution—La Sociedad de Beneficencia (The Society of Beneficence). It was not a simple task. Some of the most prominent women of Buenos Aires were from conservative Catholic families, precisely the group most alienated by Rivadavia's reforms that challenged the traditional roles of the Church. Thus, many elite women were unwilling to head an organization founded by a government tainted by such anticlerical measures. Rivadavia turned to his friend Mariquita Sánchez de Mendeville to help solve this problem. Mariquita was sympathetic to religion, but she was not a conservative Catholic. By the middle of February, Mariquita and Rivadavia finalized a list of thirteen women who would be the founding members of the new society that would be a fixture of porteño society for more than 130 years.[27]

On April 12, Mariquita, and ten other women (two were unable to attend) joined Rivadavia at the Society of Beneficence's inauguration. In his keynote speech, Rivadavia outlined the society's three main objectives: to perfect the morals of society, to cultivate the spirit of the female sex, and to focus female efforts on industry. The Society of Beneficence would be in charge of the School for Girls, the Foundling Home for abandoned children, the Women's

Hospital, and the Orphans' School. In times past, most of these activities were performed by religious organizations. Now the state was taking charge.

Continuing his speech, Rivadavia explained that the society would allow women to exercise their natural talents in a way that benefited men and all of society. Nature had granted both sexes certain gifts in equal measure, Rivadavia reasoned, but some traits were more common in one sex or the other, and it was thus the duty of each sex to exercise its special gifts on behalf of larger society. In Rivadavia's estimation, women possessed greater measures of sensibility and tenderness, and it was precisely these traits that women needed to promote in a society so corrupted by violence and by men's pursuit of vain ambition. Women, he asserted, were ideal agents to regenerate order and morality. For too long the world had unjustly made woman inferior to man, when in reality nature had granted her many superior gifts. All great achievements in human history, Rivadavia concluded, came from societies where intelligent women actively influenced their societies.[28]

MARIQUITA AND THE SOCIEDAD IN ACTION

Mariquita was exactly the kind of woman Rivadavia was talking about. A sampling of records from the Society of Beneficence shows that Mariquita was an active, passionate, and feisty member of the organization. During one meeting in 1824, the women of the society debated what kind of prizes to purchase for students receiving awards for sewing excellence at a girls' school in Monserrat, a community to the east of the main plaza with a large Afro-Argentine population. Mariquita and an associate favored a set of clothes as the prize, but other members proposed a sewing box instead. To avoid a protracted argument, the matter was put to a vote, and the sewing box was victorious. Mariquita then suggested that they should be able to find the boxes for less than eight pesos, and with the leftover budget they could order some necklaces with pendants for the girls. Mariquita assured her fellow members that if they looked hard enough they could find suppliers who sold "pretty boxes at low prices."[29] During a Sociedad meeting a few weeks later, a few girls from the Monserrat school received their awards for excellence in embroidery and sewing. Mariquita also presented the girls with the medallions she had proposed in the previous meeting.[30] Prizes for sewing and embroidery signaled the main purpose of many of the schools run by the society: to educate the girls for life in the home or for low-paying jobs.[31]

The Sociedad also arranged for the purchase of books for the schools. While some books were published locally, the Sociedad also contracted with foreign suppliers like the London-based company of Rudolph Ackermann, who produced hundreds of titles in Spanish for the Spanish American market. In 1824, for example, Rivadavia arranged for the Sociedad de Beneficencia to receive a shipment of nine hundred copies of Ackerman's geography and chemistry books. In 1826, Ackermann planned to send a shipment of books on female education. However, the Sociedad wanted to save money. Shopping for good deals was one of Mariquita Sánchez de Mendeville's strong suits. She was appointed secretary of the Sociedad in January of that year, and she and the Sociedad had already asked a local printer in Buenos Aires to reprint Ackermann's book. This saved the Sociedad some money, but showed little concern for the copyright of the London publisher.[32]

While Mariquita tried to save costs by finding cheaper books, she was adamant about maintaining high-quality instruction. In October of 1826, Mariquita and her fellow members discussed the needs of a school they were creating. The society had secured a building, but it needed remodeling. Later in the meeting, Mariquita suggested that a student from the Normal School could be used to help younger students in the new school (an approach likely inspired by the Lancaster Method favored by Jeremy Bentham and Bernardino Rivadavia). There were a number of girls from the Normal School who, Mariquita argued, were advanced in writing, singing, and embroidery and could do the job. Mariquita also reminded her fellow members that regulations called for two teachers per class. Some complained that asking the government for two salaries was too much. Mariquita quipped back that they were missing the bigger picture: "All the money will be wasted if the girls are not taught correctly."[33]

At times, Mariquita's passion for her job led her to severity. On one occasion, a teacher requested some additional supplies for her classroom. Mariquita berated the woman, accusing her of ingratitude. Such a request angered Mariquita because she had given so much of her own time, and even some of her own money, to help the school. The teacher filed a complaint with the society, citing Mariquita's harsh treatment. Mariquita defended herself by producing receipts for hundreds of pesos she had spent of her own money to help the school. Mariquita demanded that the discussion end. When it did not, she left the meeting.[34]

Questions of race also came up in the society meetings, including one instance not long after Mariquita was elected president of the Sociedad in 1830. Juana Martínez, a student at one of the society's schools, had fallen in love with a pardo—a man of part African descent. As overseers of the school where Juana studied, Sociedad members felt authorized to intervene and prohibit the relationship, "for her own happiness." Mariquita led the discussion of the issue. She asked the advice of her fellow Sociedad members, and they all concluded that their students were under their protection and thus it was "necessary to seek the best for their happiness." After some discussion, the Sociedad decided "to see if with prudence they could change her mind, and if they were unable to dissuade her, other necessary measures would be taken."[35] Surely Mariquita remembered her own romantic history, battling her mother to marry Martín, as she considered the case of Juana and her pardo boyfriend. But in her mind, the opposition of her parents in 1801 lacked all merit. For Mariquita and many other porteños, racial inequality was still legitimate grounds to oppose a marriage, at least in this case.[36]

Mariquita was an assertive leader, as seen in how she ran meetings while she was president. She also possessed a sharp wit and grating humor, as seen in an 1831 note to Juan Lasala, the director of the National Archive (the archive was another of Rivadavia's creations). "Dear Mr. Indolent: set aside that natural apathy of yours and look in that archive for some bylaws of the Sociedad de Beneficencia. Tell me if there are any there, and in case you cannot do me the favor of bringing them to me, I will come by and ask for them formally. Your ever-affectionate friend, María S. de Mendeville."[37] Mariquita was capable of edgy humor and wit, which she could easily turn to more powerful ends.

Unitarians versus Federalists in the National Congress of 1824

The Sociedad de Beneficencia was just one of dozens of organizations and decrees that emanated from Bernardino Rivadavia's energetic mind and pen. Even General San Martín, who had clashed earlier with Rivadavia over political disagreements, now supported the young minister. In a letter to a friend, San Martín wrote that "only a fool would not be satisfied with [Rivadavia's] administration—the best that has ever been seen in America."[38] From England, Jeremy Bentham wrote Rivadavia a congratulatory letter in April of 1824. "Time after time accounts of your *res gestae* found their way into our newspapers: each time they exhibit the picture not merely of the greatest statesman late Spanish

America has produced, but alas! The only one." Bentham took pride in calling Rivadavia one of his disciples.[39]

Despite all the successes and accolades, Rivadavia saw one glaring hole in his accomplishments: the provinces of La Plata were not a unified nation. Whereas in 1821 Rivadavia and Governor Rodríguez were content with the autonomy of the individual provinces, by 1824 they aspired to a national unity bound together by a constitution. The few years of their enlightened government, they hoped, had transformed society enough, at least in Buenos Aires, to enable porteños to lead the rest of the provinces toward a unifying constitution and to nationhood.[40] In December of 1824, the Rodríguez government invited delegates from across the country to participate in a Constitutional Congress.

As the new congress debated what form the constitution might take, Centralist and Federalist positions became more prominent. Centralists (becoming known more and more as Unitarians) had a number of key goals. They wanted a strong central government that could shape development across the nation, which included reforms that separated church and state. Unitarians also wanted to unify and nationalize customs duties in the country. Customs duties collected in Buenos Aires, they argued, should go to the national government and not to the Buenos Aires Province alone. Growing the economy was another major Unitarian objective, and this meant liberalizing trade relations and pushing for more religious freedom to attract non-Catholic immigrants. Unitarians also wanted to turn the city of Buenos Aires into the federalized capital of the country, thus separating it from the province of Buenos Aires.[41]

Federalists were not opposed to a constitution, but they wanted one that would guarantee a healthy dose of provincial autonomy instead of greater oversight from a central government. Federalists in Buenos Aires Province were especially angered at the prospect of losing their capital city—the crown jewel of their province—to the federal government. No government, many of them argued, was going to "decapitate" their province. The idea of separating the province from its port city pushed ranchers like Juan Manuel de Rosas toward Federalism because losing the port would greatly damage their interests in the countryside.[42] Many Federalists also wanted to keep the Catholic Church's privileged status. Federalists were numerous all over the country, and Buenos Aires's neighboring provinces of Santa Fe and Entre Ríos were especially powerful bastions of Federalism. Federalists lived in the city of Buenos Aires as well, although their main strength was in the countryside, in the greater hinterlands surrounding the port city. As will be seen below, Unitarians and Federalists would bicker even more when Bernardino Rivadavia was elected as the first president of the United Provinces in 1826.

A treaty with Great Britain. Besides discussing constitutional questions in February of 1825, national delegates approved a Treaty of Peace and Navigation with Great Britain, giving it and its citizens special status and trading rights in the Río de la Plata. British citizens would now be exempt from numerous laws that other foreign nationals were subject to. For example, English residents would no longer be forced into local militias during a military crisis, as laws from the era of the independence wars allowed. French and other foreign residents, on the other hand, were still subject to those laws. The treaty also signaled Great Britain's recognition of the United Provinces' independence.[43] The recognition by the US three years earlier was a milestone, to be sure, but Great Britain was a great power and the dominant *seafaring* power in the world, which meant it could provide additional protection to the United Provinces. Great Britain's recognition, combined with the US's Monroe Doctrine of 1823, made the likelihood of a Spanish reconquest in the Río de la Plata a remote possibility at best.

These developments directly impacted the life of Mariquita and her family because, in 1828, her husband Jean Baptiste was appointed as the first consul of France to Buenos Aires. Even though France did not officially recognize the independence of the United Provinces, the French government thought it wise to have a consul there, especially since the British were gaining a stronger foothold in the region. Jean Baptiste had in fact lobbied for the job, arguing that his wife's powerful connections in the city would make him especially useful. Mariquita was already attracted to France through her personal taste. Now her husband's new position brought a more direct connection to French politics and culture. From then on, Mariquita would be drawn into the complicated and troubled world of Franco-Argentine relations, which, as will be seen below, would haunt her for decades.

Borderland Issues: The Eastern Shore and the Southern Indian Frontier

The national congress, by now in session for over a year, also moved to consolidate and expand Buenos Aires's frontiers. This included the territory known as the Eastern Shore (Banda Oriental), the land on the other side of the Río de la Plata and the Uruguay River. The problem was that Portuguese forces had occupied the region since 1816, and in 1821 the Portuguese congress made it an official part of the Portuguese Empire. When Brazil declared independence from Portugal in 1822, it maintained its claims to the Eastern Shore. Buenos Aires however, rejected Brazil's claims and supported an anti-Brazil insurgency begun by General Juan Antonio Lavalleja in 1825. Not long thereafter, the Buenos Aires congress voted to incorporate the Eastern Shore as an official territory of the United Provinces. Brazil was incensed, and by December of 1825, the two countries were at war. Argentine forces soon invaded the Eastern Shore and within a few months scored a number of impressive victories.[44]

While the government of Buenos Aires waged a war with Brazil in the Eastern Shore, Indians and settlers clashed on the southern frontier. Even before the war with Brazil, the government of Buenos Aires had asked Juan Manuel de Rosas to go on a diplomatic mission to the Indians to negotiate with them and to delineate a new frontier line. This request was an official acknowledgment of a simple fact: Juan Manuel was perhaps the most knowledgeable and capable individual to help sort out and shape frontier and Indian policy. Juan Manuel accepted the mission, and the government authorized him to promise friendly tribes subsidies of horses, cattle, and other commodities, along with military aid against enemy tribes. In return, the government wanted Rosas to secure the release of prisoners kidnapped in raids, and to establish the frontier line extending from the settlement of Tandil (250 miles south of Buenos Aires) eastward to the Atlantic coast, 150 miles away. This was a bold request, especially since the Natives resisted the settlement of Tandil in the first place.[45]

Juan Manuel traveled to Tandil to meet personally with the chiefs from the surrounding area. Chief Chanil and Chief Lincon, leaders of the Pampa and Ranquel tribes, arrived with full military escorts, their warriors on horseback lined up in formation. Juan Manuel arrived at the meeting without a military escort, counting on his honor and reputation to protect him. As Rosas later reported, once the meeting began he allowed the chiefs to vent their feelings in what turned out to be a long and bitter debate. Rosas responded to the chiefs' concerns in an imposing but persuasive tone, hoping to gain the chiefs' approval and trust. Juan Manuel was quick to emphasize his long-standing good relations with various Native groups. In the end, the negotiations took a positive turn and the group agreed on new frontier lines.[46]

In his report to the government, Rosas emphasized the fragile nature of the peace with the Indians: if the government really wanted peace on the frontier, he insisted, it was imperative to appoint a frontier commission with the money and resources to fulfill the promises made to the tribes. Rosas's report made it back to the government in Buenos Aires, a government now presided over by Bernardino Rivadavia, recently elected as the first president of the country (see below). And while President Rivadavia was interested in the frontier, he was more occupied by ambitious political, cultural, and economic goals, as well as intense political battles. Rosas's advice went unheeded, and the agreement with the Indians unattended.[47]

Some of the chiefs felt betrayed by the government's inaction. In response, Ranquel warriors attacked along the southern frontier, laying waste to numerous estancias, killing many settlers, and stealing thousands of head of cattle. Three estancias administered by Juan Manuel himself were pillaged. When the government asked Juan Manuel to sit on yet another frontier commission a few months later, he refused. The government's neglect of his previous advice, he pointed out, was a sign that he clearly had no credibility to serve in such a capacity.[48]

The Constitution of 1826 and the Fall of Rivadavia

Even with war on two frontiers, the national convention continued working to create a unified national government. By early 1826, delegates from across the country elected a president, chosen by a majority at the convention. On February 7, thirty-three of thirty-seven delegates voted in favor of Bernardino Rivadavia. The next day Rivadavia took the oath of office as "President of the United Provinces of the Río de la Plata." Part of the oath was to uphold the constitution, protect the Catholic Church, and defend and preserve the national territory.[49] President Rivadavia immediately went to work by, among other things, creating a national bank and establishing a system to rent public lands to ranchers, and reducing the power of the Catholic Church. He also moved forward with plans to separate the city of Buenos Aires from the Buenos Aires Province, and make it the capital of the nation.[50] The constitution, however, was still in the making. In late December of 1826, the "Constitution of the Argentine Republic" was presented to congress for debate. It outlined a republican form of government with executive, legislative, and judicial branches. Notably, the document did not declare universal male suffrage as Rivadavia did earlier in the 1820s. Voting rights were restricted to wealthy and educated males over twenty years old. The new constitution also proclaimed that the central government had the authority to elect provincial governors.[51] The Constitution of 1826 was, like its 1819 counterpart, a Unitarian document in that it upheld the Centralist position to a greater degree than the Federalist stance. The national government claimed the right to intervene in provincial affairs, something Rivadavia had already proved willing to do. For example, not long after taking office, Rivadavia informed the governor of Corrientes that he, Rivadavia, had the right to delegate authority over the troops in that province, as well as oversee the defense of provincial territory.[52] Rivadavia was acting according to his vision of what a modern commander in chief would do. But to Governor Ferré of Corrientes Province and to many other Federalists, Rivadavia's attitude, and the constitution as a whole, were clear evidence of Buenos Aires's oppressive reach. Still others disapproved of Rivadavia's attack on the Church.

Although congressional delegates from around the country approved it, the constitution received harsh treatment in the provinces themselves. When the congress sent a representative to Córdoba to share the new constitution, he was kicked out of the province because it violated the principle of Federalism that the majority of the people in Córdoba supported. The constitution was rejected in other provinces as well. Facundo Quiroga, in the province of La Rioja, raised the banner of rebellion with the cry "Religion or Death!" The priest, Father Castro Barros, wrote to Facundo that "Rivadavia is endeavoring to ruin the ecclesiastical state along with our holy religion, and I am willing to die in this defense."[53]

Besides fierce internal opposition, Rivadavia's administration also faced continued pressure from foreign powers. In addition to the war with Brazil on the Eastern Shore, the new state of Bolivia, created in 1826 with the help of Simón Bolívar, was making aggressive moves on the United Provinces' northwestern border. Faced with the war with Brazil, ongoing conflicts with indigenous groups on the southern frontier, political unrest at home, and a brewing conflict with Bolivia, Rivadavia decided to resign. Declaring that he was a man of "reason" and not a man of "force," Rivadavia presented his resignation in June of 1827. The congress accepted the resignation with near unanimity, and in his stead chose as interim president Vicente López y Planes, the author of the national anthem and a close friend to Mariquita. The congress then dissolved.

President López called elections for the provincial legislature in Buenos Aires, and members of the Federalist Party won a majority of seats. The legislature then voted Manuel Dorrego as governor of Buenos Aires Province.

The Happy Experience was over. Rivadavia's time as secretary and as president had brought great things—new laws, new institutions, and new settlements. However, he resigned leaving a country bitterly divided at home and fighting a war with Brazil abroad. Rivadavia saw himself as an enlightened and progressive leader who could transform society through new constitutions and executive decrees, all while educating the people through the printing press. Only a few short years after the unity of the country dissolved in 1820, Rivadavia believed the provinces were ready for a strong Centralist constitution that would cap off Argentina's transformation from a colony to a modern nation. In the words of Rosas's nephew, Lucio Mansilla, Rivadavia forgot what he once knew: the truth of Montesquieu's maxim, echoed by Jean-Jacques Rousseau and Simón Bolívar, that laws should be *adapted* to the particular circumstances of a country.[54]

Conclusion

The early 1820s were pivotal years for Mariquita Sánchez and Juan Manuel de Rosas. She was an intimate member of the May Revolutionary crowd who, together with her husband, Martín, helped shape the early days of the republic. Mariquita suffered the humiliation of her husband Martín's failures as a diplomat, and of his descent into insanity. Her marriage to Jean Baptiste de Mendeville began a new chapter in her life, and together they played an integral part of Rivadavia's short-lived Happy Experience, which ushered in a few months of brilliant flashes and high hopes. Juan Manuel also played a role in the Rivadavian era, as he sought to pacify and expand the southern frontier with the Indians. But the hope of the Rivadavian era was short-lived. Divisions between Unitarians and Federalists deepened over power sharing, church-state relations, and the war with Brazil on the Eastern Shore—divisions capped off by the spectacular failure of the 1826 constitution. With the fall of Rivadavia, national politics again descended into chaos, which opened the door for Juan Manuel de Rosas to make a grand entrance into the political world.

CHAPTER EIGHT

The Tumultuous Year of 1829

The mob gathering in the plaza had only one thing on its mind: hurt or destroy anything French within its reach. Earlier that day, May 21, 1829, French naval forces had attacked a number of Argentine vessels at anchor in the Buenos Aires port, capturing one and burning three others. The attack only served to heighten tensions in the city, which was already under siege by Federalist armies. Enraged by the French attack, the mob made its way toward the closest thing French they could think of: the house of the French consul, Jean Baptiste Washington de Mendeville, only a few blocks away. Many of the growing mob believed that Consul Mendeville bore at least part of the responsibility for the French attack. In any case, the house was a symbolic target. Within minutes, the mob arrived at the Mendeville residence and was about to push their way past the servants and into the home. Suddenly, Madame Mariquita Sánchez de Mendeville appeared and stopped them in their tracks.[1]

The decade of the 1820s ended in many respects the same way it began, with Buenos Aires torn again by civil conflict. On top of that, a major foreign power—France—now inserted itself into the picture. The current crisis increased the frustration and disillusion of many residents in Buenos Aires and elsewhere in the United Provinces. Nearly twenty years after the May Revolution of 1810, all they had to show was a legacy of failed governments, failed constitutions, and civil war. Some porteños pondered new alternatives to solve the chronic strife, including looking to men of order such as Juan Manuel de Rosas. And thus the old friends—Mariquita, with her French connections, and Juan Manuel, with his talent for leadership and his powerful militia—were right in the thick of things again.

The Odyssey of Governor Manuel Dorrego:
To the US and Back Again

Mariquita's encounter with the mob had a direct link to the tragic story of the ex-governor of Buenos Aires, Manuel Dorrego. Years earlier, Dorrego had fought with distinction in the independence wars in Chile and Upper Peru. The young soldier, however, had a rebellious streak. He ran afoul of Supreme Director Pueyrredón in 1817, who sent him to exile. Dorrego ended up in Baltimore, Maryland, which he found to be very supportive of Spanish American independence.[2] Dorrego admired the balance he saw in the US between the federal and state governments, and believed a similar balance could exist in the Río de la Plata. When he returned to Buenos Aires in 1820, he became interim governor, then a member of the provincial legislature, where he frequently argued in favor of the American political system—a balanced federal republic in the style of Thomas Jefferson.[3] After the fall of Rivadavia's government in 1826, Dorrego was elected governor by the Buenos Aires legislature.

Governor Dorrego calls on Juan Manuel. Governor Dorrego immediately faced stiff challenges because of frontier insecurity, disunity in the provinces, and the continuing war with Brazil on the Eastern Shore. To grapple with the frontier issue, Dorrego asked Juan Manuel to serve as a frontier militia commander. He accepted the position but insisted that the government provide the resources he needed to negotiate with the Indians, who he believed could be used to develop the Pampas region. It is a good idea, Juan Manuel argued, to "civilize the savage tribes which have done us so much harm, but who could do so much good." Juan Manuel employed a two-prong policy with the Indians. As he had done before, Rosas befriended willing tribes and fought those who resisted negotiations. Rosas played a central role in porteño-Indian relations, at times even inviting Native chiefs to stay in his home. The pressure of handling the delicate cultural questions of Indian relations taxed Juan Manuel's energies. The detail and effort needed to negotiate with and host chiefs required navigation of thorny cultural differences and protocols that could be exhausting. "I could never stop worrying about the Indians," Rosas wrote once to a friend. All his anxiety and effort paid off, however. Rosas's personal diplomacy, combined with the strength of his militias, allowed him to secure and even extend the frontier lines he negotiated in 1828.[4]

The war on the Eastern Shore. Another pressing matter for Governor Dorrego was the ongoing war with Brazil on the Eastern Shore. Although Argentine forces scored some great victories, neither side was able to deliver a finishing blow. The conflict wore on, disrupting commerce and lives on all sides in the process. The British, whose trade in the Río de la Plata suffered greatly because of the war, proposed to end the conflict by creating a new country in the disputed territory of the Eastern Shore. More than three hundred years of chronic conflict, they argued, demanded such a solution. In August of 1828, Brazil and Argentina signed the Treaty of Montevideo, thus ending the war. When Governor Dorrego ratified the treaty a few weeks later, the Eastern Republic of Uruguay was born.[5] Unitarians fumed over what they saw as a treasonous pact. Many in the Argentine military also felt betrayed by Governor Dorrego and returned home dissatisfied and frustrated. One of them was Juan Lavalle, a general in the army and a staunch Unitarian.

Juan Lavalle was from a prominent porteño family with close ties to the Rozas family. According to Juan Manuel's nephew, Lucio Mansilla, the Rozases and Lavalles were all handsome people with "beautiful faces." Pure blonds also tended to run in the families. As mentioned previously, the families were so close that, as an infant, Juan Lavalle was at times suckled by Juan Manuel's own mother, Agustina, while Juan Manuel received the same from Mrs. Lavalle.[6] Juan Lavalle fought with distinction in the wars of independence alongside both San Martín and Bolívar in Chile, Peru, Colombia, and most recently in the war with Brazil. Lavalle was very upset with Dorrego's government for signing the treaty to end the war. "The patience of the people is waning," Lavalle wrote to his father-in-law, referring to Dorrego's government. The peace with Brazil, he continued, was "ignominious" because it surrendered the Eastern Shore, which rightfully belonged to the Argentine Confederation.[7]

Unitarian leaders in Buenos Aires had also lost their patience with Dorrego. The peace with Brazil was for them only the latest in a long list of debacles that afflicted the province and country. Unitarian leaders decided that more extreme measures were needed to regain control of Buenos Aires and the country. The only way to save the republic, they concluded, was for Dorrego to die. They chose General Juan Lavalle as their executioner. Lavalle agreed to the plan, and on December 1, 1828, he led his troops toward the main plaza to overthrow the governor.[8]

As the troops approached the fort, Dorrego fled through a back door and hid near the river until nightfall. Dorrego sent urgent pleas for help, and within a few days Federalist commanders rendezvoused outside the city, including Juan Manuel de Rosas and his regiment. However, Rosas and Dorrego disagreed on how to confront General Lavalle and the other Unitarian rebels. Rosas proposed a strategic retreat while Dorrego insisted on fighting.[9] On December 9, Lavelle's forces defeated Federalist troops and captured Governor Dorrego. He asked to be exiled again to the United States of America. Many of Dorrego's friends intervened on his behalf. William Brown, the Irishborn admiral of the Argentine navy (appointed interim governor), strongly urged Lavalle to allow Dorrego to leave the country. Foreign diplomats also petitioned on Dorrego's behalf. Foreign representatives, including Woodbine Parish (England) and Jean Baptiste de Mendeville (France), all called for clemency, which, they argued, would reflect much better on the nation than having Dorrego shot. Murray Forbes of the US even offered to provide a vessel to take Dorrego to exile in the US.[10]

The Unitarian leadership, however, held firm to their original plan to kill Dorrego. They bombarded Lavalle with letters, pushing him to follow through. Unitarian quills were especially busy on the night of December 12, 1828. "The fate of the country" was at stake, Juan Cruz Varela wrote Lavalle. "The people expect everything from you, and you should give them everything."[11] Salvador del Carril was especially insistent. "General, if you take action, in cold blood, the Revolution will be decided. If you do not act, you will have lost the opportunity to cut the first head of the hydra, and you will not be able to cut the rest."[12] A short while later, del Carril fired off another missive in which he blamed Dorrego's party for the last eighteen years of anarchy. "All of us are depending on you to complete your work." Del Carril concluded by placing Lavalle at the center of this historic moment. "I am convinced that if this result does not come from the omnipotence of the sword, not even the omnipotence of God Himself will deign to do it."[13]

Lavalle agonized over the situation, caught as he was between competing demands for mercy and decisive action. Finally, Lavalle made his decision and sent Dorrego a message: "Within the hour you will face the firing squad." Dorrego was thunderstruck. "Oh my God!" he exclaimed to the messenger. "My friend, give me some ink and paper and call Father Castañer, whom I wish to consult in my last moments." Dorrego took the quill and managed to write a few notes to friends and relatives. Dorrego also wrote a tender but brief note to his wife, Angelita.

My dear Angelita.

At this very moment they tell me that I will die within the hour. I know not the reasons, but Divine Providence, which I trust at this critical moment, wants it thus. I forgive all my enemies, and I plead with my friends to refrain from taking any measures to retaliate for what has happened to me.

My darling. Teach those lovely creatures. Be happy, since you have not found it in the company of this unfortunate soul. Manuel Dorrego.

On another scrap of paper he bid farewell to his two young daughters. "Be good and virtuous Catholics, for that is the religion that consoles me at this moment."[14]

Governor Dorrego faced a firing squad on December 13, 1828. As news of the execution spread, some porteños reacted with satisfaction. "This act has opened a new era in the country," del Carril wrote approvingly to Lavalle on December 15. The Unitarian revolution now needed to be spread to the rest of the country and, del Carril declared, the name of Juan Lavalle would forever be known as the "first hero of the republic."[15]

The Federalists React and a Homecoming Is Destroyed

But instead of a hero, Lavalle was now seen by many as an archvillain. The popular classes were particular enraged. As Manuel Beruti recorded in his diary, "The majority of the people received this fateful news with disgust and sadness." After all, Beruti continued, Dorrego was a hero of the independence wars, as numerous scars on his person demonstrated. Furthermore, he was popular with the people.[16]

Juan Manuel de Rosas also understood the importance of public opinion in this whole matter. While Dorrego was awaiting his fate at the hands of his executioners, Rosas hurried to Santa Fe Province to consult other Federalist leaders. Rosas believed that by overthrowing Dorrego the Unitarians had unwittingly strengthened the Federalists' hand. "This time the federal system has been absolutely solidified," Rosas wrote to Estanislao López after Dorrego was captured. Rosas sensed that popular opinion was now firmly with the Federalists, which he knew played to his advantage. "All of the lower classes of the city and countryside" were against the Unitarian rebels and "willing to enthusiastically punish the coup and uphold the law." Rosas also advised López to make good use of the press. Newspapers should "cover nothing else" but the coup, Rosas urged, adding that they should be distributed generously throughout the countryside.[17] When Rosas heard of Dorrego's execution, it only solidified his views on the matter.

When Rosas arrived in Santa Fe, he joined a Federalist conference already in session. On February 20, Federalist leaders declared Lavalle's coup of December 1 (known thereafter as the "Decembrist movement") to be an act of treason—for overthrowing legitimate authority and for illegally executing Governor Dorrego. The Federalist convention also claimed the authority to act on behalf of the nation. Estanislao López was named head of Federalist forces, with Rosas second in command.[18] López, as he did nine years earlier, prepared to invade Buenos Aires, this time in league with Juan Manuel de Rosas.

Dorrego's execution along with the threat of another invasion from Santa Fe threw Buenos Aires and its surroundings into an uproar. Weddings were canceled, trips into exile were hastily planned, and at least one significant homecoming was ruined.[19] On February 6, 1829, the British ship *Chichester* anchored off the coast of Buenos Aires. On board was none other than General José de San Martín, who was returning to his homeland "with the firm intention to live out [his] days as a private citizen." But instead of finding peace, he found civil war, and a disappointed San Martín wanted no part of it. "My saber will never be unsheathed in civil wars," he declared. On February 12, the *Chichester* raised anchor and sailed across the Río de la Plata, where San Martín had decided to pursue his objective in Montevideo.[20]

General Lavalle immediately sent emissaries to visit San Martín, with instructions to offer him the governorship of Buenos Aires Province. San Martín refused, despite hours of pleading by Lavalle's men. The Liberator restated the opinion he had held for years, a view bolstered even more by current events. "The country will not find peace, liberty, or prosperity unless it is ruled by a monarchy." Tomás Guido also begged San Martín to stay, but again he refused. In his response to requests for him to intervene, San Martín wrote that the people "seek a savior," and he knew he himself was the main candidate. Whoever ruled the country, San Martín perceived, would be forced to use violence to establish order, and that was something he could not bring himself to do. Like other educated men of his era, San Martín drew parallels between his dilemma and those of figures from ancient Roman history. "Would it be possible for me to be the one chosen to be the scourge of my fellow citizens and, like another Sulla, impose mass punishments on my country? No, never, never. I would a thousand times rather perish in the troubles that threaten it than become the instrument of such horrors."[21] The political passions and factionalism had grown so intense, according to San Martín, that it was "absolutely impossible" to unify the country "unless one or the other [parties] was destroyed."[22]

Federalist Wrath

As San Martín sailed away, so did the hopes of an easy solution for Lavalle. Instead, Lavalle faced the combined wrath of Estanislao López and Juan Manuel de Rosas, who together with their gaucho and Indian allies converged outside of Buenos Aires in April of 1829. As he advanced toward the port city, Rosas circulated a message to the surrounding areas: "For the second time, we will use our strength to reestablish authority and law in the province."[23] Rosas assured all in his path that order would soon return. "The bloody and barbarous tyranny of Lavalle is over, sir," Rosas wrote to a skeptical army commander in the town of San Nicolás, "because it is impossible that such a small force can resist the power of this army," nor can Lavalle stop "the torrent of public opinion in Buenos Aires, which is overflowing."[24] Rosas's reputation, already elevated by his previous exploits, now increased even more as much of the citizenry looked to him to avenge Dorrego's death. When Rosas finally rendezvoused with his troops outside the city, he was welcomed by deafening cries of "Viva Rosas!"—cries that signaled the growth of a collective identity among many Federalists in the province and beyond.[25]

On April 26, Federalist forces defeated Lavalle at the Battle of Márquez Bridge just outside the city. When Lavalle retreated into the city of Buenos Aires, Rosas's and López's armies promptly laid siege to it. Inside the city, Unitarians sought desperately to hold on to power. They jailed or exiled prominent Federalists like the Anchorenas and Terreros. They even considered exiling Rosas's aging father, León Ortiz de Rozas, but his Unitarian friends intervened on his behalf. In the Plaza de la Victoria, Unitarians also executed a number of Federalist prisoners captured in earlier battles. One of Juan Manuel's cousins wrote him, saying that the Unitarians had bathed the city in blood, and then exclaimed: "May God put an end to such horrors."[26]

With the city under siege, Unitarian defense forces competed with the needs of a hungry population for food and animals. Short on horses, the government was forced to requisition them from the civilian population. One day, police showed up at the home of Juan Manuel's mother, Agustina López de Osornio, and demanded she donate some horses to the city's defenses. She refused, arguing that, although she had "no opinions" and "did not meddle in politics," she could not facilitate the request because "the beasts were to be used to fight her son." The police insisted again, and were once again rejected. After the third request, Agustina told the officers that if they wanted the horses they would have to break down the stable doors. The policemen obliged. To their dismay, they found the horses and mules with their throats cut.[27] Those that knew Agustina would not have been surprised.

While Federalist forces besieged Buenos Aires, Federalists in other parts of the country also targeted Unitarians. In the western province of San Juan, for example, a precocious nineteen-year-old named Domingo Faustino Sarmiento got caught up in the action. Sarmiento was a self-taught genius with grand ideas about the world and grand ideas about himself, but in 1829 he was in trouble. He was arrested for suspected Unitarian sympathies. Fortunately for the young Domingo, a Federalist general took pity on him and brought him into his own house, thus sparing Sarmiento from a likely execution.[28] There was no way for that Federalist general to know that the young Sarmiento he saved would later be president of the nation, or that Sarmiento would become one of Juan Manuel de Rosas's most implacable enemies.

France Gets Involved: The Venancourt Incident and Mob Violence

With the city under siege, Unitarian leaders desperately needed men to defend the city, including foreign residents. Laws from the era of the wars of independence granted the government the right to "press" foreigners into military service if they had lived in the city more than four years, or if they owned a business in the city.[29] British residents were exempt from this law because of the Anglo-Argentine treaty of 1825. French citizens, however, were not, and some were forced to join local militias. Some French citizens who refused to fight were confined on prison ships in the harbor. French officials were insulted. Consul Mendeville lodged a formal complaint to the government and demanded the release of the jailed Frenchmen. When his demands were ignored, Mendeville left to Montevideo in protest, while Mariquita and the children stayed behind as she took care of some family business.

The French navy picked up where Consul Mendeville left off. Admiral Venancourt issued an ultimatum to Unitarian leaders: release French prisoners or face the wrath of French warships. When Unitarian leaders refused to comply, the French navy moved in, cannons blazing. On May 21, the French attacked an Argentine squadron where the French prisoners were being held, burning one ship and capturing three others.[30]

When news of the French attack spread through the city, an angry mob gathered at the Plaza de Mayo looking to take revenge on anything French they could get their hands on. They headed for French consul Mendeville's residence, only a few blocks away. Hearing the ruckus, the servants came out and tried to stop the mob from entering the home. Just when it looked like the mob would succeed, Mariquita appeared and commanded them to stop. The mob froze. "Madame [Mariquita] ordered us to stop twice," recalled one member of the group. Scanning the crowd, Mariquita recognized many of the faces. "She called many of us by name and told us to leave." Mariquita then unleashed a verbal barrage on the intruders. "My husband is not here! He had nothing to do with the French attacks in the harbor! There is no reason for you to be here at my home! Besides, I am more of a patriot than all of you put together! I helped make this free country! Since when were the men of Buenos Aires not gentlemen?" Stunned by the power of Mariquita's onslaught, the mob dispersed, muttering words of admiration as they left. "What a woman! She could be in the government."[31]

Having protected her home, and the honor of the French consulship, Mariquita soon joined Jean Baptiste in Montevideo, where she helped him try to protect French citizens in the area. The city was about to fall, and Juan Manuel, they both understood, was the major power broker in the region. Jean Baptiste wrote Juan Manuel and asked him to protect French residents if and when he captured Buenos Aires. Mendeville capitalized on the long-standing friendship between his wife and Juan Manuel to add a personal touch to the letter. He spoke of how often he had seen Rosas's family. "I am not unaware of how much you respect and love your parents. I think I can assure your excellency that you will be personally rewarded for all that you do on my behalf in these circumstances, and you could never render service more deserving of my attention than protecting my compatriots in my absence."[32] Mariquita also wrote to Juan Manuel personally, asking him to protect French citizens as he entered the city. Juan Manuel responded positively to the Mendevilles' overtures. "Please put me at the feet of my dear Mariquita," he wrote to Jean Baptiste, "and receive the regards of my brothers Prudencio and Gervasio. If you would deign to include me among your closest friends, you will have honored me."[33]

French officials later concluded that Jean Baptiste was negligent of his consular duties during the 1829 siege and the French attack, and he was officially reprimanded for leaving his post. They also decided that although Mendeville was not the most able and courageous diplomat, his wife, Mariquita, with her connections to Juan Manuel, was a valuable asset and reason enough to keep Jean Baptiste at his post. As one French official later remarked, the French understood that Mariquita and Juan Manuel had been friends since infancy, although their paths later diverged. They had grown up together, and both actively shaped their own lives. Mariquita was a woman who "little by little became accustomed to the elegance of European life while [Juan Manuel] emerged from quasi barbarism through his own will and education."[34]

The Mendevilles soon returned to Buenos Aires, where Mariquita rejoined the Sociedad de Beneficencia and Jean Baptiste resumed his consular duties, writing memos to his superiors suggesting that the French found a colony in Patagonia and move into the Malvinas Islands.[35]

Rosas and Lavalle Make a Deal

The French attack dealt a powerful blow to Juan Lavalle's position and to Unitarian hopes. In fact, Rosas had encouraged the French to attack precisely to weaken Unitarian influence. For Rosas, approving of the French intervention was justified because Lavalle's government was illegal and illegitimate. Therefore, French actions did not violate true Argentine sovereignty. In a letter to the French commander, Rosas lauded Venancourt's actions, stating that they showed that France recognized the illegality of the Unitarian position. Rosas even advised the French to keep the captured Argentine ships until they could be returned to the properly constituted Argentine authorities.[36]

Faced with an increasingly impossible position, Lavalle decided to sue for peace. Not wanting to waste time with intermediaries, he mounted his horse and rode straight into Juan Manuel's camp. When the stupefied guards informed their visitor that Rosas was out inspecting the troops, Lavalle asked for some yerba mate to drink, and for Rosas's bed. Both were provided, and soon Lavalle was fast asleep. When Rosas returned late that night, he ordered his men to let Lavalle rest undisturbed.[37] In the morning, Rosas greeted Lavalle like an old friend. In what came to be known as the Cañuelas Pact, they agreed to end hostilities and call elections with candidates that both Unitarians and Federalists approved of. On June 25, Lavalle issued a proclamation in which he swore "to forget all offenses, because I have found my opponents to be fellow porteños willing to consecrate their honor for their country."[38]

Lavalle's fellow Unitarian leaders, however, openly disregarded the Cañuelas Pact. Rosas was not amused. "It is a horrifying picture," Rosas wrote a friend, "if faith in agreements is destroyed and if trust is lost. All will be desolation and death."[39] Lavalle was also frustrated. If the new governor cannot control the factions, Lavalle confided to Rosas, the province will "relive the year 1820, and the blood of our compatriots will flow in torrents." Lavalle also worried that one party would have to "cut the throat of the other" for there to be a decisive victory.[40] Nonetheless, Rosas still believed a positive outcome was possible. "I dare to predict," he wrote a close friend, "that if general Lavalle unites firmly with me, the country will be saved. To say it even better: the great family of the Argentine republic will soon see the long-awaited day of the great work of national consolidation." Then, referring to himself in the third person, Rosas mused about the future and his possible role in it. "Juan Manuel de Rosas is a good man, an honorable farmer, a friend of the laws and the happiness of his country, a country in which he has investments, a wife, children, parents, siblings." And, Rosas continued, "what will be his aspirations after the lessons taught by the history of all revolutions in the world?"[41] At thirty-five years old, Juan Manuel was proposing himself as a solution to the problems in Buenos Aires and beyond. In the meantime, General Lavalle believed it best to leave the country, at least for a while. He soon moved with his family across the river to Montevideo, Uruguay.

Ladies and Gentlemen, Your Newly Elected Governor, Juan Manuel de Rosas

One of the first things interim governor Viamonte did was try to reorganize Buenos Aires's provincial legislature. Viamonte wanted to call elections to choose a completely new set of representatives. Juan Manuel de Rosas, however, wanted the old legislature restored—the one in place when Dorrego was governor. When Viamonte and others resisted, Rosas sent menacing signals. In a letter to his cousin, Rosas warned that if the old legislature was not restored, the current government would lose his confidence, and he "and everyone else would be very unfortunate."[42] Viamonte finally gave in, and the old legislature reconvened on December 1, 1829, exactly one year after the Decembrist uprising sparked the war.

One of the new legislature's first items of business was to choose a new governor. Congressman Tomás de Anchorena, Juan Manuel's cousin, proposed that the new governor, whoever he was, be granted extraordinary authority to deal with the troubles in the province, just as other provincial leaders had been given in past times of crisis. Although the election was still pending, everyone knew that Rosas was the likely victor. The proposal sparked intense debate in the legislature. One opponent expressed concerns that a governor with *facultades extraordinarias*, as they were called in Spanish, would be above the law. Another worried that such powers could easily lead to tyranny. But such opposition was drowned out by an overwhelming majority of delegates who favored increased powers for the new governor. On December 8, the legislature elected Juan Manuel de Rosas as governor and granted him *facultades extraordinarias* for a period of six months to enable him to restore order to the province. Rosas's inauguration on December 8 was met with popular acclaim while the president of the legislature, Felipe Arana, welcomed Rosas as the "Savior of the Fatherland."[43] Soon, the governor's supporters revived the comparisons of Rosas to the Roman hero Cincinnatus.[44]

A conversation with an Uruguayan. The next day, Governor Rosas met with a representative from the new nation of Uruguay. During their conversation Rosas shared some of his philosophies on social and political leadership. "I have always had my own system of doing things," Rosas told his visitor, "and I will tell you frankly how I have done it." Rosas spoke of how he admired the great leaders of the country, even Bernardino Rivadavia, for their talent and skill. "But in my view they all made a great error: they led the upper classes well, but they despised the lower classes and rural dwellers who are the men of action." Those were the very groups that, according to Rosas, caused much of the disorder in all revolutions. He thus endeavored "at all costs" to "gain influence over these people" to contain and guide them. He worked and sacrificed to make himself "into a gaucho like them, to speak like them, to do whatever they did, to protect them," and to make himself "their representative and look after their interests." Such an approach might earn him scorn from some quarters, he admitted, but they did not understand that his intentions were always to instill "obedience to authority and to the laws." Rosas told his Uruguayan visitor that he did not belong to any one party. "They all think I am a Federalist. No sir. I don't belong to any party but my country." In the end, Rosas concluded, "all I want is to avoid maladies and reestablish institutions."[45] This remarkable statement came at the dawn of Rosas's formal political career, but it emerged from concepts and ideas he had developed since his childhood days among the gauchos and Indians at his family's estancias. To those ideas he added his experiences as a militia commander, rancher, and now, provincial governor.

Immediately following his appointment, Rosas issued a proclamation to his province and another to the whole country, both of which revealed some of his objectives and his political style. He urged the people to prevent the return of "maleficent winds of discord" in the province. "May the days of my rule be paternal," he concluded. "The health of the Province is my only aspiration, and the good, the rest, and the security of all is my principal devotion."[46] In his circular to the other provinces, Rosas blamed Unitarians for attempting a "premature perfection" in national organization. Unitarians believed erroneously that they could rush things, that "enlightenment could be converted into the right to force time and events." Conversely, Rosas promised that under his rule the will of the people would serve as the "fundamental base of the organization of the Republic."[47] His predecessors all failed to establish a unified constitutional order, and Rosas was in no hurry to tempt fate again.

Juan Manuel de Rosas (and Simón Bolívar) Take a Hemispheric View

Juan Manuel also cast Buenos Aires's plight in a broader national and even hemispheric context. He warned that if the United Provinces did not keep chaos at bay, then their independence could still be threatened. Spain, he reminded everyone, was attempting to reconquer Mexico at that very moment. (Spanish forces had indeed landed in Veracruz, Mexico, only a few weeks earlier, only to be repulsed by General Santa Anna, among others.) Rosas implied that Buenos Aires could be next on King Ferdinand's agenda.[48]

Rosas's assessment of the situation in part paralleled Simón Bolívar's view of the hemisphere. In a stroke of serendipity, Bolívar wrote a short analysis of the state of Spain's former American colonies in 1829. Bolívar began his "Glance at South America" with a section on the "Argentine Republic," as he called it. He started with Argentina but, he felt compelled to explain, "not because [Argentina] stands in the vanguard of our revolution, as her own citizens have claimed in their excess of vanity." Instead, Bolívar spoke first of Argentina "because it is the farthest south while at the same time presenting the clearest perspectives regarding every kind of anarchic revolution." Bolívar decried the divisions that had plagued Argentina since its independence. "Blood, death, and every crime" were the results of a "federation combined with the rampant appetite of a people who have broken their chains and have no understanding of the notions of duty and law." In the Río de la Plata region, he continued, "every election is plagued with confusion and intrigue," and everything "is decided by force and faction." Bolívar did not mince words when analyzing Juan Lavalle, who sparked the conflicts of 1829 with his execution of Governor Dorrego. Bolívar, who knew Lavalle personally, labeled him as a "reckless, immoral man . . . whose career has followed the steps that lead a criminal to the gallows."

But Bolívar did not see these as faults unique to Argentina. "Its history is the history of Spanish America," he continued, and the same problems existed across the hemisphere, "with no difference from one country to another" except in some details. "If Buenos Aires manages to abort a Lavalle, the rest of America finds itself overrun by Lavalles. If Dorrego is assassinated, assassinations are rife in Mexico, Bolivia, and Colombia."[49] To be sure, Bolívar was not in the best of moods in 1829 because the country he had created, Gran Colombia, was falling apart and his popularity had plummeted. Nevertheless, Bolívar's views paralleled roughly those of San Martín and Rosas.

What remained to be seen was which party or faction would emerge victorious. Which party would subdue the anarchy and unify the country? Juan Manuel Rosas was determined that the Federalists would triumph, with him in the lead on the governor's seat in Buenos Aires. Balancing differing regional demands, it seemed, was a hemispheric problem, as Simón Bolívar already knew. US president Andrew Jackson would soon face similar problems with the Nullification Crisis of the early 1830s, which threatened to break up the US.[50]

Rosas's Administration: Laws, Symbols, Words, and Rituals

The Sociedad de Beneficencia was eager to reach out to Governor Rosas to secure continued government support. Mariquita was chosen as one of the two Sociedad members to officially greet him. Although they had been friends since their childhoods, Mariquita was a bit wary of Juan Manuel as a politician. She already knew that his style was not her style. His emphasis on unity and conformity was at odds with her preference for dialogue and tolerance. Despite Mariquita's wariness of Juan Manuel, the Sociedad knew that her friendship offered a direct connection to the government. A few weeks after Juan Manuel became governor, Mariquita was elected unanimously as the new president of the Sociedad de Beneficencia. The previous president was a Unitarian.[51]

While Rosas enjoyed enormous popularity, his government still faced daunting obstacles. Unitarians were looking for any way they could remove him from power, and the Unitarian general Paz controlled Córdoba Province and was making alliances with other parts of the interior. The Federalist Party also suffered from internal divisions, some based on the long-standing issue of national organization. The most divisive issue among the Federalists, however, was the contentious question of whether or not Rosas should continue to wield extraordinary powers.

Rosas dealt astutely with the opponents within his own party. For years, he had demonstrated an acute awareness of the power of common people, and he also understood the power of symbols, language, and words in shaping public opinion. From the beginning of his first government, Rosas carefully chose the words he used to describe his followers as well as his enemies. In some ways, Rosas engaged in a war of words as much as a war of the sword. Rosas instructed his Federalist supporters to start using the word *cismáticos*—those that promote *cismas* (schisms)—to refer to his opponents within the Federalist Party. His loyal followers, on the other hand, Rosas called "Apostolic" Federalists. These religious adjectives referenced the great schisms of Christian history and gave the current political debate a sacred religious element. Rosas presented himself as the representative of the true Federalism—Apostolic Federalism—while the Cismático Federalists were frauds who promoted discord and division.[52]

Rosas also recognized the symbolic power of the fallen governor, Manuel Dorrego. In one of the first major events of his administration, Rosas presided over the reburial of Dorrego. Even before Rosas's election as governor, he had promoted the glorification of the ex-governor. Although Rosas had been critical of Dorrego many times when he was alive, he recognized that Dorrego's overthrow and summary execution were potent symbols of the disorder and lawlessness caused by Unitarians. And so the governor praised Dorrego's name and made sure others did as well. In gratitude for Rosas's veneration, Angelita Dorrego presented Rosas with her dead husband's saber.[53]

As the carriage carrying Dorrego's remains approached its destination, Rosas allowed people from the crowd to pull the carriage the final few blocks to the cemetery. Rosas delivered the funeral oration at the tomb, where he lauded Dorrego as the "first magistrate of the Republic," who was "sentenced to die in the silence of the laws." Dorrego's death, Rosas continued, was the "blackest stain in the history of the Argentines," but a stain now washed clean "by the tears of a just, thankful, and sensible people."[54] Manuel Dorrego was now a kind of Federalist demigod.

With Rosas now in the governor's seat, and the first great martyr of Federalism laid to rest in an appropriate tomb, the future looked promising for the Federalists. They were in firm control of Buenos Aires Province, and Rosas enjoyed wide popularity. Most active Unitarians were in exile, Federalists dominated the legislature, and the population was on high alert for any evidence of opposition. Rosas was everywhere praised as the "Restorer of the Laws." But Rosas was not satisfied with perceived popularity. He wanted his support to be overwhelming. He moved to neutralize any remaining support for the exiled Unitarians. The governor decreed that anyone who expressed support or sympathy toward Lavalle's Decembrist revolution would be "punished as a rebel." And anyone who supported the December 1 uprising in any fashion needed to unequivocally declare the uprising to be illegal, and even evil. In addition, Rosas's supporters organized a public burning of all anti-Rosas materials published during Lavalle's uprising. Rosas also implemented other practices to promote the unanimity of opinion he felt was needed to stabilize society. Soon after taking office, he decreed that all public employees wear a red ribbon to signify their support of the regime.[55] Ribbons would frequently carry texts such as "Long Live the Federation" and "Death to the Unitarians," or a variation on the theme, like "Death to the Savage, Dirty, and Wicked Unitarians."

Although Rosas enjoyed popularity in his home province, he firmly believed he was surrounded by threats elsewhere. Unitarian exiles, he knew, were already

FIGURE 8.1 A red ribbon of the confederation period with Rosas's image on it and the letters "F o M" (Federation or Death) followed by "Long Live the Federalists, Death to the Savage, Filthy, Traitorous Unitarians." Courtesy of the Museo Histórico Nacional, Buenos Aires.

plotting to overthrow him. The Unitarian general Paz, with a large army, controlled Córdoba Province, and in August of 1830 he signed a pact that united nine of the thirteen provinces and designated him (Paz) as the "supreme chief." In addition, Unitarians from Uruguay supported a revolution in Entre Ríos. And from his exile in Montevideo, Juan Lavalle decided that Rosas needed to be overthrown. Lavalle organized an invasion of the province of Corrientes only to have it fail.

Perceiving threats on all sides, Rosas worked tirelessly to form an alliance of his own. The result of his efforts was the Federalist Pact of January 1831, which included the provinces of Buenos Aires, Santa Fe, Corrientes, and Entre Ríos. This agreement was in reality a loose confederation, with each province maintaining most of its sovereignty.[56] With this alliance, Rosas believed Federalists could defeat the Unitarian general Paz and his allies. Estanislao López led the Federalist attack against Paz's forces, and a few months later General Paz was captured after his horse was snared by the bolas of a Federalist soldier. Estanislao López reported the news gleefully to Rosas and even sent the governor the very bolas that disabled Paz's horse. General Paz's capture destroyed his alliance, and soon Rosas incorporated all the provinces into the Federalist Pact. Despite their victory, Rosas still worried that General Juan Lavalle would invade from Uruguay at any moment, and that he might find support from Unitarians remaining in Buenos Aires. To prevent the possibility, López advised Rosas to exterminate all Unitarians. "If this was a personal matter, we could be generous. But this is something else, for it determines the best interest of the people, their joy and peacefulness."[57]

For Rosas to continue to govern effectively, he felt like he needed to maintain his extraordinary power as governor, which the legislature voted periodically to reextend to him. Although Rosas called it an "odious power," he argued that it was still needed to quell domestic disorder and defend against threats from European powers. The issue came up again in 1831 and 1832, always with intense debates. In May of 1832, he returned the extraordinary powers to the legislature, but he did so with a warning. Rosas argued that "those who [saw] themselves as more enlightened than the rest" were shaping the debates, even though they were in the minority. A society *not* governed by extraordinary powers, Rosas warned, would unleash the "passions" and "immorality" that had provoked "that terrible episode" of 1829.[58] Later that year, the legislature reelected Rosas as governor *without* granting him extraordinary powers. Rosas declined the appointment. One of Rosas's friends wrote him a letter assuring him that the legislature meant no offense. Provincial lawmakers, his friend continued, hoped Rosas would remain in office. And, his friend pleaded, "may heaven grant that you be loved and not feared!"[59]

The legislature recognized that Rosas was indispensable, but they hoped he would govern without extraordinary power. Rosas disagreed. "It seems to me you haven't seen clearly on this issue," he responded. "After this I can do no more. Responsibility for the evils that will come are no longer the government's or the governor's. The true responsibility will lie with the representatives of the people."[60] Rosas's attitude toward the new government seemed to be "Keep order if you can."

Conclusion

1829 was a pivotal year for both Mariquita and Juan Manuel. Their growing prominence in porteño society tied them both to the great events of the age. Conflicts between Federalists and Unitarians continued and were only intensified by Lavalle's overthrow and execution of Governor Dorrego. The civil unrest that followed provided a catalyst for the rise to power of Juan Manuel de Rosas. The crisis of 1829 also catapulted Mariquita Sánchez de Mendeville, as the wife of the French consul, directly into the complex world of Franco-Argentine relations. As governor, Juan Manuel was more than just an old friend she might disagree with. His personality and his policies now governed and shaped Buenos Aires, none of which sat well with Mariquita's vision for her city or her country.

CHAPTER NINE

Mariquita and Juan Manuel Part Ways

Juan Manuel looked at the piece of paper in front of him with disgust. It came from Mariquita, and she was asking him to accept the new candidate for the French consulship in Buenos Aires. Pondering the signature with its last name of Mendeville, he marveled over how much his old friend had changed. He wrote her a stinging note. "I used to know a María Sánchez who was a good and virtuous Federalist. I can't recognize her anymore in the letter I received with your signature." Instead of the signature of a loyal friend, Juan Manuel continued, all he saw was a "coquettish blabbermouth little Frenchy."[1] Governor Rosas, now serving for the second time, had long since grown tired of French attempts to pressure him on political and economic fronts. And now Mariquita, his old friend, was applying pressure in her own way on behalf of France.

This 1836 exchange between Juan Manuel and Mariquita signaled a growing rift between the old friends. The beginnings of this rift could be seen as early as 1829. After serving from 1829 to 1833, Juan Manuel left the governor's seat and undertook a successful military and diplomatic campaign along the southern Indian frontier. Then, in 1835, he was reelected governor by the Buenos Aires legislature, this time granting him more power than ever. All of these developments were full of drama and intrigue. Porteño politics were volatile, and civil war threatened to break out in Buenos Aires and in other provinces. Juan Manuel accepted the governor's seat in 1835, but only after the legislature granted him sweeping powers to rule as he saw fit. What Buenos Aires needed, he believed, was a strong hand that could stamp out disorder and division and create a culture of unanimity that could withstand the divisions that threatened to disrupt porteño society. Governor Rosas's coercive activities provoked intense opposition, which in turn pushed him to more violent reactions, all of which created a cycle of violence in the country. Juan Manuel's policies alienated his old friend Mariquita Sánchez enough for her to choose to leave the country, a departure that anticipated a greater wave of exiles to follow.

Rosas's Frontier Campaign of 1833

Before Juan Manuel left office in late 1832, he made final arrangements for an expedition to the Indian frontier on the southern fringes of the Buenos Aires Province. In his words, it was vital to move against "enemy Indians" while building stronger ties with friendly tribes. By so doing, Rosas asserted, the territory extending to the Río Negro and Patagones would be opened up, and the "frontier line" would be "completely secure."[2] The project had been in the planning stages for months and included cooperation from neighboring provinces. On March 22, 1833, Rosas left his estate in the Guardia del Monte and headed south. Besides his gaucho soldiers, Rosas counted on hundreds of Indian allies among his men. As his force progressed south across the Pampas, Rosas established a line of guard posts manned by soldiers and garrisoned with horses, to facilitate communication with the capital. Within a few weeks, the expedition traveled nearly five hundred miles south to the banks of the Río Colorado, where Rosas set up his headquarters. For protection, Rosas and his men bivouacked inside a large square made up of wagons and artillery pieces. Rosas understood, more than most, the dangers posed by the Native tribes, for this was not far from where his own father, Don León, was captured by Indians back in 1785.

From their base on the river, Rosas's forces fanned out into the surrounding region, negotiating with tribes willing to make peace, and battling those that did not. In the process, Rosas's forces freed hundreds of Hispanic captives kidnapped in various Indian raids. At least two of the rescued had been kidnapped in Tucumán Province, more than a thousand miles to the north, a testament to the power, mobility, and interconnectedness of the Native tribes.[3]

An observant visitor. On August 13, 1833, a most interesting visitor arrived at Rosas's camp, a young naturalist from England on a scientific voyage. His name was Charles Darwin, and he was traveling around the world on a British warship, the *Beagle*. Darwin knew of Rosas and his reputation, and the young Englishman was willing to go to great lengths to see the famous leader. Darwin arranged an ambitious journey, starting with a visit to Rosas's camp, followed by a trek northward across the Pampas to then rendezvous with the *Beagle* in

FIGURE 9.1 Rosas on the Southern Desert Campaign of 1833. Courtesy of the Archivo General de la Nación, Buenos Aires.

Buenos Aires a few weeks later. The *Beagle* dropped him at the coastal settlement of Carmen de Patagones in early August, and from there he set off on a two-day ride to Rosas's camp, with a guide, an Englishman, and five gauchos as companions.

While traveling to Rosas's camp, Darwin was fascinated by the gaucho way of life. On the first afternoon, Darwin recorded in his journal, one of the "lynx-eyed" gauchos chased down a cow, slaughtered it, and barbequed it for dinner. "We here had the four necessities of life 'en el campo,' pasture for the horses, water (only a muddy puddle), meat, and firewood." He could not help but admire certain aspects of life on the Pampas. There was "high enjoyment in the independence of the Gaucho life," Darwin mused, "to be able at any moment to pull up your horse, and say, 'Here we will pass the night.'" The whole scene was indelibly printed on Darwin's mind. "The death-like stillness of the plain, the dogs keeping watch, the gypsy-group of Gaucho making their beds round the fire, have left in my mind a strongly marked picture of the first night, which will never be forgotten."[4]

When he finally arrived at Rosas's camp, Darwin was unimpressed at first. Most of the soldiers, he noted, were a mixture of blacks, Indians, and Spaniards, and in Darwin's eyes, such a "villainous banditti-like army was never before collected together." Darwin then turned his attention to observing the

Indians in the camp. "The men were a tall, fine race" while many of the young women deserved "to be called even beautiful." The women spent most of their days chipping stones to be used in the bolas—one of the preferred weapons of the Natives—made up of three rounded stones, each tied into a long cord, all three of which would then be attached together to form a weapon that could ensnare, disable, or kill an animal or human enemy.[5]

On the second day, Rosas granted Darwin an audience. He found Rosas to be "enthusiastic, sensible, and very grave," and in their discussions Rosas never cracked a smile. Darwin, nevertheless, was impressed. "I was altogether pleased with my interview with the terrible General," Darwin wrote in his journal. "He is worth seeing, as being decidedly the most prominent character in S. America." Darwin concluded that Rosas was "a man of extraordinary character," and that he had "a most predominant influence in the country, which it seems probable he will use to its prosperity and advancement."[6] Darwin informed Rosas that he intended to travel through the Pampas back toward Buenos Aires, making observations along the way. Rosas willingly provided Darwin with letters instructing the post commanders of the Pampas to provide him shelter and horses as needed. The English visitor thanked Rosas for his hospitality and took his leave.

Darwin was fascinated by Rosas and was even more intrigued by the intense loyalty he possessed among almost the entire population. Darwin tried to understand the origin of such loyalty as he conversed with locals during his travels. He found no shortage of stories about Rosas, stories that burnished the general's reputation as a man of honor and a man of order—a kind of first among equals. Darwin recorded a few of these stories in his journal, including one about Rosas's rule regarding knives. As Darwin told the story, Rosas issued a rule on his estates that his workers were not allowed to carry knives on Sundays. Sundays were days of rest but also days of drinking and gambling, a potent combination that led frequently to knife play, injury, and even death. To prevent this loss of manpower, Rosas prohibited the carrying of weapons on Sundays. One Sunday, however, Rosas left his house with his knife still in his belt. One of his foremen pointed out the error, perhaps thinking that Rosas would simply return the knife to his house. Instead, Rosas insisted that the foreman apply the proper punishment and put Rosas himself in the stocks. A bit fearfully, the foreman obeyed. After a while the foreman decided to release the captive general even though the allotted time had not elapsed. Once free,

Rosas declared that the foreman had broken the law by releasing him early, and the foreman went into the stocks. Darwin perceived that such stories "delighted the Gauchos, who all possess[ed] high notions of their own equality and dignity." Through such behavior, and by "conforming to the dress and habits of the Gauchos," Darwin found that Rosas had achieved "an unbounded popularity in the country, and in consequence a despotic power."[7]

Darwin heard stories like this and others as he and his guide made their way north toward Buenos Aires on horseback. They traveled from military outpost to military outpost as Darwin took in more of the scenery and more of the frontier culture. One night he stayed at a post commanded by a black army lieutenant who, Darwin learned, had been born in Africa. Darwin was impressed, calling his African host the most "civil and obliging man" he met during the trip. Darwin also experienced the Indian question at close range. His guide was always on the lookout for Indian patrols and once told Charles to load his pistol and jump on his horse when an attack appeared imminent.[8] Darwin was impressed that all the Argentines he met were completely convinced that the war against the Indians was justified because it was waged against savages. "I never saw anything like the enthusiasm for Rosas, and for the success of the 'most just of all wars,'" against the Indians. "Who could believe in this age that such atrocities could be committed in a Christian civilized country?"[9] Perhaps Darwin was unaware that British troops and settlers were, at that very moment, engaged in a similar struggle against the aboriginal population of Australia.

As Darwin made his final approach to Buenos Aires to rendezvous with the *Beagle*, he ran into trouble. "A violent revolution" had broken out, and no traveler was allowed in or out of the city. Darwin found himself "to a certain degree a prisoner." The revolution, Darwin found out, was started by supporters of Juan Manuel de Rosas, who wanted him to return to the governorship. The local commander informed Darwin that Buenos Aires was under siege and impossible to enter. Fearing he might be left behind by the *Beagle*, Darwin pulled out a name he hoped would make a difference. He told the commander of his recent meeting with Rosas and how the general had treated him kindly. According to Darwin, "magic itself could not have altered circumstances quicker than did this conversation." With his Rosas connection opening the way, Darwin soon received permission to enter the city.[10]

In his journal, the English naturalist could not resist commenting on the uprising, which he believed was illegitimate. The current revolution, he wrote, "was supported by scarcely any pretext of grievances." However, Darwin acknowledged, "it would be very unreasonable to ask for pretexts" in a country where governments changed hands so often. As a case in point, Darwin cited that "in the course of nine months (from February to October, 1820), [Buenos Aires] underwent fifteen changes in its government."[11] In Buenos Aires, Darwin reunited with the *Beagle* and set off on the journey that would eventually take him to the Gálapagos Islands, and to fame. But before he observed his famous finches on the Galápagos Islands, Darwin observed the gauchos, Indians, and the natural history of the Pampas. He also observed the rise of Juan Manuel de Rosas.

Encarnación Ezcurra de Rosas and the Revolution of the Restorers

The uprising that almost kept Darwin from his rendezvous with the *Beagle* was known as the "Revolution of the Restorers." The main protagonist of the revolution was none other than Encarnación Ezcurra de Rosas, Juan Manuel's wife. While Rosas was on the southern frontier of the province, his wife, Encarnación, took it upon herself to represent and defend her husband's reputation—and his political position—at any cost.

Encarnación was deeply involved in the ongoing struggle between factions within the Federalist Party. "Liberal" Federalists supported provincial autonomy—the key doctrine of Federalism—but they opposed giving extraordinary powers to the governor. More conservative Federalists approved of such powers. In pro-Rosas-speak, as seen above, these groups were labeled Cismáticos (promoters of schism) and Apostólicos (true, apostle-like followers of Rosas). In the local elections of 1833, the liberal Federalists triumphed. In celebration of their victory, some victorious liberals defecated outside the homes of prominent Apostólicos and cleaned themselves with the pro-Rosas voting lists. Meanwhile, in the legislature, General Tomás de Iriarte delivered a speech against the threat of dictatorship, a clear reference to where he and others believed Rosas would lead them if he returned to the governor's seat. The liberal Federalist press also attacked Rosas supporters by mocking red ribbons and criticizing the idea of granting extraordinary faculties.[12]

In the face of such opposition and insult, Encarnación and other Apostolic

Federalists redoubled their efforts. A pro-Rosas paper was published, called *El Restaurador de las Leyes* (The Restorer of the Laws), named in honor of Rosas. Encarnación kept Juan Manuel apprised of all developments through letters, including her activities on his behalf. He in turn offered advice, encouraging her to cultivate the support of all social classes, including people of color. He suggested that she invite Apostólico leaders and others into her home, and that she speak to the mothers of the free slaves who were fighting under him on the frontier. Encarnación agreed, and soon her home became a crossroads of many segments of porteño society, including gauchos, mulattoes, and blacks.[13] Encarnación also met with local leaders from various regions in the countryside to garner their support. Encarnación's efforts earned her a nickname among her supporters: the Heroine of the Confederation. "The masses are ready more and more each day," she wrote Juan Manuel on September 14, 1833. The people would be even more ready, she added, if Apostólico leaders were more courageous. "I prefer those with an axe and a pick.... No one enters here except the truly committed." Encarnación also singled out individuals she thought were threats to the cause. "We need to go after the priest Vidal," she told her husband. "He is a miscreant who has played a big role in the present misfortunes." When Juan Manuel's opponents attacked Encarnación in the press, she passed that information along to her husband as well. "By the enclosed papers you will see how your wife's reputation stands. But, she assured her husband, "nothing intimidates me. They will pay dearly for their crimes. Everything, everything, is going to hell! There is no patience for these criminals, and we wait for men to start knifing each other to death in the streets."[14]

The animosity between the pro- and anti-Rosas press became so intense that Governor Balcarce charged the editors of the most extreme newspapers with disturbing the peace. He ordered the editors of the two most fanatical papers to appear in court. One of them was the editor of the pro-Rosas paper *The Restorer of the Laws.* On the morning of October 11, the day of the trial, pamphlets appeared throughout the city saying that "the Restorer of the Laws" would be put on trial later that morning. Many people mistakenly believed that Juan Manuel de Rosas himself was going to be put on trial, a misunderstanding Rosas's supporters encouraged and perhaps intended. Within a few hours, a large crowd showed up outside the courthouse and began chanting in support of Rosas, forcing a suspension of the trial. The crowd then dispersed into the countryside to recruit more followers to resist the government. They soon returned and laid siege to the city in what became called the "Revolution of the Restorers."[15]

Although Juan Manuel appeared to be far removed from developments in the capital, the letters between him and Encarnación show he was well informed and very much involved. Encarnación took to writing "Federation or Death" in the top left corner of some of her letters to Juan Manuel. In one letter she asserted that loyal Federalists needed to "pulverize" their enemies because the country "would experience no happiness as long as even one Decembrist" remained alive. Encarnación's choice of wording was telling: she was equating her liberal Federalist enemies (Cismáticos) with Unitarians—those who had supported Juan Lavalle and the execution of Governor Dorrego in December of 1828. An Apostolic victory would assure "happiness for the country" and "tranquility for families." Meanwhile, she added referring to her husband, "I will not stop directing my pleas to my friend," hoping that he will realize "the necessity of exterminating" the enemies of order to bring peace to the country. Encarnación underlined part of her farewell in the letter: "Your eternal friend, Encarnación Ezcurra de Rosas."[16]

Meanwhile, pro-Rosas forces continued to besiege Buenos Aires. The pressure of the siege forced Governor Balcarce to resign on November 7, 1833. A few days later Balcarce's house was looted. Some houses of prominent liberal Federalists were also sprayed with gunfire. Many liberal Federalists got the message and fled the country soon thereafter, including General Tomás Iriarte, who had warned about the threat of dictatorship in the legislature. In the meantime, José Viamonte was again chosen to serve as interim governor.[17]

La Sociedad Popular Restauradora and the Mazorca

Encarnación Ezcurra did not care for Governor Viamonte either, and she was disgusted by the lukewarm actions of many prominent porteños who supposedly supported her husband. She wanted more action. One day, one of Encarnación's associates, Tiburcio Ochoteco, approached her with an idea. While living in Spain years before, he had seen the power of political clubs that organized to oppose King Ferdinand VII's excessive rule. Ochoteco believed that a similar organization would be useful to Apostolic Federalists. He proposed to Encarnación the formation of a club open only to the most dedicated, zealous, and fanatic Rosas supporters. Encarnación Ezcurra agreed and became the club's main patron. It was called the Sociedad Popular Restauradora (Popular Restoration Society).[18] Ochoteco was the club's first president, and it soon boasted a growing membership. This was a new type of club in Buenos Aires because it reached out to all classes of people, especially the lower classes. Earlier clubs like San Martín's Sociedad Patriótica, or the masonic lodges of the independence era, were geared toward the elite. These types of elite societies had become very unpopular by the early 1830s in Argentina as well as elsewhere in the hemisphere. Race-based associations had also existed for decades, especially among Afro-Argentine groups, but they were not secret, nor were they particularly political in nature. The Popular Restoration Society, then, represented something new: a secretive political club that opened its doors to all, including the popular classes.[19]

Members of the Popular Restoration Society took it upon themselves to support Rosas in a variety of ways. They could be found at political gatherings lauding Rosas's virtues. They might also be found shouting insults outside the homes of prominent anti-Rosistas, pressuring them to change their behavior or perhaps leave the country. On one occasion, society members even publicly insulted Rosas's cousin, Nicolás de Anchorena, whom they deemed as too mild in his support of the Apostólico cause. Popular Restoration Society members also sprang into action when ex-president Bernardino Rivadavia returned to Buenos Aires on April 28, 1834. His arrival set off a wave of fear about escalating political unrest. Governor Viamonte ordered Rivadavia to leave immediately, and five hours later he was gone. Nevertheless, the next night, Popular Restoration Society members fired shots at the homes of two government ministers, resulting in the first death caused by the club. Minister García was hosting a tertulia at his home when the shots were fired outside. A young guest, Enrique Bedlam, went out to investigate and was shot to death. Encarnación did not mention Bedlam's death in her next letter to Juan Manuel, but she did boast about the impact of the whole affair and her role in it. "The bullets I had fired on the 29th had great effect," she wrote, for "they caused the flight of that wicked priest Vidal back to his homeland [of Uruguay]."[20]

Not all members of the Popular Restoration Society believed in violence or wanted to engage in it personally. Thus, over the next few months, a very small but radical wing of the club took shape, made up of men willing to use violence as a political tool. They took upon themselves the name Mazorca. The origin and meaning of the name are not clear. "Mazorca" means an ear or a cob of corn, and some claim the name was born after Rosas gave a gift of corn to the club. The unity of the kernels in the ear of corn also represented the tight union of Rosistas in the Mazorca—an elite club within a club. Other variations of the name's origin were more violent. The corncob, some said, signified what would happen to enemies of the society: they would have a corncob introduced into their bodies in a most uncomfortable manner (a known form of torture at the time). Some also saw the name Mazorca as signifying *mas horca*, or "more hanging," pointing to the killings committed by the group (*horca* meaning gallows). In practice, the Mazorca encompassed all of these meanings at different times. It was a small, close-knit, zealous group of followers willing to do just about anything to protect Rosas's name and Rosas's power. But after the death of Enrique Bedlam outside the tertulia, the Popular Restoration Society and its radical wing, the Mazorca, focused on strengthening support for Rosas and laying the foundation for the return of the "Restorer of the Laws."[21] But it would not be long before they returned with a vengeance.

Rosas Gives His Answer to the Constitutional Question

In October of 1834, Governor Viamonte called for elections to choose a new governor. Rosas was again the obvious candidate. The legislature elected Rosas, but *without* the extraordinary powers he demanded if he were to accept the office. Over the next few months, the legislature tried three more times to convince Rosas to accept his election with normal authority, and each time he declined. Yet even though Rosas was not the governor, he was still seen as the main power broker in the region.

As such, Federalist leaders around the country sought Juan Manuel's opinion when it came to the pressing issue of national unification. Was it not time, asked many Federalists, to create a national constitution? The moment seemed propitious, especially since Rosas's faction of Federalists—the Apostólicos— controlled much of the country. Rosas had heard that question before, and his response was always firm: the country was not ready for a more robust national organization. "If I let myself be guided by my heart-felt desires," Rosas wrote to one provincial governor, "I would be the first to call for [a constitutional] assembly." However, he continued, "experience and repeated disappointments have shown me the dangers of a resolution based only on enthusiasm instead of on sound counsel, reason, and on the practical study of the situation."[22]

Juan Manuel had similar discussions with General Facundo Quiroga, his close ally from the province of La Rioja. When trouble erupted between provinces in the northwestern part of the country, Juan Manuel nominated Facundo to mediate the conflict. Governor Viamonte agreed. In December of 1834, Juan Manuel wrote Facundo a long letter outlining his views on the constitutional question—views Juan Manuel wanted Facundo to share with the governors in the North. Juan Manuel wrote as a civilian, having rejected the governor's seat, but he nevertheless still possessed enormous influence in the province and throughout the country. His letter to Facundo turned out to be a lengthy discourse on why, in Juan Manuel's view, the United Provinces were not ready for another attempt at a national constitution.

At first, Juan Manuel talked about how the idea of a unifying constitution was dear to his heart. However, he pointed out, attempts to achieve that goal in recent years had failed miserably. "The results tell the tale eloquently," Juan Manuel wrote. Scandal followed upon scandal, and the republic now found itself in a "dangerous state" that destroyed all hope of a happy solution. With all that had happened, Juan Manuel wondered if there was anyone who really thought "a national constitution would be the remedy." He emphasized repeatedly that a strong foundation needed to first be in place before a constitution could be attempted. Who forms an "ordered whole," or an army, without first having a strong foundation? "Who forms a robust and living being with dead and broken limbs?" In short, Juan Manuel concluded, "we completely lack the elements for a unified government." He accused the Unitarians and Masons, among others, of corrupting many provinces and thus making them unfit to join a national government. The United States of America, Rosas pointed out, was slow to incorporate new territories as states, not doing so until they could manage themselves. The Argentine provinces, he implied, were not ready to manage themselves, let alone create a constitution to unite the country. Such an attempt, Rosas affirmed, as in times past would cause a "most frightful catastrophe." In closing, Juan Manuel wished Facundo Quiroga a successful trip, which would save their "compatriots from so many dangers that threaten them."[23]

An American Dilemma: Political Ideals versus Realities

Juan Manuel de Rosas's letter showed how he confronted a similar dilemma that beset other leaders during the 1820s and 1830s in Spanish America and beyond: how to balance political ideals with practical realities. This problem was so vexing throughout the hemisphere that it merits some additional attention.

One of the main questions Rosas and others faced was the following: to what degree should newly formed Spanish American republics follow models from Europe or the United States? The US had a federalist system that tried to balance states' rights with the power of the federal government. During his exile in the US, the late governor Manuel Dorrego had studied the American system and tried to convince his fellow porteños and others to follow it. But according to many in Argentina and beyond, the US system gave too much power to the states, which led to factionalism and discord. In Venezuela, for example, Simón Bolívar, shared his thoughts on the matter. "In my opinion, it is a miracle" that the United States of America "endures with such prosperity and that it does not fall apart at the first manifestation of trouble or danger."[24] A few years later, the American Civil War, with its six hundred thousand dead, would in part bear out some of Bolívar's concerns.

Bolívar had grappled with similar questions when considering the formation of a republic twenty years earlier in the 1810s. Were Venezuela and its people capable of "maintaining in proper balance the difficult undertaking of a republic?" Bolívar asked in his famous *Jamaica Letter* of 1815. "Is it conceivable that a newly liberated people can be launched into the sphere of freedom without their wings disintegrating and hurling them into the abyss, like Icarus?" At the Congress of Angostura in 1819, Bolívar again argued for a more realistic approach to politics. "Legislators. It is unlikely that we can achieve what the human race never achieved, what even the greatest, wisest nations never accomplished. Untrammeled freedom, absolute democracy, these are the reefs on which republican hopes have ever shattered." To help guide these new, immature states, Bolívar suggested "concentrating all power in a president" with "sufficient authority to carry on the struggle against the difficulties inherent in [the] current situation." In short, Bolívar concluded, "let us not aspire to the impossible."[25] And when Bolívar presented his draft constitution to the newly formed nation of Bolivia in 1826, he spoke of the dangers facing a constitutional order. "Tyranny and anarchy form a vast ocean of oppression surrounding a tiny island of freedom that is perpetually pounded by the violence of the waves and hurricanes that seek unremittingly to sink her. Behold the sea you hope to traverse in a fragile boat, its pilot utterly unskilled."[26] Despite these grave concerns, Bolívar moved boldly forward with his constitutional experiments.

Yet he died in 1830, a sick and broken man of forty-seven years who had been banished from his own homeland of Venezuela.[27]

Rosas, meanwhile, was much more pessimistic than Bolívar about hopes for constitutional success, and Bolívar's spectacular struggles may have even inspired part of Rosas's pessimism. For now, Rosas wrote to his friend Quiroga, a loose confederation was the best the United Provinces could possibly hope for. Quiroga kept Rosas's letter with him and studied it assiduously in preparation for his mission to the northern provinces.

A Gory Assassination and a New Election

Quiroga finished his mission to the North successfully and embarked on his return trip to Buenos Aires. But getting back to Buenos Aires safely could be tricky, especially in times of political discord. Over the years, Facundo Quiroga had made many enemies, even within the Federalist Party. The powerful Reinafe family in the province of Córdoba, for example, had clashed with Quiroga since the early 1830s. As it turned out, Quiroga's route home from his northern mission passed through Córdoba. Quiroga's friends for months had warned him to take the long way around Córdoba to avoid the Reinafe family. He ignored the advice. On February 6, a few miles outside the city of Córdoba, an armed group of horsemen intercepted Facundo's carriage. "What is the meaning of this?!" Quiroga shouted, leaning his head out of the carriage window. The answer came in the form of a bullet through the eye. Facundo fell dead. The letter from Juan Manuel, still in his pocket, was stained with his blood. All but one of his escorts were killed, and the assassins slit the throats of all the bodies.[28]

News of Facundo's assassination sent a wave of panic through the city of Buenos Aires. The killing of such a prominent leader, many feared, would spark a new round of civil war. The Buenos Aires governor resigned, and the legislature offered the governorship to Rosas again. This time they agreed to grant him the powers he wanted. Not only did legislators offer him the extraordinary powers he had wielded in 1829, but they also granted him the *suma del poder político*, or the plenitude of public power. These powers meant that Rosas, if he so chose, could exercise all three governmental powers—executive, legislative, and judicial.

As Juan Manuel pondered the meaning of his new position and powers, the troubled state of the country weighed heavily on his mind. His feelings boiled over in a letter written to a foreman on one of his ranches. After giving some instruction relating to oxen, Rosas turned his pen toward politics. "The honorable Dorrego," Rosas began, "was shot by a firing squad at Navarro by Unitarians." He then continued with a list of other Federalists killed treacherously. General Villafañe was killed while traveling between Mendoza and Chile; General Latorre was run through by a Unitarian lance even after he surrendered and was in prison; Coronel Aguilera suffered a similar fate; General Quiroga's throat was cut while traveling through Córdoba, along with sixteen others who accompanied him. After finishing the grisly list, Rosas exclaimed: "How about that! Have I, or have I not described the true state of this land? But even these will not be enough for the men of enlightenment and principles! Those wretches! I was foolish enough to get involved with such idiots. Now they will see. The response will be frightful, and Argentine blood will flow freely."[29] Facundo's assassination seemed to push Juan Manuel to a tipping point. In his way of thinking, he understood how the game was played and, he implied, he was going to play it better than anyone else, even if it meant that blood would flow in the streets.

While Rosas was pleased with the legislature's decision, he wanted more democratic support of his election and of his extraordinary powers. In his mind, the legislature's vote was not enough, nor was his apparent popularity among the people. Tempestuous times, Rosas knew, rendered fragile any type of political power. Rosas wanted his election, in his words, to be "so authentic that it could never be put in doubt." Rosas hoped to achieve such authenticity through a plebiscite—a public vote—which took place in late March of 1835. All males in the province, regardless of wealth or color, would be able to vote simply yes or no on Rosas's governorship. Rosas made great efforts to get people out to vote. In the end, more than nine thousand men voted in his favor, with only four voting against.[30] Periodic elections continued throughout Rosas's time in office, and elections were part of the republicanism that the governor and his supporters claimed to defend.[31]

Although many anti-Rosistas abstained from voting, the result was a resounding victory for Rosas. The legislature had elected him and chosen to grant him extraordinary powers. Now the people gave him an overwhelming stamp of public approval. For Rosas and his supporters, this was a victory for democratic sentiment. For Rosas's opponents, the plebiscite provided additional proof that the right to vote needed to be kept out of the hands of the common people, and that the land of Argentina naturally produced popular classes inclined toward barbarism. And while the plebiscite indicated that Rosas was extremely popular with the lower classes, many of the wealthier class approved of him as well because Buenos Aires, as a hub of merchant and export activity, depended on peace and security for the economy to flourish.[32]

Juan Manuel Returns as Governor

On the morning of April 13, 1835, the color red enveloped the city of Buenos Aires as Juan Manuel de Rosas prepared to officially take the governor's seat for the second time. Red had become a symbol of Rosas ever since his red-clad regiment mobilized during the anarchy of 1820. As Rosas made the short carriage journey from the congress to the fort, thousands of people lined the streets and gathered on their balconies and rooftops, showering flowers on the procession as it went by. Residents hung whatever red items they could from their windows, including shawls, tablecloths, and bedspreads, among other items. Soon after the procession began, twenty-five members of the Popular Restoration Society unhitched the horses from Rosas's carriage and pulled it through the streets themselves. As they entered the plaza, the procession passed under a triumphal arch and was greeted by soldiers in formation.

Members of the Popular Restoration Society also made a fashion statement that day. They all wore red vests and mustaches. It seemed to be a fairly spontaneous decision, because many did not have time to grow their own and thus wore fake or painted-on mustaches. The mustaches were most likely meant to symbolize unanimity in support of Rosas, but also to distinguish society members from the clean-shaven style that was typical among some liberal Federalists and Unitarians.[33]

Rosas addressed the public without a smile. He was chosen, he said, almost unanimously, by citizens of the city and countryside, to wield "limitless power, that, despite its odious nature," he had "deemed to be absolutely necessary to pull the country out of the abyss of misfortune in which it [was] sadly immersed." Rosas counted on protection from heaven against a "corrupt faction of men" who sought to destroy religion and undermine society. "Divine providence has put us in this terrible situation to test our virtue and determination," Rosas continued. "May we fight to the death against the impious, the sacrilegious, the thief, the murderer, and above all the perfidious and the traitors who dare to mock our good faith. May not even one of these monsters be allowed to remain among us."[34]

Symbols, images, and a culture of unanimity. Immediately after taking office, Rosas, as he had done in 1829, initiated policies to eradicate opposition and create a unanimity of opinion. Within his first few weeks of office, Rosas dismissed large numbers of public workers and military officials suspected of not being loyal to his government. His picture began to appear in churches, and processions honoring his likeness became common around the city. Rosas also ordered executions within his first month in office. Over the next months and years, Rosas would dedicate a large portion of the provincial budget to military and police activities—institutions of social control—to help ensure order and stability.[35] Rosas also renewed red ribbons as an outward show of support for Federalism, but this time it was even more pervasive. Men would wear ribbons on their hat or chest while women would wear a red ribbon in their hair. Red stamps also began to appear in top corners of many government documents as well, emblazoned with the inscription "Long Live the Federation! Death to the Savage Unitarians."[36] The governor's likeness even made its way onto various items of female fashion. Mariquita owned a pair of white gloves with the image of his face on them. At least one tortoiseshell comb (*peinetón*), so popular in the 1830s, had Rosas's profile carved into the top middle, while across the base of the comb the artisan had carved out an intricate "Federation or Death."[37]

Juan Manuel also promoted the proliferation of images of himself as well as of his wife, Encarnación. Although he resisted posing for pictures, he and his ministers understood the power of image in public spaces. And artists did not have to worry much about exaggerating the looks of their subject, for Juan Manuel was almost universally recognized as a handsome man. One of the most popular images of him to emerge during his second governorship was painted by Cayetano Descalzi in the late 1830s. The image was so popular that Descalzi went to France himself to have it engraved for mass production. Even though Rosas's government had chronic conflicts with France, everyone knew that the best engravers were in Paris. The engraved version became known as *Rosas el Grande* (Rosas the Great). Soon it could be seen everywhere, including churches. On April 12, 1842, the *Gaceta Mercantil* advertised "magnificent pictures recently arrived from Europe of his excellency the illustrious Restorer of the Laws," emphasizing that they were "made in Paris by the premier engraver of the Royal French School."[38]

FIGURE 9.2 Anonymous portrait of Encarnación Ezcurra and her husband, Juan Manuel de Rosas. Courtesy of the Museo Histórico Nacional, Buenos Aires.

FIGURE 9.3 *Portrait of General Juan Manuel de Rosas* by Cayetano Descalzi. Courtesy of the Museo Histórico Nacional, Buenos Aires.

FIGURE 9.4 *Rosas the Great*, engraved portrait by the firm of Julien and Lemercier (Paris) of Juan Manuel de Rosas based on the original painting by Cayetano Descalzi. Courtesy of the Museo Histórico Nacional, Buenos Aires.

In addition to fashion and images, Rosas throughout his career was meticulous in his use of the print media to define his regime and to define his enemies. For example, in letters and in his political discourse, Rosas began labeling all his opponents simply as "Unitarians," even though many of his critics were moderate Federalists from within his own party (those that wanted him to be governor but without the extra powers, for instance). Federalists who opposed him, he argued, lost the right to be called Federalists. And besides, if anyone opposed his government, they were essentially in league with the Unitarians who had sought his overthrow since 1829.

Rosas also cultivated public opinion through newspapers and other publications. Pedro de Angelis, an Italian immigrant, wrote pro-Rosas literature geared toward the upper classes, especially through the newspaper *El Lucero*.[39] Meanwhile, popular journalists turned out pro-Rosas material in newspapers and broadsheets, especially during Rosas's first government. Frequently, these materials were written in the colloquial style of the gauchos, or of the Afro-Argentine population. Luis Pérez, for example produced over thirty newspapers between 1830 and 1834, some with titles like *El Gaucho* and *Little Black Girl*. "He has arrived, thanks be to God," one article declared, "our beloved patron, the long-awaited one of the people, the genius of the nation."[40]

Another way Governor Rosas and his officials bolstered support among the people was by presenting his government as a great defender of a republic, perhaps even a holy republic. Part of this idea is found in an article by Pedro de Angelis, perhaps the governor's most skilled defender and publicist. After reviewing the maladies that had plagued the country since 1810—from anarchy to civil war to secret conspiracies—de Angelis declared: "Such was the situation the General was called upon to triumph over and organize." De Angelis continued, arguing that the "vast majority of the country wanted, and still wants today, independence, tranquility, and order—things that were lost during the cruel conflicts that tore apart the republic."[41] On top of that republican identity, Rosas and his supporters added a layer of religious wording and imagery. "Apostolic" Federalists defended the republic against enemy evildoers. Porteños saw images of their governor displayed prominently throughout the city, including in churches. Pedro de Angelis hoped that when people saw a picture of the governor, they would see him as the great defender of their republic, even of their Holy Federation, as some began calling the country.[42]

For many, the regime's combination of heavy-handed policies and a softer approach in the media bore fruitful results. From his self-imposed exile in France, General San Martín looked approvingly on Rosas's return to power. "I am convinced that when men refuse to obey the law, there is no alternative to force," San Martín wrote to his friend Tomás Guido in December of 1835. The futile quest for a stable society had limped on ever since the English invasions of 1806, San Martín continued. "Twenty-nine years in search of liberty" had failed, leaving the country "with a legacy of oppression, personal insecurity, destruction of fortunes, indiscipline, venality, corruption, and civil wars." These "great evils" needed to be vanquished, and, San Martín believed, "any government that establishes order and stability" is legitimate and legal. "I am sure you think the same, as do all those who love their country."[43] Did San Martín see things clearly from across the Atlantic, or would he have thought differently if he lived in Rosas's Buenos Aires?[44]

Foreign Pressures and Domestic Economic Disputes

Besides dealing with internal political divisions, Rosas faced grave challenges in foreign relations during the 1830s. The French continued to pressure him on trade issues. British investors demanded repayment of the Baring Brothers loan (from the Rivadavia era), and those investors pressured the British government to lean on Argentine authorities.

In addition, in 1833, the British occupied Argentine territory—the Malvinas Islands in the South Atlantic. Claimed by Spain, though contested by the British, the islands were a popular destination for British and American ships hunting for fish, whales, and seals. After the May Revolution of 1810, porteño officials sent a governor and a few settlers to the islands. When Argentine officials attempted to restrict unbridled sealing and whaling by British and American vessels, the foreigners retaliated. "The Government of Buenos Ayres can certainly deduce no good title to these Islands," declared the US secretary of state, Martin Van Buren, in February of 1831.[45] Van Buren's words were not idle talk. In late 1831, the USS *Lexington* arrived in the Malvinas Islands to address the "piracy" of Argentina. In the end, the affair caused an official break in US-Argentine relations, a break that would last for almost a decade. To make matters worse for Argentina, the actions of the USS *Lexington* opened the door to the British, who, in 1833, occupied the islands and claimed them for the British crown. Governor Rosas, when he returned to power in 1835, protested the British occupation but did not let it sour his good relationship with the British government and the British community in Buenos Aires.

US officials assessed Rosas rather critically. According to US representative Baylies, Rosas was ill-educated but exhibited "certain qualities which gave him a commanding influence with the gauchos." The governor possessed "much personal beauty," Baylies continued, including a "large commanding figure and a fine face." Rosas was also a "Rubeo" (blond), which helped him win over the people. In addition, Rosas was highly skilled "in all Athletic exercises." Baylies worried openly about the dangers of having so many powerful traits concentrated in one person. Rosas's tremendous power "would transform a patriot into a Tyrant and an angel into a demon." As evidence of this, the American diplomat cited sixteen executions without trial in previous months.[46]

Besides pressures on the diplomatic front, Rosas also faced domestic economic disputes. Many interior provinces pushed for a more equitable and protected economic organization of the country. A number of key questions stood out. First, how would the customs duties, paid by foreign merchants bringing goods into the country, be collected and distributed? Who, in the end, had the right to control trade on the Paraná and Uruguay Rivers? It was a complicated question since those rivers ran along Argentine borders, but they also touched territory belonging to Uruguay, Paraguay, and even Brazil. What role did Buenos Aires play in that equation? Finally, would Argentina's economic policy protect local industry by implementing protective tariffs, or would it follow more of a free-trade model?

Rosas, as leader of the Argentine Confederation, was granted by the other provinces authority to negotiate foreign relations for the whole country, due to Buenos Aires's port and strategic location on the coast. That authority also included the right to preside over economic policy, at least as it pertained to tariffs and other aspects of international trade. Unitarian leaders in the 1820s had crafted laws that allowed Buenos Aires to control the river trade. Rosas kept those laws in place, which meant that Buenos Aires claimed the right to control the river trade on the Paraná River from the Atlantic Ocean all the way up into Paraguay—over a thousand miles.[47] Rosas and his government claimed that Buenos Aires was the national port and that all shipping coming into the country needed to stop in the port of Buenos Aires to pay customs duties before it could travel upriver. Federalists from the interior wanted those customs duties to be shared among all the provinces. Buenos Aires Federalists, however, argued that the basic tenet of Federalism was provincial autonomy, which meant that each province should control its own politics *and* its own resources. The river and port were resources of Buenos Aires, which meant it collected and kept those tariffs. Rosas upheld porteño Federalism, and although many of the interior provinces chafed under its yoke, for the time being Rosas's Federalism was preferable to the interventionist and radical solutions the Unitarians offered.[48]

Another pressing issue was that of economic protection. Foreign competition, especially from the British, threatened to undermine many local industries in Argentina. British textile producers, for example, could produce, ship, and sell ponchos at a lower cost than many local producers in Argentina. The same was true for any number of other goods. Local industries in Argentina lobbied the government to place tariffs on foreign goods; this would level the playing field between foreign and local products. This issue also highlighted the division between provinces that depended on exports and those geared toward internal markets. Export-oriented provinces like Buenos Aires preferred more of a free-trade model because that meant foreign countries would put less tariffs on Argentine exports. The estancieros of Buenos Aires, then, preferred free trade because it benefited their export business. Textile producers in the interior, however, demanded protection because they could not compete, at least for the moment, with foreign goods. Rosas, himself an estanciero who preferred free trade, tried to balance these demands. His solution was the Customs Law of 1835, which placed tariffs on a few items, although by and large Rosas upheld a free-trade system with foreign powers, especially the British.[49]

Rosas and the Popular Classes

In addition to his other duties, Governor Rosas always paid close attention to his relationship with the lower classes, including Indians, people of color, and gauchos and other rural dwellers. His Indian policy of negotiation combined with punitive expeditions against uncooperative tribes persisted. Whenever possible, the governor sought opportunities to build relationships with indigenous groups. In 1834, for example, a friendly chief gave Rosas a gift of a number of children captured from the Ranquel tribe. When Rosas found out one of them was the son of a Ranquel chief, Rosas took the boy, named Panguitruz, and had him baptized with the Christian name of Mariano Rosas. After living among the settlers for six years, Mariano Rosas returned to his people, where he eventually became a powerful chief.[50] For friendly Indians, such as Chief Cachul, Rosas was a great friend and ally. "Juan Manuel is my friend. He has never deceived me. I and all of my Indians would die for him," Cachul stated. "If it were not for Juan Manuel, we would not live, as we do now, in brotherhood with and among the Christians. As long as Juan Manuel lives, we will all be happy and live a tranquil life with our wives and children. The words of Juan Manuel are the same as the words of God."[51] Those that would not negotiate, however, felt Rosas's wrath.

Rosas also continued his appeals to porteños of African descent. In addition to reaching out to them in newspapers, Rosas and his family attended various Afro-porteño celebrations. Rosas also finally put an end to the slave trade in 1839, with pressure from the British. While the trade had been prohibited during the May Revolution, it lingered on in reduced form.[52] By declaring an end to the trade, Governor Rosas further ingratiated himself to blacks in the city. This act, and the gratitude it generated for Rosas, was captured in a remarkable tapestry painted by Doroteo Plot. The tapestry depicts Rosas presenting his decree to a group of slave women in 1839. The proclamation in Rosas's hands reads "Federation. Liberty, no more Tyrants." Meanwhile, broken chains lie at the women's feet. The women, in turn, carry Federalist banners emblazoned with "Long Live Liberty," "Long Live the Restorer of the Laws," and of course, "Death to the Savage Unitarians." Overlooking the scene, an angel flies through the air trumpeting "Not one slave will ever again groan in chains in the Plata." Their bitter cry has ended, the angel continues trumpeting, thanks to Rosas's generosity, compassion, and humanity. "I bring forth this precious gift to the sorrowful African" (see figure 9.6).

Rosas's courtship of the lower classes, especially the blacks and mulattoes, did not sit well with his opponents. Many exiles railed against this distortion of classes and ethnicities. José Antonio Wilde later recalled fondly the days when Afro-Argentines knew their place in society. But then came "the time of Rosas, and all was disrupted, demoralized, and corrupted." Indeed, according to Wilde, many black servants became informants for Rosas in his network of spies, who accused reputable families of being Unitarians. Domestic servants in many homes, Wilde continued, became "so haughty and insolent" that many porteño families "came to fear them as much as they did the Mazorca."[53] Some of his enemies even gave Rosas a nickname: "the Mulatto."[54]

FIGURE 9.5 *Candombe Federal during the Era of Rosas* by Martín Boneo. Rosas and members of his family attend an Afro-Argentine festivity. Courtesy of the Museo Histórico Nacional, Buenos Aires.

FIGURE 9.6 *The Female Slaves of Buenos Aires Show Their Freedom and Gratitude to Their Liberator* by Doroteo Plot (1841). Courtesy of the Museo Histórico Nacional, Buenos Aires.

Rosas was a hands-on administrator, and he frequently intervened personally in a variety of cases, both criminal and civil. Exercising the plenitude of public power granted him by the legislature, Rosas was known to read police files and issue sentences himself. Some he would send to prison; others to the firing squad. Rosas's wrath could be turned away on special occasions and by special people. Sometimes he would pardon individuals on special days, such as on the anniversary of his wife's death.[55] On another occasion, Rosas's mother intervened to save an imprisoned man named Almeida, suspected of being a Unitarian. When Agustina heard about it, she sent an angry letter to her son. "That man is neither a Unitarian or a Federalist. He has no party. He is a good citizen. This is how Juan Manuel de Rosas makes enemies, because he only listens to his sycophants." Juan Manuel begged forgiveness from his mother and assured her the man would be set free.[56]

Mariquita Disillusioned

Juan Manuel de Rosas's policies alienated and angered his old friend Mariquita Sánchez de Mendeville. Juan Manuel's style, his absolute faith in his rectitude, and his willingness to coerce others into conformity stood in stark contrast to her ideals of openness and modernism that she sought to foster in her tertulias and otherwise. Juan Manuel, to her, seemed like a relic of the colonial past.

One example of Juan Manuel's backwardness, according to Mariquita and others, was his use of what some called court jesters or buffoons. Charles Darwin noted in his journal that Rosas kept two buffoons, "like the barons of old." Both of them were of African descent. Darwin met one of them while visiting Rosas in 1833, and the buffoon shared a story that Darwin later recorded in his journal. At a social gathering, the buffoon asked Rosas if the musicians could play a certain piece of music. After asking Rosas a number of times, Rosas told him curtly, "Go about your business for I am engaged." When the buffoon asked again, Rosas responded, "If you come again I will punish you." When the buffoon persisted one more time, Rosas laughed. Hearing the laugh, the buffoon knew he was in trouble. "I rushed out of the tent," he told Darwin, "but it was too late; he ordered two soldiers to catch and stake me. I begged by all the saints in heaven he would let me off; but it would not do." According to the buffoon, "when the general laughs he spares neither mad man nor sound." The man seemed quite uncomfortable relating the incident, although Darwin's description of staking makes the discomfort understandable. "Four posts are driven into the ground, and the man is extended by his arms and legs horizontally, and there left to stretch for several hours."[57]

Another observation of Rosas's buffoons came from William Henry Hudson, a young English boy who grew up on a ranch outside of Buenos Aires. The young Hudson relished the times when he came into the city. In his memoirs, he described his first visit. "Perhaps the most wonderful thing I saw during the first eventful visit to the capital was the famed Don Eusebio, the court jester or fool of the President or Dictator Rosas." Hudson was playing at the house of an Anglo-Argentine family when someone opened a window above them and cried out: "Don Eusebio!" He did not understand what that meant, but all the other children did. They all ran quickly to the window in hopes of catching a "glimpse of the great man in all his glory." The children then piled out of the house to watch the procession coming down the street. There, dressed in a general's scarlet uniform and a three-cornered hat came Don Eusebio. "He marched along with tremendous dignity," Hudson recalled, "his sword at his side, and twelve soldiers, also in scarlet, his bodyguard, walking six on each side of him with drawn swords in their hands." The children stared in amazement at this "splendid spectacle." The scene became even more interesting when one of Hudson's friends whispered to him that if anyone "laughed or made any insulting or rude remark, he would instantly be cut to pieces by the guard."[58] Mariquita would later reference Rosas's buffoons as evidence of the "brutish and harsh" society Rosas was promoting, something she feared was spreading throughout the city and province (see figure 9.7).[59]

A New French Consul and Mariquita's "French" Identity

Tensions between Mariquita and Juan Manuel increased when the two were again drawn into the chronic turbulence of Franco-Argentine relations. France continued to pressure Rosas to sign a treaty of friendship and commerce. Meanwhile, French officials decided to replace Jean Baptiste de Mendeville as consul. Both Mariquita and Jean Baptiste resented the move, but they both nevertheless tried to smooth the way for the new consul. But Rosas rejected the first

FIGURE 9.7 Anonymous portrait of Eusebio of the Holy Federation. Eusebio was one of Rosas's buffoons. Courtesy of the Museo Histórico Nacional, Buenos Aires.

proposed replacement and was dragging his feet with the next candidate—the Marquis de Payssac, who arrived in Buenos Aires in April of 1835. The Mendevilles organized a welcome banquet in his honor. Although a new consul was in town, Mariquita hoped Jean Baptiste could remain in Buenos Aires. But it was not to be. Jean Baptiste left for France in late 1835 in preparation for his new assignment in Quito, Ecuador.

The new candidate for consul, the Marquis de Payssac, sought to ingratiate himself to Rosas and his wife, Encarnación. At the same time, Payssac felt somewhat threatened by Mariquita, who, everyone knew, had wanted her husband to remain the consul in Buenos Aires. Nevertheless, in letters to French officials Payssac praised Mariquita as a woman of "superior spirit." He also complimented Encarnación Ezcurra de Rosas. She was, in his estimation, about forty years old, "more little than big," and did "not appear to be in good health." Nevertheless, he continued, Encarnación could speak with great power if called upon. "I do not say that Madame Rosas carries a pair of pistols or a dagger in her belt . . . but I would say that if her husband or her country was in danger, this woman would be capable of great commitment and effort that only courage could inspire."[60]

Despite Payssac's attempts to gain the governor's confidence, Juan Manuel still refused to recognize the new French consul. Mariquita agreed to write Juan Manuel on Payssac's behalf. Her attempts to influence his foreign policy caused the governor to send Mariquita a playful but pointed note, cited at the beginning of this chapter: "I used to know a María Sánchez who was a good and virtuous federalist. I can't recognize her anymore in the letter I received with your signature, which is one of a coquettish blabbermouth little Frenchy."[61]

Mariquita responded in an equally familiar way in a richly layered letter.

I don't want to leave any doubt as to whether a French or American woman has written you. I will tell you that ever since I married a Frenchman, I have served my country with even more devotion and enthusiasm. And I will always do so, as long as you don't oppose France, for if such is ever the case, I will become a Frenchwoman because my husband is French, and he is in the service of his nation. You of all people should approve of such behavior, since you would put [your wife] Encarnación in the stocks if she did not wear your red ribbon. And not only am I following your own doctrine, but also that of honor and duty. What would you do if Encarnación turned Unitarian on you? I know what you would do. Thus, my friend, it is for you to decide if I am American or French. I love you like a brother and I would feel like you were declaring war on me. Until then, allow me to speak with the frankness of our long-time friendship, and know that I am your friend.[62]

Their familiarity with one another is evident in this frank, humorous, and mildly insulting exchange. Also evident is Juan Manuel's sensitivity to Mariquita's meddling in affairs of state on behalf of a foreign nation exerting pressure on him. Mariquita's response highlights the issue of female identity, especially a married woman's identity, and particularly the identity of women married to foreigners. Mariquita Sánchez de Mendeville was obviously Argentine, but did her marriage to a Frenchman affect her identity? The answer to that question had political, legal, and cultural elements to it.

Her marriage made her subject to her husband in the Hispanic tradition. But what was her *legal* identity? From the French perspective, according to the Code Napoléon, "the foreigner who shall have married a Frenchman, shall follow the condition of her husband." Mariquita, then, at least according to the Napoleonic Code, was French, as were her children by Mendeville since "every child born of a Frenchman in a foreign country is French."[63] Ideas of citizenship and nationality in emerging nation-states were still forming at this time, and it appears that Argentine practice, still based on colonial law codes, did not relinquish nationality of Argentine women married to foreign men.[64] But in practice—for Juan Manuel as he read Mariquita's letters on behalf of French citizens and consuls, and perhaps for the mob that showed up outside her home in 1829—Mariquita's marriage gave her a strong French streak that colored, and perhaps stained, her Argentine identity. The essential question Mariquita laid before Juan Manuel was profound: Should loyalty to one's husband trump loyalty to one's country? And what if private patriarchy put a woman in conflict with the patriarchy of the nation-state? In this case, Mariquita was caught between three patriarchs: her husband and the states of France and Argentina. And it would not be the last time.

Governor Rosas finally did accept Payssac as the new French consul. On May 1, 1836, Payssac threw a grand ball to which he invited all the prominent porteños. Rosas sent his daughter Manuelita, along with her cousins. In his letters back to France, Payssac boasted of his triumph at the ball, but also spoke ill of Mariquita. In fact, Payssac's wife feared that Mariquita was involved in a plot to kill her husband, possibly by poisoning. But just three weeks later, Payssac suddenly died. Rumors immediately began to circulate that he had indeed been poisoned, and some mentioned Mariquita as the prime suspect. Such was the pressure on her that Mariquita felt compelled to write a letter to French officials to declare her innocence and protect her honor. "I dare not only Mr. de Vins, sir, but also the whole world, to find even one thing I've done to damage or hurt anyone." Mariquita lamented that it would be difficult, if not impossible, to rid herself of the dishonor of the accusations against her. But she at least wanted French officials to know the truth so that they would not spread false rumors. "I declare, sir, and I swear on what is most sacred, that I never did anything to hurt Mr. de Vins."[65] The scandal surrounding the death of Vins de Payssac only added to Mariquita's growing disillusion with the state of things in Buenos Aires. Many of her friends were already in exile. Others of her circle, however, seemed happy to remain in Buenos Aires. Her good friend Tomás Guido, for example, was one of Rosas's government ministers.

In the end, Mariquita decided to leave Buenos Aires and move across the river to Montevideo, at least for a while, where she could be away from the restrictive environment Juan Manuel had created. This was a self-imposed exile on the part of Mariquita because, unlike many others in Buenos Aires, Juan Manuel had not threatened her with any harm. But for her, Rosas's Buenos Aires was suffocating, and in late 1836 she asked immigration authorities for her passport. Governor Rosas, already known for intervening in matters great and small, took a particular interest in her request. Her decision to leave his city was a blow to him, perhaps even an insult, especially because he knew that *he* was the reason she was leaving. Rosas sent Mariquita her passport, along with a note: "Why are you leaving?" he asked. Her response: "Because I'm scared of you, Juan Manuel."[66]

And so Mariquita moved to Montevideo, taking her youngest son, Enrique, with her. As the baby of the family, Enrique was dear to Mariquita's heart, even more so because he had always been a sickly child. Jean Baptiste visited them on his way from France to his new posting in Ecuador.

In that same year, illness also struck the family of Juan Manuel—when his loyal partner, Encarnación Ezcurra, died after a long illness. Encarnación had

FIGURE 9.8 *Portrait of Manuelita Rosas* by Prilidiano Pueyrredón (1851). Courtesy of the Museo Nacional de Bellas Artes, Buenos Aires.

been a stalwart supporter of Juan Manuel, not just in the traditional role of wife, but also as a political player who could act in her own right. Her death was a big loss to Rosas, but he compensated for it by elevating his daughter, Manuelita, to take her mother's place in his political world. Rosas claimed he needed her at his side, so much so that he forbade her from getting married, even though she was in love with Máximo Terrero, the son of one of Rosas's business partners. Manuelita honored her father's requests, and her charm had a softening effect on Rosas's policies.[67] As will be seen below, Manuelita was admired even by many of Rosas's enemies, who saw her as an unfortunate captive of her father's political machinations.

Conclusion

When Mariquita Sánchez left Buenos Aires in self-imposed exile, it served as the symbolic closing of the doors of a certain vision of Buenos Aires held by many porteños of her era—that of a modern, cosmopolitan, and liberal nation born of Enlightenment and revolution. But it was a vision that had, thus far, been out of reach for Buenos Aires and its sister provinces, even before Governor Rosas came to power. And, it was apparent, he would take his time to reconstitute the body of Argentine society with a constitution. In the meantime, he would stamp out dissent and create a culture of unanimity. Mariquita's departure also signaled the end of her influential salon that had been a cultural and political center of the port city.

CHAPTER TEN

The Rosas Regime under Fire

On this day, of all days, Mariquita Sánchez de Mendeville should have been happy. It was Saturday, May 25, 1839. Twenty-nine years earlier, in 1810, the cabildo had voted to create the first autonomous government in Buenos Aires. Mariquita had been there with her beloved Martín during all the celebration and intrigue. But instead of celebrating this day, Mariquita was depressed. She let her feelings gush out in her diary. "The 25th of May, 1839! I am all but banished from my homeland for detesting tyranny and ignorance. What a strange destiny is mine." Adding to the strangeness of that Independence Day in 1839, French forces were helping Argentine exiles plan and carry out an invasion of Buenos Aires to overthrow Governor Juan Manuel de Rosas—something the exiles called "the Great Enterprise." Mariquita understood the irony of celebrating Argentine independence and sovereignty on one hand while encouraging foreign meddling in her country on the other. Mariquita blamed everything on Juan Manuel and hoped for his speedy overthrow. "We live in a hell that tests the patience of those who work and hope, with prudence, to strengthen the Great Enterprise. How much work, how much disappointment, how many impossibilities to defeat one man!" Mariquita went on. "Oh how he has destroyed society! How much disorder, to put in order, this crusade, this veritable crusade to redeem Christian captives!"[1] While Rosas had gained some of his fame for rescuing captives, Mariquita turned the tables and accused him of kidnapping a whole nation.

Many types of disorder plagued Argentina before, during, and after 1839. Between 1833 and 1845, foreign powers encroached on Argentine territory, and Rosas's enemies applied constant pressure on his regime, launching more than one attempt to overthrow his government. At times, Mariquita was closely involved in these anti-Rosas activities. But Rosas managed to survive all threats, leaving Mariquita and thousands of others languishing in exile and wondering if the tyrant might stay in power forever.

Mariquita and the Generation of 1837

Although Mariquita was very unhappy to be in Montevideo on May 25, 1839, she was, in reality, free to travel back to Buenos Aires whenever she pleased. After all, her exile was self-imposed (Rosas had not ordered it). For example, just a few months after she left Buenos Aires initially, she returned to attend the baptism of one of her grandchildren. Mariquita's social position in the city, however, was greatly diminished because of her well-known antipathy toward Governor Rosas's regime. It was also known that her son Juan was engaged in anti-Rosas activities in Corrientes Province. Clear evidence of Mariquita's fall from favor came when her daughter Albina, who still lived in Buenos Aires, was rejected as a member of the Sociedad de Beneficencia. Members of the society, Rosas asserted, should be overt supporters of the Federalist cause, and the patriotism of Albina's extended family—namely her mother and brother—did not fit the definition of Federalist patriotism.[2]

While back in Buenos Aires, Mariquita connected with a group of young liberal intellectuals, many of whom were friends with her son Juan. These included writers, poets, and statesmen such as Esteban Echeverría, Juan Bautista Alberdi, Juan María Gutiérrez, José Mármol, and Domingo Sarmiento, among others, many of whom came of age during Rivadavia's progressive governments of the 1820s. This group, later known as the "Generation of 1837," brought the Romantic Movement to the shores of the Río de la Plata and to Latin America. They also hoped to change politics and culture in Buenos Aires and beyond, and to create a new and powerful identity for the Argentine nation.[3] They were unified by the belief that the factionalism that had characterized Argentine politics in previous decades needed to be replaced by a "regeneration" of the ideals of the May Revolution. "We are not Unitarian, nor are we Federalists," declared the group's leader, Esteban Echeverría. They wanted the warring factions in the country to follow their lead toward a bright future. Mariquita was a perfect symbol of the unrealized ideals of the May Revolution. During their years in exile, Mariquita would serve as a friend and inspiration for the group, as well as a kind of surrogate mother. At the same time, for Mariquita, this vibrant group of youths rejuvenated her connection to ideals she cherished—those of enlightenment, reform, and republicanism.

The group met frequently at a bookstore in the city center where they discussed the latest in political and cultural developments in Argentina and the world (thus receiving the name Salón Literario, or Literary Salon). Together they began publishing a newspaper called *La Moda* (The Fashion), in which they promised to deliver tasteful analysis of society and culture in Europe and Argentina. The lead story in the first edition, for example, was "The Latest French Fashions," which talked about the advantages of new furniture designs in Paris.[4] The editors openly declared support for Rosas's government. In actuality, however, they offered a qualified support. In essence, the editors of *La Moda* invited the Rosas regime, and the rest of Argentina, to follow their vision of a regenerated Argentine society. Readers did not get far in *La Moda*'s pages before encountering obvious criticisms of Rosista politics and culture. It was not long before the Salón Literario was under government surveillance.

One of *La Moda*'s main goals was to elevate women's position in society through female education, which, they asserted, was sorely lacking in the Río de la Plata. In their current state, *La Moda*'s editors asserted, women were seen as little more than pretty decorations, domestic administrators, or the providers of momentary pleasure, all of which were "far removed from the true and brilliant destiny of women."[5] The scant education available to women in the 1830s, the editors continued, only prepared them for a small fraction of their existence—that of finding a husband. For many parents, "the sole destiny" of their daughters was a "mercenary marriage" to whoever paid "the most." This, they argued, amounted to little more than a "legalized prostitution" that bound young women to men they did "not love, if not detest." Such arrangements all too often ended up badly. Therefore, women should "prepare themselves for all stages and contingencies of life." Addressing women directly, the editors concluded: "Rise up and stand alongside men in the place God has given you in the throne of Creation."[6]

Mariquita no doubt agreed with these ideas. Her work with the Sociedad de Beneficencia had focused on female education since the early 1820s. Mariquita's personal experience served as additional inspiration for the publication. After all, her parents had attempted to force her to marry a man she did not love. Mariquita's life also showed why female education was necessary. Her life was a model of how an educated woman could influence broader society. And now that the contingencies of life had taken her husband, Jean Baptiste, far away to Ecuador, Mariquita was forced to make it on her own, in essence as a single woman and mother. The editors of *La Moda* surely knew Mariquita's story and many others like it.

The thirteenth issue of *La Moda* dealt with another subject close to Mariquita's heart: cultured conversation. According to *La Moda's* editors, the quality of conversation in Buenos Aires was sorely lacking. Salons existed, to be sure, but they offered only "calculated frivolities" and an "eternal fiction of sentiment." If someone wanted to enjoy fruitful exchanges on compelling subjects like philosophy and freedom, they would be sorely disappointed by porteño salons, for "the happiness of mankind [was] not discussed there, nor the rights of the people." Sadly, their meditations were consumed "only by little white clouds that beautify the heavens!" All these problems could be solved, the editors affirmed, by women—the "beautiful sex"—if they were properly educated. The earth would then turn into an "immense paradise" when women learned "to encircle the soul of Brutus with the graces of Cleopatra."[7] This was a call for a regeneration of the ideals that Mariquita had incorporated into her own salon in its heyday: educated women needed to promote better conversation—better sociability—and thus better morality in society.[8]

Although *La Moda* couched this and other arguments in generic reformist language, it was clear that its editors despised certain elements of culture in Rosas's Buenos Aires. The subject was all the more sensitive because Rosas's daughter, Manuelita, hosted a prominent salon of her own. Was Manuelita the sponsor of mere frivolities? Whether or not Rosas saw things that way, his tolerance was waning for the wit, satire, and thinly veiled criticism of *La Moda*. The paper was shut down after its twenty-third issue.

After Governor Rosas's crackdown on the paper, many members of the Salón Literario began to leave Buenos Aires. Before they did, Esteban Echeverría reorganized them into a group called La Joven Generación Argentina (the Young Argentine Generation). The group committed itself, in an eloquent oath composed by Echeverría, to promote the ideals and promises of the May Revolution of 1810, including association, progress, fraternity, Christianity, freedom from backward traditions, and the emancipation of the "American spirit." Juan Bautista Alberdi left for Montevideo (as did others). José Mármol landed in jail for a short while before heading to Montevideo as well. Others went to interior provinces of the country. Esteban Echeverría, for the time being, felt safe at his brother's ranch a few miles outside of Buenos Aires. Mariquita herself would soon return to Montevideo, where she would entertain many of the members of the Young Generation in her home or maintain contact with them through letters. Indeed, letters to and from friends and family became Mariquita's life-line—especially her letters to her daughter Florencia Lezica.

The Malaise of Exile in Montevideo, the "New Troy"

Although Montevideo was a refuge for Mariquita, it was the troubled capital of a troubled country. Because Montevideo served as a safe haven for exiles, and because it was such a thorn in Rosas's side for so many years, the context of the city deserves a bit of explanation.

After its independence in 1828, Uruguay suffered bitter factionalism that paralleled the divisions in Argentina. By 1838, two men claimed the presidency of Uruguay at the same time: the more conservative Manuel Oribe, and the more liberal Fructuoso Rivera. By the early 1840s, Oribe controlled much of the countryside while Rivera controlled Montevideo, where Mariquita and many other exiles lived. Juan Manuel de Rosas dreamt of overthrowing the city using Manuel Oribe's armies, thus destroying the cradle of his enemies. By 1842, Oribe's armies had laid siege to Montevideo, Rivera's stronghold. Meanwhile, Governor Rosas's navy blockaded the port of Montevideo as well. More than ever before, the residents of the city felt like they lived on an island of freedom. Montevideo gained a reputation in these years of being just that: an outpost of liberty fighting against the tyranny of Rosas, as well as the tyranny of the European powers that supported him. As such, Montevideo attracted numerous exiles from around the Atlantic World. One of the more famous of these was Giuseppe Garibaldi, the Italian freedom fighter who was exiled to the Americas in the late 1830s. After spending some time in Brazil, Garibaldi came to Montevideo in 1842 and soon organized a fighting force of volunteers, the Italian Legion, to fight against Oribe's forces.[9] Because it was so besieged on all sides, Montevideo came to be known by many as the "New Troy."[10]

Life in Montevideo was not easy for Mariquita, especially because most of her family was elsewhere. Her husband, Jean Baptiste, was at his new post in Ecuador, and Mariquita never joined him. Her oldest son, Juan Thompson, was in Corrientes, a province that had opposed the regime since the late 1830s, and he would soon move to Europe.[11] Her oldest daughter, Clementina, had married a Frenchman and moved to France, never to return to Argentina, while her daughters Florencia and Albina remained in Buenos Aires. Julio and Carlos Mendeville were back and forth to school in Europe. So Mariquita came to Montevideo with only her youngest son, the charming but sickly Enrique.

Enrique's ill health continued in Uruguay. Jean Baptiste stopped by to visit his family on his way to Ecuador, perhaps not knowing that it would be the last time he would see his son. Enrique died on April 18, 1838, leaving his mother and the rest of the family "swallowed up in the most profound sadness." Enrique had the sweetest of dispositions, wrote Mariquita's son-in-law, and although Enrique had been sick for years, no one could reconcile with his passing. "Destiny has shattered the hope of a loving mother," Mariquita's son-in-law continued. "Only time can alleviate the pain."[12] That time was long in coming, if it ever did. On the anniversary of Enrique's death a year later, Mariquita could barely say anything in her diary. "I don't have strength even to write."[13]

Enrique's death intensified her loneliness and increased her desire to return to Buenos Aires, but a Buenos Aires without the tyrant Juan Manuel in the governor's house. Ironically, the governor's brother Gervasio was in Montevideo. "He is the opposite of his brother," Mariquita wrote to her son Juan Thompson, and although Gervasio Rosas was not mixed up in the revolt, "he openly disapproves of his brother's system." For Mariquita, Gervasio Rosas's disaffection with his brother symbolized how the Rosas regime had become an embarrassment to Argentina and an insult to humanity. "What a picture of horrors and crimes these lands present to the philanthropic philosopher who sees only brothers in the human race!"[14]

Rosas's Time of Troubles: Juan Lavalle and the French

Part of the "picture of horrors" Mariquita referred to was a vicious cycle of violence that plagued the Río de la Plata. Liberal Federalists and exiled Unitarians despised Rosas's authoritarian ways and disapproved of the extraordinary powers granted him by the Buenos Aires legislature. Rosas, in turn, repressed dissent, enforced unanimity, and exiled or killed his most outspoken enemies. From exile, his opponents, in word and deed, constantly harassed Rosas for his authoritarianism and also planned and staged rebellions of various kinds. In reaction, Rosas intensified his repression with each hint of conspiracy and intrigue. Thus the cycle of violence went on, each side blaming the other. Rosas's reactions got even more intense when his opponents teamed up with foreign powers, and that is exactly what happened in 1838 with France.

Old disputes—the same ones Jean Baptiste de Mendeville faced as consul—continued to plague Franco-Argentine relations. In 1838, France still sought to sign a treaty of friendship and commerce with Rosas, an agreement that among other things would provide more trade opportunities and give French citizens more protection. Rosas had rebuffed French advances throughout the 1830s. With Rosas facing civil unrest and a possible conflict with Bolivia, foreign residents were again coerced into armed service. French consul Aimeé Roger demanded that Rosas stop forcing Frenchmen into the local militias. When Rosas refused, Consul Roger called in the navy. Admiral Leclerc soon arrived and ordered Rosas to abolish the forced recruitment of French citizens and grant France most-favored-nation status. When Rosas again refused, Admiral Leclerc blockaded the port of Buenos Aires in late March of 1838. Soon thereafter French forces also occupied Martín García Island in the middle of the Río de la Plata.

Patriotic Argentines, even many who opposed Rosas, could not ignore France's violation of Argentine sovereignty. Even Juan Lavalle himself felt a nationalistic fervor when he heard news of the French action. But Lavalle also wanted to overthrow Rosas, and in the end he decided that French intervention was a necessary evil, one that might help rid Buenos Aires of the greater evil of Rosas's regime. Lavalle and the exiles in Montevideo and elsewhere saw the French intervention, and the disaffection it was causing in Buenos Aires, as an opportunity to challenge Rosas. Lavalle began formulating a plan to build an army in Uruguay that would, with French logistical support, invade Buenos Aires and defeat Rosas. The invasion would be aided by a simultaneous anti-Rosas uprising in the city of Buenos Aires, as well as a rebellion in the countryside south of the city, where many ranchers were hurt by the French blockade. French officials responded favorably to Lavalle's plan and began supporting the rebels, seeing it as an opportunity to get rid of Rosas and thus challenge British dominance in the region. On paper, this coordinated, three-pronged rebellion, supported as it was by French forces, looked formidable, and it boosted Mariquita's hopes that she would soon return home for good.

Governor Rosas was quick to invoke national honor and sovereignty in the face of French intervention. He also argued that the sovereignty and honor of all Spanish America was at stake. In a letter to the governor of Corrientes, Genaro Berón de Astrada, Rosas was clear: by working together, the provinces could be truly free. Resisting French imperialism would give Argentina international respect and would prevent it from becoming a slave to foreign interests. If they defended their "sacred oath of liberty," their bravery would be recorded in the "illustrious pages of American history." On the other hand, Rosas continued, if the confederation caved in to foreign pressure, the sovereignty of all the Americas would be in jeopardy, and Argentina "would be cursed by the free peoples of the world, especially the American republics." "I am firmly resolved," Rosas concluded, "not to retract one word you have seen in my letter."[15]

Rosas pointed to French aggression elsewhere in Spanish America to illustrate his arguments. In 1838 France was supporting Bolivia in disputes against Argentina and Chile, and there was at least one proposal by a governor of Córdoba to defeat Rosas by partitioning the country and creating a new nation under French protection. French misdeeds were even more evident in Mexico. In 1838 French warships appeared off the coast of Veracruz and demanded 600,000 pesos of reparations payments for past injuries to French property, including a French chef's claim that his pastries had been stolen by Mexican soldiers nine years earlier. When Mexico did not comply, the French bombarded the fortress of San Juan de Ullúa in Veracruz, then landed troops in what became known as the "Pastry War." General Santa Anna, of Alamo fame, led part of the resistance to the French advance, losing his leg to French cannon fire.[16] For Rosas and his government, the Pastry War in Mexico, French intrigue in Bolivia, and their blockade of Buenos Aires showed France's malevolent imperial designs in the hemisphere and beyond.

FRANCE IN THE AMERICAS

Rosas was correct in many respects. France was indeed bent on extending its influence in Spanish America, part of its attempt to revive French power across the globe. In the 1830s, for instance, French troops were in the process of conquering Algeria in North Africa. And by the time the French bombarded Veracruz and blockaded Buenos Aires in 1838, some French thinkers had begun referring to Spanish America as "Latin America," putting it in the same linguistic and cultural family as other Latin-speaking countries of Europe.[17] Because France styled itself as the enlightened and benevolent leader of all Latin peoples, it claimed the right to assert its influence over Latin America. But for Rosas and his supporters, whether in Veracruz or Buenos Aires, French intervention was far from justified or benevolent, and they did their best to expose French abuses in the media and in official communications.

French officials, meanwhile, tried to deflect accusations of being an evil empire. They attempted to communicate their benevolent intentions, at least to their allies in Montevideo, during the anniversary of the May Revolution in 1839. Mariquita, in tune as usual with the latest developments, knew in advance what the French were planning. "Tomorrow the French squadron will salute the Argentine flag," she wrote in her journal on May 24, 1839. "This order has been given to show this is a war only against Rosas" and not against the Argentine people.[18] The next day, as planned, French warships anchored off Montevideo saluted the Argentine flag. Writing in her diary later that day, Mariquita reflected on the sovereignty dilemma. "The French ships have raised the Argentine flag on the highest mast and saluted it with a cannonade. What a strange sensation for thoughtful Argentines! What things could be said! It is an anomaly for some. It is a beautiful demonstration that [Argentine] independence is not being attacked. Each person sees this according to their own ideas."[19]

Mariquita herself was one of those "thoughtful Argentines" who could see the French intervention from a variety of perspectives. One example was her reaction to the news that France and Mexico had signed a treaty ending the brief Pastry War. In her diary, Mariquita analyzed the whole situation with a bit of patriotic sarcasm. "News from North America has arrived. All has been resolved. Mexican honor is satisfied, after seeing their beautiful castle (worth millions) demolished, after losing all their magnificent artillery, and having to pay 600,000 pesos of indemnification."[20] France came, saw, bombarded and destroyed, and collected money, and all was now supposedly well. This was Mariquita, the American patriot, criticizing an abuse of power.

Two days later, however, Mariquita's political preferences of the moment spurred her to revise her assessment of French actions in Mexico. "A treaty has been signed and all is concluded. The destroyed castle has been returned to its ancient owners, and those who have endeavored to portray the French as conquistadores will have to come up with something new."[21] Thus Mariquita experienced what Juan Lavalle and many others did as well: patriotic indignation toward foreign intervention, but an indignation trumped ultimately by their anti-Rosas sentiment.

Across the river in Buenos Aires, Rosas fumed at what he saw as the exiles' treasonous collaboration with France. The porteño press followed his lead. One porteño newspaper referred to Mariquita, insultingly, as "Madame" Mendeville. She had been called that before as the wife of the French consul, but in the Buenos Aires of 1839, blockaded as it was by the French navy and threatened with a French-backed invasion, "Madame" was meant as a slur. But when Mariquita heard about the article, she embraced the label with relish. "I don't know this enemy that has given me the name Madame to show my Frenchification. How happy I'd be if all they find out is that I deserve this title!"[22]

MARIQUITA GRAPPLES WITH FREEDOM'S BIRTHRIGHT

While Mariquita embraced French aid, she criticized the United States and Great Britain for supporting Rosas. The Americans, she argued, erred by accepting "the old and discredited opinion that this country is not mature enough for a liberal government."[23] In that statement Mariquita implied that freedom belonged to Argentines as well and was not something only Europeans and Americans could enjoy. Mariquita was thus grappling with one of the greatest problems of the Age of Revolution: How much liberty, in actuality, can be enjoyed by a particular society? And who makes those decisions? As seen above, Simón Bolívar had labored over this same question, declaring in 1819 that freedom "is a succulent food that is hard to digest."[24] Bolívar gleaned part of that principle from one of his favorite authors, Jean-Jacques Rousseau, who argued in *The Social Contract* that true freedom and liberty were not equally accessible to all people. "Liberty, not being a fruit of all climates, is not within the reach of all peoples."[25] Mariquita refused to accept the notion, implied by British and American policies, that Rosas's tyranny was the only way Buenos Aires could be governed at the moment. Juan Manuel perhaps embraced it too wholeheartedly.

In a note to Echeverría, Mariquita did not hide her suspicion that old-fashioned greed motivated foreign support of Rosas (something she called "interest"). "What power interest has over nations and individuals—a sad reflection for the two of us, not rich, but without self-interest."[26] Mariquita also noted the irony when an English diplomat urged Uruguayan authorities to suppress the slave trade on the one hand while British officials supported Rosas's tyranny on the other. British policy, she concluded cynically, means that "the slaves are freed and the whites enslaved!"[27]

Mariquita's son Juan Thompson was even more critical of British support for the Rosas regime. The British supported Rosas, Juan believed, because Rosas's policies favored British interests not only in Argentina but also on a global scale. "Many say that England would in no way prefer this kind of government," Juan wrote in his journal in 1838. "Wrong, Wrong. It benefits [England] to have no factories other than their own, and that the peoples of the South America do not progress in areas where English commerce has a strong foothold." For Thompson, English policy toward South America was clear: "Self interest, vile self interest."[28] What England feared, Thompson continued, was that France would take advantage of the current situation to gain influence in the Río de la Plata. But like his mother, Juan Thompson welcomed French influence. France had a lot to offer new countries, especially the "love of liberty." England, on the other hand, wanted only to extract "gold and all kinds of other products." However, Juan Thompson understood that France could not risk too much in the Río de la Plata because it had other imperial concerns to consider in North Africa, where France had just conquered Algeria a few year earlier. If France and England went to war over their differences in Argentina, France might risk losing "fertile Algeria," because it would be impossible for France to fight on two fronts. As Thompson wrote in his journal, to understand the present situation in the Río de la Plata, it would be "extremely useful to know the current state of politics in Europe."[29] For Juan Thompson, France's intervention against Rosas in the Río de la Plata and its conquest of Algeria were both examples of France's love of liberty.

Mariquita's Hope and Frustration

Mariquita's hope for the success of Lavalle's army was also mixed with frustration and cynicism. Mariquita kept her finger on the pulse of exile activity. She attended meetings, received daily reports, and read British and French newspapers. But the turbulence of life in Montevideo, and the unpredictable political situation, could make life very confusing. Montevideo was a "veritable tower of Babel," she confided to her diary.[30] "Here there is much waiting. . . . No one says anything. No one asks anything. Deaf noise, revolution, mystery, desire, and fear are the order of the holy day."[31]

While France was a backdrop of great-power support, on the ground in Montevideo it was General Juan Lavalle that symbolized their liberation. "I have seen Lavalle, and I have great hope for what is to come," Mariquita wrote in her diary on April 25, 1839. Mariquita was present at a meeting between Lavalle and other leaders of the resistance. "I looked at that group of men, aged more by adversity than by time, and I thought in silence what many of them might be saying: 'after so much effort, we have to begin again to conquer our country and our liberty.'" For Mariquita, the Lavalle family represented true civilization. The general and his wife had four children, two boys and two girls, all of whom were "good looking" in Mariquita's estimation. "When I find a family that can play a role and influence civilization, my heart finds repose, in the same way that it is tired of all the torments of barbarism." There are "a thousand little things" that set the Lavalles apart, and meeting them "brings an inexplicable pleasure to those that feel it." Mariquita could hardly bear to think of the discrepancy between the societies and cultures on each side of the river. As she gazed at Lavalle, his family, and the other exiles, she could not help but remember Rosas's buffoon Eusebio and the other crazies back in Buenos Aires. "Oh, what pain, what torment, my friend, is the brutish and harsh society to one whose heart has long been sensitive and accustomed to the sweetness of refined culture."[32]

If Lavalle was the great Argentine hope, Mariquita also recognized that French support was key to any liberation attempt. For Mariquita, France had always represented philanthropic philosophy and universal brotherhood. It was the land of civilization, the land of polite conversation where women and men of goodwill would gather and speak of the finer things of life. Now, in the Río de la Plata, France was lending its military might to the cause of civilization. "France is the only thing that supports our hope to conquer liberty," she confided to her diary in June. And as for the Argentines who have been wary of France, they are now "becoming convinced that only at [France's] side can they find real help in the grand enterprise."[33] Even General Lavalle himself admitted: "Were it not for the French, we would not have anything to eat."[34]

Despite French support to the exiles, key aspects of Lavalle's strategy began to fall apart. One problem was that plans for the uprising against Rosas were never kept very secret. In fact, Rosas had known about them for a while. Many months earlier, in August of 1838, Juan Thompson wrote in his journal: "Rumors have spread that the revolution has been discovered."[35] Those rumors were true. Rosas was aware of the plans, but allowed them to proceed for the time being so as to expose as many conspirators as possible. Rosas soon learned that the leader of the conspiracy in Buenos Aires was Colonel Ramón Maza, the son of one of Rosas's close friends, Manuel Maza, who was also the president of the Buenos Aires provincial legislature. In late June 1839, Rosas ordered Ramón Maza's arrest. When the word of the conspiracy began to spread, vigilantes also jumped into action. That very night members of the Mazorca converged on the congress building and, cornering the elderly Maza in his office, murdered him at his desk. The younger Maza died at the hands of a firing squad the next day. A few months later, in November, Rosas also defeated the uprising of disgruntled ranchers in the southern part of the province—the "Libres del Sur" rebellion.[36]

Juan Lavalle's Invasion

In spite of these major setbacks, General Lavalle finally launched his invasion in January of 1840. Instead of following his original plan of attacking Buenos Aires, Lavalle decided to move first against Corrientes Province before challenging Rosas in Buenos Aires. Mariquita's hopes ran high as the invasion began. But along with hope came trepidation. Waiting nervously for news of Lavalle's invasion, Mariquita wrote to her son Juan. "Here we are awaiting the political Messiah, more anxious than those who waited for Him." Amid hopes for salvation, Mariquita also observed a general "sadness and discouragement" in the exile community.[37] That was not news to Juan, who for months had detected disillusion. "Despite the strong support of the French," he recorded in his journal, "I see my countrymen asleep. The effects of the despotic yoke are more fatal to the spirit of a people than opium in its largest dose."[38]

When news of Lavalle did arrive, it was disappointing. His actions in Corrientes proved to be a stalemate, and Lavalle and his men boarded French vessels and headed downriver to Buenos Aires. Lavalle marched his force to the outskirts of Buenos Aires, hoping to spark a popular uprising against Rosas. Some residents joined Lavalle's force eagerly. Among them was Esteban Echeverría, who had been living quietly on his brother's ranch near the city. However, the popular uprising against Rosas never materialized, and Lavalle decided to pull his forces out of the province. Echeverría and many others were forced to flee as Rosas's soldiers began taking revenge on any who collaborated with the invasion. Echeverría made his way to the river where he boarded a French ship that took him to Uruguay.

Not long after leaving Buenos Aires, Echeverría penned a poignant description of what it meant to be exiled.

Nothing is more sad than to emigrate! . . . To be violently forced to leave one's country, without time to think except of how to save oneself from the grasp of tyranny, leaving behind family and friends under its yoke; and furthermore, the country mutilated and bloodied by a band of assassins, such is a real death-sentence, a storm that no one can comprehend without suffering it themselves. . . . Emigration is death; we die for our loved ones, we die for our country, because we can do nothing for them.[39]

Mariquita may well have answered those sentiments in the postscript to her diary, which she dedicated to Echeverría: "You may cry, perhaps, and console yourself with the thought that, even though we are so unhappy, our brothers in other parts of the world are loving one another and enjoying the fruits of civilization." Even as the exiles deplored, as Mariquita put it, "the events that have separated us from that civilization," they still held on to hope for a future day when men would be "created here as they are there, as children of the kingdom of God." Mariquita could hardly bring herself to dream. "When might that day come, my friend? I don't know. I fear the civil war will not end with us. The resentment and hate have such deep roots."[40]

The Terror

Rosas, as usual, reacted to threats against him with swift and brutal energy. His response this time was even greater because it was a combined domestic and foreign threat. His immediate orders were to capture and kill those who allied with Lavalle, "sweeping them as with a broom," so that the whole province would be purged of "savage and godless" Unitarians. Rosas also ordered that "all their possessions, lands, and cattle be confiscated and given to faithful Federalists." Thus everything Echeverría left behind was taken away. He especially lamented the loss of his guitar and his books, especially "those chosen ones I brought from France."[41]

Besides eliminating the specific threats to his regime, Rosas unleashed a wave of violence that came to be known as "The Terror." Rosas and his agents made lists of enemies that would be targeted. Nevertheless, many decisions were made without much due process, as Rosas frequently acted as judge, authorized as he was to exercise the plenitude of public power. Rosas's anger only intensified when, in 1841, a package arrived for him at his home in Palermo. Manuelita opened it only to discover an elaborate device designed to explode when opened. Fortunately for Manuelita, the "infernal machine" did not go off.[42] In this tense environment, the Mazorca jumped into action and committed a variety of nocturnal assassinations, beatings, and intimidations. Over the next few years, especially during times of political crisis, the Mazorca murdered an estimated eighty individuals, although the actual number is likely higher.[43] And the psychological effect of these killings was also surely greater than their numbers. But it was not indiscriminate killing. As one biographer put it, Rosas's "cruelty had its chronology." State violence reached its peak during the times when the regime was most threatened by external and internal forces, most notably between 1838 and 1842, during the French blockade and Lavalle's invasion.[44] As far as total numbers killed by the regime, Rosas's government reported 500 executions between 1829 and 1843, while his opponents claimed a total of nearly 6,000 for the same period, including over 3,700 having their throats cut. Later estimates put the number of executions at just over 2,000.[45]

Even being suspected of possible Unitarian sympathies could put someone in mortal danger. Such was the case of Tomás Martínez, who was baffled that his name came up as a Unitarian sympathizer, something he strongly denied. Martínez feared for his life and considered fleeing to Montevideo. He turned for help to his friend Tomás de Anchorena, who was also Rosas's cousin. Anchorena obliged and wrote Rosas a letter, asking if Martínez could be exonerated from any association with anti-Rosistas. "As far as I am concerned," Rosas wrote in answer to his cousin, "there is no problem with Tomás Martínez leaving for Montevideo. . . . He is the one who needs to decide what suits him best." The governor then added a menacing observation: "Cousin, I perceive at this time a great irritation against the savage Unitarians, and above all against foreigners. Who knows what will become of this country, and all of its inhabitants, both good and evil, if God carries out his punishment?" And while Mr. Martínez might not be a savage Unitarian, Rosas doubted if even he could convince Martínez's accusers otherwise. Perhaps it was better that he did go into exile, Rosas concluded. And when Martínez returns, "we shall see if something can be done so that he is not considered a suspect."[46] In these statements, Rosas admits that, at this particular time in Buenos Aires, death could await even those erroneously accused of being Unitarian sympathizers. And, at this moment, the governor was not going to do much to change things.

Peace with France and the End of Lavalle

Even as Rosista agents crushed rebellions and repressed dissent, Rosas pursued a diplomatic solution to his problem—at least the *French* portion of his problem. By 1840, France was ready for a diplomatic resolution as well. A number of French diplomats, including Admiral Mackau, traveled to Buenos Aires to negotiate with Rosista authorities. Rosas made sure the French were well treated—arranging for his daughter Manuelita to help host the group initially. The outcome of the negotiations was the Mackau-Arana Treaty, which ended the French blockade and granted France the commercial treaty it had sought the last fifteen years. Rosas happily reported the outcome of the negotiations to a friend on November 6, 1840. "Vice admiral Mackau is coming to see me. I am heading to the city to receive this courtesy, to congratulate him, embrace him." The good feelings between them, Rosas continued, "cannot be explained." In the meantime, Rosas busied himself getting ready to receive the transfer of Martín García Island, which the French had occupied for the last many months.[47]

General Lavalle was now in dire straits. Abandoned by France, and suffering from desertions among his own ranks, Lavalle beat a steady retreat northward, hoping to join the Coalition of the North—a group of provinces that declared opposition to Rosas. One night in La Rioja Province, Federalist soldiers approached the house where Lavalle was hiding and sprayed it with gunfire. Lavalle suffered a mortal wound and died a few hours later. His supporters managed to escape with his body and flee toward Bolivia, with Federalist forces in hot pursuit. With the body rotting, Lavalle's men decided to remove the flesh from the bones, and various parts of his body were buried in Argentina and Bolivia.[48]

Lavalle's failed invasion and Governor Rosas's peace with France combined to leave exiles in Montevideo and elsewhere disconsolate. Mariquita reflected on the state of affairs in a letter. "I am not a strong woman, and I'm sick and tired of my bad luck," she wrote her daughter Florencia. "It could be pride on my part, but I think I deserved many things that didn't turn out for me in life, and the constant pain, with only myself to comfort me, is wearing me down."[49]

If Domingo Sarmiento was disillusioned, he hid it behind a wall of anger and in volumes of anti-Rosas diatribes. Writing in 1842 from his exile in Chile, Sarmiento tried to put a positive (and anti-Rosas) spin on the current situation. In the Chilean newspaper *Mercurio*, Sarmiento noted that Rosas was again facing one of his crises, "which [threatened] him periodically each year," and from which he could only escape by cutting throats and shedding torrents of blood. Sarmiento latter added that although "Free men have been defeated a thousand times" by Rosas, not once has "the tyrant been able to rest freely." And despite all of his power, Sarmiento concluded, Rosas's position is "as precarious as it has been in ten years."[50]

While for Sarmiento those words signified his and others' courageous perseverance, Juan Manuel de Rosas could read those same lines and see them as a kind of confession: Sarmiento and his fellow exiles admitted, openly and defiantly, that they had never left Rosas's government in peace for even a moment, even though he had been appointed by the legislature, and even though his election had been validated by a plebiscite. Sarmiento boasted that Rosas's government faced constant conspiracies, some backed by foreign powers. Governor Rosas and his supporters highlighted this and other kinds of opposition as part of an ongoing conspiracy against his republic.[51] What other choice did he have as governor but to strike fast and hard to protect his government and the country against these constant threats? And the threats continued.

Trade, Commerce, and Foreign Intervention

Even as the menace of Lavalle's invasion receded, an old conflict resurfaced that gave exiles renewed hope. At issue was the freedom to navigate and trade on the Paraná River, which was navigable from the mouth of the Río de la Plata all the way to Paraguay. Since the early days of independence, officials in Buenos Aires had maintained that Buenos Aires possessed the right to control the river trade that passed by its borders—policies that Rosas continued to enforce. As economies in the region grew, other provinces increased their protests of Buenos Aires's stranglehold on river commerce.[52] Brazil, Paraguay, and Uruguay were also affected by these policies. The province of Corrientes, bordered on the west and east by the Paraná and Uruguay Rivers respectively, was particularly perturbed by Buenos Aires's claims. Since the late 1830s, Corrientes had often opposed Rosas, and then in 1844, Corrientes officially declared a trade war against Buenos Aires Province.[53] Meanwhile, the exile community tried to turn another provincial leader against Rosas. Justo José Urquiza, the Federalist governor of Entre Ríos, was becoming powerful enough, many believed, to challenge Rosas for national leadership. For the time being, however, Urquiza resisted these overtures and remained loyal to Rosas.

England and France were also hoping for a change in the politics of river trade. Although Rosas was friendly to British interests and had recently made peace with France, foreign merchants still saw Rosas's control of river trade as detrimental to commercial development. In addition, Rosas's constant meddling in Uruguayan affairs also disrupted trade in the larger region. The Empire of Brazil also resented Rosas's constant interventions in Uruguay. In short, Rosas was seen by many as a disruptor and an impediment to economic growth in the whole Río de la Plata. Exiles took advantage of this dissatisfaction and lobbied England and France for another round of interventions against the Rosas regime.

England and France were already considering the situation as an opportunity to expand their share of trade in the region. In early 1845, French and British officials in Buenos Aires presented Rosas with some demands if he wanted to avoid European intervention: Rosas needed to evacuate his forces from Uruguayan territory and lift his naval blockade of Montevideo.[54] Rosas, unsurprisingly, rejected the demands. In response, British forces attacked the Argentine ships blockading Montevideo, and British soldiers occupied the city of Colonia, Uruguay, as well as Martín García Island. England and France also began amassing a fleet, including steam-powered warships, capable of forcing its way up the Paraná River—1400 miles from Buenos Aires to Asunción, Paraguay.

Despite these setbacks, Rosas and his ministers believed they could ultimately withstand the Anglo-French intervention. The British and French navies were powerful, but they would be unable to control every city up and down the river, much less the countryside surrounding those cities. Even if the Europeans blockaded ports along the river, those cities could easily resupply with the bounties of the interior. Thus, Rosas concluded, any foreign occupation along the river would be ineffective. Rosas was also convinced that the British and French had no stomach for a large-scale war or occupation. This conviction derived from a simple truth that Rosas expressed to his ministers: overall commerce would suffer "along with the majority of English and French commerce."[55] In his calculations, the British would not tolerate that scenario very long.

Rosas initiated various plans to impede and harass the invaders. Rock-filled boats were sunk in the main channels of the Paraná River to obstruct the passage of warships. Rosas also created a new army division to defend the river, commanded by his brother-in-law, Lucio Norberto Mansilla (father of the younger Lucio who wrote so much about Rosas). General Mansilla supervised the fortification of strategic spots along the Paraná River, from which Argentine forces could shell passing ships. One of the key defense points was a place called the Vuelta de Obligado, located on a pronounced bend in the river about a hundred miles from Buenos Aires. At Obligado, General Mansilla placed numerous cannons as well as a regiment of soldiers.

Rosas also engaged in a war of words against the Anglo-French intervention. Just as he did in 1839, Rosas and his ministers portrayed the current action as a threat not only to Argentine sovereignty, but to the sovereignty of all America. In August of 1845, Defense Minister Arana asked the other provinces for help "in defense of the independence of the American continent."[56] A few weeks later, *La Gaceta Mercantil* stated that "America" would rise up to defend its "independence and safety."[57] Rosas and his ministers knew that threats to Spanish American sovereignty in the hemisphere were real in 1845. Mexico, at that very moment, was being pressured by the United States of America to sell all of California and to concede the United States' annexation of Texas, which

Mexico still viewed as a rebel state (an issue that would spark war between the two neighbors only a few months later). The Age of Imperialism was far from over in the Americas.

By mid-November, an English and French fleet was ready to head upriver. The force consisted of a number of traditional warships as well as heavily armed paddleboats with steam engines. Dozens of merchant ships also accompanied the fleet, eager to cash in on the promise of new trading opportunities.

The Battle of Obligado, November 20, 1845

By November 18, the Anglo-French fleet had sailed one hundred miles upriver, unopposed. Knowing of the concentration of forces at the Vuelta de Obligado, the vessels anchored three miles below the fort while commanders drew up final battle plans. The forts at Obligado, they knew, had substantial artillery and numerous soldiers. The British also learned that the Argentines had spread heavy chains across the river, held up by a line of boats anchored in the river.

Meanwhile, the Argentines made their own preparations. General Mansilla gave a rousing speech to his men. "Look at them, comrades, there they are!" The foreign invaders, he asserted, are an "insult to our national sovereignty." He challenged his men to resist using the "burning enthusiasm of liberty. Let the cannons sound!" He then pointed to the flag flying above the fortress. "Our first duty is to die, every one of us, before seeing it brought down."[58]

At 8:30 a.m. on November 20, the Anglo-French fleet began its push toward the Argentine positions. As soon as the first vessels came within range (about nine hundred yards), Mansilla's guns unleashed furious cannonades. The shots hit the fleet like a hailstorm. Cannonballs battered hulls, shattered rigging, and shredded sails. Only moments into the battle, a thirty-two-pound ball decapitated an English officer. The French ship *San Martín* took particularly heavy fire and was forced to retreat downriver. The British and French returned fire as best they could. At noon, a group of British armorers and a blacksmith rowed up to the chains spanning the river and cut out a large section. Two paddleboats steamed through, anchored a few hundred yards upriver, and began shelling Argentine positions. At about 5:00 p.m., after nearly seven hours of dueling cannon fire, the English deployed a landing party that began scaling the cliffs to the forts. After a brief skirmish, the Argentines withdrew and the British took control of the whole area.[59]

FIGURE 10.2 *Battle of Obligado*. The Anglo-French fleet confronts Argentine forces in 1845. Courtesy of the Museo Histórico Nacional, Buenos Aires.

After the Battle of Obligado, convoys of ships headed upriver toward Asunción, Paraguay, finding pockets of resistance along the way. British officer Astley Cooper Key, who commanded the British ship *Fanny*, told his mother all about the battle in a letter. "Again it has pleased Providence to watch over me in the midst of danger! Would that I deserved it!" Although we were expecting Argentine resistance, Key continued, "we found much more than we expected." Only one person on his boat was wounded, he told his mother—"*your boy*." Key had sustained a "trifling" injury to his ankle when a chain cable was shot away. Other boats were not as lucky. The battered French vessel *San Martín* lost thirty-five men dead out of a crew of one hundred. Key estimated British and French losses at a little less than a hundred. The Argentines, he figured, lost many more.[60]

News of the battle soon reached Buenos Aires. "Argentine territory has been attacked by Anglo-French forces," the *Gaceta Mercantil* announced a few days later. In eight hours of battle, General Mansilla and his men displayed heroically that the Argentines were "firmly committed to defend their independence and their honor." Remarkably, the *Gaceta Mercantil* also praised the invaders for their honorable conduct after their victory, an indication that Rosas was leaving the door open for a diplomatic resolution to the conflict. The paper reported that Anglo-French forces did not engage in any pillaging and respected homes and businesses wherever they went.[61]

Reports of Argentina's resistance also spread throughout the Americas and across the Atlantic. British officials in London wondered how long, and how hard, Rosas would resist. They reached out to the exiled general San Martín for his opinion on the matter. San Martín answered on December 28, 1845. His "deepest conviction" was that the intervention would ultimately fail. He explained why: Rosas was too stubborn to give in to foreign pressure, and he was too popular with the people. "All the people will unite and take active part in the fight," San Martín concluded.[62] Though this was not the answer British officials were hoping for, San Martín's belief that Argentines would resist likely conjured up memories of the failed English invasions of 1806 and 1807. In particular, diligent British policy makers surely heard echoes of General Whitelocke, the British commander during the second invasion, who declared that Buenos Aires could never be subdued.

Two weeks later San Martín wrote another letter, this one to Governor Rosas himself, in which the Liberator passed judgment on the whole enterprise. The intervention was a "patently unjust aggression and abuse of power by England and France." Were it not for his ill health, San Martín added, he would have offered his services in defense of his country so that Argentina would know that "it still [had] an old defender of its honor and independence."[63]

The Anglo-French Intervention and the Monroe Doctrine

The Anglo-French incursion also caught the attention of the United States of America. The Monroe Doctrine of 1823 warned European powers against interference in the Western Hemisphere.[64] One group of senators wanted the United States to invoke the Monroe Doctrine and vigorously oppose the Anglo-French actions. Senator John Calhoun, however, issued a strong rebuttal to the idea. Although Calhoun believed that the Anglo-French intervention was an outrageous abuse of power, he did not believe that the United States could take the responsibility to protect the "whole family of American states."[65] Calhoun's position mirrored that of President Polk, who, in 1845, was too preoccupied with his plans to expand into the Mexican territories of Texas and California to consider any action in the southern hemisphere. Nor did President Polk want to upset the British precisely when he was negotiating with them regarding the boundary of the Oregon Territory.[66] The Monroe Doctrine would not save Buenos Aires in 1845, just as it did not save the Malvinas Islands in 1833.

Back in Argentina, just as San Martín predicted, Rosas refused to cave in. Even though the Anglo-French fleet was victorious at Obligado on November 20, Rosas simply set up cannons at other locations along the river. Over the next many months, Argentine artillery units fired on as many unauthorized vessels on the river as they could. The British continued to suffer losses. The guns placed near the city of San Lorenzo were particularly deadly. In early 1846, for example, the cannons of San Lorenzo shot up the British steamer *Lizard*, killing four men, including two officers. At about the same time, another British schooner attempted to sneak past San Lorenzo during the night but ran aground on one of the many sandbars dotting the river. The captain tried all night to push off the bar but failed. When the breaking dawn revealed his predicament, the Argentines opened fire. The captain and crew hastily abandoned ship and escaped in rowboats, leaving behind guns, ammunition, mailbags, and, most importantly, the British colors—all fine prizes for the Argentines, and humiliating losses for the British.[67]

More than six months after the Battle of Obligado, Argentine forces were still inflicting damage on British and French shipping along the river, and no end appeared in sight. Rosas seemed determined to continue such harassment, apparently unconcerned about the ongoing blockade of Buenos Aires. The city and province could provide all of their basic needs from the bounties of the Pampas while the British and French merchants suffered heavy losses. Rosas pointed this out by politely offering to supply meat to British residents in Buenos Aires during the British naval blockade of the city.

And so it was that after many months of such harassment by Argentine forces, the British and French began peace talks with Rosista officials. Negotiations dragged on for months until finally, on November 24, 1849, Rosas signed the treaty officially ending hostilities. England agreed to evacuate Martín García Island, and it recognized Argentina's rights to control the navigation of the Paraná and Uruguay Rivers. Although the British and French achieved a short-term victory at the Battle of Obligado in 1845, in the long run the guns of San Lorenzo and elsewhere frustrated the Europeans' plans to force open the river trade.

Posing In Times of Trouble

Although both Mariquita and Juan Manuel went through hard times during the early to mid-1840s, they both took time to pose for talented artists traveling through their lands. In 1842, the Frenchman Raymond Monvoisin was in the Río de la Plata region. He visited Rosas and felt inspired to paint a portrait of him clad in a poncho. Although Rosas was notorious for his refusal to pose for portraits, Monvoisin affirmed that Rosas did indeed pose for him on more than one occasion.[68] Not long afterward, Mariquita had her chance. Maurice Rugendas came through Buenos Aires while she was back in the city in 1845. She was more than happy to pose for him. Rugendas responded by placing her in a romantic setting at her home in San Isidro, sitting under an ombu tree—one of the icons of the Pampa region (see figs. 10.3 and 10.4).

The Politics of Foreign Intervention

Rosas's resistance to French and Anglo-French intervention earned him accolades from around Latin America and the world. General San Martín was so pleased that he sent his saber from the independence wars to Rosas as a gift, in gratitude for defending Argentina against foreign interlopers. The Venezuelan statesman Andres Bello praised Rosas for "conduct in the great American question" that placed him "in the leading ranks of the great men of America." The "American question" was, according to the British diplomat Lord Howden, "a determination never to admit the right of any European power to intervene, in hostility or protection, in the affairs of this Continent." This was something taught even to children. Howden found that the "the only political idea sedulously instilled into every boy in the streets is that there is one great European conspiracy against American Independence throughout the whole American world."[69]

For Rosas's enemies, however, Rosas's knack for survival was odious and frustrating. Domingo Sarmiento and others continued to hope for, and justify, foreign intervention to get rid of Rosas. Writing from his Chilean exile in August of 1845, just as the Anglo-French intervention was heating up, Sarmiento blamed Rosas for all European imperialism dating back to the 1830s. "Wouldn't it be correct to say that the European intervention is the ultimate sad

FIGURE 10.3 *Portrait of María Sánchez de Mendeville* by Jean Maurice Rugendas (1845). Courtesy of the Museo Histórico Nacional, Buenos Aires.

FIGURE 10.4 *Portrait of Juan Manuel de Rosas*
by Raymond Auguste Quinsac Monvoisin (1842).
Courtesy of the Museo Nacional de Bellas Artes,
Buenos Aires.

consequence brought by that monstrous tyrant?" Sarmiento went on to argue that the great powers of the world had an obligation to intervene in the affairs of lesser states, especially for the purpose of opposing barbarism. "Will France and England, leaders of the civilized world, remain aloof when it comes to America?"

The answer, Sarmiento implied, was no. "We also agree," he continued, "that the 'rights of peoples' should be modified in its application in the Americas. We believe that because each part of America is powerless to influence others, lacking foreign policy or commercial interests substantial enough to give them influence over others, that Europe, with its commercial and political strength, is necessarily called to action against a subversion like that which is happening on the shores of the Río de la Plata, to contain the damage caused by retrograde and barbarous powers." As the most powerful Christian nations, France and England were able to influence the world, "intervening in the Orient, in Europe, and in the West, each time tranquility [was] threatened anywhere on earth."[70] These were the same arguments that imperialists in Europe made as they justified carving up the world, and in Sarmiento's view it was Rosas's backwardness, rather than imperial avarice, that was to blame.

Conclusion

For much of his rule, Juan Manuel de Rosas faced determined and even vitriolic opposition from his Argentine opponents. Rosas's authoritarianism, and his coercive policies to impose unanimity of opinion, alienated Mariquita Sánchez de Mendeville and others like her, who since May of 1810 had dreamt of building a liberal republic on the shores of the Río de la Plata. In addition to domestic opposition, Rosas also experienced extreme pressure from foreign powers. The United States and England violated Argentine sovereignty in the Malvinas / Falkland Islands in the early 1830s, with England occupying them indefinitely after 1833. France also pressured Rosas to grant most-favored-nation status, and used a naval blockade of Buenos Aires in the process. Mariquita and others also gratefully accepted French support of General Juan Lavalle's anti-Rosas invasion in the early 1840s. Even his British allies turned against Rosas in 1845 during the dispute over navigation on the Paraná River.

But Rosas survived, and by 1845 Mariquita and many other exiles had grown weary of the ebbs and flows of plots, conspiracies, and failed rebellions and interventions. Mariquita, for her part, focused on her life, which included extended stays in Río de Janeiro as well as back in Buenos Aires, and as always, she dreamt of going to France.

CHAPTER ELEVEN

Mature Exile and Mature Tyranny

In September of 1847 Mariquita was short on money, again, and her rent was overdue. She rented a home in Montevideo and paid for it with rents and other remittances from her properties in Buenos Aires. But her financial situation in exile was precarious at best, in part because it was sometimes hard for her to collect rent. One tenant in Buenos Aires was especially delinquent, but it was a delicate matter because the man was intimately connected to the Rosas regime. "To think of collecting my rents from the government"—Mariquita explained to her daughter Florencia—is "absurd under these circumstances." Mariquita hoped that Rosas's brother Gervasio could help her: "But without doubt he is wary of taking my side in public, and it doesn't seem proper for me to insist." The rent in this case had not been paid in years. "But how can one think of such things? Such is life, and each day I get poorer."[1] Why was this case so difficult? The delinquent renter in question was none other than Ciriaco Cutiño, the head of Rosas's dreaded Mazorca.[2]

Mariquita's life in exile was not an easy one. In Montevideo, she tried to re-create her tertulia as best she could, entertaining guests and writing countless letters to friends and family. During her exile Mariquita wrote hundreds of letters, and through those letters she maintained and deepened friendships, offered comfort, and dispensed advice. Money was always tight, however, and Mariquita constantly sought financial succor from wherever she could find it. Rosas, meanwhile, remained in power, but only after surviving foreign interventions. After the death of his wife, Encarnación, the widowed Rosas took solace in the arms of one of his servant girls. Meanwhile, new opposition from within the country threatened his regime by the late 1840s.

Mariquita, Esteban Echeverría,
and the Young Generation in Exile

Mariquita's home in Montevideo was a destination for many of the exiles—especially the members of the Young Generation. With Rosas's dictatorship in full swing, the ideals of the May Revolution seemed in retreat—ideals of a modern republic with a constitution that balanced power between federal and provincial governments; that promoted education and the rights of women. In exile, Mariquita was a symbol of those ideals—a living piece of the May Revolution.

Mariquita developed particularly close ties with three of her son Juan Thompson's friends. In December of 1838, Juan María Gutiérrez, a member of the Young Generation, was excited that his friend Juan Bautista Alberdi would soon be visiting their "good friend" Mariquita in Montevideo. "She is very capable, and she loves and understands our ideas in admirable fashion. She is an amazing talent, and we have a thousand reasons to love her. Take care of her, as your spiritual affinity obliges you to." Gutiérrez later added: "I love her more than my own mother because she has done so much and I owe her many favors of infinite consideration."[3]

Mariquita also became close friends with Esteban Echeverría. When she was in Montevideo, they exchanged letters that included some of his writings, possibly including the "The Slaughterhouse," a short story that would soon be recognized as a pioneering work of Romanticism in Argentina. It was also a dramatic and powerful anti-Rosista tract. "The Slaughterhouse" deserves close attention for what it reveals about the Rosas regime and, just as importantly, for what it reveals about the prejudices of the author, Esteban Echeverría, and many of his compatriots.

"THE SLAUGHTERHOUSE"

The story tells of a tragic encounter between a young Unitarian man with a mob of people at what Echeverría portrays as a grotesque slaughterhouse near Buenos Aires.[4] For Echeverría, the slaughterhouse represented the city and province of Buenos Aires under the rule of Governor Rosas. A montage of images sets the scene. At a massive slaughterhouse, animal carcasses litter the ground. Pictures of Rosas and his deceased wife, Encarnación, cover the walls. A mixed-race crowd fights over scraps of meat and fat. Butchers scream at the crowd. "Hey there, black witch, get out of here before I cut you open." Black women in blood-soaked mud fight over cow intestines, lungs, and other bovine parts while two black women drag away the entrails of an animal. Nearby, "two young boys practicing the handling of their knives [slash] at one another with terrifying thrusts."

When a well-dressed young man rides by on his horse, all activity at the slaughterhouse stops. "Here comes a Unitarist!" yells one of the butchers. The young man's appearance says it all. He wears a fancy coat and his sideburns are long and thin, in European style. He is not wearing a red ribbon *or* a black insignia of mourning for Encarnación Ezcurra. To make matters worse, he uses an English saddle instead of traditional gaucho riding gear. It is clear, by his appearance, that this rider is an enemy of Rosas and his dear wife. "The son of a bitch," says one onlooker. "To the gibbet with him!" says another. "All these cocky Unitarists are as showy as the devil himself!"

Soon the young man is pulled off his horse, tied up, and interrogated by a slaughterhouse official. Why doesn't he wear the red ribbon as Rosas ordered, the official asks, or a black sash of mourning for his dead wife? The young man responds defiantly: ribbons are for slaves; and he does wear a sash of mourning, but he wears it in his heart, "in memory of my country, which you, infamous wretches, have murdered." His audacious response riles up the crowd even more. "Take the pants off this arrogant fool and beat him on his naked ass." The young man struggles mightily against his captors' attempts to undress him. All of a sudden, "a torrent of blood [spouts], bubbling from the young man's mouth and nose, and [flows] freely down the table." The murderers are shocked. "The savage Unitarist has burst with rage," one of them says. "We just wanted a bit of fun."

Throughout the story, Echeverría makes sure that his readers understand the purpose of the tale: the story is meant to show "the savage ways" that social conflicts are settled in the country. Echeverría compares the trial of the young Unitarian to the trial of Jesus. And in the end, Echeverría concludes that the butchers of the slaughterhouses are the "apostles" who characterize Rosista society: "It is not difficult to imagine what sort of federation issued from their heads and knives." They would label as a "savage Unitarist any man who was neither a cutthroat or crook, any man who was kindhearted and decent, any patriot or noble friend of enlightenment and freedom."[5]

Echeverría's story portrays the arbitrary brutality the Rosas regime could produce, especially the vigilante justice some of his followers meted out, with the Mazorca being the most notorious. As portrayed in the story, records of the time show instances of police drawing guilty conclusions based on how people dressed and groomed themselves. At the same time, however, Echeverría—a self-proclaimed "friend of enlightenment and freedom"—reveals in the story that his (and others') enlightened views included a healthy contempt for the lower orders of society. Echeverría portrays blacks and mulattoes with particularly unglamorous images.

The ruling class's contempt for the poor and people of color predated the Rosas regime, but when Rosas successfully courted the favor of the popular classes, elite disdain for the lower orders only magnified. That increased disdain, in turn, pushed the masses, colored and otherwise, further into the arms of Rosas. Indeed, support from people of color was vital to the Rosas regime since blacks and mulattoes made up close to 25 percent of Buenos Aires's population at this time. How many blacks or mulattoes would be attracted to Echeverría, or his way of thinking, after reading "The Slaughterhouse"? Meanwhile, Rosas and his family, as well as the pro-Rosas press, continued to openly cultivate the support of African descendants.

Mariquita's Salon in Exile

Across the river, Mariquita tried to re-create her salon in exile. But Montevideo was not Buenos Aires. She was without her spacious mansion, money was always a problem, and she was a bit self-conscious at first because she could not entertain as she was accustomed to in Buenos Aires.[6]

As mentioned above, Mariquita rented a home in Montevideo, although her finances were always tight.[7] To make matters worse, the cost of living in Montevideo was high. Rosas's naval blockade of Montevideo in 1840 created chronic shortages and higher prices. It was especially difficult to get good wine and other spirits. Mariquita's reduced circumstances are evident in the following note to Juan Bautista Alberdi regarding a dinner with Esteban Echeverría, who by this time was also in exile in Montevideo. "Echeverría has promised to eat with me today. See if the offer tempts you, but don't think it will be anything grand. It will be just the two of us. Tell me if you are up to it."[8]

On another occasion, she wrote Alberdi to lament that he was too ill to dine with her. "I regret not having the pleasure of eating with you today. . . . I am of the same mind as Victor Hugo: the life of a Romantic is pernicious,

and their stomachs are not irrigated, but are in need of tonics and good wine and corn stew." In the meantime, she hoped Alberdi would be ready for a get-together the next Tuesday evening, even if they did not have good wine because of the blockade. Be sure to "come over and drink something, even if it is just some sugar water." Mariquita promised him a piano-harp duet. "Don't think it will be a tertulia," she warned him, "but I will have something good." In her postscript, Mariquita thanked Alberdi for a book he lent her, apparently part of their habitual exchange of literature. "The book is a gem. I return it with a thousand thanks. And consistent with the custom, I send you this bit of verse to make you laugh. I will tell you later who the author is."[9] The author may very well have been Mariquita herself, who was known to dabble in writing poetry.

When Mariquita could not meet with her young intellectuals in person, she kept up a lively correspondence through mail. She wrote consistently to her daughter Florencia, but she also wrote to a host of others as well. Her many letters reveal that one of Mariquita's main roles was to bring comfort and relief to suffering souls. "My dear friend, your fine letter has brought great comfort to the heart of Nieves," wrote Justa Fouget to Mariquita in 1840.

"You can't imagine, friend, how much we have missed you during this time."[10] In another letter, Justa Fouget confessed to Mariquita: "You are my salvation from far and near, and you always find ways, with your endless kindness, to commiserate and sweeten the sad loneliness of your friends."[11] Mariquita also kept up a strong correspondence with a number of her male friends. Tomás Guido thanked Mariquita for one of her letters that "came to mitigate my sorrows" after he lost a family member.[12] Rivera Indarte, one of the most prolific producers of anti-Rosas literature, wrote a poem in honor of Mariquita on her birthday, referring to her as "sweet, dear Godmother."[13]

Mariquita in turn was also buoyed up by letters from others, including male friends like Juan María Gutiérrez, another friend of her son Juan. "I am very thankful for your letter," Mariquita wrote Gutiérrez in an undated note. She had "been sad for a while" and thus his letter "could not have come at a better time." She then turned to one of her favorite subjects: French salons and the delightful characters that populated them. "Let's move on to our Madame Recamier, of whom I have received much news of late through people I have spoken to." She was very beautiful, although not a great intellect. "But I will tell you a *secret*: She was an *incomplete being* and could not feel passions" (referring to Madame Recamier's rumored inability to have sex). Recamier's life went forward without troubles, Mariquita continued, and her beauty was preserved "because no one could alter her; and because she did not favor any of her admirers, they were all resigned to the fact." Mariquita finished her letter with a humorous story about three of the most iconic figures from the golden age of French salons that she so admired: the salon hostesses Germaine de Stael and Madame Recamier, along with Charles Maurice Talleyrand-Périgord, a prominent French diplomat and socialite (commonly known simply as Talleyrand). One day when all three were at a salon, Talleyrand could not stop complimenting both of them. The women decided to put him to a test: which one of them did he favor most? The conversation that followed was carried on with great wit by all three. Madame de Stael finally presented a scenario to settle the question once and for all: if both of them were drowning at the same time, which woman would he save first? After a pause, Talleyrand responded that of course he would save Madame Recamier . . . because Germaine would swim all by herself. "Can you see how gracefully he flattered both of them?" Mariquita asked Gutiérrez. "Well, my friend, how enchanting are the gatherings of refined society! I have enjoyed my share of it, and it makes me feel my loneliness more deeply."[14] Mariquita loved the idea of France, or the *ideal* of France, and it shimmers in much of her writing.

These notes and letters capture Mariquita's exiled salon in miniature. Food, French authors, romantic ideals, music, book exchanges, and discussions of literature. Although reduced in circumstances, Mariquita was still able to serve as a mentor for a younger generation of Argentine thinkers, including the likes of Juan María Gutiérrez, who went on to be an important statesman. "Among the friendships that influenced the formation of Gutiérrez, we should not forget the Señora de Thompson de Mendeville," Alberdi later wrote. She was vital to Gutiérrez's development because of the "great influence she had on his education and character as a man of society and the world. Madame Mendeville has been the second mother of Gutiérrez, in his intellectual and social formation."[15] The historian Pastor Obligado, who knew Mariquita, praised her for such mentorship. "How great the influence of a distinguished woman, who discreetly polishes the education of whoever surrounds her! This is one of the outstanding merits of a grand lady in the political and social sphere."[16]

Mariquita to Rio de Janeiro and Back Again

On July 14, 1846, Mariquita announced to Florencia that she was moving to Rio de Janeiro for a few months. It was a big decision because it meant no more easy trips across the river to visit family in Buenos Aires. She tried to reassure Florencia, who she knew would be fearful for her safety. "I am going to a delicious country, where I have people waiting eagerly for me, and where I will lack for nothing." She would be traveling safely as a passenger on a warship and in the company of two good servants. "Don't cry," she chided Florencia. "For once in my life can I do what I want?" Besides, she continued, in Rio she would be free from the "craziness" of Montevideo with its "hellish politics." Mariquita made it clear she was looking forward to some rest, even from her favorite activities. Her house in Montevideo was an "inferno of people that don't let me do anything." She was always "making and receiving visits, going from tertulia to tertulia, nothing more."[17] Rio would be a respite from her harried life. And besides, the cost of living in Brazil was a lot cheaper.

Mariquita absolutely loved Rio. The city impressed Mariquita in a number of ways, especially the low cost of living. She was also struck by how even the wealthiest of women engaged in business dealings personally, without compromising their honor. "The milk I drink comes from the estate of a Marquise, who will collect payment at the end of the month." In turn, the elite classes of Rio also found Mariquita delightful, especially when she spoke to them in Portuguese. "I told them if they give me a piece of land, that I'll stay."[18] In all, Mariquita spent a splendid seven months in Rio. "I have never had a season of better health," she told Florencia.[19]

Even though she was having a grand time, Mariquita still missed friends and family in Montevideo and Buenos Aires. "I feel homesick when I think of my daughters. Then I cry." As always, she kept in touch as best she could through letters. "Hardly a day goes by that I don't write," she told Florencia in September.[20] But by November of 1846, she was ready to go home. "I think I will soon leave this place," she wrote Florencia. "I cannot be so far from everyone. Montevideo is half of my home, and they love me so much there." Plus, she added, from Montevideo it was so easy to hop over, "like the mail," to Buenos Aires for a visit.[21]

Back in Montevideo, Mariquita's financial struggles continued to weigh heavily on her mind. She even played the lottery on occasion in hopes of striking it rich.[22] Gervasio Rozas, Juan Manuel's brother, helped administer some of her properties in Buenos Aires, which was of great help to her. Gervasio also offered to help Mariquita in another matter. He asked for the hand of Mariquita's widowed daughter, Florencia Lezica. In their notes exchanged on the subject, Mariquita praised the Rozas family but in the end advised her daughter that the Rozases were too hard for people like her and Florencia. In the end, even though such a marriage proposal offered monetary and political advantages, Mariquita advised Florencia to remain single.[23]

Mariquita's struggles, financial and otherwise, at times brought out her spiritual side. As seen above, Mariquita at times had trouble paying her rent on time. She recounted to Florencia what she did on one such occasion when things were particularly bad. "I got serious and had a talk with God, as if He were me, to ask for consolation." She turned to her cherished book, Eckartshausen's *God Is the Love Most Pure*, and recited one of her favorite prayers from it, perhaps a few lines from "Trust in God during Times of Trial," which reads: "I find myself a prisoner, and I see that only you are able to help me."[24] Her prayer brought immediate results. "I had my book in hand. . . . And can you believe it! Someone called and a gentleman brought me five ounces [of silver]. I immediately went and paid rent on the house." In the end the experience inspired Mariquita to dispense some sage advice to her daughter: "We go through life and God will give us strength. . . . I never tire of giving thanks to God because, my dear daughter, good health and a clear conscience are great benefits. One can better endure trials if you have these two supports."[25] On another occasion, money from the house rented by Cutiño—years behind in payment—arrived at Mariquita's door. Mariquita attributed it to a special intervention from the Rosas family. "Manuelita must have heard of my predicament," she told Florencia.

Back in Montevideo, Mariquita became friends with the French count Waleski and his wife, Marie-Anne, who went first to Buenos Aires and then on to Montevideo as part of a French diplomatic mission (trying to settle disputes stemming from the Anglo-French intervention in 1845). Mariquita's friendship with the Waleskis boosted her confidence regarding an insecurity that had bothered her for years: Mariquita doubted her own ability to speak French fluently. Years earlier her husband, Jean Baptiste, perhaps as a kind of mental abuse, had told Mariquita that her French was not good enough to function in French society. This may have been one of the reasons Mariquita never hazarded a trip to France. Mariquita confided her fears to Florencia. Jean Baptiste "believed that I would not like life in Europe, mostly because of my poor French." However, her successful trip to Rio and her friendship with the Waleskis made Mariquita believe she could thrive in the elite circles of Europe. "I am about to write [Mendeville] that the Countess Waleski said, the first time I met her, that she could not believe I was not French. When I left, she asked me to come see her again soon." Mariquita also overheard the countess tell another visitor: "I feel like I know Madame Mendeville well, for the feeling of familiarity she has inspired in me, and because I like her manners and her style."[26] Whether Mariquita spoke fluent French or not, the countess, like Mariquita, was a consummate host who clearly knew how to make her guests feel comfortable.

France and the Politics and Culture of Travel

Although Mariquita's hopes of traveling to Paris were fading, she still held on to the possibility. Her dream persisted perhaps because she still admired France, and surely Paris looked even more attractive compared to Mariquita's struggles in Montevideo. In addition, Mariquita kept reading more and more about the wonders of Paris. Her favorite French novelist, Honoré de Balzac, wrote that taking a stroll—a *flânerie*—through Paris was a way of life for resident and visitor alike. "Ah! To wander over Paris! What an adorable and delectable existence is that! Flânerie is a form of science, it is the gastronomy of the eye."[27]

Mariquita's wanderlust was well known to her friends. Juan Bautista Alberdi, for example, even referenced Mariquita's itch to travel in the journal he kept during his own exile. "Last night I dreamt of Paris, and other travel destinations," Alberdi wrote while sailing the Atlantic in 1844. "I am destined to suffer thus all my life—I am a true Madame Mendeville." And, he added, he would be dreaming of such things until he was "gray and wrinkled."[28]

Alberdi did finally visit Paris in the 1840s. Making his way eagerly to the Palace of Versailles, Alberdi was enchanted by the fountains and gardens. His visit inside the palace, however, was somewhat disappointing. "The bed was not as tall, and it was so short that it looked like it was made for someone of regular stature. It is beautiful but compares unfavorably to something made today." Versailles's failure to measure up characterized what Alberdi concluded about France, and Europe as a whole, as he prepared to return home. "How I long to see myself in those countries. How beautiful is America! How comforting! How sweet! Now I know. Now that I've come to know these countries of hell; these selfish people, of vice, and prostitution. We [Americans] are worth a lot and we don't even know it. We attribute more value to Europe than it deserves."[29] After seeing the supposed wonders of Europe, Alberdi gained a new appreciation for his homeland and its potential.

Mariquita's son Julio also traveled to France during Mariquita's exile. After returning to Buenos Aires after one trip to Paris, Julio visited one of Mariquita's favorite pen pals, Justa Fouget, who shared part of their conversation with Mariquita in a letter. Justa told Mariquita that she and Julio had started to talk about porteño women. Julio spoke of how he, while in France, told the women of Paris that the porteñas dressed in the latest French fashion and read all the famous French authors. According to Julio, the Parisian women did not believe him. Justa Fouget gave Julio a biting response: "I told him to tell those ladies" that Argentine women have all but forgotten the old French authors and now they are reading all the new ones, like "Victor Hugo, Lamartíne, Dumas, Sue, de la Viña, Kock, Gorlan, Marceline, Valmore, Orago, Ducange, Nodier, Balzac, and I didn't continue the list so as to not appear pedantic." Justa finished her letter to Mariquita with a compliment: "Why were you not born in the century of Louis the XIV as a marquesa or a countess? Who would cite the letters of [Madames] Sévigné and Maintenon if you had been their contemporary?"[30] This may well have been, to Mariquita's ears, one of the greatest compliments she ever received.

Rosas's own nephew, Lucio Mansilla, became quite a Francophile. He traveled to France as a teenager in the late 1840s, the first of many trips. "Say what you want," he challenged his readers in one of his memoirs, but "there's no other place like Paris."[31] But Mansilla had to be careful about his French proclivities, for he had his uncle Juan Manuel to consider, who spent years sparring with French officials and French gunboats. After one extended trip to France, young Lucio returned to Buenos Aires, in 1851, dressed like a Parisian. Soon after arriving, one of his first stops was to pay his uncle Juan Manuel a visit. "God bless you, uncle!" young Lucio declared upon arrival. "God be with you, nephew!" Rosas responded. After a lengthy conversation in which uncle Juan Manuel assessed the state of Lucio's character, Rosas offered his nephew some reassurance. "I am very happy with you, that you have not come back transformed into a gringo" (*agringado*). In Lucio's words, "I had not returned (which was true), behaving like so many who go to Europe as big as a trunk but return like little pouches. I may have returned dressed as a Frenchman, that was true, but I was still an American stallion to the marrow of my bones . . . I was proud: I had not returned *agringado*."[32]

Anti-Rosas Literature in Torrents

When exiles were not traveling, many of them took up their pens to trumpet the evils of the Rosas regime. Mariquita was friends with many of them. Few were more prolific than Domingo Faustino Sarmiento. During his exile he traveled widely, including to North America where he became friends with Horace and Mary Mann, pioneers in the public education programs of the United States of America, programs he sought to imitate in Latin America. He settled for a number of years in Chile, where they recognized his talents enough to appoint him minister of education in the 1840s. Along with his ministerial duties, Sarmiento found ample time to unleash tirades of vitriol against the Rosas regime. Rosas's forces, he wrote, plagued the land with "torrents of blood" and "spontaneous throat cutting." "The hand of disgrace has hovered over us for ten years, without hardly a pause."[33] And it was from Chile that Sarmiento penned his most famous anti-Rosas tract: *Facundo, or Civilization and Barbarism*. The thesis was in the title. For Sarmiento, Facundo Quiroga and, by association, Juan Manuel de Rosas were the products of an empty and brutal land that could not help but create barbarity, which in turn needed to be transformed by civilization. For Sarmiento, Rosas's regime was a reflection of Rosas's life as a rancher on the barbarous Pampas.[34]

While Sarmiento shot verbal arrows from across the Andes, exiles in Montevideo did their part to ravage Rosas in the printed word. José Rivera Indarte produced volumes of anti-Rosas literature, including a book titled *Tables of Blood* and another called *It Is a Saintly Act to Kill Rosas*. He and others also produced anti-Rosas newspapers, including one called *Muera Rosas!* (Death to Rosas!). "A cry is heard from hell," reads the opening line of the first edition, "like a thunderclap" echoing eternal wrath. A bolt of lightning from Buenos Aires provides an answer: "Death to Rosas."[35]

The poet José Mármol also wrote anti-Rosas material that was so eloquent that he became known by some as the "poetic hangman" of Rosas. He showed some of that eloquence in an editorial in a Montevideo newspaper on May 25, 1848. "Thirty-eight years! 100 battles in the war for our independence. The Generation of 1810 is in its tomb while the generation of their children finds itself in holy misfortune." And through it all, "the May Revolution is shouting: Carry on! And we do carry on."[36] His best-known anti-Rosas writing was his epic novel, *Amalia*. The harrowing opening scene—one of betrayal and grisly murder of Unitarians by the Mazorca—sets the tone for the whole story.[37]

José Mármol took a particular interest in Manuelita Rosas, whom he and others saw as an unfortunate victim of her father's tyranny. He even addresses her directly in one of his publications, *Manuela Rosas*. In it, Mármol offers to be the first to "raise a voice" on her behalf and seek "the justice" she deserves. "Poor woman! Manuela Rosas's world is an orgy in which the senses are, without her knowing it, dulled and snuffed out." For Mármol, despite the terrible environment, Manuelita's virtues still manage to shine through. Manuelita "listens and receives everyone with cordiality and sweetness. The masses find kindness in her words and in her countenance, while the upper classes find courtly manners, education, and talent."[38]

Juan Manuel and Eugenia Castro

Although Mármol's poetic claim about the generation of 1810 being in the tomb was an exaggeration, it was true that Mariquita and Juan Manuel were feeling their mortality. Mariquita had lost a husband in Martín, then her son Enrique, and in essence she had lost her second husband as well, who now lived in Ecuador. Juan Manuel also suffered loss. Encarnación passed away from an illness in 1839. Juan Manuel mourned the loss of the faithful and energetic Encarnación, as did the whole city and province. Not long after her death, however, he sought the comfort of a new companion.

Eugenia Castro lived on one of Rosas's estates, where her father worked as a ranch hand. When her father passed away, Rosas became the executor of his will and the guardian of his two children, Eugenia and Vicente. When Eugenia was about thirteen years old, Rosas brought her into his home to help care for the ill Encarnación. Eugenia endeared herself to everyone in the family by the way she cared for Encarnación, and for anyone who was ill, Manuelita and Juan Manuel included. She also soon became Rosas's preferred *cebadora* (server) of his yerba mate, which had its own kind of ritual. Eugenia did her best to be meticulous in every aspect of this tradition. She heated the water to just the right temperature, poured it into the small gourd with the correct amount of crushed yerba leaves inside, placed the bombilla (straining straw) in the drink just so, and then handed it in the appropriate way to the person receiving it. Several rounds of mate could be shared among friends, all using the same gourd and straw.[39] If it was just the two of them, Eugenia and Juan Manuel likely drank together. Serving mate the correct way was no small affair. A few years later, the speaker of the second part of the epic poem *Martín Fierro* tells the story of one malefactor who killed his wife for giving him a cold mate.[40] The speaker is unsure if the story is true, and in any case, Eugenia Castro was in no such danger.

Soon after Encarnación died, Eugenia became Juan Manuel's intimate companion and ended up bearing him six children between 1840 and 1852. The dynamics of the relationship are not clear, including the question of coercion and consent. It would have been hard for Eugenia to resist the advances of a man, thirty years her senior, who wielded as much power as the governor. From her lowly social and political station, Eugenia likely had little choice in the matter. Nevertheless, over time she seemed to be content with their relationship.[41]

Such interactions between patron and servant were not uncommon in the Río de la Plata. The illegitimate children born of these unions were occasionally recognized by their fathers and given some education, and they formed a kind of second class of citizens in Buenos Aires. Rosas, however, never officially recognized his illegitimate offspring. Rosas nicknamed Eugenia "the Captive" because she spent most of her days inside the walls of Rosas's spacious estate. The nickname referenced the long history of Indians kidnapping female settlers along the frontier and forcing them to become brides for Native warriors. It may have been simply an amusing nickname, or it may point to a clearer picture of Eugenia's vulnerable position in the house of Juan Manuel de Rosas.

Some commentators on Rosas's relationship with Eugenia might be tempted to say, as Darwin did of Rosas's buffoons, that this illegitimate family was another example of the governor behaving like the "barons of old." Perhaps it is so. But nearly a hundred years after Rosas created his illegitimate family with Eugenia, an infant girl was born out of wedlock into the family of Juan Duarte and Juana Ibarguren. The major difference was that in this latter case, Juan Duarte had a legitimate family simultaneously in another city. The illegitimate baby's name was Eva, and she would go on to become the famous Evita Perón.[42] Some old barons, like old habits, die hard.

The place where Eugenia spent most of her time was Rosas's newly built home, located away from the city center. Rosas called his estate San Benito de Palermo, based in part on the name of one of the original inhabitants on the land back in the 1580s (an Italian). Perhaps a greater influence on Rosas's choice was the fact that the patron saint for Afro-Argentines was Saint Benito, a son of Moorish slaves who died in 1589 in a monastery in Palermo, Italy.[43]

Rosas apparently took pleasure in his children by Eugenia. He was especially fond of his daughter Angela. To some observers, Rosas seemed more relaxed with his children by Eugenia because he did not feel any pressure to educate them. He did enjoy their company. For fun, Angela and some of her siblings would dress up in soldiers' uniforms and go through makeshift military maneuvers, to the great delight of their father. Rosas even gave Angela the endearing nickname of "Little Soldier." Rosas also found another useful job for Angela and her siblings: keeping a watchful eye on Manuelita and her boyfriend, Máximo Terrero. Rosas even taught his younger children a song to sing as they spied on the couple. "The rations my country gives me turn me into a sentinel. He is alert! Attention, sentinel, attention! Yes sir!"[44]

Growing Opposition to Rosas: The Rise of Justo José Urquiza

Even as Juan Manuel enjoyed life with Eugenia and her children, clouds began to gather over his regime. This was evident in the deterioration of Rosas's relations with Justo José Urquiza, the powerful governor of Entre Ríos Province, and the second most powerful man in the confederation. In May of 1851, Governor Urquiza refused to renew his consent to Rosas's position as head of the Argentine Confederation. Urquiza was also organizing a new army to challenge Rosas, an army made up of Argentines as well as foreigners.

Urquiza had been a faithful ally of Rosas in previous years. In 1845 he led a smashing victory against Fructuoso Rivera in Uruguay. After the battle, Urquiza sent a few trophies to Rosas, including the bolas and saber of the defeated commander. Rosas was "deeply pleased" by the gifts and informed Urquiza that they would be placed in a museum in Buenos Aires "to perpetuate the memory of glorious acts" carried out in the name of "independence and liberty."[45] But relations between the two began to sour two years later. In November of 1847, Urquiza commanded forces that defeated a Unitarian uprising in his province. In victory, Urquiza chose a path of reconciliation instead of retribution. Without Rosas's permission, Urquiza granted generous terms to his vanquished foe. When Rosas heard about it, he ordered Urquiza to demand a new and more harsh treaty. When the defeated commander refused, Urquiza inflicted another defeat even bloodier than before.[46]

Governor Rosas also criticized Urquiza's government for being too lenient in the language they were using in provincial documents to describe enemies of the state. Rosas had long believed in the power of words to convey messages. His own letters almost always contained at least one (and frequently more) derogatory adjectives when referring to his enemies. He insisted that others follow suit. By the mid-1840s, however, Governor Urquiza's province of Entre Ríos had relaxed its use of labels, referring to opponents of Federalism simply as "savages" instead of the more specific "Savage Unitarians." For Rosas, this was problematic because some of his enemies were also using the lone term "savages" to describe supporters of Rosas. For Rosas, this opened the door for confusion. In 1847, Rosas's minister Arana sent a letter to all governors urging them to use the correct phrase—"Savage Unitarians"—when describing regime enemies. Without such clarity, the "confusion of words" would lead to "the anarchy of ideas," which would then allow the Unitarians to further "their designs of disorder, desolation, and blood." It was thus indispensable to present a united front of correct wordage across the country so that future generations would also use the appropriate epithets for the Unitarians, a group who, according to Arana, had perpetrated "execrable acts and dark treason," not only against the Argentine Confederation but against "all of America."[47] Governor Urquiza and many others chafed under these criticisms.

After his military victories in 1845 and 1847, Urquiza understood that he was the most powerful man in the country, second only to Rosas. Urquiza resented the way Rosas had handled the question of Urquiza's lenient treaty, and the meddling with word choice in provincial documents made things worse. Urquiza bided his time for an opportunity to exact his revenge. In the meantime, he began building an army that could challenge Rosas's leadership of the confederation.

The Love Story of Camila O'Gorman and Ladislao Gutiérrez

While military and political opposition to Rosas grew, a tragic love story also undermined his regime. On December 12, 1847, a scandal rocked the city of Buenos Aires. A young girl from a prominent family, Camila O'Gorman, a friend of Manuelita Rosas, disappeared from her home. Camila's disappearance was even more problematic because, on the same day, Father Ladislao Gutiérrez, the priest of the O'Gorman's parish, also disappeared. It soon became clear that the couple ran away together.

As soon as Camila's father, Adolfo O'Gorman, realized the truth, he quickly penned a letter to Governor Rosas. His purpose was to inform Rosas of "the most atrocious act ever heard of in this country." According to Mr. O'Gorman, the priest Ladislao seduced Camila, and he urged Governor Rosas to dispatch soldiers to intercept the fugitives who, he figured, were most likely trying to flee the country. A few days later, Bishop Miguel García wrote Governor Rosas to inform him of the scandal as well. He begged the governor to do everything possible to minimize the damage to "the honor of the church and to the priesthood."[48] Soon, Rosas sent letters to all the provincial governors asking them to apprehend the fugitives if they were found. The priest Ladislao was to be brought back in chains, Rosas instructed, while Camila would be sent to the House of Spiritual Exercises.[49]

Rosas responded to Father García's letter by lecturing the cleric on the ramifications of the scandal. If such an incident was not punished severely, Rosas reasoned, it would reflect poorly on the Church. Appropriate punishment would also deter others from committing such acts of "demoralization, libertinage, and disorder." Rosas also questioned the Church's wisdom in placing such a young priest in the O'Gorman parish. And, Rosas implied, perhaps the fugitives could have been apprehended if the Church had told him sooner.[50]

Camila and Ladislao were eventually discovered in Corrientes Province, where they lived under false names. As news of their capture spread, so did petitions for mercy for Camila. Manuelita Rosas may have tried to intervene on behalf of her friend Camila.[51] In the end, Governor Rosas decided that they both should die, and on the morning of August 18, 1847, the couple faced the firing squad together, despite some reports that Camila was pregnant. Just the year before, Rosas had disbanded the Mazorca, and the days of terror had subsided.[52] But now, Camila and Ladislao's death by firing squad revived the image of Rosas the executioner, an image that fueled his opponents and fatigued his supporters and those that tolerated him.

Mariquita Back in Buenos Aires

At about the same time Camila O'Gorman's tragic saga was playing out, Mariquita returned to Buenos Aires, this time for an extended stay. She had long grown weary of the life of an exile, and for all she knew, Rosas was going to rule forever. Mariquita's childhood friendship with Juan Manuel, though greatly damaged, still protected her from any danger. As Juan Bautista Alberdi later pointed out, Juan Manuel used the informal and friendly "tu" when speaking to Mariquita—a sign of great familiarity. At the same time, however, Mariquita knew enough to keep a low profile. She reopened her tertulia, although it did not have the political element of its early years. Although Mariquita was somewhat marginalized for political reasons, her home was still well respected, even among the extended Rozas family. Lucio Mansilla, Governor Rosas's nephew, remembered that although Mariquita rarely visited his home, she and her family remained symbols of refinement in the city. "My mother always referred to them as exemplars of culture, and she would often send me to visit her. Miss Mariquita's home on Florida Street . . . with its enormous patio, was a mansion that filled me with respect and awe."[53]

And Mariquita and Manuelita were still friends, as seen in an undated note

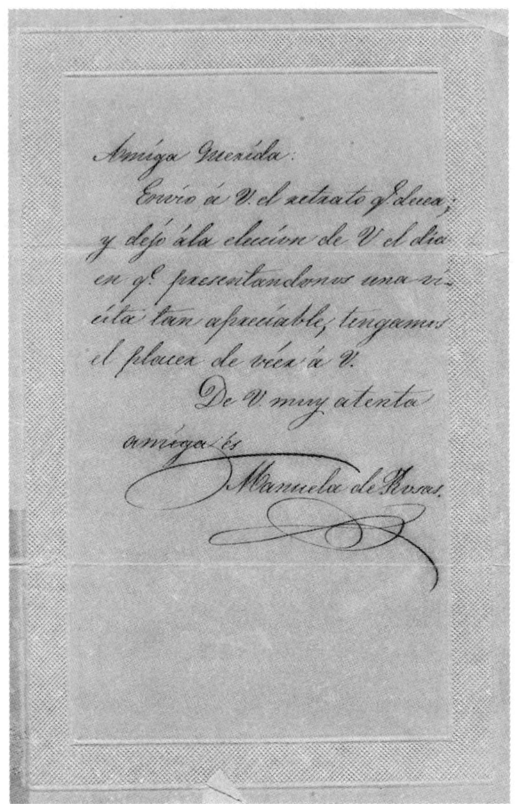

FIGURE 11.2 Note from Manuelita Rosas to Mariquita Sánchez inviting her for a visit. Courtesy of the Museo, Biblioteca y Archivo Histórico Municipal de San Isidro Dr. Horacio Beccar Varela, San Isidro, Argentina.

from Manuelita found later among Mariquita's papers. "Dear Friend," Manuelita wrote on exquisite stationary. "I send you the picture you asked for, and I leave it to you to choose the day you will pay us a nice visit and we have the pleasure of seeing you. Your very attentive friend, Manuelita."[54] It was a nice gesture at least, with the open-ended invitation perhaps indicating Manuelita's understanding that Mariquita might feel awkward making an official visit.

Mariquita did enjoy visiting, as always, even more so because she was alone, a fact that made her resent her absent husband, Jean Baptiste, even more. The two exchanged letters occasionally, although recently, as she told Florencia, Jean Baptiste's missives had only served to perturb Mariquita further. With each letter "my enthusiasm greatly diminishes, and each letter from Mendeville takes ten years off my life. What miserable luck I have!" Wasn't it strange, she asked Florencia, "that my friends write me with more affection than my husband? From three thousand leagues away, he takes up a pen to fill letters with cruelties and problems. I know you will tell me I am stupid to pay attention to his jabs."[55] Making matters worse, Mariquita heard that Mendeville was living well in Quito, in stark contrast to her situation. "This is Rivadavia, part II, who forced an unhappy life on his wife, who had to wash and iron while he lived in grand style." In the meantime, according to Mariquita, Rivadavia did not pass his inheritance on to his family. Mariquita worried that Mendeville would do something similar to her. "My jewel will do the same, no doubt. What a brute of a man!"[56]

Conclusion

Mariquita did her best to re-create her life during her exile in Montevideo. Although she was without her husband, she enjoyed the personal company of Esteban Echeverría, Juan Bautista Alberdi, and other members of the exile community. These relationships gave her comfort and purpose, but through them she also helped shape a younger generation of Argentine statesmen and politicians. The exiles' hopes for Rosas's demise were again dashed. Nevertheless, the rise of General Urquiza in Entre Ríos, and the execution of Camila O'Gorman and Ladislao Gutiérrez, signaled storm clouds on the horizon for the Rosas regime, and new rays of hope for Mariquita and her fellow exiles.

CHAPTER TWELVE

New Beginnings and New Ends

Mariquita had seen and heard the noise of battle before. But this time, back in Montevideo, it was the rumor of battle that gave her fits. The story on the morning of February 3, 1852 was that a massive battle was being fought on the outskirts of Buenos Aires. Her thoughts turned immediately to her family and friends living in Buenos Aires. As the hours wore on, bits of news trickled in to Montevideo: a colossal conflict; thousands of dead on the battlefield; hundreds executed by firing squad; looters sacking the city. But Mariquita had no idea if her family was safe amid all the violence. The unknown unnerved her. In a panic, she scribbled off a note to Florencia, perhaps just to calm her own nerves. "Consider my state of mind not having any word of you. . . . Think of how I must feel! Never have we gone this long without news. Never have we desired it more." After what seemed like an eternity, a ship from Buenos Aires arrived at the docks of Montevideo. Mariquita's grandson Enrique was there. He sprinted back to his grandmother's house. Out of breath, he could barely deliver the news: Rosas had been defeated![1]

Rosas was defeated by his former ally, Governor Justo José Urquiza of Entre Ríos, at the Battle of Caseros on February 3, 1852. His defeat, followed immediately by his exile to England, was greeted with jubilation by Mariquita and by thousands of other exiles spread throughout the Americas and Europe. Mariquita returned to Buenos Aires and tried to re-create her life and, in part, renew her long-distance relations with her husband, Jean Baptiste. But her and others' hopes for the creation of a unified nation were frustrated by the province of Buenos Aires, whose leaders refused to ratify the newly written constitution. Meanwhile, Juan Manuel de Rosas sought to make a life for himself in England, even as he tried to defend his reputation and his properties back in Argentina.

Governor Urquiza's *Pronunciamiento* and the End of the Rosas Regime

General Urquiza defeated Governor Rosas in February of 1852, but the enmity between the two dated back at least to 1847. As mentioned above, that year Rosas forced Urquiza to rescind a generous treaty he had signed with a defeated Unitarian foe. But discontent with Rosas was also fed by long-standing resentment of Rosas's dominance of the river trade, of Buenos Aires's control of the customs revenues taken at the port of Buenos Aires, and, of course, of Rosas's refusal to organize a constitutional convention.

Rosas, nevertheless, still enjoyed significant support. He maintained his authority through a yearly ritual in which he would circulate a letter to all the provinces asking governors and legislatures to reapprove him as the head of the Argentine Confederation. This letter was usually unanimously approved by all, except for the occasional years when provinces like Corrientes declared themselves in opposition to the regime. In recent years, however, Rosas had also been circulating his request to resign from his position, citing declining health and his desire to return to the peaceful ranching life. Each time his resignation was heartily rejected by the provinces.[2]

But that changed in 1851. In January of that year, newspapers in Entre Ríos began publishing anti-Rosas tracts. And when the letter of Rosas's reappointment arrived in Entre Ríos in April, Governor Urquiza said "no." On May 1, the Entre Ríos legislature officially rejected Rosas as the head of foreign relations for the confederation, and thus reclaimed Entre Ríos's right to freely navigate the Paraná and Uruguay Rivers, and to conduct foreign relations on their own. On May 25, the anniversary of the 1810 revolution, Urquiza sent a letter to all the provinces inviting them to join his *pronunciamiento* (pronouncement or uprising) against the Rosas regime. Urquiza called Rosas the "new Cromwell" (after the English dictator from the 1650s), who for the last twenty years had subjugated Argentines to the "most degrading dictatorship." Urquiza's goals were "liberty, unification, and war against despotism." Provincial documents in Entre Ríos now contained the heading "Death to Enemies of National Organization," referring to Rosas's refusal to ever call a constitutional convention. Governor Rosas responded in kind, as official documents in Buenos Aires started off with the declaration, usually handwritten: "Death to the crazy, savage, gross, evil Unitarian Urquiza."[3] Governor Rosas was now labeling as a

Unitarian a once-staunch Federalist ally—a practice Rosas had employed since the early 1830s.

The war of words would soon become a clash of armies. Although only Corrientes Province joined him at first, Urquiza successfully invaded Uruguay and defeated Rosas's ally General Oribe, thus breaking the years-long siege of Montevideo. Urquiza also signed an alliance with Uruguay and Brazil, both of whom were tired of Rosas's constant interference in Uruguayan affairs. Brazil and Uruguay also contributed thousands of soldiers to the "Great Army" that Urquiza was building in Entre Ríos. As news of Urquiza's uprising spread, many exiles returned to join the effort, including Domingo Sarmiento, among others.

As tension over the imminent invasion increased, Mariquita again felt uncomfortable in Buenos Aires. Fearing that her well-known distaste for the Rosas regime might make her a target of reprisals, she returned to Montevideo in October of 1851. The move left Mariquita depressed. She wrote Alberdi that her heart was "in a prison" and her spirit was "completely alone." She found solace in the piano and in doing, in her words, other "womanly" tasks. "I never liked doing them, but since despotism is in fashion, I have placed myself under the despots of embroidery and other nonsense of school girls. And thus we go on living, sometimes like idiots, other times soaring to the highest regions of the mind. . . .When will we see the end of this universal battle? What will remain after so much destruction?"[4]

The Last Battle

As it turned out, the answer to Mariquita's existential questions came quickly. Urquiza's Ejercito Grande (Great Army) left Entre Ríos in December of 1851 with more than twenty thousand men, including a few thousand from Brazil and Uruguay. This time, it seemed, more than ever before, the odds were stacked against Buenos Aires. Even the ever-confident Rosas made contingency plans to go into exile in case he was defeated. Anticipating an escape by sea, in late January he filled nineteen large trunks with important documents and moved them from his estate in Palermo to one of his homes in the city, not far from the port. Interestingly, Rosas did not arrange transfers of money in case he was forced to flee. Manuelita also sent a number of chests by ship to England. When news of Manuelita's shipments leaked out, critics of the Rosas regime lambasted the whole affair in a newspaper in Montevideo. The British were guilty of trafficking in ill-gotten goods, for surely these items were stolen from Rosas's enemies. "We are not saying that Manuelita stole them; only that she must have accepted them as gifts" from her father "or as presents laid at her feet by the thieves that fill the court of San Benito."[5]

By February 2, Urquiza's army of twenty-four thousand men had marched, essentially unopposed, to within a few miles of Buenos Aires. Rosas joined his troops, leaving Manuelita in charge of the house. Even under these stressful circumstances, Manuelita performed her duties admirably. One foreign visitor from the US at the time observed that she took care of official business "with great spirit and energy, receiving all visitors—official, diplomatic, and private—as usual, in the salons of the Quinta, and conducting with ability and dispatch the affairs of the Home Department of Government."[6]

From across the river, Mariquita eagerly awaited any tidbit of news. She knew all too well that Rosas had survived many threats before, against her most ardent wishes. But this time, Mariquita reasoned, was different. Urquiza's army was large and powerful, while Rosas's forces had suffered serious blows. Rosas's main commander, for example, resigned just as Urquiza approached Buenos Aires. Taking it all together, could Mariquita allow hope to again enter her heart?

As she contemplated the real possibility of Rosas's fall, her feelings were tender toward all of her friends and acquaintances—on both sides of the political divide. "Tell me, how is Guido?" she asked Florencia on January 30, 1852, referring to her close friend that was one of Rosas's ministers. Mariquita also had great concern for members of Juan Manuel's family. "And how has Agustina been after the arrival of [her son] Lucio? What a world! Poor mothers! . . . And what about Manuelita? Can you believe that I think of her often? Can you believe that I love her? Poor girl—she has gone through so much!"[7]

At 9:00 a.m. on February 3, the armies met in battle near the ranch of the Caseros family, a few miles southwest of Buenos Aires. It was a monumental clash between Urquiza's twenty-four thousand against Rosas's twenty-three thousand. Hours later, a steamboat pulled up to the dock in Montevideo with the news. Ironically, the steamboat was called *Manuelita Rosas*. Mariquita's grandson was at the dock, and then sprinted to tell her the news that Rosas was defeated. Mariquita could not contain her joy.

Her first instinct was to write. "I grabbed a pen as big as a stick because the finer ones don't write well enough," she wrote giddily to Florencia on the day of the battle. Using her big pen, Mariquita let her hopes and frustrations of the last twenty years spill onto the page. "You can imagine how my pulse is, my head, my heart. If I see Liberty returned to my country, and that God has preserved my loved ones, how I will thank Him. . . . I can't stop crying. I can't do anything. I pace back and forth in a stupor, waiting for passage back to the land of my sorrows."[8]

But Mariquita's joy was mixed with dread. She was elated that Rosas was defeated, but she knew nothing about the safety of her loved ones, even as she heard horror stories of looting and executions. With each passing hour Mariquita feared the worst. She cloistered herself in her home and canceled her normal activities. Finally, a letter from Florencia arrived saying all was well. Mariquita breathed a sigh of relief in her response. "Thank God for your letter, because not hearing from you turned all my joy to bitterness." Mariquita was so worried that she refused to attend the theater, as was her custom, because she felt it was "a crime to amuse myself without knowing if you were alright, or if you were sick, what with all the tumult and looting."[9]

"Long Live Urquiza and his brave companions!" Mariquita began one of her next letters to Florencia. "I am crazy for Urquiza. What language! What moderation! Everything is the way I like it! It seems like I have returned to 1810." After asking Florencia about some of her male friends, Mariquita turned her attention to women. "I can't wait to go and see all of my female patriots."[10] Soon Mariquita would be back home in the Buenos Aires she loved, which she also called the "land of my sorrows."

Juan Manuel's Turn in Exile

Juan Manuel, meanwhile, took refuge aboard an English warship anchored in the river. As his forces were overrun on the battlefield, Juan Manuel, wounded in the hand, hastily wrote a letter of resignation to the legislature of Buenos Aires. "Honorable Representatives, the time has come to return to you the office of governor of the province, as well as the plenitude of power with which you deigned to honor me." Rosas believed he had done his duty to the best of his abilities. "If we did not do more in the sacred support of our independence, of our integrity, and of our honor, it is because we could do no more."[11]

Juan Manuel then mounted his horse, Victoria, and galloped home, where

Eugenia Castro helped him organize his things. He packed some clothes, gathered his trunks of documents, grabbed what money he could, and headed for the docks where an English ship awaited him. He asked Eugenia to come, along with two of their six children—his favorites, Angela (the Saldadito) and Ermilio. Eugenia said no. She would stay with all of her children, even if it meant facing an uncertain future. Rosas was displeased, but there was little time to persuade her.[12] On the evening of February 3, Rosas and Manuelita boarded an English ship, the *Centaur*, which remained at anchor for a few days just off Buenos Aires, much to the consternation of the interim government. Finally, on February 10, Rosas and Manuelita sailed for England. The voyage was long, arriving in England on April 19, where Rosas was greeted with a salvo of cannons from the fort at Davenport. He continued on to Southampton, on the southern coast of England, where he rented a hotel room for the next few months while he tried to sort out his precarious situation.[13]

The Constitution of 1853

As Juan Manuel sailed into exile, Mariquita and others placed their hopes on the broad shoulders of General Urquiza, "the Victor of Caseros," as many now called him. But Urquiza wanted to be a benevolent victor. His motto the last many months, "Neither Victors Nor Vanquished," indicated his intention to pursue reconciliation instead of revenge. On February 4, the day after the battle, Urquiza appointed Mariquita's old friend Vicente López y Planes (the composer of the national anthem) as governor of the province. Urquiza also called for a convention in the city of Santa Fe (in the province of Santa Fe), where delegates from around the country would gather to write a constitution.

Many of Mariquita's friends influenced the constitutional debates. This was especially true of Juan Bautista Alberdi. After Rosas's defeat, Alberdi immediately began writing a book, and within a few weeks published *Foundations and Points of Departure for the Political Organization of the Argentine Republic*, which was soon disseminated throughout Argentina. Based on his extensive studies of various constitutions, including the US's, Alberdi proposed a system that would recognize the rights of the people, but did so through systems of indirect representation.[14] General Urquiza read the book and was impressed enough to send Alberdi a letter thanking him for writing a "thoughtful book" that would be "an important tool of cooperation" in the upcoming discussions.[15] Alberdi shared the book—and the letter from Urquiza—with Mariquita. She was duly impressed. "What joy I felt reading your little book, along with the beautiful letter Mr. Urquiza wrote you! I am very pleased to think that you will have a very beautiful page in our history."[16]

Only a few months later, however, Mariquita's optimism was in tatters. Soon after his victory, Urquiza expressed a sentiment common at the time: "After overcoming a powerful tyranny" like Rosas's, "all other [problems] appear smaller."[17] In reality, some things got worse, much to the chagrin of Mariquita. Porteño elites, led by Bartolomé Mitre, calculated that Urquiza's innovations would reduce the power of Buenos Aires relative to the other provinces. On September 11, 1852, porteños rose in rebellion, took over the government, and recalled their delegates from the Constitutional Convention in Santa Fe. Urquiza ultimately decided to negotiate with Buenos Aires rather than try to reconquer it. It was clear that, even with Rosas out of the picture, deep divisions still existed between Buenos Aires and her sister provinces. In fact, it would take ten long years before the country could be unified.

Mariquita's Frustrations Return

The political situation left Mariquita depressed, and she vented her frustrations to Alberdi. "Ahh my friend, how much I would give for a long hour of conversation!" Regarding the situation of their "unfortunate country," Mariquita admitted, "It is better that I don't say what I think." But she did feel comfortable lamenting the vicious attacks in the press against Urquiza and his representatives, including their good friend Juan María Gutiérrez, who, although from Buenos Aires, was representing Entre Ríos Province at the Constitutional Convention. Mariquita wanted to share more with Alberdi, but she knew that the mail was not safe. "If I had faith that this letter would get to you without complications, I would tell you more. But when there is no security, neither the mind nor the pen flow."[18]

Even without representatives from Buenos Aires, Juan María Gutiérrez and the other delegates continued to work. The result was the Constitution of 1853, which established a republic with a bicameral legislature. All the provinces but Buenos Aires ratified the constitution. In 1854, Urquiza was elected president of the Argentine Confederation, with its capital in Paraná, a city along the banks of the river by the same name. Buenos Aires Province, meanwhile, functioned as its own country, a division that would last into the early 1860s. Both Urquiza and Mitre sought recognition from foreign powers. Urquiza appointed Juan Bautista Alberdi as an envoy to Europe to seek support. Buenos Aires did the same. While in Madrid, Alberdi had an awkward encounter with his counterpart from Buenos Aires. It was none other than Juan Thompson, Mariquita's son.[19]

Mariquita supported Urquiza and the new constitution, and she was perplexed by her home province's refusal to join the union. Her letters throughout the 1850s are full of laments about politics. The bitter political infighting in Buenos Aires offended her sense of universal brotherhood. She spoke of the problem in a letter to her grandson Enrique Lezica. One politician from Buenos Aires, she wrote, referred to the whole Santa Fe Province (the site of the Constitutional Convention) as one big cow pasture. Such attitudes "do much harm," she warned her grandson. "The customs of each region should not be the object of insults." Mariquita used an example close to the heart of all Argentines—drinking the yerba mate tea—to emphasize her point. "Our mate, for example, is it not piggish? To drink from the same straw?" Those who have been insulted, she added, will never accept an outsider who engages in insults. "If Buenos Aires has strengthened itself, it is for that very reason that it should not insult its victims."[20] Mariquita believed, enough to share it with her grandson, that the porteños' hunger to maintain a dominant position over the rest of the provinces was at the center of the current political problems in the country.

Indeed, Mariquita wished that everyone would exhibit more respect. "In politics, as with religion, I am very tolerant," she wrote Alberdi in 1856, while he was in Paris on a diplomatic mission. "All I ask for is good faith. But the idea of tolerance is unknown here." She assured him that, if he read porteño newspapers, he would "blush at the language used to insult opponents." Many porteños, she found, hated Urquiza more than Rosas. "Don't read this letter to anyone," she pleaded, "because around here I have been labeled an 'Urquicista.'" Although she was not embarrassed of her sympathies, she nevertheless did not want to "start the people murmuring." Mariquita finished the letter in typical Mariquita style. "Don't forget to send me some of your writing, and the memoir you have written lately—I am eager to see them. . . . Stay healthy and happy, and enjoy that Paris I long for. Admire all that it has to offer, and don't forget your old friend."[21]

Rosas's Trial and Confiscations in Absentia

Although many porteños focused their disgust on Urquiza, they did not forget about Juan Manuel de Rosas, whom they sought to prosecute to the full extent of the law, and perhaps beyond. In one of their first acts after the Battle of Caseros, the Buenos Aires legislature declared that all of Juan Manuel's properties, including horses and cattle, would be confiscated. These included properties that belonged to Manuelita by inheritance from her mother's side, which, from a legal perspective, had nothing to do with Rosas or his government. Rosas protested these and other actions vigorously from Southampton, England. One of his closest friends back in Argentina was Josefa Gómez, a family friend who became Rosas's informal representative in Buenos Aires during his exile. Through Josefa Gómez and other friends and intermediaries, Rosas petitioned Urquiza to rescind the confiscations. As a rancher and politician himself, Urquiza sympathized with Rosas's plight. Later in 1852 Urquiza revoked the confiscations, which allowed Rosas's representatives to sell some of his property and thus provide the ex-governor with much-needed income. Thanks to Urquiza's magnanimity as well as support from some English friends, Rosas rented a comfortable residence in Southampton.[22]

Any prospects of a luxurious exile, however, were interrupted by two events in late 1852. On October 23, Manuelita married Máximo Terrero. Rosas had opposed their marriage while he was in power, in part because she was one of the main instruments in his government. In exile, he still coveted her close support. But Manuelita finally felt justified in pursuing her own romantic desires. Rosas accused Manuelita of abandoning him, and he refused to receive the couple's visits for years afterward, although they wrote him often from their home in London.[23]

About the same time Manuelita got married, Rosas received news of the September 11 uprising, when anti-Urquiza forces rebelled and took over the government of Buenos Aires. Much to Rosas's chagrin, the legislature reconfiscated all of his properties. Rosas protested again through letters, arguing that the province of Buenos Aires had no right to judge him, and that he needed an income to be able to live with some comfort. A "decent" living, according to Rosas, meant money for rent, servants, and a horse and carriage. Rosas also had significant medical bills, at least according to his son Juan, who complained that unscrupulous physicians were overcharging his father.[24]

FIGURE 12.1 Juan Manuel de Rosas's Burgess Farm, which he rented near Southampton, England. Courtesy of the Archivo General de la Nación, Buenos Aires.

Fortunately for Juan Manuel, friends in Buenos Aires, particularly Juan Nepomuceno Terrero, advanced Rosas some money each year, based on the value of his properties. Nevertheless, he was still chronically short on cash. On one occasion he was forced to sell the gold-encrusted scabbard that the Buenos Aires legislature gifted him after his 1833 frontier campaign.[25]

Juan Manuel the Farmer

But Juan Manuel's manhood was offended by his dependence on others. By 1858 he accepted that he might never recover his confiscated properties, so he took matters into his own hands by renting a farm to help pay his own expenses. To that end Rosas rented Burgess Farm, a five-hundred-acre piece of land a few miles outside of Southampton, where he raised a variety of animals and crops. Manuelita and Máximo were recipients of the literal fruits of his labors. In one letter, Manuelita thanked her father for the "splendid, fresh, and delicious" produce. She especially enjoyed the chickens, eggs, squash, cherries, apples, pears, and cucumbers.[26]

Although he was not a regular socialite, Rosas did, on occasion, attend dinners and other social events. And he apparently was not completely lacking in female company. When Juan Bautista Alberdi visited him in 1857, he noted that Rosas kept himself busy with "whores" and his "memoirs."[27] Some asked why Rosas did not remarry, a question he answered, at least in part, in a letter to his "Little Soldier" Angela, his favorite daughter with Eugenia. "I have not remarried because I don't have the means of taking care of a woman, and I don't want to marry a rich woman." Rosas also told his daughter Manuela that he interacted with Englishwomen of all walks of life, many of whom asked him for advice on various topics. They even asked him for the secrets of Manuelita's beautiful hair.[28]

When not engaged in ranching and farming, Rosas spent his time reading books and writing letters. Among his favorites included works from golden-age Spanish literature and Greek and Roman classics.[29] He also read attentively the news and other literature from Argentina and elsewhere that arrived ever more frequently by steamship. With great interest, Rosas also read books that began to be published about his era. He read a newly published four-volume history of Colombia, for example, where he undoubtedly found parallels between his career and Simón Bolívar's. In fact, while reading it, Rosas found evidence from Bolívar's life that Rosas used to justify his request for money to ensure a respectable lifestyle in England.[30]

Rosas surely had mixed sensations when he first handled Manuel Bilbao's *The History of Rosas*, the first full biography written about the ex-governor since his fall from power. After glancing it over, Rosas vented his frustration over Bilbao's *History of Rosas* to Josefa Gómez in the spring of 1868. "For now, the little I have seen of it, I have found errors, weaknesses, and falsehoods of such seriousness that any intelligent person who reads closely could not help but recognize them."[31] The obvious errors and distortions, in Rosas's eyes, caused him to reflect on the nature of history. Slander, Rosas surmised, especially when it is well rewarded, would always have more historians than the truth. This was also true with another recent publication: the memoirs of the Unitarian general Paz. Rosas found so many errors that he could not believe that Paz himself was the author. "Why don't they list the real authors?" he asked Josefa. Rosas found both Bilbao's *History of Rosas* and Paz's memoirs lacking in documentary evidence and objectivity. Why had they ignored different perspectives? Why did these authors ignore the disorder of the time? Why did they discount the assassinations of Dorrego and other leaders? And why did they not recognize Rosas's magnanimity and generosity when dealing with the captured General Paz himself?[32] Undoubtedly, many of Rosas's enemies wished he had practiced this kind of measured objectivity in his judgments and decrees while he was in power.

Rosas also corresponded with Eugenia Castro and her children, although not as often as they would have liked. Eugenia had refused Rosas's invitation to go with him into exile (with his two favorite children). Her choice, though noble, assured that she would struggle financially. Eugenia sent Rosas repeated letters—in 1852, 1853, and 1854—asking for support and wondering why he had forgotten her and the children. When Rosas finally responded in 1855, he chastised Eugenia for not coming with him to England, blaming it on her "damned ingratitude." Nevertheless, Rosas added, once his possessions were returned to him: "I could facilitate your trip here, with all of your children."[33]

Eugenia, in turn, took four years to answer that letter. Greeting him as her "dear father and sir," Eugenia recounted how she and her children had fallen on hard times, which prevented her from writing. But even though she was destitute, she continued, she tried not to inconvenience anyone. Margarita Ezcurra, Encarnación's relative, was always kind to help. All but two of the children were still living at home with her. Mercedes, the oldest, was married with two children. "I have never forgotten you, nor will I ever forget you," Eugenia promised. She in turn urged Rosas not to forget them. "The girls send a thousand greetings. Please don't forget this poor, unfortunate soul, and don't forget to send best wishes my way." She signed: "I am, as always, your most humble servant. Eugenia."[34]

Rosas's long delays in responding provoked sadness in his children. Angela, his Little Soldier, wrote him on May 21, 1866, asking him a question that burned in her heart: "Why have you so forgotten me, after having loved me?" She pleaded with him to send her a picture, "because I want to see you" and "I want you by my side." Angela continued pulling at heartstrings. "The tender times of my childhood are over," but someday, she hoped, "maybe you will remember me." She closed with "an embrace from your beloved soldier, Angela Castro."[35]

Rosas Receives Visitors in Southampton

Although Rosas spent much of his time alone with his servants and animals, he periodically received visitors. Manuelita and Máximo eventually made their peace with Rosas, but the hundred miles between their home in London and his in Southampton made their visits infrequent. Rosas occasionally entertained other visitors as well. One of them described the interior of his house. Boxes and trunks of documents were everywhere. Two clocks hung on the chimney, not far from a picture of the Virgin of la Merced (a gift from Eugenia). There was a shelf full of books, the most used being a Spanish-English dictionary, a testament to Rosas's love of words and to his attempts to learn the tongue of his new land.[36]

Another visitor was Vicente Pérez Rosales, a wealthy Chilean statesman with a conservative bent, who visited Rosas in 1855. Pérez Rosales fancied himself an astute observer of history and politics. Few figures intrigued him more than Juan Manuel de Rosas. Pérez Rosales was planning a trip to Europe, and he hoped to pay Rosas a visit along the way. In the first leg of his trip, Pérez Rosales traveled from Chile to Buenos Aires in May of 1855. He immediately sought out connections that would facilitate an audience with Rosas once he arrived in England. As he shared later in his memoirs, Pérez Rosales knew exactly what to do: "I asked Señora [Mariquita] de Mendeville." Mariquita, whom Pérez Rosales referred to as a "respected matron of Buenos Aires's high society," had invited him to her home for a visit, where she and her family welcomed him warmly. He asked her if any of Rosas's family still lived in the area. Thanks to Mariquita's network, Pérez Rosales soon met "one of the loveliest women" he had ever seen. Delighted that he wanted to visit Rosas, she pulled out one of her calling cards, wrote one word on the back of it, and gave it to Pérez Rosales as a letter of introduction.[37]

Once in England, Pérez Rosales called on Rosas at his residence in Southampton. "I heard the firm voice of a man who seemed to be accustomed to command, ordering that I be admitted." Pérez Rosales described the sixty-two-year-old Rosas as "above medium height, and sturdily built" with a "white and ruddy" complexion, "two beautiful blue eyes, an aquiline nose, and thin, but perfectly marked lips." He was a bit surprised to find Rosas dressed like an Englishman since many in Buenos Aires insisted that the former governor always dressed in gaucho or military attire. Initially Rosas was reserved toward his Chilean visitor, but as soon as he read the word on the back of his relative's calling card, Pérez Rosales wrote that he "rose from his seat and stretched out his arms to me, calling me his *paisano* or countryman" (perhaps revealing the word on the card). Rosas showed Pérez Rosales his domicile, including his many documents. "Do you see all this, paisano?" Rosas asked, referring to the boxes of papers lying everywhere. "Well, these are the private archives of my government. Here you can find not only the documents that vindicate my conduct, but also many of those that prove the perfidy of my enemies, some of whom are ingrates and almost all of whom are wicked men. One day all these documents will be made public, and that's what I'm working on now." Over the next few days, Pérez Rosales and Rosas had lunch together and shared yerba mate numerous times. Mate, Pérez Rosales noted, "seemed to be his favorite drink," and he took it "without sugar."[38]

Juan Bautista Alberdi also visited the ex-governor in England. "Last night I met Rosas," Alberdi wrote in his diary on October 18, 1857. General Urquiza (now president) commissioned Alberdi as a representative of the Argentine Confederation and sent him to Europe to obtain recognition from England and other foreign powers. The two met at the home of a mutual acquaintance. After introductions, Rosas asked Alberdi to thank President Urquiza, whose earlier intervention helped him have a decent life in England. Rosas quickly warmed up to Alberdi, calling him variably "paisano," "Mr. Minister," or "Juan," his first name. Touching on politics, Rosas rejected Buenos Aires's right to pass judgment on him. Rosas also spoke to Alberdi about the pleasures of English country life, especially the magnificence of English horses.[39]

Alberdi perceived that Rosas was well accepted in English society. Even though the ex-governor spoke English very poorly, he did so confidently, without pausing. Rosas, Alberdi observed, "has the manner of a man accustomed to seeing the world from above. Nevertheless, he is not a braggart nor is he arrogant." In that way, Alberdi concluded, Rosas was like the English lords—"the most gentle and amicable people in the country." Looking back on his trip, Alberdi concluded that Rosas, with only one exception, treated him better than any other porteño in Europe. During their meeting and afterward, Alberdi found his view of Rosas shifting. In exile during much of Rosas's regime, Alberdi had formed an idea of Rosas as a great monster and tyrant. But after meeting him in person, that view softened. "His respectful attitude toward the [confederation] and its national government made me less suspicious of him."

Alberdi admitted that he found it hard to believe that the Rosas sitting before him, separated as he was from his accoutrements of power, had dominated Buenos Aires Province and the country so thoroughly. Meeting Rosas personally led Alberdi to believe, more firmly than before, that it was the historic role of the province of Buenos Aires that was the source of Argentina's problems. Rosas alone was not to blame.[40]

Alberdi's more nuanced view of Rosas was evident in a letter he wrote to Manuelita in which he urged her to convince her father to sit for a photograph. Photographic technology arrived in the Río de la Plata in the early 1840s and quickly grew in popularity. Mariquita sat for a daguerreotype image, but Juan Manuel refused the new technology, and he tried to dissuade Manuelita from having her image taken as well. Rosas's s stubbornness continued in exile. Manuelita, however, disregarded her father's aversion and began sitting for numerous photographs over the next few years.[41] Likewise, Alberdi believed that a photograph of Rosas in exile would help his image in Buenos Aires. Rosas, Alberdi found, looked so well in Southampton, and—according to some views of the time—fine facial and head features denoted intelligence. "I believe that active and sustained exercise of intelligence over many years develops and modifies the material configuration of the head," Alberdi wrote Manuelita not long after he visited her father in Southampton.[42] Alberdi implied that Rosas's good and intelligent looks, if captured in a photograph, could counter the negative image of Rosas being portrayed in Buenos Aires. Indeed, in the same year that Alberdi visited the ex-governor, Rosas was put on trial by criminal courts in Buenos Aires. The verdict and sentence: guilty of high treason, punishable by death.[43] Rosas never did sit for a photograph.

As the years wore on, however, the number of visitors to Rosas's home diminished. He seemed to pass most of his time on his farm. He lamented his lonely and frugal state to Josefa Gómez in a letter from 1864. "I don't smoke, I don't use snuff or drink wine or any other liquor. I don't attend dinners nor do I make or receive visits. I don't go out or attend the theater, or participate in any other diversions. My clothes are those of a commoner. My hands and face are sunburned, testaments to how much I work each day to support myself. My food is a piece of grilled meat, and my yerba mate, nothing more." What disappointed Juan Manuel most was that he did not have the money to publish his defense against "cruel enemies" who constantly published "unjust calumnies" against him.[44]

Mariquita Back in the Saddle

While Juan Bautista Alberdi was on his European mission for the confederation, Mariquita took a big step toward returning to a semblance of her old life. Despite her sympathies with Urquiza, Mariquita was appointed secretary of the Sociedad de Beneficencia in 1857. This was fortuitous timing, for that very year the Sociedad was in the midst of a campaign to bring back the remains of its founder, Bernardino Rivadavia, who had died in 1845 while in exile in Spain. The repatriation of Rivadavia's remains was a massively symbolic act used by the government of Buenos Aires to shape national identity and national unity. In their own ways, Mariquita and Juan Manuel were key parts of the symbolism of Rivadavia's return.

Mariquita was intimately linked to Rivadavia. In 1823 he chose her as a founding member of the Sociedad de Beneficencia. Mariquita was also an enthusiastic supporter of Rivadavia's reforms in the 1820s. Rivadavia was exiled after his failed 1826 constitution, and he became one of the most despised

Unitarian figures in the official history of the Rosas era. But changes in political systems inevitably include redefinitions of heroes and villains alike. After the Battle of Caseros, Rosas became the great villain of the new official history, a history that now hailed Rivadavia as one of the great founding fathers of Argentina. The new government in Buenos Aires decided it was time to reposition bodies to align heroes and villains with the current political climate. With Rosas exiled in England, it made sense for Rivadavia's body to return to his homeland.

On August 20, 1857, Rivadavia's remains arrived at the docks of Buenos Aires and were transported the few miles to La Recoleta Cemetery. Thousands of onlookers paid homage along the way. Mariquita attended the ceremony at Rivadavia's tomb, a ceremony that included speeches by María Carreras (the current Sociedad president), José Mármol, Domingo Sarmiento, and Bartolomé Mitre. All of them touched on similar themes: the Argentine family had been broken, and it was now being reunited with the help of the remains of one of its great founding fathers.

Speaking first, María Carreras praised Rivadavia as a pioneer in women's rights. He was "the first in our country to understand" that women "could and should share many of the concerns of public life." Rivadavia, she continued, also saved women from degradation by giving them education so that they could better raise patriotic children. "He tried to create good citizens by first creating good mothers."[45] José Mármol, the vice president of the senate, followed. With this act of repatriation, he asserted, the Argentine nation has gathered "the bones of her great sons banished by the hatred of tyrants" and "returns them to our universal mother." Taking his turn, Sarmiento referred to the ceremony as a gathering of the "great Argentine family to receive the remains of [their] son who died in a strange land." Bartolomé Mitre declared the repatriation a "victory" for Rivadavia, but not a victory of armies. Instead, Rivadavia's true victory was found in each child attending the schools he founded. His victory was also evident in all the women, especially the "priestesses of beneficence," who cared for the sick, who educated poor girls, and who were parents to the orphans. "These are the ideas [Rivadavia] spread over this earth."[46]

With their founder buried in a place of honor in La Recoleta Cemetery, the Sociedad continued its actions of beneficence, founding schools for girls and opening a hospice for insane women, an act that for Mariquita surely conjured up painful memories of her first love, Martín. Another significant issue the Sociedad confronted was the question of racial segregation in schools. As always, the Sociedad was a major sponsor of education in the city. In 1850s Argentina, as in most of the hemisphere, schools segregated white and non-white students. Although the issue of segregated classrooms was not open to debate, some members of the Sociedad thought it appropriate for all the girls, regardless of color, to attend the same awards ceremony, which happened every few months. There was sharp disagreement among the members. When the issue went to a vote, ten voted to integrate the ceremony while eleven voted against the measure. Mariquita voted to keep the awards ceremony segregated. She defended her position, arguing that she did not want the other women to get the wrong idea. It "has not been my intention to cheat the colored classes of their education." Mariquita believed in a "prudent separation of the two classes so as to avoid future problems and unpleasantness."[47] The persistence of racial hierarchies was in part the "bondage of old habits" that Alberdi would later refer to—habits that would continue in Argentina. It is significant that nearly half the women voted more progressively than Mariquita on this issue. But in a hemisphere where racial and social hierarchies still reigned supreme, perhaps it was more significant that ten women voted in favor of integrating the ceremony in the first place.

As secretary of the society, Mariquita also dealt with the energetic intervention of her old friend Domingo Sarmiento, who in 1861 was superintendent of schools in Buenos Aires Province. Sarmiento was eager to implement modern educational methods, including in the schools run by the Sociedad. After a thorough review of the Sociedad's educational efforts, Sarmiento issued a critical report, questioning the efficacy of the curriculum and the level of learning. He also believed that some of the funds used by the Sociedad could be better used elsewhere. True to her personality, Mariquita shot back boldly in a letter to Sarmiento. "What a move my old friend has pulled on me with that sinister report against this poor Sociedad!" She instructed Sarmiento: do "not start a fight with me." She then outlined how the budget was spent and asked for even more money for various materials, including a globe. She accused Sarmiento of being "unjust" in his report. "Don't make war against us, because we can do much good by working together. For my part, I don't pay attention to your recriminations because I believe they come from your passion for education, and for that I forgive you."[48] For Mariquita, who had worked on behalf of the Sociedad's educational programs since 1823, Sarmiento's report was a stinging rebuke not only to her, but also to the legacy of Bernardino Rivadavia, who had founded the Sociedad. Mariquita composed a few verses in honor of the incident. "What say you, my young girl, of the sad incident, when Rivadavia was killed by the boys of Sarmiento?"[49]

Mariquita and Jean Baptiste

For Mariquita, the 1850s also brought a rebirth of good feelings toward her husband, Jean Baptiste. His health was declining, particularly his eyesight. Mariquita even thought of rejoining him if he received a favorable transfer. "In my dreams, I'm not sure why, I see myself going to Chile," she wrote Alberdi in January of 1851. And if Mendeville was appointed there, "I would leave instantly."[50] New appointments, however, were not forthcoming for Jean Baptiste. His ill health forced him to retire from his post in Ecuador, and by 1853 he had returned to France where his sister helped care for him.

A sampling of her letters to Jean Baptiste after 1853 reveal a Mariquita full of tenderness and concern for her estranged husband, as well as a resurgence of her hopes to visit Paris. "Two mail bags have come without letters from you, and I tremble because of your eyesight," she wrote in October of 1853. "If my funds permitted, I would visit you, but since I don't have the money to travel to Paris without overburdening you, I cannot comfort myself by visiting and helping you in your trials." She assured Jean Baptiste, "It would be a great pleasure to show you my unalterable affection."[51] But her desire to care for the ailing Jean Baptiste, and her longing to visit Paris, were still not enough to get her on a boat. Money for the trip surely could have been raised between Jean Baptiste, Mariquita, and their children, but there were many reasons Mariquita chose not to travel. She still felt insecure about speaking French, and trans-Atlantic travel at her age was also daunting. And after not seeing Mendeville for fifteen years, perhaps the prospect of reintegrating their lives may have been too difficult.

With little hope of seeing Jean Baptiste, Mariquita poured her heart out in letters. "I assure you that you don't suffer your illness more than I do," she wrote him in 1860.[52] "If my sacrifices could give you back your sight, I would do something." She was also pleased to hear that Jean Baptiste had moved to Paris, where "pleasures and comforts" consoled both "the stomach and the spirit."[53]

Mariquita also empathized with Jean Baptiste as he faced the ills of aging.

"There is no remedy, my friend, against getting older. In a century of great discoveries, no progress has been made on this point. From now on it is all gray hair and wrinkles." But Mariquita was not going to go gently into the night of old age. "If you saw me battle this enemy, you would with good reason envy my genius." And battle she did, on a daily basis. Mariquita had a number of recipes for age-combatting ointments and pomades. One mixture to preserve her hair included cocoa butter, sweet almond oil, and wax. Another concoction to combat wrinkles called for a dose of lily juice, honey, and wax, which Mariquita recommended be applied on a nightly basis. Another one of her age-battling tactics was to stay active. "I write constantly, I sew, mend, and patch." Her grandchildren also kept Mariquita on her toes. "I play some popular piano pieces, and if the granddaughters want to dance, I can play the latest polkas and other things." Besides keeping her young, playing with the grandchildren distracted Mariquita from other realities of life. "Do you know why I live this busy life? So I don't think and go crazy." As she looked around Buenos Aires, Mariquita could not help but see all the properties she used to own, and she tried not to dwell on what might have been had she been able to preserve more of her wealth and property.[54]

Jean Baptiste passed away in France in 1863. Mariquita hoped to inherit money as well as various items from her husband of forty-three years. However, Mendeville's family in France moved to disinherit Mariquita and her children by claiming that her marriage to Mendeville was not legal in France because it was only a religious ceremony. Argentine law codes in 1820, when they wed (and still in 1863), left marriage completely in the hands of the Catholic Church. Marriage in France, on the other hand, had been controlled by civil authorities since the days of the French Revolution. Mariquita feared that many items in Jean Baptiste's possession were already sold. She did not have legal representation in France, so she turned to her friend Juan Bautista Alberdi, who was living in France at the time, and asked him to represent her family in this legal matter.

Besides the larger questions of inheritance, there were a few items in particular that Mariquita wanted back from Mendeville's estate. She wanted any family portraits, as well as three medals from the wars of independence. These were "two large silver medallions" commemorating the Battles of Salta and Tucumán, and a gold medallion depicting the liberation of Lima by General San Martín. Mariquita explained that the medals "were sent to me by the two generals, an honor bestowed on only a few, but that no other woman in the country received. You know how much joy it would bring me to recover them."[55] Mariquita eventually recovered the family portraits. Unfortunately, as feared, she found out that the medallions had been sold to collectors, who refused to sell them back.[56] As for other items, Mariquita heard that Jean Baptiste had a few thousand francs to his name when he died, and there were stories that he owned mines in Quito as well—items that she asked Alberdi to check on in France.[57] To her dismay, she never received anything else.

The whole situation made Mariquita divulge to Alberdi things she had never told anyone before about her long history with Jean Baptiste. When she met him, he was in a "most unhappy" state. He came to Buenos Aires with no resources and was forced to give piano lessons to survive. "I married him, and my fortune became his. I had no influence beyond his caprice. I was very unhappy." Two other suitors desired her hand, "both of them superior to him." But, she admitted, "I deceived myself." Finally sharing the story, she told Alberdi, was a great relief to her heart. "But let's stop talking about it."[58]

Although Mariquita did not receive the inheritance she hoped for from her husband's estate, she was surrounded by a supportive family in Buenos Aires that gave her great joy and comfort. Juan Thompson, her oldest child, returned from Spain that year and moved in with her. Florencia was also still in Buenos Aires, and Julio was close enough to visit in Montevideo.

Mariquita remained active even in her old age. In 1866, a young intellectual, Santiago Estrada, asked her to write a memoir of growing up in the colonial period. Mariquita was happy to oblige and soon produced *Memories of a Colonial Life*. In 1866 Mariquita was also elected president of the Sociedad de Beneficencia, a post she had occupied thirty-five years earlier during Rosas's first governorship. Besides the traditional focus on educating poor girls, the year 1866 happened to be the height of Argentina's war with Paraguay, a war that claimed the lives of thousands of Argentines. Included among the dead was the son Rosas had with Eugenia Castro. Coincidentally, Rosas's bitter enemy Domingo Sarmiento also lost his son—his only child—to the war. Mariquita and the Sociedad organized aid for the wounded returning from the front. Also, cholera broke out in the city that year, which occupied the time and talents of Mariquita and her fellow Sociedad members.

In June of 1868, Mariquita stopped attending Sociedad meetings. She sensed the end of her life was near. In a letter to Juan María Gutiérrez on June 20, 1868, Mariquita admitted she had been "thinking a lot about my final journey, and whenever I can I put papers in order."[59] In early October she wrote her final testament. Mariquita Sánchez de Thompson de Mendeville died on October 23, eight days before her eighty-third birthday. Much of the city mourned her death, as seen in a tribute to her in *La Tribuna* newspaper. She was buried in La Recoleta Cemetery in a ceremony attended by members of the Sociedad de Beneficencia and other dignitaries.[60]

Twilight in Southampton

Juan Manuel de Rosas outlived his old friend Mariquita Sánchez. He also outlived his lover, Eugenia Castro. In November of 1876, "Little Soldier" Angela Castro informed Rosas in a letter that her mother had passed away. Eugenia was fifty-two years old. Rosas responded on December 3. "My dear Little Soldier," he began. "It is with feelings of pain and satisfaction that I received your dear letter of the 21st of last month." Rosas was saddened by the death of their "dear Eugenia," but was happy that Angela had done her duty before God of assisting her mother until the end. "Yes, we should never forget our mothers. As for me, I always keep mine close." Mothers deserved praise, Rosas continued, for myriad reasons: they risk their lives to give birth; they nourish children with the milk of their breasts; they care for children during times of illness; and they teach and counsel through hard times. Rosas promised that, now that Eugenia was gone, Angela would receive what had been promised to her mother, whom he praised for her "unwavering faithfulness in caring for Encarnación, Manuelita, and I in our illnesses." Rosas finished the letter complaining about his economic situation. "I continue to be poor—very poor, and in a sad state, working as always to help make ends meet in my miserable financial condition. Goodbye, my dear little soldier. I bless you on behalf of your mother Eugenia, your mistress Encarnación, and me, at 83 years, nine months and three days. I am, as always, your loving patron, Rosas."[61]

As Rosas pointed out to his Little Soldier, he was feeling his age. Despite his advanced years, Rosas still spent hours riding his horse around his farm and carrying on his business. But in early March of 1877, Rosas contracted pneumonia. The robust body of yesteryear was no more, and Rosas died on

FIGURE 12.3 *Portrait of General Juan Manuel de Rosas in His Final Years* by Fernando García del Molino. Courtesy of the Museo Histórico Nacional, Buenos Aires.

March 14, 1877, just days before his eighty-fourth birthday. He stated in his will that, in the short term, he wanted to be buried in the Catholic cemetery of Southampton. However, once "my country recognizes, along with its government, the justice owed me for my services," he wanted his body taken back to Argentina for a dignified though modest burial.[62] Meanwhile, back in Argentina, José Mármol had already prophesied that "not even the dust of his bones will be had in America."[63]

Mariquita and Juan Manuel in Argentine History and Imagination

On September 30, 1989, Mariquita Sánchez and Juan Manuel de Rosas were once again neighbors. This time, however, it was not in the sumptuous houses of early nineteenth-century Buenos Aires. Instead, it was in the most luxurious cemetery in the land—La Recoleta. After 112 years buried in England, Juan Manuel finally returned, by boat, to his home province. A large procession accompanied his remains from the dock to the cemetery. A select few, full of emotion, pulled the carriage carrying the coffin, escorted by horsemen dressed in traditional gaucho attire. Some observers claimed that a few of the escorts were dressed like members of the Mazorca. Thousands watched in silence, while others shut their windows and doors in disgust. If onlookers looked closely, they might have understood the significance of who was marching with whom. In the procession, descendants of Juan Manuel de Rosas walked together with descendants of Juan Lavalle, as well as with descendants of other enemies of Rosas. After a brief ceremony in the cemetery, Rosas's remains were laid to rest in a family tomb.[1] Just over a hundred paces away, angling toward the cemetery's entrance, lay his old friend Mariquita Sánchez de Thompson de Mendeville.

The repatriation of Juan Manuel de Rosas in 1989 occurred during an extremely sensitive political moment for Argentina. Understanding the context of that moment helps reveal the controversial role Rosas played, and continues to play, in Argentine society. Presiding over the events of the repatriation was the newly elected president of Argentina, Carlos Saúl Menem, who hoped the return of Rosas would help heal a bitterly divided nation. Most recently, those divisions stemmed from a brutal Cold War military dictatorship that tortured and killed thousands of civilians between 1976 and 1983. But President

Menem also said he wanted to heal wounds that dated back to more remote times Mariquita and Juan Manuel. In one of his inaugural addresses, President Menem declared that he wanted to be president "of Sarmiento and Rosas." He just as well could have said he wanted to be president of Mariquita and Juan Manuel.

The image and legacy of Mariquita and Juan Manuel remained vibrant and active after their deaths. In life, Mariquita was hailed as a key player in the nation's founding and development. After death, that reputation was solidified in history and art. The postmortal state of Juan Manuel de Rosas's reputation, on the other hand, was laden with controversy, as his image became a symbol, depending on one's perspective, of all the promises or problems of Argentine history.

The Legacy of Mariquita

As news of Rosas's defeat reached Montevideo in 1852, Mariquita declared to her daughter: "I am going to write the history of the women of my country. They are real people."[2] In a way she did write it, in her own style, through the letters she wrote in her court battle with her mother in 1804, and through her records as secretary of the Sociedad de Beneficencia, as well as through her memoirs, diaries, and countless letters. And even before her death, others started writing about her as well. Foreign travelers and residents like the Frenchman Arsene Isabel and the Englishman William Parish Robertson, for example, included high praise for her in their letters and memoirs. After her death, Mariquita's friend Vicente Fidel López included a glowing description of Mariquita and her salon in his multivolume history of Argentina published in the 1880s.[3] In Pastor Obligado's 1903 *Tradiciones argentinas*, Mariquita played a prominent role in three chapters, one of which portrayed her as a key player in the creation of the national anthem.[4]

Another "text" that fixed Mariquita as an influential player in porteño society was a painting by a Chilean artist. Pedro Subercaseaux produced a number of paintings to commemorate the 1910 centennial celebration of the Latin American independence movements, including one portraying the first performance of the Argentine national anthem.[5] In his memoirs, Subercaseaux explained how he composed the work. "I put together my group of subjects: some young ladies dressed in 'imperial' fashion, alongside which are painted representations of [General] San Martín . . . and a few other men. At the clavichord sat the accompanist for the singer, Mariquita Thompson, who was meant to be the principal figure in the piece."[6] Though not meant to be historically accurate in a literal sense, Subercaseaux's painting went on display in Buenos Aires museums and provided visual reinforcement of Mariquita's influential position in the creation of revolutionary society after May of 1810. The painting's popularity also demonstrates that, by the early 1900s, Mariquita was a key figure in the contested identity of Argentina, an identity still very much in flux even after one hundred years of independence.[7] The vision of Mariquita depicted in Pastor Obligado's *Tradiciones* (1903) and Subercaseaux's painting (1910) made its way into primary-school textbooks, ensuring that generations of Argentine children would remember Mariquita as the first person to sing the national anthem. As discussed in chapter 6, even if evidence does not support the literal accuracy of Subercaseaux's painting, it does nevertheless reflect the larger truth that speaks to the influence of Mariquita's tertulia (see fig. 4.1).[8]

Other historians soon illuminated more about Mariquita's remarkable life. In 1923, Antonio Dellepiane wrote a biography of Mariquita, which he declared would help inaugurate a long-neglected subject: the study of notable women in Argentine history.[9] In the early 1950s, Clara Vilaseca edited a large collection of Mariquita's letters.[10] Another press published Mariquita's memoirs of growing up in the viceroyalty. Since then, three biographies of Mariquita have been published in Spanish. The first was by Mariquita's descendant Ricardo Zavalía Lagos (1986), followed by María Sáenz Quesada (1995), and then Graciela Batticuore (2011). Together, they capture Mariquita in all of her triumphs and tragedies and complications: rebellious child; patriot of 1810; tertulia hostess; long-suffering wife and mother; Francophile; administrator; mentor; Romantic; anti-Rosista; exile; moderate Federalist; grandmother; writer. Mariquita has also been the subject of at least one novel; and her piano (which still plays) and other of her possessions, as well as Subercaseaux's painting of her singing the national anthem, have been displayed prominently in the Museo Histórico Nacional in the neighborhood of San Telmo, Buenos Aires.[11]

Mariquita's sumptuous mansion on Florida Street is all gone, replaced by a myriad of stores on Calle Florida, one of the great shopping streets of the world. If Mariquita could walk out of her house today, she would find herself face to face with a McDonald's and other businesses, many of them foreign.[12] Juan Manuel's principal residence, his Palermo estate, is now a large park.

Juan Manuel after Death

Juan Manuel de Rosas's postmortal journey through the history and imagination of Argentina has been a much more turbulent affair. The most controversial and contested aspects of Rosas's life were his actions as provincial governor and as the head of the Argentine Confederation. But before Rosas was governor and brigadier general, he was Juan Manuel the boy, the husband, the father, the rancher. He was Juan Manuel the Indian agent, Indian fighter, and militia commander who rose to power after previous governments failed repeatedly to craft a viable constitution. At one level, there is no debate about *what* Juan Manuel de Rosas was as a leader. During his exile, he described his ideal leadership qualities. In a way he may have been him describing how he viewed himself. "For me the ideal of good government would be paternal autocracy, intelligent, disinterested, and indefatigable . . . I have always admired the autocratic dictators who have been the first servants of their people."[13] Here Rosas in a sense admits that he was an autocratic dictator (who was also tireless). Yet opinions diverge dramatically regarding the next part of his description: to what extent was Rosas paternal, intelligent, disinterested, and a servant of the people? As backdrop to these questions lies another: to what extent was Rosas's rule legitimate, usurped, popular, or coercive? And if he had any legitimacy to begin with, did his actions in office justify attempts to remove him by any means necessary?

During his life Rosas had eloquent literary proponents as well as the official Rosista press to laud his name. Rosas's exiled enemies, on the other hand, produced volumes of anti-Rosas tracts that painted him in the worst of lights. After the Battle of Caseros in 1852, Bartolomé Mitre made the anti-Rosas perspectives part of the standard history of the nation. In 1857 Mitre published a collection of biographies entitled *Galería de celebridades argentinas* (Gallery of Argentine Celebrities), which helped establish what might be called a new "mainstream" view of Argentine history. Rosas was not included, but Mitre did mention him and his fellow Federalist strongmen as examples that were to be shunned by all Argentines.[14] The growing anti-Rosas perspective came into full view when news of Rosas's death arrived in Buenos Aires in 1877. Faced with the prospect of pro-Rosas manifestations, the national government decided to suppress any veneration of his memory. Any public demonstration in favor of "the tyrant Rosas" was prohibited. Instead, the government declared that the *victims* of Rosas's tyranny would be honored.[15]

But Rosas also had his defenders after his exile and after his death. His popularity endured, especially among the rural and lower classes.[16] He had intellectual allies as well. The Chilean statesman Vicente Pérez Rosales, who visited him in Southampton in 1855, defended Rosas while at the same time recognizing the difficulty of passing historical judgment on him. In his 1882 memoirs, Pérez Rosales argued that the histories of Rosas were so polemical that "the impartial outsider, if he is to be fair, must suspend his judgment until he is better informed."[17] While recognizing the difficulty of passing historical judgment so early, Pérez Rosales nevertheless felt comfortable stating some "indisputable" facts about Rosas. He "challenged France, spat in the face of England, heaped scorn on Brazil, and managed at the same time to struggle against his implacable domestic enemies and maintain his extraordinary power."[18] Even Domingo Sarmiento admitted later that Rosas "was a republican who used all of the artifices of the popular representative system," and that he "was the expression of the will of the people, as the elections surely demonstrate."[19]

New Perspectives on Rosas and the Rise of Revisionism

Around 1900, some Argentine historians began writing more even-handed histories of Rosas, such as Ernesto Quesada's *La época de Rosas* (1898). According to Quesada, Rosas was not the monster that Unitarians and their successors portrayed. Instead, Rosas was a man of his time who, perhaps with greater ability than his cohorts, governed using methods acceptable at the time.[20] Despite some positive treatment, most academic historians continued with negative attitudes toward Rosas.

Beginning in the 1920s and 1930s, a new generation of writers began producing pro-Rosas materials. This movement, known as Revisionism, was pushed especially by conservative nationalists who, like nationalists elsewhere, resented the influence of liberalism in the world. In addition, many nationalists in Argentina feared the masses of immigrants coming to Argentine shores—immigrants who brought dangerous ideas like socialism, anarchism, and communism, which, if not checked, might overrun Argentine culture and identity.[21]

Argentine nationalists fixated on Juan Manuel de Rosas as a model of a powerful Catholic leader who resisted foreign aggression. Nationalists also saw in Rosas someone who lived his life guided by local creole, or gaucho, customs and values—values present in the popular epic poem *El gaucho Martín Fierro* by José Hernández. These values, nationalists asserted, were authentically Argentine. Manuel de Anchorena, a nationalist politician and also a descendant of Rosas, captured this view. "We should mention that we consider [Rosas] to be the most gaucho of all Argentines of all times. We have already indicated that he lived and died like a gaucho. Up to his last moments, as he made up his will, in his use of bolas and the lasso, and in spending even the last days of his life on horseback, he honored the verses of Martín Fierro."[22]

For Anchorena and other nationalists, it was an insult to the nation that Juan Manuel de Rosas, their great hero, was buried in England of all places, the biggest foreign exploiter of all! Thus, in the 1930s, Rosas supporters founded the Pro-Repatriation Committee, dedicated to bringing Rosas back to Argentine soil. In 1938, nationalists also founded the Juan Manuel de Rosas Historical Institute, whose purpose was to produce the true history of Rosas, free from the distortions of "official history," as many of them referred to the standard history taught in schools and universities. Many of the histories produced by nationalist writers, however, suffered from the same distortion as some of the early anti-Rosas official history. For the extreme Revisionist, Rosas could do no wrong. Moderate and left-leaning academics at times felt it their duty to combat extremist politics by continuing to cut Rosas down to size, especially since many saw the Rosas legacy in the military governments that ruled Argentina frequently after 1930.

JUAN PERÓN AND ROSAS

The pro-Rosas movement also found an ally in Juan Domingo Perón, president of Argentina from 1946 to 1955. This was true especially after Perón went into exile after his overthrow in 1955, when he was trying to gain support from as many groups in Argentina as he could.[23] In a 1970 letter to Manuel de Anchorena, Perón praised Rosas's legacy. In "the fight for liberation, Brigadier General Don Juan Manuel de Rosas deserves to be the archetype that inspires and guides us, because for more than a century and a half of shameful colonialism, he has been one of the few who knew how to honorably defend national sovereignty."[24]

Perón's time in exile corresponded with the surge in revolutionary movements in Argentina and around the world, inspired by a variety of figures including Marx, Lenin, Trotsky, Mao, and, more recently, Fidel Castro and Argentina's own Che Guevara in the Cuban Revolution of 1959. Meanwhile, military governments ruled frequently in Argentina. By 1970, groups of armed revolutionaries, such as the Montoneros, were active in many Argentine cities. By the early 1970s, political violence in Argentina was so bad that Juan Perón was allowed to return from exile and run for office again. When Perón was elected president for the third time in 1973, he appointed Manuel de Anchorena as ambassador to Great Britain and gave him two main tasks: resolve the Malvinas/Falklands conflict, and arrange for the return of Rosas's remains. Anchorena helped arrange for Rosas's return, but just as the repatriation was about to move forward, Argentina descended into chaos and everything was put on hold.[25]

From Military Dictatorship to Democracy

Juan Perón died in office in 1974, without solving the divisions in Argentine society. Nor could his successor, his vice president and third wife, Isabel Perón. On March 24, 1976, Argentine military forces overthrew the government and instituted a dictatorship, vowing to save the country from a communist takeover. The military government targeted armed rebel groups but also used state terror against thousands of unarmed civilians labeled as enemies of the state, including left-leaning students, labor leaders, social activists, and intellectuals, among others. Many victims were "disappeared" without a trace, dumped into mass graves or cast into the river or ocean from airplanes. Numerous babies of executed mothers were taken and adopted out to military families or to other collaborators.[26] Persistent economic crises and declining popularity drove the military government in 1982 to gamble on invading the Malvinas Islands and reclaiming them from the British. After losing the war with Great Britain that followed, the Argentine military allowed civilian elections. In 1983, Raúl Alfonsín of the Radical Party was elected president. President Alfonsín initiated an intense investigation of human rights violations during the dictatorship, an investigation that resulted in the conviction of many top military commanders. These convictions in turn led to a spate of military uprisings by dissident soldiers protesting the mistreatment and humiliation of the armed forces. Some Argentines feared another military coup.[27]

The question of repatriating Rosas's remains gained new life with the return of democracy. And while Alfonsín's government did not have time, or perhaps the desire, to deal with the Rosas question, filmmakers took up the topic of Rosas. In 1983, María Luisa Bemberg directed *Camila*, which told the story of the fateful love affair between Camila O'Gorman and the priest Ladislao Gutiérrez. Although the film was ostensibly about the brutality of the Rosas regime, Bemberg used Rosismo as a metaphor for the state violence of the recent military dictatorship while at the same time reinforcing many traditional notions of Rosista society.[28]

In 1989, newly elected president Carlos Saúl Menem also planned to use Rosas as a metaphor. As Menem took office, inflation stood at astronomical levels, military-civilian relations were tense, and relations between rival political groups were conflictive. Menem believed that he, as president, could bridge all these divides and cure the wounds that history had inflicted on his country. Menem perceived that these wounds originated not only in the recent history of state terrorism, but also in the more remote history of the conflicts between Rosas and his opponents in the nineteenth century. It was in his inaugural speech that he declared that he wanted to be "president of Rosas and Sarmiento."[29]

To help in this healing process, Menem reached out to the Pro-Repatriation Committee. Menem believed that bringing Juan Manuel de Rosas back to Argentina would be a powerful symbol of reconciliation. In particular, Menem wanted to address long-standing divisions between nationalists (Rosistas) and liberals (anti-Rosistas), as well as grapple with the most pressing problem of the moment—the sour civilian-military relations. In fact, the idea was to make Rosas's repatriation a preamble for something big: President Menem planned on pardoning the military commanders convicted for crimes during the recent dictatorship. To that end, Menem sent a commission to England that successfully arranged for the exhumation and repatriation of Rosas's remains.[30]

As the process moved forward, Argentines debated the merits and the meaning of Rosas's return. Many groups praised the repatriation as an act of national reconciliation and national unity. But others opposed the repatriation as well, especially because they associated Rosas's return with President Menem's plan to pardon military officials. The idea of pardoning military commanders was more controversial than the repatriation of Rosas, with polls putting opposition to the pardons at 70 percent of the population. Meanwhile, even ardent critics of Rosas seemed willing to accept his remains.[31] María Sáenz Quesada, who would later write a biography of Mariquita Sánchez, was the director of a major museum in Buenos Aires at the time. Before the repatriation, she was happy to have Rosas stay buried in England, although she did recognize that he had a right to return, and she felt comfortable once it happened.[32] The editor of the prominent newspaper *La Nación* declared that he was not opposed, necessarily, to the repatriation. However, he wanted Argentines to never forget that "the era of Rosas forms a dark and painful history of the nation." Nevertheless, he continued, it could be the time to embrace the "hope that liberty and harmony among men can put Argentina back on the path of economic and cultural growth."[33] The editor's name was none other than Bartolomé Mitre, a direct descendant of the same Bartolomé Mitre who fought Rosas at the Battle of Caseros, and who founded *La Nación* in 1852, right after Rosas was overthrown.

Rosas Returns

Rosas's remains were exhumed on September 21 in Southampton, England, placed in a coffin, and loaded onto a plane. After stops in France and the Canary Islands, the crew headed for Brazil, with a few members of the repatriation committee on board. When the plane entered Brazilian airspace, Manuel de Anchorena swelled with emotion as he remembered the prophecy of José Mármol that not even the dust of Rosas's bones would return to America. Once in Brazilian air space, Anchorena declared: "We pulverized the ignominious judgment of Mármol."[34] The plane landed first in the city of Rosario, a few hundred miles northwest of Buenos Aires. President Menem's speech at Rosas's welcome ceremony applied to Rosas's Mazorca of the 1840s, but also to the death squads of the recent dictatorship. The parallels were intentional. "As we welcome Brigadier General Juan Manuel de Rosas, we are also saying goodbye to an old country, wasted, anachronistic, absurd. . . . We proclaim that there is no more time or place for a country where thinking differently was cause for death and persecution."[35] Reconciling with the remote past of Rosas, Menem implied, would help open the door to reconcile with the more recent past of the dictatorship.

After the ceremony in Rosario, Rosas's remains were loaded onto a small naval boat, which then headed downriver toward Buenos Aires, passing the site of the Battle of Vuelta de Obligado along the way. At the docks in Buenos

Aires, President Menem gave another speech in which he signaled his future plans to pardon military officials. "There are still wounds that need to be closed, and I, president of the Argentines, promise before God and my people that I will suture those wounds once and for all, so that we might march forth in national unity toward the nation dreamed of by Juan Manuel de Rosas, Justo José Urquiza, Sarmiento, Quiroga . . . and all the great men and caudillos born in this promised land."[36]

A large procession accompanied Rosas's remains the fifty-five blocks to La Recoleta Cemetery. At the tomb, a priest delivered the funeral oration, an oration that captured the essence of nationalist feelings about Rosas that had been developing over the last century. The prayer also revealed much about nationalist culture, and about culture and politics in late twentieth-century Argentina. In his prayer, the priest asked that all Argentine citizens, the young in particular, see in Juan Manuel an example of "the ideal gaucho and patriot." In so doing, he continued, may the youth shun "the idols of foreign influences" and reject "ideas imported" from the empires that Rosas "confronted without conceding ground." The priest also prayed for the souls of all who had died fighting for Argentine freedom—from the wars of independence to the Battle of Obligado to the Malvinas War. As he closed, the priest asked that "the firm and patriotic austerity and honor of Juan Manuel be an example to our men of government."[37] Rosas's remains were then laid to rest in a family tomb just a few yards from Mariquita Sánchez's.

The repatriation proved to be the beginning of a kind of miniexplosion of Rosista symbolism and iconography in the country.[38] In 1992, Rosas appeared on the new twenty-peso bill, with images of Manuelita and the Battle of Obligado on the back.[39] Monuments to Rosas also appeared in various parts of the country.[40] In 2003, a porteño politician introduced a bill in congress to take a section of Sarmiento Avenue in Buenos Aires and rename it Juan Manuel de Rosas Avenue. The proposal sparked immediate controversy, with more than a hundred people debating the idea in a public meeting.[41] In 2012, President Cristina Fernández de Kirchner (from the Peronist Party) established a new entity with a long name: "The National Institute of Argentine and Ibero-American Historic Revisionism—Manuel Dorrego." The main objective of the Dorrego Institute, as it came to be called, was to write the forgotten and neglected history of Argentina, especially the history of certain figures like Juan

Manuel de Rosas, Manuel Dorrego, and other "popular" leaders of the past. The institute came under heavy fire from academic historians who feared that the government was sponsoring one "official version" of history and imposing it on the rest of the country. In 2015, newly elected president Mauricio Macri closed the institute, citing its lack of plurality.

Despite continued controversy, scholarship on the Rosas era has flourished since the return of democracy in 1983. Since then, historians have produced numerous works that, without excusing his excesses, have revised large portions of the traditional scholarship on Rosas. Rosas brought order where others before him had failed. And while it was true that he was a powerful rancher, and that he wielded extraordinary powers as governor, Rosas nevertheless was constrained by existing social and political traditions. All the while he and his ministers went to great lengths to cultivate votes and public opinion in favor of his regime, both among the popular and upper classes.[42]

Mariquita and Juan Manuel Together Again

La Recoleta Cemetery is impressive and for the most part peaceful. It is full of illustrious Argentines, many of whom, like Mariquita and Juan Manuel, opposed each other during their lifetimes. Even the very land the cemetery is built on is a reminder of the great conflicts of Argentina's past. In the 1820s, Bernardino Rivadavia confiscated land from an order of Catholic priests and used it to create a public cemetery—all part of his radical reforms that helped spark the unrest that led to the rise of Juan Manuel de Rosas in the first place. That contested ground became, in 1989, Juan Manuel's final resting place, not far from his old friend Mariquita.

I have strolled through La Recoleta many times. It is a fine retreat on a Sunday afternoon when the archives are closed. Outside, one can find any number of souvenirs, from mate gourds to small leather maps of Argentina, and much more. Once inside, visitors can check the large map for the location of prominent historical figures. Many of the great ones of Argentine history are there, including a number who appear in this book. Moving out into the cemetery itself, obelisks, columns, and monumental sepulchers dot the narrow pathways, making it a true necropolis—a city of the dead. No tomb can compete with Evita Perón's for popularity. Sometimes someone is praying there,

FIGURE E.1 Mariquita's tomb, La Recoleta Cemetery, Buenos Aires. Photo courtesy of the author.

FIGURE E.2 Juan Manuel's tomb, La Recoleta Cemetery, Buenos Aires. Photo courtesy of the author.

while frequently there are so many bouquets of flowers piled around her crypt that it is hard not to walk on them as you sidestep past. Juan Manuel's tomb sometimes has some flowers on it, and Mariquita's even fewer.

As I have walked back and forth between their tombs—113 steps by my stride—I have paused and wondered, "What would Mariquita and Juan Manuel whisper to each other, if they could, 150 years after their deaths?"

Might they whisper about how they were, in some ways, perfect foils for each other? The woman and the man, the urbanite and the rural dweller, the progressive and the conservative, the democrat and the authoritarian, the Europhile and the nationalist? But they might also whisper about how they were very much alike. Their families were close friends; they resisted their parents' attempts to control their marriages; they were both shaped by the convulsions of the English invasions; and they both had Federalist sympathies, although his were much more pronounced. After a lot of whispering, they might even agree that they were both republicans, in their own way. Were they both patriotic? "But you were such a Frenchy," Juan Manuel might whisper. "But you were so cozy with the British," Mariquita might retort.

They might also share how they were masters of their respective spheres, from which they both wielded power: Juan Manuel from his office at his San Palermo estate, or on horseback commanding soldiers or overlooking his lands, and Mariquita from her illustrious tertulia, or through her activities of the Sociedad de Beneficencia, or in her mentoring of young women and men. They might have a very interesting chat about the influence of women in their lives: their mothers, Magdalena and Agustina, along with their daughters, Florencia and Manuelita. Adding Encarnación Ezcurra and Eugenia Castro to the equation makes for a potent mix of female power in both of their lives. And if I were able to interject an additional question into their conversation, I might ask to what extent did Mariquita reinforce or challenge the attitudes of her day toward race, class, and gender? And what about Juan Manuel?

If talking about the political struggles of their days, Juan Manuel might argue that Mariquita and her cohorts dreamed a little too idealistically about rushing to implement an enlightened republic in the Río de la Plata. She might counter that Juan Manuel lacked the faith to use his considerable talent and popularity to promulgate an enduring constitution during his long rule. In hindsight they might both agree that the struggle of ideals—between what might have been and the reality of what was—sparked civil wars from Buenos

Aires to Bogotá to Bull Run in the nineteenth century. A conversation about these and other questions, it is hoped, emerges from the previous pages.

Besides strolling between their tombs, I experienced another part of the Mariquita-Juan Manuel rift during one of my trips to Argentina. I was conducting research for this book in the National Archive in Buenos Aires. One day, the archive staff informed me that a descendant of Rosas had heard that I was writing a book about him, and she wanted to meet me. This woman, I was told, would come to the archive one day to see me. A few days later I left on a short trip to Patagonia. When I returned to the archive, I learned from the staff that the person came while I was away. "She asked what documents you were looking at," the archivist told me. At the time I was looking for material on Mariquita in the records of the Sociedad de Beneficencia. The archivist continued the story. "When we told her you were looking for things on Mariquita, she said, 'I am not really interested in seeing him anymore.'" She knew, as did I, that Mariquita turned from friend to foe of Juan Manuel and became, at least for a while, one of his most vociferous opponents. For her, Mariquita and Juan Manuel could not mix, even 150 years after their deaths.

I left the archive that day with a reaffirmed commitment. I would indeed write about these two friends—Mariquita and Juan Manuel—friends who became enemies in the turbulent beginnings of Argentina.

Argentina: The name of the country, the Argentine Republic, officially named after 1862. The term Argentina derives from the name of the river—the Río de la Plata—that runs by Buenos Aires. The early Spanish explorer Juan de Solís named the river the Silver River (Río de la Plata). Argentum is the Latin name for silver. The names for the political organizations of Argentina before 1862 included United Provinces of the Río de la Plata and the Argentine Confederation. See also **Río de la Plata**.

Banda Oriental: A region of land on the Eastern Shore of the Río de la Plata, roughly the territory of modern Uruguay. This is the land on the east of the Uruguay River, and on the other side of the Río de la Plata, north of Buenos Aires (sometimes called the Northern Shore). During the colonial period, it was a highly contested territory between Spain and Portugal, lying as it does on the border between the two empires. After independence, Argentina and Brazil fought a war over this territory in the mid-1820s, which resulted in the creation of the independent state of Uruguay. **Orientales** were people from the Eastern Shore. See also **Montevideo**.

cabildo / cabildo abierto: The cabildo was the town council that usually met in a building—also called the cabildo—typically located in the city center. In Buenos Aires, the cabildo was in the main plaza, along with the fort and the cathedral. A cabildo abierto was an expanded town council where the prominent men of the city joined with the regular members of the council to debate and vote on policy. This usually occurred during times of crisis.

Creole/criollo: A term for a Spaniard born in the Americas, as opposed to a Spaniard born in Spain (thus a "peninsular" Spaniard), or as opposed to a mestizo (a person of mixed Spanish-Indian ancestry) or other racial categorizations. Throughout the colonial period (roughly 1500–1810), Creoles increasingly developed identities tied to their regions of birth. Meanwhile, especially in the latter half of the eighteenth century, the Spanish crown grew more distrustful of their Spanish American subjects, favoring instead Spaniards from Spain. By the twentieth century, *criollo* also came to denote a version of local Argentine culture and identity.

estancia/estanciero: An estancia is a multiuse landed estate. Many estancias were cattle ranches, although they might also be used in various other stock raising and agricultural activities. An estanciero is the person who owns the estancia. Juan Manuel de Rosas came from a family of estancieros. Estancias characterized the centrality of cattle raising in the early nineteenth century, as well as Argentina's export-led economic growth of the nineteenth and twentieth centuries, which included wool, wheat, and other agricultural commodities.

Federalist/Federalism: One of the dominant political ideologies of the early to mid-nineteenth century. Federalism was the ideological position that favored provincial rights over the rights of a central government. Federalists resisted attempts to create a strong national government centered in Buenos Aires in the 1820s, and a fierce struggle between Federalists and Centralists (see **Unitarians**) continued for much of the nineteenth century. Juan Manuel de Rosas emerged as a powerful Federalist leader in the late 1820s and, as governor of Buenos Aires Province, led the Argentine Confederation under the banner of Federalism until his overthrow in 1852.

gauchos: A term used loosely to describe rural dwellers who made their living off the land. Typically they were associated with the cattle, horses, and other animals so abundant on the plains of Argentina (the Pampas), although gauchos existed throughout the country. They could be workers on someone's ranch, or be itinerant laborers moving from place to place. Gauchos were expert horseman used to working with knives and lances, and groups of gauchos could be mustered into formidable cavalry units.

Juan Manuel de Rosas: A wealthy rancher and militia commander who became governor of Buenos Aires Province from 1829 to 1833, and from 1835 to 1852, during which time he also served as the head of the Argentine Confederation before being overthrown in 1852. He enjoyed strong support from many of the popular classes, but also from other ranchers, and from the British government and merchant community, among others. The provincial legislature granted him power to rule by decree, and he frequently exercised that right on all fronts (executive, legislative, and judicial). His heavy-handed rule was characterized by oppressive measures that in turn sparked various anti-Rosas movements among Argentines as well as interventions by foreign powers.

José de San Martín: An Argentine general who spent much of his early life fighting for the Spanish army in Spain. He returned to Argentina in 1812 and helped build an army that liberated Chile and parts of Peru from Spanish rule. He was asked by many to get involved in Argentine politics after independence, but he refused because he did not want to get involved in civil wars. Instead he chose to live in Europe for the last thirty years of his life. From exile, he expressed support for Juan Manuel de Rosas's rule.

Iberian/Iberia: Someone from Iberia—the peninsula where Spain and Portugal are located—although, in Spanish America, Iberian usually denoted someone from Spain. Within Spain, however, lived various groups of people with different languages and cultures. Over the last many centuries, Spanish kings and queens unified these various groups into the empire and country that came to be called Spain (Portugal managed to remain independent). However, within Spain there are areas that cherish their regional identity and still speak their own languages—Galicia, Basque Country, and Catalonia being some prominent examples. These identities came to the New World as well.

Indians: In the Americas, the term Indian has historically been used as the generic word for indigenous peoples. Believing that they had arrived on the outskirts of Asia, Spaniards began referring to Natives they encountered in the New World as Indians. Although hundreds and even thousands of different Native groups existed, Spaniards frequently lumped them all together as Indians. The label Indian became a legal definition within Spanish law as well. Prominent groups in the narrative that follows include the Araucanian, Charrúa, Mapuche, Pampa, Ranquel, Tehuelche, and Querandí tribes, among others.

mate (yerba mate): Mate, or yerba mate, is a bitter tea made from the finely chopped leaves of the yerba mate plant. Mate was drunk by indigenous groups before the arrival of the Spaniards, but throughout the colonial period it became a common drink among residents of all ethnicities in the Río de la Plata region. Juan Manuel de Rosas and Mariquita Sánchez enjoyed mate. It is still enormously popular in Argentina and many surrounding countries today, and it has experienced a kind of globalization, appearing in various beverages.

Mariquita Sánchez: Born to a wealthy merchant family in Buenos Aires, Mariquita was an influential woman who—along with her husbands (she was widowed and remarried)—played an influential role in Buenos Aires society and culture. A friend of Juan Manuel de Rosas in her youth, she disliked him as a governor, and went into exile during much of his rule.

Montevideo: The port city on the other side of the Río de la Plata from Buenos Aires, in what is now Uruguay. Montevideo, and all the territory on the Eastern Shore of the Uruguay River, was contested by Portugal and Spain during the colonial period, and then by their successor states, Brazil and Argentina, after independence. Finally, in 1828, Montevideo became the capital of a new country—Uruguay. During Governor Juan Manuel de Rosas's rule, Montevideo became a preferred place of exile for many fleeing Rosas's tyranny. Rosas supported one faction (the Blancos) in Uruguay, while the Colorados faction, centered in Montevideo, offered refuge to exiles. The two sides fought a long civil war from 1838 to 1851, during much of which time Rosas supported the Blancos' efforts to overthrow Montevideo.

negro/mulato/pardo/moreno: Words to describe the racial makeup of Africans and their descendants in the Río de la Plata region. *Negro* means "black" in Spanish, and when used in racial terms, *negro* could mean someone of pure African blood. *Mulato* and *pardo* and *moreno* denote mixtures of various levels of black and white, and perhaps indigenous, which meant that the individual referred to was not a first-generation African. Spaniards were very attentive to racial identity and levels of race mixing, as were other racial and ethnic groups. Morenos, for example, frequently saw themselves as distinct from "blacks," who were darker and had closer ties to Africa, or might have been born in Africa.

orientales: See **Banda Oriental**.

Pampas: The massive plains that cover large portions of central Argentina, Uruguay, and southern Brazil. In addition to their native flora and fauna, these fertile lands became home to massive herds of cattle, horses, and sheep, as well as a flourishing agricultural zone. Large ranches (estancias) emerged on the Pampas in the late 1700s and into the 1800s, especially after wars with the Native tribes opened up more land for European settlement. Pampas is also the name of an indigenous tribe of the region.

peninsular: Meaning something or someone from the Iberian Peninsula. In particular, a Spaniard born in Spain—on the Iberian Peninsula—was known as a *peninsular*. See also **Creole**.

Plaza Mayor / Plaza de la Victoria / Plaza de Mayo: The main plaza in downtown Buenos Aires and the center of the city. The most important buildings of the city surrounded the plaza, including the cathedral, the cabildo (town hall), the fort, and later, the Casa Rosada (the equivalent of the White House in Argentina). During the colonial period it was known as the Plaza Mayor (Main Plaza). After the English invasions of 1806–1807, however, its name was changed to Plaza Victoria (Victory Plaza), and later, Plaza de Mayo (named in honor of the May Revolution of 1810). It continues to be a major symbolic center of Argentina. For example, it is where the Mothers of the Disappeared have marched each Thursday since 1977.

porteño/porteña: Someone or something from the port city of Buenos Aires and its surrounding region. The endings of many Spanish words denote the "gender" of that word. A porteño (ending in an "o") is a man or boy from Buenos Aires, while a porteña is a woman from Buenos Aires. This frequently means from the actual city of Buenos Aires, although porteño can also be used more loosely to signify being from the larger region surrounding the port city. Porteño also might be used to refer to other nouns. Porteño culture, for example, would mean the culture of Buenos Aires, etc.

Río de la Plata: The River Plate or River of Silver is a river (estuary is a better word for some geographers) created at the confluence of two great river systems—the Paraná and Uruguay Rivers—that come together just northwest of Buenos Aires. It was named by the early Spanish explorer Juan de Solís, who found Natives with silver objects in its upper reaches. The Río de la Plata opens up into the Atlantic Ocean. The river makes part of Argentina and Uruguay's border with each other, and Buenos Aires and Montevideo are located along its shores. Navigation and trading rights up the Río de la Plata and its estuaries (the Paraná is navigable all the way to Paraguay) were a source of major disagreement and violence among the Argentine provinces themselves, but also with foreign powers in the nineteenth century.

Simón Bolívar: A wealthy Venezuelan revolutionary who helped liberate Venezuela, Colombia, Ecuador, Peru, and Bolivia. He, along with General José de San Martín of Argentina, are known as the two great "Liberators" of South America. Bolívar was well known in Argentina, and in the early 1820s he incorporated many Argentine soldiers into his armies that would achieve the final victories against Spanish royal forces. A soldier and a statesman, Bolívar's troubled career corresponds with the trials of Argentina's early nation-building efforts. Periodically throughout this book, Bolívar's thought and experiences will be touched on because he ruminated about Argentina. His difficulties, along with Argentina's, are a reminder that most of the American republics, including the USA, struggled with similar issues in the postindependence era.

Unitarian: Unitarians were a political group that believed that a strong, centralized state was needed to shape Argentine politics, culture, and society. In general, Unitarians were progressive-minded in that they wanted to adopt what were considered "modern" political ideas, such as a republican form of government and the separation of church and state. Their focus on strong central authority, and challenging the traditional role of the Catholic Church, provoked conflict with the **Federalists** and more conservative elements in Argentine society. The early efforts to write a constitution (such as the Constitution of 1826) in Argentina all failed because they were deemed by a majority of the country as too Centralist (too "Unitarian") and too liberal. During the Rosas era, "Unitarian" was used by Rosas and his supporters to describe many enemies of the state even though they might not have been part of the original Unitarian movement.

NOTES

INTRODUCTION

1. Fradkin and Gelman, *Juan Manuel de Rosas*, 383. See also Gelman, *Rosas, estanciero*, 11–12.

2. Zavalía Lagos, *Mariquita*, 170.

3. The term "Enlightenment" is used broadly in this instance, recognizing that there were significant differences between what some have called the "Northern Enlightenment" (France, England, and beyond) and the "Catholic Enlightenment" as found in the Iberian Peninsula. By the early nineteenth century, there was substantial convergence of these two traditions. See Chiaramonte, *Ilustración*, 13. See also Fernández Sebastián, "Toleration and Freedom," 196. Brazil, with its independent monarchy, was the notable exception to the republican rule.

4. Myers, "Identidades porteños," 39–40.

5. For the emergence of feminism in Argentina and elsewhere, see Lavrin, *Women, Feminism, and Social Change*.

6. Polasky, *Revolutions without Borders*, 273. For more on porteños' connections in the Atlantic, see Adelman, chap. 1 in *Republic of Capital*.

7. The historiography on Rosas is immense. The most recent Spanish biography of Rosas is Fradkin and Gelman, *Juan Manuel de Rosas*. The standard treatment of Rosas in English has been Lynch's *Argentine Dictator*. Lynch also provides a useful introduction to the historians and travelers who wrote on Rosas. For an excellent discussion of the historiography of Rosas, especially as relevant to the definition of *caudillismo*, see Goldman and Salvatore, *Caudillismos rioplatenses*. See also Etchepareborda, *Rosas*, especially chaps. 1 and 2. For a sample of pro- and anti-Rosas scholarship over many decades, see Barbará, *Con Rosas*.

8. Fowler, *Santa Anna*.

9. Dusenberry, "Juan Manuel de Rosas."

10. Even Domingo Sarmiento, a harsh critic of Rosas, acknowledged that Rosas had a republican streak and was upheld by a strong popular and democratic sentiment. See Sarmiento's thoughts in Chávez, *Vuelta*. For examples of the debates about Andrew Jackson and the contrasting views of historians, see Wilentz, *Rise of American Democracy*; and Howe, *What Hath God Wrought*. For Wilentz, Andrew Jackson was a major force in the rise of democracy in the United States. Howe,

on the other hand, sees Jackson's legacy as one of broken promises and white supremacy.

11. Fradkin and the late Gelman argue that the term "caudillo" can only be used if it loses its pejorative connotation, and if it acknowledges the substantial institutional base of power Rosas employed. For an excellent discussion of how scholarship over the last many decades has reshaped the view of Rosas, see Fradkin and Gelman's *Juan Manuel de Rosas*, chap. 10; and Gelman, *Rosas bajo fuego*. Fuente has also produced a more nuanced view of caudillos in his *Children of Facundo*. See also Goldman and Salvatore, *Caudillismos rioplatenses*. Adelman designates Rosas's rule as "quasi-law." *Republic of Capital*, 110–20. For another recent example of new scholarship on the Rosas regime, including the role of Rosas's wife, Encarnación, in key aspects of his regime, see Di Meglio, *Mueran*. See also Myers, *Orden y virtud*; Salvatore, *Wandering Paysanos*; and Goldman, "Orígenes," 118–22. For a useful introduction to the older contours of the debates on caudillismo, see Lynch, *Caudillos in Spanish America*.

12. For an examination of the rising power of the popular classes in the Río de la Plata region, see Lyman Johnson, *Workshop of Revolution*; and Di Meglio, *¡Viva el bajo pueblo!* For a hemispheric perspective on the rise of popular republican movements, see Sanders, *Vanguard of the Atlantic World*.

13. Scholars for decades have examined the emergence of modern political activity in Western societies. Salons and tertulias have been discussed as part of that process in Europe and the Americas, as have the role of popular classes. Habermas's *Structural Transformation of the Public Sphere* sparked increased interest in what he called a "public sphere"—which included spaces like salons, cafés, and taverns—where new kinds of sociability enabled the growth of political activity outside the traditional state apparatus. Habermas's theories have sparked much debate. For an overview of scholarship on public spheres in Latin America, see Uribe-Uran, "Birth of a Public Sphere"; and Piccato, "Public Sphere in Latin America." For examples of the role of plebeians in politics, see Lyman Johnson, *Workshop of Revolution*; and Di Meglio, *¡Viva el bajo pueblo!* For a recent example of an "incipient" plebeian public sphere in Venezuela, see Soriano, *Tides of Revolution*. See also Guerra's edited volume, *Espacios públicos*. Chap. 4 of my book further discusses these issues.

14. Lynch, *Simón Bolívar*, 201–2; Fowler, *Santa Anna*, 301–2.

15. Adelman, *Republic of Capital*, 5–7.

16. For a useful discussion of the notion of empire in Latin America, see Knight, "Britain and Latin America."

17. For further discussion of contingency, or "altered historical sequelae," see Adelman, "Age of Imperial Revolutions," 319–21; and Langley, introd. of *Age of Revolution*. For uncertainty during the American Revolution, see Beeman, *Plain, Honest Men*, ix–x.

18. Myers, "La revolución en las ideas," 393–417; Mayo, chap. 5 in *Porque la quiero tanto*; Dueñas-Vargas, *Of Love*.

19. See earlier endnotes in this introduction for a long list of works on Rosas.

20. Lynch, *Argentine Caudillo*. Lynch incorporated some of the new scholarship into his abridgment, but he says: "I have preferred to leave the new research in the hands of its authors identified in the bibliography, and to keep my own text intact as part of an ongoing debate on a controversial figure" (viii).

21. Some notable exceptions are Szurmuk's excellent chapter on Mariquita in her *Women in Argentina*; Chambers, "Letters and Salons"; and Jeffrey Shumway, chap. 4 in *Ugly Suitor*.

22. Obligado, *Tradiciones*. Dellepiane published *Dos patricias ilustres*. Vilaseca, *Cartas*. Mizraje, *Mariquita*. Zavalía Lagos, *Mariquita*. Sáenz Quesada, *Mariquita*. Batticuore, *Mariquita*.

23. For further discussion of Argentina's contested past, see Goebel, *Argentina's Partisan Past*. See also Nicolas Shumway, *The Invention of Argentina*. Shumway outlines a number of competing "guiding fictions," created by various Argentine writers and politicians, that had their root in the nineteenth century but are still visible in contemporary Argentine society.

24. As Fernández Sebastián writes, "We should avoid the 'presentification' of the past worlds, respecting as far as is possible the radical alterity of the past worlds that we study; all of which surely implies an effort to understand—to the extent to which this is possible—the actor in their own terms." "Toleration and Freedom," 196.

25. See, for example, Crosby, *Ecological Imperialism*. For more on the Spanish Empire at its zenith, see Parker, *Phillip II*.

26. For useful surveys of early Argentine history, see Jonathan Brown, *Brief History of Argentina*; Sáenz Quesada, *La Argentina*; and Rock, *Argentina*.

27. See Schmidt's account of the first settlement. "Going Wild," 23–26.

28. Scobie, *Buenos Aires*, 6.

29. Dellepiane, *Rosas*, 21–22. See also Ibarguren, *Rosas*, 9.

30. Borucki, *Shipmates to Soldiers*, 19–20. For the increase in the "pardo" label as the nineteenth century progressed, see Edwards, "Mestizaje," 92–93.

31. Borucki, 6. Lyman Johnson in *Workshop of Revolution* has also conducted voluminous research on black artisans in Buenos Aires. For population estimates of Buenos Aires, see Goldberg, "Población negra y mulata," 75–99.

32. For a nineteenth-century example, see Cutrera, *Subordinarlos*.

33. Adelman, *Sovereignty and Revolution*, 15, 23. Smuggling was in part why the crown made Buenos Aires into a new viceregal capital. Now trade was legalized and thus taxable.

34. Prado, *Edge of Empire*, 15–17, 61–62. See also Jonathan Brown, *Socioeconomic History of Argentina*, 22.

35. Adelman, *Sovereignty and Revolution*, 16.

36. Sarreal, *Guaraní and Their Missions*.

37. See the example of Cipriano de Melo in Prado, chap. 6 in *Edge of Empire*. See also Prado, *Colônia do Sacramento*.

38. Kendall Brown, *Bourbons and Brandy*; Premo, *Children*.

39. Adelman, *Republic of Capital*, 23–26. See also Assadourian, *Sistema*.

40. Adelman, *Sovereignty and Revolution*, 58; Borucki, *Shipmates to Soldiers*, 32.

41. Ratto, "Allá lejos," 47–48.

42. The Mapuches (known as Araucanians by the Incas, who bequeathed the name to the Spaniards) conquered many local tribes and transformed indigenous society on the pampas. Palermo, "Compleja integración hispano-indígena." See also Cutrera, *Subordinarlos*; and Jones, "Calfucurá and Namuncurá."

43. For more on ranchers in the late colonial period, see Mayo, "Landed But Not Powerful," 761–79; for a reference to Clemente López, see p. 776.

CHAPTER ONE

1. As transcribed in Ibarguren, *Rosas*, 8. Dellepiane disputes that the news would have been spread at that hour of the night, but it seems reasonable that such good news, especially because it was from the patron's family, would be spread around no matter what the hour. See footnote in Dellepiane, *Rosas*, 21.

2. Gálvez, *Rosas*, 16–17.

3. Ibarguren, *Rosas*, 10–11. The exchange was mediated by Chief Calpisqui.

4. Sáenz Quesada, *Mujeres*, 17.

5. Richard A. Fletcher, *Moorish Spain*.

6. For more on the merchant community in Buenos Aires, Spaniard and otherwise, see Socolow, *Merchants of Buenos Aires*.

7. Most women married when they were still minors, while under greater control of their parents (see chapter 2). Because women were usually much younger than their husbands, they would become widows at a relatively young age. A prominent writer in colonial Lima advised young women to willingly marry "rotten old men," and then after their husband's death they could choose a man to their liking. Socolow, *Women*, 56.

8. Sáenz Quesada, *Mariquita*, 23–24. Mariquita's home address was San José (near Florida 200 today), Santa Lucia (Sarmiento), Santísima Trinidad (San Martín) and Merced (Cangallo), with the house fronting the first three streets. For a street plate of Buenos Aires from this era, see Socolow, *Merchants of Buenos Aires*, 73.

9. While she is mostly known as "Mariquita," she is sometimes referred to as "Marica," of which "Mariquita" is an endearing diminutive. Because of the connotation of the term "Marica" in many Hispanic societies today, I have chosen to translate any reference to her as "Marica" to the more common "Mariquita."

10. For a detailed discussion of the home, see Batticuore, *Mariquita*, 110–16.

11. Sáenz Quesada, *Mariquita*, 22.

12. Sánchez, *Recuerdos*, 23, 28–29. In her memory, Mariquita may have exaggerated the scarcity of goods in Buenos Aires. While Spain's monopoly system was cumbersome, contraband trade was ubiquitous, which helped keep Buenos Aires in good supply of the latest wares from the Atlantic World.

13. Sánchez 26, 32, 33. Although she wrote this memoir in the 1860s, and her memories, like those of others, may be influenced in part by the experience of the intervening years, her memoir is nevertheless a valuable source on the colonial period.

14. Sánchez, 27–28.

15. Sánchez, 14–15, 32–33. For more discussion of gauchos, see Slatta, *Gauchos;* and Salvatore, *Wandering Paysanos.*

16. Sánchez, 41–42.

17. Sánchez, 47.

18. Sánchez, 57.

19. Sánchez, 48–49.

20. Sánchez, 29 April 1839, in Mizraje, *Mariquita,* 61.

21. Eckartshausen, *God Is the Love Most Pure,* 29.

22. "La letra con sangre entra" in Sánchez, *Recuerdos,* 55.

23. Sánchez, 55–56.

24. Zavalía Lagos, *Mariquita,* 26. See also Sáenz Quesada, *Mariquita,* 25–26.

25. Dellepiane, *Dos patricias ilustres,* 21.

26. For an excellent study on what activities slaves and other working-class porteños worked in, see Lyman Johnson, *Workshop of Revolution.*

27. Mansilla, *Rozas,* 25.

28. Sánchez, *Recuerdos,* 54.

29. Mansilla, *Rozas.*

30. Mansilla, 25–26. Mansilla said the practice was reciprocated by Mrs. Gonzalez de Lavalle.

31. Mansilla, 24. Gálvez, *Rosas,* 16.

32. Mansilla, 29.

33. Ibarguren, *Rosas,* 11.

34. Mansilla, *Rozas,* 25, 29.

35. Mansilla, 26.

36. Mansilla, 26.

37. This description of riding in a galera is taken from Parish, who journeyed in one such carriage from Buenos Aires to Mendoza. See his *Buenos Ayres,* 325.

38. Dellepiane, *Rosas,* 27.

39. Mansilla, *Rozas,* 23.

40. Mansilla, 27–28.

41. Slatta, *Gauchos,* 8–9.

42. Slatta, *Cowboys of the Americas.*

43. Dueling in the Río de la Plata region was more common among the popular classes than the elite during this time period. Such duels are found in the poetry of José Hernández in his epic poem *El gaucho Martín Fierro* as well as in Eduardo Gutiérrez's *El Gaucho Juan Moreira.* Hudson discussed the prevalence of knife dueling in his memoir, *Far Away,* 137–39. See also Chasteen, "Violence for Show."

44. Taken from Rosas's dictionary published years later, *Gramática y diccionario.*

45. Mansilla, *Rozas*, 32–33.

46. Mansilla, 34–35. Irazusta does not dispute Mansilla's story, but he does dispute his conclusions. Rosas, according to Irazusta, was simply not made for storekeeping—it was not his destiny. *Vida política*, vol. 1, pt. 1, 17. There is also some disagreement in the sources about the conflict that caused the blowup between Juan Manuel and his parents.

47. Gálvez, *Rosas*, 16.

48. Saldías, *Historia de la confederación*, 1:13.

49. See the prologue in Ellis, *American Creation*.

50. Letter from Juárez to Deán Funes, as quoted in Ibarguren, *Rosas*, 14–15.

51. Decree of Viceroy Arredondo as quoted in Ibarguren, *Rosas*, 15. So worried was the viceroy about the spread of French ideas that he offered half of any confiscated property to the person who turned in French conspirators. For ship seizure and other anti-French action, see Lyman Johnson, *Workshop of Revolution*, 154–57.

CHAPTER TWO

1. "Expediente promovido por el alférez de fragata de la real armada, Don Martín Jacobo Thompson," 1804, legajo 21, AGN.

2. Sáenz Quesada, *Mariquita*, 31.

3. To see the variety of things done to preserve religious and racial purity, see Nalle, *Mad for God*. For more on the treatment of Moorish peoples, see Tueller, *Good and Faithful Christians*.

4. From documents copied in González Lonzieme's *Martín Thompson* appendix.

5. Socolow, chap. 2 in *Merchants of Buenos Aires*.

6. Patriarchy, then, took many different forms. As Premo outlines, depending on the context, patriarchy might refer to the unequal relationship between men and women, husbands and wives, but it also includes "intergenerational" relationships between parents and children, which might include a mother's control over her children (especially in the absence of the father). *Children*, 9–10.

7. Boyer, "Women, La Mala Vida," 252–55.

8. For an excellent study of the long history of marriage conflicts, including the Pragmatic of 1776, see Seed, *Love, Honor, and Obey*.

9. González Lonzieme, *Martín Thompson*, document 3, 133–34.

10. For more on the Casa de Ejercicios, see Jeffrey Shumway, *Ugly Suitor*, especially chap. 4.

11. Azamor y Ramírez, *Matrimonio*, 402.

12. For more studies that look closely at questions of marriage and marriage-conflict cases, see Jeffrey Shumway, *Ugly Suitor*; Cicerchia, *Vida privada*; Socolow, "Acceptable Partners"; and Porro, "Juicios de disenso."

13. Martín Thompson v. Magdalena Trillo, legajo 21, AGN.

14. For some examples of such behavior, see Jeffrey Shumway, *Ugly Suitor*, especially chap. 4.

15. Letters found in Martín Thompson v. Magdalena Trillo, legajo 21, AGN.

16. Martín Thompson v. Magdalena Trillo, AGN.

17. Martín Thompson v. Magdalena Trillo, AGN.

18. Sáenz Quesada, *Mariquita*, 39–40.

19. Batticuore, *Mariquita*, 63.

20. According to Mansilla, Rosas was not a sensual or licentious character. *Rozas*, 40.

21. See the case of Antonio Garmendia and the opera singer Angela Tani. 1825, 7.5.15.56, AHPBA. For a heartbreaking withdrawal from a relationship, likely under parental pressure, see Fortunato Rangel sobre disenso, 1826, 7.5.15.58, AHBPA.

22. Lyman Johnson and Rivera, *Faces of Honor*. Over time, the concept of honor came to be associated with the lower classes as well if they followed accepted societal norms, especially related to marriage and family.

23. Getting pregnant out of wedlock was not the end of the world if the offending couple got married. Even if a child was born to unwed parents, as long as neither parent was married at the time of the pregnancy, that child would be called a "natural" child and could still become legitimate if the parents married. If one or both of the parents had been married to someone else at the time of the pregnancy, then the child was labeled as coming from an adulterous union and could not be legitimized through marriage. Juan Manuel and Encarnación did not have to worry about all that.

24. Many historians have told a version of this story. See Bilbao, *Rosas*, 102; Ibarguren, *Rosas*, 40; Gálvez, *Rosas*, 17; and Dellepiane, *Rosas*, 36–37. Later in life Rosas downplayed the letter in question, saying it was more of a love letter. See letter to Josefa Gómez, 2 May 1869, in Raed, *Cartas confidenciales*, 118.

25. Sáenz Quesada, *Mujeres*, 54.

26. For an in-depth discussion of the Bourbon Reforms and children, see Premo, chap. 5 in *Children*.

27. Ginestá, *Conservador*. The term "Enlightenment" had different meanings throughout Europe, including in the Iberian Peninsula. Sometimes called the "Catholic Enlightenment," this reformist way of thinking was rooted more firmly in the Catholic faith and tended to pursue new ideas in science and technology rather than in religion and politics. See Fernández Sebastián, "Toleration and Freedom," 159–62.

28. For more on the critique of wet nurses, see Premo, *Children*, 169–70.

29. Ginestá, *Conservador*, 13–14, 20, 35–36, 39–40.

30. "Su merced." See Sánchez, *Recuerdos*, 55–56, 59.

31. Sánchez, 59–60.

32. "Satirilla Festiva," in *Telégrafo Mercantil*, 17 January 1802, 39–40.

33. "Satirilla Festiva," 17 January 1802, 39–40. The phrase *que lindo ejemplar* (what a beautiful example) could also be translated as "what a beautiful specimen," as in a reference to an animal. Thus, in another translation, and perhaps a more accurate one, the editors added an additional layer of insult to these behaviors. Thanks to Gabriel Di Meglio for this insight.

34. "Satirilla Festiva," in *Telégrafo Mercantil*, 24 January 1802, 54–56.

35. Fernández Sebastián, "Toleration and Freedom," 159–62. See also Adelman, *Sovereignty and Revolution*, 145–46.

36. Premo, introd. of *Enlightenment on Trial*.

37. "We should take advantage of the efforts of the wise Europeans to spread the knowledge." From *Correo de comercio*, as cited in Chiaramonte, *Ilustración*, 11.

38. Fernández Sebastián, "Toleration and Freedom," 167.

CHAPTER THREE

1. Sánchez, *Recuerdos*, 63–65.

2. Adelman, *Sovereignty and Revolution*, 13–14.

3. However, Prado has illustrated that Spanish American merchants, particularly in the Río de la Plata region, used neutral trade, as well as their connections with Brazilian and Portuguese merchants, to mitigate the severity of these disruptions. *Edge of Empire*, 59–60.

4. Adelman, *Sovereignty and Revolution*, 103–5. He concludes that "the resumption of war again in December of 1804 put a permanent end to the Spanish mercantilist era."

5. Racine, *Francisco de Miranda*. See also Goodman, *Republic of Letters*, 1–3. Citizens of the Republic of Letters were dedicated to intellectual endeavor and progress. They valued reciprocal exchanges of ideas, through letter writing and the sharing of books and other literature. They also valued a more egalitarian form of friendship that differed from the values of the absolutist monarchies dominating much of Europe in the eighteenth century. Members of the Republic of Letters sought to remain citizens of their countries while also remaining loyal to the ideals of the Republic of Letters.

6. Popham, *Trial of Sir Home Popham*, 91.

7. Popham, 92.

8. Ian Fletcher, *Waters of Oblivion*, 11–12.

9. Popham, app. in *Trial of Sir Home Popham*.

10. Popham, 94–95.

11. Popham to Marsden, app. in *Trial of Sir Home Popham*.

12. In a letter to his friend Thomas Marsden, Popham assured him: "You will, I have no doubt, find [in speaking to London merchants], that Buenos Ayres is the best commercial situation in South America." Buenos Aires was "the grand centre and emporium of the trade of all its provinces, and is the channel through which a great proportion of the wealth of the kingdom of Chili and Peru annually passes." App. in *Trial of Sir Home Popham*.

13. Ian Fletcher sees Popham's plan as a kind of piracy, but clearly Popham, Baird, and Beresford saw it differently. *Waters of Oblivion*, 19.

14. Fletcher, 21.

15. Beruti, *Memorias curiosas*, 46.

16. Beresford calculated that $1,086,208 was going back to England on the ship *Narcissus*. Ian Fletcher, *Waters of Oblivion*, 30–31.

17. Sánchez, *Recuerdos*, 64.

18. The 71st Highlander Regiment is Scottish, meaning that perhaps a more accurate name for the invasions would be the "British" rather than the "English" invasions, although it would require a change to over a century of tradition. Thanks to Gabriel Di Meglio for this insight.

19. Sánchez, *Recuerdos*, 65–66.

20. Sánchez, 65–66. A few years earlier, one ill-clad American colonial militiaman described the spectacle of approaching British troops as "the prettiest men he had ever seen." Fischer, *Paul Revere's Ride*, 204, 206, 216.

21. As quoted in Gallo, *Great Britain*, 76.

22. Lyman Johnson, chap. 5 in *Workshop of Revolution*; see also Di Meglio, *¡Viva el bajo pueblo!*, 78–79. No documentary evidence reveals extraordinary slave activity, but elite fear was palpable.

23. The fear of Haiti was hemisphere-wide. See Adelman, *Sovereignty and Revolution*, 94; and Soriano, *Tides of Revolution*. For an example of the impact of the Haitian Revolution on the USA, see White, *Encountering Revolution*.

24. Decree by General Beresford, n.d., in Instituto Cultural, *Invasiones inglesas*, 109–10.

25. Beruti, *Memorias curiosas*, 46–47.

26. Gillespie, *Gleanings and Remarks*, 52.

27. Gillespie, 52–53.

28. Sánchez, *Recuerdos*, 66–67.

29. Gillespie, *Gleanings and Remarks*, 69. Some spellings updated here.

30. Ian Fletcher, *Waters of Oblivion*, 33–34, from Captain Pococke's memoirs from 19 July 1806.

31. Indeed, many Spaniards and royalists in this time period referred to the English and other Protestants simply as "northern heretics." See Fernández Sebastián, "Toleration and Freedom," 162.

32. Gillespie, *Gleanings and Remarks*, 88–90.

33. Ibarguren, *Rosas*, 21.

34. Chief Loncoy was later rewarded for his services. See Cabildo of 18 February 1807, in Instituto Cultural, *Invasiones inglesas*, 130.

35. As quoted in Ian Fletcher, *Waters of Oblivion*, 41–42.

36. Rivarola's "Romance heroico," in Instituto Cultural, *Invasiones inglesas*: "A estos héroes generosos; una amazona se agrega; que oculta en varonil traje; triunfa de la gente inglesa: Manuela tiene por nombre; por patria: Tucumánesa."

37. Years later, Juan Manuel wrote a friend about his being assigned to a cannon. Rosas to Josefa Gómez, 2 May 1869, in Raed, *Cartas confidenciales*, 117.

38. As quoted in Ibarguren, *Rosas*, 22.

39. Peña's story is reconstructed using his petition to be recognized for his

conduct in the battle. See "Pedido de Francisco González de la Peña," 15 September 1807, in Instituto Cultural, *Invasiones inglesas*, 95–97. Even leaving room for some possible exaggerations, other accounts of the battle reveal its intensity so as to render Peña's account credible.

40. Peña, "Pedido," 95.

41. Ian Fletcher, *Waters of Oblivion*, 44–47.

42. For more on ways the porteños raised money for the city's defense, see Grieco, *Politics of Giving*.

43. Cabildo of 14 August 1806, in Instituto Cultural, *Invasiones Inglesas*, 116–17.

44. Cabildo of 14 August 1806, 116–17.

45. Rosas referred to this commendation later in his life, in a letter to Josefa Gómez, 2 May 1869, in Raed, *Cartas confidenciales*, 117.

46. As quoted in Ibarguren, *Rosas*, 22.

47. Rivarola, "Romance heroico."

48. Gillespie, *Gleanings and Remarks*, 112.

49. Rosas to Josefa Gómez, 2 May 1869, in Raed, *Cartas confidenciales*, 117.

50. Liniers, proclamation to the city of Buenos Aires, in Instituto Cultural, *Invasiones inglesas*, 93–94.

51. Lieutenant Colonel Guard to Lieutenant General Whitelocke, 8 July 1807, in Chelsea College Court Martial, *Trial of George Whitelocke*, app. 12.

52. Whitelocke also offered to accept Liniers's surrender, which Liniers refused. See Colonel Elio to General Whitelocke, 3 July 1807, in Chelsea College Court Martial, *Trial of George Whitelocke*, app. 11.

53. Lyman Johnson, *Workshop of Revolution*, 258.

54. Report by Major Nichols, 5 and 6 July 1807, in Chelsea College Court Martial, *Trial of George Whitelocke*, app. 12.

55. Letter from Whitelocke to Rear Admiral Murray, 6 July 1807, in Chelsea College Court Martial, app. 12.

56. Treaty between General Whitelocke and Santiago Liniers, 7 July 1807, in Chelsea College Court Martial, apps. 9–10.

57. Letter from Cabildo of Buenos Aires, 25 May 1808, in Instituto Cultural, *Invasiones inglesas*, 98–99.

58. López y Planes, "El triunfo argentino."

59. Anonymous, "Bolero II," in Instituto Cultural, *Invasiones inglesas*, 218–20.

60. Cabildo of 15 October 1807, and Cabildo of 29 October 1807, in Instituto Cultural, *Invasiones inglesas*, 137–38. The lottery was eventually expanded to include widows and children of slaves killed in battle.

61. Lyman Johnson, *Workshop of Revolution*, 265. For more on these and other benefits granted to widows, orphans, and slaves during these years, see Grieco, "Family and Political Authority," 69–71.

62. "Un esclavo que luchó," 29 March 1808, in Instituto Cultural, *Invasiones inglesas*, 192–93.

63. Blanchard, "Institution Defended," 253–72.

64. And many of them were now armed. See Lyman Johnson, *Workshop of Revolution*, 259.

65. Lyman Johnson, 256.

66. "Panegírico histórico poético al Excelentísimo Señor Virrey Marqués de Sobremonte," in Instituto Cultural, *Invasiones inglesas*, 220–21. Chiaramonte also argued that the invasions awoke a great patriotism in the city.

67. Saavedra as quoted in Instituto Cultural, *Invasiones inglesas*, 30.

68. Calvera, "Revoluciones, minué y mujeres," 166–75.

69. Gillespie, *Gleanings and Remarks*, 76–77.

70. Elena, "Steam-Age Eldorado." See also Matthew Brown, *Informal Empire*.

71. Juan Manuel, later in life, claimed that he had two letters given by city leaders to his parents, acknowledging his participation in the city's defense against Whitelocke's invasion. Rosas to Josefa Gómez, 2 May 1869, in Raed, *Cartas confidenciales*, 117. Other historians dispute that Rosas ever fought in the second invasion.

72. Pueyrredón, Cabildo of 5 September 1806, in Instituto Cultural, *Invasiones inglesas*, 126.

73. Parish, *Buenos Ayres*, 70.

74. Sánchez, *Recuerdos*, 70. Goldgel recognized this dual impact of the English invasions in Mariquita's writings. See his *Prensa, moda y literatura*, 116–17.

CHAPTER FOUR

1. Taken from a description of Mariquita's tertulia by Vicente Fidel López, whose father, Vicente López y Planes, was a close friend of Mariquita's. This is more of a composite sketch of her salon. López, *Historia de República Argentina*, 135–38.

2. Batticuore, *Mariquita*, 125.

3. As quoted in Polasky, *Revolutions without Borders*, 273.

4. Higonnet, *Paris*, 18–19, 30. By the time of Mariquita's youth, more and more tourists were also making their way to Paris from all over the world, as seen in the proliferation of travel guides in the latter half of the eighteenth century.

5. Kale, *French Salons*, 204.

6. See Renan's chapter in Guerra, *El espacio público*. See also Blossom, chap. 1 in *Nariño*.

7. For more discussion of the role of salons in Spanish America, and for examples of postindependence tertulia hosts, including Mariquita, see Chambers, "Letters and Salons."

8. See letters from Lord Chesterfield to Master Stanhope, in 1740 or 1741, and on 23 January 1752, in *Lord Chesterfield's Letters*, 247–48.

9. When she did come back to Philadelphia, Anne Bingham impressed John Adams with her political wisdom. See Furstenberg, *When the United States Spoke French*, 162–63, 187–88.

10. As quoted in Kale, *French Salons*, 86–89.

11. Tertulias in Buenos Aires were usually much more informal than Parisian salons, although Mariquita's tertulia was known to approximate the Parisian version. See Myers, "Una revolución," 119–20.

12. Gillespie, *Gleanings and Remarks*, 67–68.

13. J. P. Robertson and W. P. Robertson, *Letters on South America*, 107–8.

14. Nin's description is found in the footnote in Vilaseca, *Cartas*, 151. Obligado referred to sixty couples dancing in the great room, in his *Tradiciones*, 261.

15. López, *Historia de República Argentina*, 136.

16. J. P. Robertson and W. P. Robertson, *Letters on South America*, 107.

17. J. P. Robertson and W. P. Robertson, 112–13.

18. Adelman, *Sovereignty and Revolution*, 25.

19. Spanish officials were unable to fully embrace the free-trade model. See Adelman, 41–42.

20. Moreno, "The Landowners Petition," in Nouzeilles and Montaldo, *Argentina Reader*, 66–70.

21. As quoted in Lynch, *Simón Bolívar*, 30. The moderate nature of the American Revolution is perhaps what allowed the union of the young United States to survive its first few decades, time enough to withstand its brutal civil war that finally came and cost more than six hundred thousand lives. See Ellis, *American Creation*, 18–19.

22. As early as 1788, a French traveler noted that Washington had already been compared to Cincinnatus. "The comparison is doubtless just," for the "celebrated General is nothing more at present than a good farmer." Warville, *New Travels*, 368.

23. Bolívar, "Oath Taken in Rome," in *El Libertador*, 113–14.

24. There is some discussion about when the oath was composed and in what form. For Bolívar's reference to the oath and its significance, made in a letter he sent to his tutor in 1824, see Lynch, *Simón Bolívar*, 27.

25. For an excellent discussion of this process, see Goldman, "Buenos Aires," 47–69.

26. Lynch, *Spanish American Revolutions*, 236–38.

27. See Saavedra's autobiographical selection in Senado de la Nación, *Biblioteca de mayo* 2:1052.

28. Sáenz Quesada, *Argentina*, 214–15.

29. Di Meglio, *¡Viva el bajo pueblo!*, 93.

30. Sáenz Quesada, *Argentina*, 214–16.

31. Carranza, *Oratoria argentina*, 20–22.

32. Halperín-Donghi, *Politics, Economics, and Society*, 208–9.

33. *Gazeta de Buenos Ayres*, 7 June 1810, 1–3.

34. *Gazeta de Buenos Ayres*, 9 August 1810, 166. Members of the lower classes also donated to the cause. See Halperín-Donghi, *Politics, Economics, and Society*, 159.

35. *Gazeta de Buenos Ayres*, 9 August 1810.

36. Halperín-Donghi, *Politics, Economics, and Society*, 159.

37. *Gazeta de Buenos Ayres*, 16 August 1810, 173.

38. *Gazeta de Buenos Ayres*, 16 August 1810, 178–80.

39. Prado, *Edge of Empire*, 163–64.

40. Vera, *British Book Trade*, 2, 9.

41. *Gazeta de Buenos Ayres*, 15 November 1811, 14.

42. For a deeper discussion of porteño centralism at this time, see Segreti, *Bernardino Rivadavia*, 58–68.

43. Gallo, *Struggle*, 7–8.

44. *Gazeta de Buenos Ayres*, 27 December 1811, 62.

45. Monteagudo, "Observaciones didácticas," 48–49.

46. *Gazeta Ministerial*, 26 June 1812. The note is signed 30 May, so this could be before the donations of the men, which were recorded in the early weeks of June. For more on female contributions, see Grieco, "Family and Political Authority," 83.

47. Dellepiane, *Dos patricias ilustres*, 29–30; and Sáenz Quesada, *Mariquita*, 61–62.

48. *Gazeta Ministerial*, 26 June 1812. For more on the emergence of print culture during this time, see Acree, chap. 1 in *Everyday Reading*.

49. Supplement of *Gazeta Ministerial*, 12 June 1812, 50.

50. *Gazeta Ministerial*, 12 June 1812 (Mexican rebellion), and 19 June (Philadelphia editorial).

51. *Gazeta Ministerial*, 19 June 1812, 44–46.

52. *El Grito del Sud*, September 1812, as well as nos. 8, 9, 10, and 11. The editors proposed on September 20 that a multijudge panel hear each case to ensure that parents were not abusing their authority over their children.

53. Obligado, *Tradiciones*, 261.

54. J. P. Robertson and W. P. Robertson, *Letters on South America*, 109, 112.

55. J. P. Robertson and W. P. Robertson, 112–13.

56. San Martín had previously associated himself with masons in Spain. See Lynch, *San Martín*, 22.

57. Halperín-Donghi, *Polics, Economics, and Society*, 217–18.

58. Segreti, *Bernardino Rivadavia*, 70.

59. Lynch, *San Martín*, 46.

60. Gallo, *Struggle*, 22–23.

61. Lynch, chap. 4 in *San Martín*.

62. Obligado, *Tradiciones*, 64. Buch argues in *Juremos con gloria* that no one mentions a connection between Mariquita's salon and the anthem at all in nineteenth century.

63. "Memoria sobre la necesidad de contener," as found in the John Carter Brown Library. Copy of original thanks to Grieco and Di Meglio. See also Szuchman, *Order, Family, and Community*, 119.

64. Rosas to Josefa Gómez, 2 March 1869, in Raed, *Cartas confidenciales*, 118.

65. Lynch, *Argentine Dictator*, 15.

66. *Gazeta Ministerial*, 12 June 1812.

67. Ibaguren, *Rosas*, 41.

68. Rosas to Josefina Gómez, 2 May 1869, in Raed, *Cartas confidenciales*, 117.

69. Myers, "Una revolución," 120.

70. Mariquita Sánchez's tertulia functioned without twenty-first-century social-science theory. Nevertheless, Mariquita's tertulia fits into the realm described by Kale in that salons in France "always filled some sort of institutional vacuum at the intersection between public and private life left by the decline of certain cultural, social, or civic institutions and the rise of others that had not yet taken root." *French Salons*, 2–4. Furstenberg also found that salons and other social gatherings helped prop up the fledgling USA in the instability of the early days of its republic. *When the United States Spoke French*, 156.

CHAPTER FIVE

1. González Lonzieme, *Martín Thompson*. McCullough discusses the perils of trans-Atlantic voyages in the late 1820s and 1830s. Long sea trips would have been all the more precarious in 1815 when Martín Thompson embarked on his mission to the USA. *Greater Journey*, 12.

2. As quoted in Barba, *Quiroga y Rosas*, 231.

3. Artigas, "Proclama de Mercedes," 11.

4. As quoted in Street, *Artigas*, 373.

5. Artigas's *Reglamento provisorio de la Provincia Oriental para el fomento de su campaña y seguridad de sus hacendados* in Street, *Artigas*, 376–79. Street argues that whereas previous attempts to help inhabitants settle land was meant to stop Portuguese settlement, Artigas's goals were to develop the province and help those who really needed the land. See 227.

6. Bushnell, *Reform and Reaction*.

7. Kale, *French Salons*, 99–100.

8. Lynch, *Simón Bolívar*, 91–92.

9. Both quotes as cited in Ibarguren, *Rosas*, 54.

10. *El Censor*, 10 October 1816, 1–2.

11. For a close look at the various forces at work in 1816, see Di Meglio, *Trama de la independencia*.

12. Argentine Declaration of Independence.

13. *El Censor*, 25 July 1816, 1–5.

14. These were the choices put forward by many, including *El Censor*, 22 August 1816.

15. Ignacio Alvarez, letter of appointment of Martín Thompson, 16 January 1816, in González Lonzieme, *Martín Thompson*, 204.

16. Letters naming Martín Thompson as deputy to the US, 16 January 1816, and letter to President Madison, 16 January, both in González Lonzieme, 203, 207.

17. Gregorio Tagle and Ignacio Alvarez, instructions to Martín Thompson, 16 January 1816, in González Lonzieme, 206.

18. Gregorio Tagle and Ignacio Alvarez, instructions to Martín Thompson, 16 January 1816, in González Lonzieme, 206.

19. Thompson to the Directory, 20 May 1816, in González Lonzieme, 208.

20. Thompson to the Directory, 23 August 1816, in González Lonzieme, 209.

21. Thompson to the Directory, 23 August 1816.

22. The accusation was true. Thompson was recruiting men in and around Philadelphia, while in Baltimore, Maryland, ships were being outfitted to prey on Spanish ships in 1817. Di Meglio, *Manuel Dorrego*, 146.

23. Fitz, *Our Sister Republics*, 170–71.

24. For records of Bouchard's agreements with Kamehameha, see State of Hawai'i Archives, folders 402-2-9 and 402-2-10, Chronological File, 1790–1849.

25. John Quincy Adams to G. Hyde de Neuville, 5 December 1817, in Manning, *Diplomatic Correspondence*.

26. Vicente López to Thompson, 10 January 1817, in González Lonzieme, *Martín Thompson*, 234.

27. Pueyrredón to President James Madison, 10 February 1817, in González Lonzieme, 236.

28. Vicente López to Thompson, 20 February 1817, in González Lonzieme, 238.

29. Sáenz Quesada, *Mariquita*, 71–72.

30. Taylor, *Civil War of 1812*.

31. Belgrano to Guemes, 18 January 1817, in Belgrano, *Epistolario*, 309–10. Regarding the inclination toward monarchy in this era, as one scholar put it, "the United States was once again an island in a sea of monarchies hostile to republicanism." John J. Johnson, *Hemisphere Apart*, 33.

32. Belgrano to Manuel de Ulloa, 10 October 1816, in *Epistolario*, 297–99. In his next letter to Ulloa, Belgrano proposed a constitutional monarchy with an Incan monarch.

33. Burgin, *Argentine Federalism*.

34. William Spence Robertson, *France and Latin-American Independence*, 130–35. If the American revolutions were successful, the Russian continued, they would provide the world a horrible example of anarchy and of threats against "rights of legitimacy" (134–35).

35. William Spence Robertson, 144.

36. William Spence Robertson, 145.

37. Lynch, chaps. 4 and 5 in *San Martín*.

38. Rivadavia to Richelieu, as quoted in William Spence Robertson, *France and Latin-American Independence*, 158–59.

39. As quoted in Piccirilli, *Rivadavia y su tiempo*, 438–40 (spelling of Chile is modernized here).

40. Dessolle to Hulot, as quoted in William Spence Robertson, *France and Latin-American Independence*, 164.

41. See William Spence Robertson, 172–73, for the enormous list of conditions for the "French Plan" to be accepted.

CHAPTER SIX

1. As quoted in Ibarguren, *Rosas*, 49.

2. Complete letter found in Pradere, *Su Icconografía*, 18–19.

3. As quoted in Carranza, Rodriguez, and Ventura, *Manual de historia política*, 86. The constitution also outlined a number of rights that were common in other constitutions of the age.

4. As quoted in Street, *Artigas*, 373.

5. Segreti, "Desacuerdos," 364–65.

6. As quoted in Ibarguren, *Rosas*, 58.

7. As quoted in Ibarguren, 56.

8. As quoted in Celesia, *Aportes*, 36–37.

9. See Fradkin and Gelman, *Juan Manuel de Rosas*, 127–28, for how Rosas and his partners expanded their holdings. See also 388–89.

10. Gálvez, *Rosas*, 15.

11. See Gelman, *Rosas, estanciero*.

12. Celesia, *Aportes*, 42. See also Fradkin and Gelman, *Juan Manuel de Rosas*, 138–39.

13. Fradkin and Gelman, 391.

14. Cutrera, *Subordinarlos*, 25.

15. From *Abeja Argentina*, as quoted in Fradkin and Gelman, *Juan Manuel de Rosas*, 141.

16. *Gazeta de Buenos Ayres*, 19 January 1820.

17. Ibarguen, *Rosas*, 51–52.

18. Di Meglio, chap. 4 in *¡Viva el bajo pueblo!*

19. Lamadrid, *Memorias*, 2–3.

20. Gelman, *Rosas, estanciero*, 46.

21. Lamadrid, *Memorias*, 17–19.

22. Celesia argues, however, that the Córdoba delegation played a major role in the peace process. *Aportes*, 46–47. See also Bilbao, *Rosas*, 111–12.

23. Bragoni, *Carrera*, 198–202. See also Chambers, *Families*, especially chap. 1.

24. Bragoni, 251–58.

25. Iriarte, who lived during these events, claimed that Carrera did his best to stop the brutality. *Biografía del brigadier general*, 56–57.

26. As quoted in Carranza, Rodriguez, and Ventura, *Manual de historia política*, 91.

27. Caldcleugh, *Travels in South America*.

28. Caldcleugh, 1:237–39.

29. Caldcleugh, 1:264.

30. Caldcleugh, 2:100.

31. Caldcleugh, 2:121–22. "Reales" is a modernized version of Caldcleugh's "rials."

32. Caldcleugh, 2:166–67.

33. Caldcleugh, 2:167. López defeated Ramírez's army and eventually captured and beheaded him.

34. Caldcleugh, 2:176.

35. Caldcleugh, 1:215, 162–63, 122.

36. Caldcleugh, 2:122.

37. Caldcleugh, 1:233.

38. As quoted in Ibarguren, *Rosas*, 63.

39. Di Meglio, *¡Viva el bajo pueblo!*, 208–9.

40. Ibarguren, *Rosas*, 64.

41. Fradkin and Gelman, *Juan Manuel de Rosas*, 431. Fradkin and Gelman here refer to Rosas wielding these powers, but the same point—of their ancient and institutional use—applies for when Rodríguez wielded them as well.

42. As quoted in Ibarguren, *Rosas*, 65.

43. As a young officer in Spain, San Martín witnessed the murder of his close friend by a mob, which, according to Lynch, seemed to shape his distrust of the masses (and perhaps of democracy). *San Martín*, 17. Similarly, Alamán in Mexico witnessed mob violence in 1810, an experience that likely gave him a significant conservative bent for the rest of his life. *Historia de México*, 50–52.

44. Rosas, "Segunda memoria of Rosas," in Saldías, *Rozas y su época*, 1:279–90.

45. Rosas, "Manifiesto del coronel de caballería," in Pradere, *Su Icconografía*, 18–19.

46. As quoted in Gallo, *Struggle*, 50. For more on Father Castañeda, see Troisi, *Sócios incómodos*, 124–25.

47. Caldcleugh, *Travels in South America*, 1:169–71.

48. Beruti, *Memorias curiosas*, 328.

49. Reproduced in the front matter of Goñi Demarchi, Scala, and Berraondo, *Rosas, Washington, y Lincoln*.

50. Ibarguren, *Rosas*, 65.

CHAPTER SEVEN

1. Halperín-Donghi, *Revolución y guerra*, 352.

2. *Gazeta de Buenos Ayres*, 10 March 1819, 495.

3. Sánchez to Joaquín, 26 May 1817 (Sáenz Quesada corrects the date to 1819), in Vilaseca, *Cartas*, 28.

4. Sáenz Quesada, *Mariquita*, 74.

5. W. P. Robertson to General Miller, in *Letters on South America*, 112.

6. Mariquita had two other suitors besides Mendeville. See Sánchez to Alberdi, 27 May 1863, in Vilaseca, *Cartas*, 359.

7. Meyer Arana, *Las primeras trece*, 52.

8. Zavalía Lagos, *Mariquita*, 125.

9. Batticuore, *Mariquita*, 97.

10. Sáenz Quesada, *Mariquita*, 81 (age difference), 83 (son's note).

11. As quoted in Zavalía Lagos, *Mariquita*, 126.

12. Batticuore, *Mariquita*, 262.

13. Halperín-Donghi, *Revolución y guerra*, 351.

14. Sáenz Quesada, *Argentina*, 270.

15. As quoted in Gallo, *Struggle*, 19.

16. Gallo, 32.

17. Gallo, 57.

18. L. M. Simon to investors, 11 March 1825, folder HC 4.1.1, BBA.

19. See, for example, an 1849 petition from investors to Juan Manuel de Rosas, for him to start repayments to creditors in England. Folder HC 4.1.13.22, BBA.

20. Gallo, *Struggle*, 34–36.

21. Piccirilli, *Rivadavia*, 222–24. Known as the Lancaster method.

22. Gallo, *Rivadavia*, 43.

23. From Castañeda, *Doña María Retazos*, 219–20.

24. Belsunce et al., *Buenos Aires*, 142.

25. See, for example, *Observador Americano*, 4 November 1816. See also Jeffrey Shumway, chap. 6 in *Ugly Suitor*.

26. Meyer Arana, *Las primeras trece*, 22–23, fol. 1.

27. Meyer Arana, 92. The Sociedad de Beneficencia lasted until Juan Perón merged it into other state institutions. See Guy, *Women Build the Welfare State*, 159–71.

28. *Abeja Argentina*, in Senado de la Nación, *Biblioteca de mayo* 1:142–47.

29. *Libro de actas*, sala 7, tomo 1, folio 1, AGN.

30. "Acta 42 de la Sociedad de Beneficencia," *Libro de actas*, 13 May 1824, sala 7, tomo 1, folio 41, AGN.

31. Guy in *Sex and Danger* explores the precarious conditions of women in nineteenth- and twentieth-century Argentina. For a collection that speaks to the breadth and depth of Guy's contributions, see her *White Slavery*.

32. Vera, *British Book Trade*, 40–41, 110. For Mariquita's appointment as secretary, see Sáenz Quesada, *Mariquita*, 99.

33. "Acta 33 de la Sociedad de Beneficencia," *Libro de actas*, 18 October 1826, sala 7, tomo 1, folio 93, AGN.

34. "Acta 45 de la Sociedad de Beneficencia," *Libro de actas*, 23 April 1827, sala 7, tomo 1, folio 112, AGN.

35. "Acta 118 de la Sociedad de Beneficencia," *Libro de actas*, 8 October 1830, sala 7, AGN.

36. Race was still a powerful motivator in marriage-conflict cases between parents and children, although as the nineteenth century progressed, some judges began to modify colonial laws and customs, especially for poor sectors of society. See Jeffrey Shumway, "Purity of My Blood," 201–20.

37. Sánchez to Lasala, n.d., caja 6, notas, AGN.

38. As quoted in Halpeín-Donghi, *Revolución y guerra*, 364.

39. As quoted in Gallo, *Struggle*, 44. Bentham had a penchant for calling people his disciples. The two later had a falling out. See also Gallo, *Rivadavia*, 143–44.

40. For more on Rivadavia's idea of creating a nation, see Myers, "Identidades porteños."

41. Piccirilli, *Rivadavia*, 399–400.

42. Gallo, *Rivadavia*, 147–48. Di Meglio, *Manuel Dorrego*, 247–48.

43. See Gallo, chap. 5 in *Rivadavia*.

44. Prado, *Ege of Empire*, 179–80.

45. Fradkin and Gelman, *Juan Manuel de Rosas*, 143–44.

46. Rosas, "Memoria que elevó el coronel al gobierno de Buenos Aires," in Saldías, *Rozas y su época*, 1:302–3.

47. Lynch, *Argentine Dictator*, 30.

48. Ibarguren, *Rosas*, 92–93.

49. For a detailed discussion of this process, see Segreti, *Bernardino Rivadavia*, 346–49.

50. Segreti, 366–84.

51. Segreti, 406–9.

52. Ibarguren, *Rosas*, 99.

53. As quoted in Enrique Arana, *Juan Manuel de Rosas*, 303.

54. Mansilla, *Rozas*, 42.

CHAPTER EIGHT

1. Zavalía Lagos, *Mariquita*, 167–68.

2. Di Meglio, *Manuel Dorrego*, 144.

3. Di Meglio, 265.

4. Ibarguren, *Rosas*, 102, 107.

5. At first open to allowing Easterners to decide their own fate, the war became so unpopular that Dorrego accepted Great Britain's mediation and the creation of a new state. See Di Meglio, *Manuel Dorrego*, 314–18.

6. Mansilla, *Rozas*, 25. Lucio also emphasized that the Lavalles and Rosases were from "pure blood, without mixture, truly colonial blood."

7. Pasquali, *Juan Lavalle*, 156, 162.

8. Di Meglio, *Manuel Dorrego*, 333–39.

9. Di Meglio, 344–45.

10. Ibarguren, *Rosas*, 119.

11. Varela to Lavalle, 12 December 1829, in Irazusta and Rosas, *Vida política*, vol. 1, pt. 1, 155.

12. Del Carril to Lavalle, 12 December 1828, in Irazusta and Rosas, 151–52.

13. Del Carril to Lavalle, 14 December 1828, in Irazusta and Rosas, 154.

14. Note to wife as found in Di Meglio, *Manuel Dorrego*, 350.

15. Del Carril to Lavalle, 15 December 1828, in Irazusta and Rosas, *Vida política*, vol. 1, pt. 1, 156. News of Dorrego's assassination also made the papers in the US. *The*

Evening Post in New York, for example, published translated letters from the slain governor's wife and brother. See *Evening Post*, 21 May 1829, 2.

16. Beruti, *Memorias curiosas*, 401.

17. Rosas to López, 12 December 1828, in Irazusta and Rosas, *Vida política*, vol. 1, pt. 1, 158–59.

18. Irazusta and Rosas, 164–65.

19. In June of 1829, for example, Juan Alagón refused to give his permission for his daughter to marry because of the tumultuous state of the country at the moment. See "Juan Alagón con Ubaldo Méndez," 1829, 7.5.14.6, AHPBA; and Jeffrey Shumway, chap. 3 in *Ugly Suitor*.

20. As quoted in Pasquali, *San Martín, confidencial*, 236, note 173. "Unsheathed" as quoted in Ibarguren, *Rosas*, 122.

21. Lynch, *San Martín*, 211–13.

22. San Martín to Bernardo O'Higgins, 13 April 1829, as transcribed in Ibarguren, *Rosas*, 124–25. Lynch, *San Martín*, 212–13.

23. As quoted in Irazsusta and Rosas, *Vida política*, vol. 1, pt. 1, 165.

24. Irazusta and Rosas, 166.

25. Fradkin, *Fusilaron a Dorrego*, 67–69.

26. As quoted in Ibarguren, *Rosas*, 121.

27. Mansilla, *Rozas*, 26–27. For a possible reaction to such requisitions, on 7 September 1829, *El Lucero* published a decree from the government protecting private citizens from unauthorized seizure of property.

28. Sarmiento described this incident years later in a letter to the general who saved him. See Sarmiento to General José S. Ramírez, 26 May 1848, in Córdoba Province, *Compilación de leyes*, 266–67.

29. Document in Fitte, *Agresión francesa*, 19–20.

30. Sáenz Quesada, *Mariquita*, 112–13. For many Argentines this was one of the most egregious violations of national sovereignty in their history. See also Fitte, 7.

31. This is a reconstruction of Mariquita's words based on eyewitness accounts. As quoted in Zavalía Lagos, *Mariquita*, 167–68. Late in her life, Mariquita wrote a letter to Juan Bautista Alberdi in which she talked about how she had "done things that were more than heroic with her husband. Twice his consulate was in ruin" and she had "saved it." Sánchez to Alberdi, 27 May 1863, in Vilaseca, *Cartas*, 359.

32. Mendeville to Rosas, 12 May 1829, as transcribed in Fitte, *Agresión francesa*, 90.

33. Rosas to Mendeville, 27 May 1829, as transcribed in Fitte, *Agresión francesa*, 146.

34. See selection from French diplomat Alfred Brossard in Fitte, *Agresión francesa*, 143–44.

35. See Mendeville's letter in Fitte, *Agresión francesa*, 217–23.

36. Rosas to Admiral Venancourt, n.d., as transcribed in Irazusta and Rosas, *Vida política*, vol. 1, pt. 1, 169–70.

37. Pasquali, *Juan Lavalle*, 219–20.

38. Pasquali, 221.

39. Pasquali, 226. Rosas gave instructions through Félix de Álzaga.

40. Pasquali, 225. "My head is a labyrinth," he wrote Rosas in early July.

41. Rosas to Ángel Pacheco, 24 July 1829, in Saldías, *Rozas y su época*, 2:327–28. Sarah Chambers examines the image of the national family as it played out in Chilean nation building. See her *Families*.

42. As quoted in Ibarguren, *Rosas*, 138.

43. Irazusta and Rosas, *Vida política*, vol. 1, pt. 1, 196.

44. *Gaceta Mercantil*, 27 October 1831, as found in Myers, *Orden y virtud*, 270–71.

45. Recollection of a Mr. Vazques of Uruguay, as transcribed in Irazusta and Rosas, *Vida política*, vol. 1, pt. 1, 197.

46. Rosas, "Proclamation of 8 December 1829," in Irazusta and Rosas, 198.

47. Rosas, "Circular to Provinces," 12 December 1829, transcribed in Irazusta and Rosas, 200–1.

48. Rosas, "Circular to Provinces."

49. Bolívar, "A Glance at South America," in *El Libertador*, 95–97.

50. Howe, *What Hath God Wrought*, 395–410.

51. Sáenz Quesada, *Mariquita*, 119.

52. Fradkin and Gelman, *Juan Manuel de Rosas*, 244–45.

53. For more on Rosas's use of Dorrego's image, see Dellepiane, *Rosas*, 46.

54. Transcription of Rosas's speech as found in Irazusta and Rosas, *Vida política*, vol. 1, pt. 1, 199.

55. For the documents granting Rosas extraordinary power, as well as the early decrees of his government regarding supporters of Lavalle and the ribbons, see Myers, *Orden y virtud*, 125–28.

56. For an excellent discussion of the various ideas associated with Federalism, and what was truly "federal" versus "confederal" in this time period, see Goldman, "Orígenes." See also Chiaramonte, "Federalismo argentino." The Federalist Pact of 1831 was more akin, according to Chiaramonte, to the Articles of Confederation of the USA.

57. As quoted in Ibarguren, *Rosas*, 156.

58. See letter from Rosas to the legislature in Myers, *Orden y virtud*, 156.

59. As quoted in Ibarguren, *Rosas*, 165.

60. Ibarguren, 165.

CHAPTER NINE

1. As cited in Zavalía Lagos, *Mariquita*, 168. The phrase has multiple translation possibilities: "una francesita parlanchina y coqueta."

2. Fradkin and Gelman, *Juan Manuel de Rosas*, 237.

3. For more on this mission and the Spanish captives, see Socolow, "Spanish Captives," 73–99.

4. Darwin, *Voyage of the Beagle*, 76.

5. Darwin, 78–79.

6. Darwin, 79–81.

7. Darwin, 80, 81.

8. Darwin, 85–86. If the guide sensed danger, they would ride deep into one of the many swamps that dot the pampas and then make their way on foot in an attempt to escape their attackers. When Darwin was not worried about Indians, he was on the lookout for jaguars. See his entry from 12 October (139–41).

9. Darwin, 109.

10. Darwin, 145.

11. Darwin, 146. "Since leaving South America," Darwin later wrote, "we have heard that Rosas has been elected, with powers and for a time altogether opposed to the constitutional principles of the republic."

12. For more on these developments, see Di Meglio, *Mueran*, 30–40.

13. Fradkin and Gelman, *Juan Manuel de Rosas*, 245–46.

14. Letters from Ezcurra de Rosas to Rosas, 14 September and 2 October 1833, in Ezcurra de Rosas, *Doña Encarnación*, 8–9, 11–12.

15. Di Meglio, *Mueran*, 45–49.

16. Letter transcribed in Celesia, *Aportes*, 482.

17. Di Meglio, *Mueran*, 49–50.

18. Di Meglio, 55–56.

19. Di Meglio, 63.

20. Ezcurra de Rosas to Rosas, 9 May 1834, in Ezcurra de Rosas, *Doña Encarnación*, 12.

21. Lynch, *Argentine Dictator*, 215–18; Fradkin and Gelman, *Juan Manuel de Rosas*, 257. For more on the origin of the term "mazorca," see Di Meglio, *Mueran*, 67–68.

22. As quoted in Ibarguren, *Rosas*, 157.

23. Rosas to Quiroga, 20 December 1834, as transcribed in Irazusta and Rosas, *Vida política*, vol. 1, pt. 2, 237–45.

24. Bolívar, "Angostura Address," 15 February 1819, in *El Libertador*, 36.

25. Bolívar, 23.

26. Bolívar, "Address to Constituent Congress of Bolivia," 25 May 1826, in *El Libertador*, 54.

27. Arana, epilogue of *Bolívar*.

28. Ibarguren, *Rosas*, 206. Ibarguren says that the stain is Facundo's blood, as did an archivist who showed me the actual letter in the AGN.

29. As quoted in Ibarguren, *Rosas*, 207.

30. Numbers reported by *La Gaceta*. See Ternavasio, *Revolución del voto*, 202–3; Di Meglio lists ten votes again in *Mueran*, 69–70.

31. Fradkin and Gelman, *Juan Manuel de Rosas*, 317–18.

32. Ibarguren, *Rosas*, 142–43.

33. Di Meglio, *Mueran*, 70.

34. As quoted in Ibarguren, *Rosas*, 210.

35. Garavaglia, "Apotéosis del Leviathán," 135–68. For more on the administration of justice during this era, see Barreneche, *Administration of Justice*.

36. For an example of the red seal, see Francisca Canicoba, "Sobre disenso," 1842, 7.5.15.20, AHPBA. For more on mottos and ribbons, see Acree, *Everyday Reading*, 60–63.

37. I saw this comb, with Rosas's profile and "Federation or Death" carved into it, on display the Municipal Museum in Colonia, Uruguay. For more on Rosas and fashion, see Root, *Couture and Consensus*.

38. Vertanessian, *Retrato imposible*, 31–32.

39. For a sampling of de Angelis's writings, see Myers, *Orden y virtud*, 165–208.

40. For more on Pérez, see Acree, *Everyday Reading*, 51–59. For *Black Girl* quote, see Fradkin and Gelman, *Juan Manuel de Rosas*, 436.

41. *Gaceta Mercantil*, 1 January 1844, as transcribed in Myers, *Orden y virtud*, 227.

42. For more on the "holy" nature of the republic, and for an excellent discussion of the multiple ways Rosas's government appealed to a variety of classes, see Salvatore, "Expresiones Federales," 192.

43. As quoted in Lynch, *San Martín*, 216.

44. For Lynch's discussion of this question, see Lynch, *San Martín*, 216–17.

45. Van Buren to Forbes, 10 February 1831, in Manning, *Argentina*, vol. 1 of *Diplomatic Correspondence*, 3–4.

46. Baylies to Livingston, 24 July 1832, in Manning, *Argentina*, vol. 1 of *Diplomatic Correspondence*, 132–33.

47. Whigham, *Politics of River Trade*, 57

48. It was clear that Buenos Aires Province benefited the most from a strict interpretation of Federalist dogma. See Ibarguren, *Rosas*, 159.

49. For more on this and other economic issues during the Rosas era, see Burgin, *Argentine Federalism*.

50. Gatica, *Yo quiero la paz*, 33–35.

51. As quoted in Sule, *Rosas y sus relaciones*, 13. Ratto in "Caciques" has the same quote as coming from Chief Cachul.

52. Borucki, *Shipmates to Soldiers*, 50–54; Andrews, *Afro-Argentines*, 56–57. Rosas had slaves on his estates, and he even revived the slave trade, under certain circumstances, in 1831, before he signed the agreement with the British. See Lynch, *Argentine Dictator*, 119–24.

53. Wilde, *Buenos Aires*, 176.

54. Fradkin and Gelman, *Juan Manuel de Rosas*, 300. For more on Rosas's relations with Afro-Argentines, see Salvatore, "Integral Outsiders."

55. Ibarguren, *Rosas*, 242–43.

56. Mansilla, *Rozas*, 29.

57. Darwin, *Voyage of the Beagle*, 81. Darwin says that this technique derived from staking cowhides to dry them in the sun.

58. Hudson, *Far Away*, 109–10.

59. Sánchez, 25 April 1839, in Mizraje, *Mariquita*, 58.

60. As quoted in Sáenz Quesada, *Mariquita*, 135.

61. As cited in Zavalía Lagos, *Mariquita*, 168.

62. Sánchez to Rosas, ca. 1836, as found in Mizraje, *Mariquita*, 327–28.

63. France, *Code Napoleon*, bk. 1, chap. 1, title 1, articles 10 and 12. For a larger discussion of French nationality, see Weil, *How to Be French*.

64. But this would become an issue later in the century. See Augustine-Adams, "'She Consents Implicitly.'" See also Guy, "Parents before the Tribunals: The Legal Construction of Patriarchy in Argentina," in *White Slavery*.

65. Sáenz Quesada, *Mariquita*, 143.

66. As cited in Zavalía Lagos, *Mariquita*, 170. Juan Thompson, Mariquita's son, heard rumors that she had been arrested in her own house by Rosista authorities. See his journal in Piccirilli, app. of *Juan Thompson*, 177.

67. See Sáenz Quesada, chap. 3 in *Mujeres*.

CHAPTER TEN

1. Two diary entries from Sánchez, 25 May 1839, and 11 June 1839, in Mizraje, *Mariquita*, 70, 78.

2. Sáenz Quesada, *Mariquita*, 146.

3. For a thorough discussion of the Generation of '37, see Myers, "Revolución en las ideas"; and Nicolas Shumway, chaps. 5–6 in *Invention of Argentina*.

4. *La Moda*, no. 1, 18 November 1837.

5. *La Moda*, no. 5, 16 December 1837, 3.

6. *La Moda*, no. 9, 13 January 1838, 1–2. The Generation of '37 admired Saint Simón, as did Mariquita (in part for his treatment of women's rights). Writing a few years later, in *Senhora*, the Brazilian author Alencar also criticized the selling of women through the dowry system of marriage.

7. *La Moda*, no. 13, 10 February 1838, 1.

8. This fits well with what Goodman says about the role of salons and the role of women as arbiters of a higher morality. *Republic of Letters*, 7–8.

9. Sanders, *Vanguard of the Atlantic World*, 25–28. The population included 11,431 natives and 19,758 resident foreigners, including 5,324 French, 4,305 Italians, 3,406 Spanish, 2,553 Argentines, 1,344 Africans, 659 Portuguese, and 606 English, among a few others.

10. See, for example, the memoirs of Iriarte regarding the "New Troy." *Memorias*, 184.

11. A letter from Sebastián Lezica to his brother, Faustino (Florencia's husband), indicated that Jean Baptiste was prepared to receive Mariquita in Quito. Nothing came of the idea. Sebastián Lezica to Faustino Lezica, 3 July 1839, AL/AZL.

12. Faustino Lezica to Sebastián Lezica, 18 March 1838, AL.

13. Sánchez, 18 April 1839, in Mizraje, *Mariquita*, 54.

14. Sánchez to Juan Thompson, 26 November 1839, in Vilaseca, *Cartas*, 31. Here

Mariquita expresses solidarity with other like-minded peoples of the world, a kind of universalism that may fit into what Sanders has termed "American republican modernity." *Vanguard of the Atlantic World*, 6–8.

15. Rosas to Astrada, 19 June 1838, in Ternavasio, *Correspondencia*, 171–74.

16. Fowler, *Santa Anna*, 190.

17. Charlip and Burns place the term in the 1830s, while Hollaway has it in the 1850s. See Burns and Charlip, *Latin America*, 29–32; and Holloway, *Latin American History*, 7–8. Thanks to Steve Bunker for the references.

18. Sánchez, 24 May 1839, in Mizraje, *Mariquita*, 69–70.

19. Sánchez, 25 May 1839, in Mizraje, 70.

20. Sánchez, 7 June 1839, in Mizraje, 76.

21. Sánchez, 9 June 1839, in Mizraje, 77.

22. Sánchez, 27 April 1839, in Mizraje, 60.

23. Sánchez, 21 April 1839, in Mizraje, 55–56.

24. Bolívar, "Angostura Address," 1819, in *El Libertador*, 34.

25. Rousseau, *Social Contract*, bk. 3, chap. 8: "That All Forms of Governments Do Not Suit All Countries."

26. This was in her diary, but she addressed Echeverría in her entry. Sánchez, 21 April 1839, in Mizraje, *Mariquita*, 55–56.

27. Sánchez, 28 May 1839, in Mizraje, *Mariquita*, 72.

28. Thompson, journal entry from 22 August 1838, from his journal in app. of Piccirilli, *Juan Thompson*, 126–27.

29. Thompson, journal entry from 27 August 1838, in Piccirilli, 182.

30. Sánchez, 29 April 1839, in Mizraje, *Mariquita*, 61.

31. Sánchez, 18 May 1839, in Mizraje, 67.

32. Sánchez, 25 April 1839, in Mizraje, 57–58.

33. Sánchez, 24 June 1839, in Mizraje, 83.

34. Sánchez, 20 July 1839, in Mizraje, 97.

35. Thompson, journal entry from 21 August 1838, in Piccirilli, *Juan Thompson*, 176.

36. Segreti, Ferreyra, and Moreira, "Hegemonía de Rosas," 418. See also Gelman, chap. 2 in *Rosas bajo fuego*.

37. Sánchez to Juan Thompson, 3 February 1840, in Vilaseca, *Cartas*, 32.

38. Thompson, journal entry from 28 August 1838, in Piccirilli, *Juan Thompson*, 183.

39. As quoted in Weinberg, *Esteban Echeverría*, 131.

40. Sánchez, postscript, 1840, n.d., in Mizraje, *Mariquita*, 113.

41. Weinberg, *Esteban Echeverría*, 129–30.

42. Ibarguren, *Manuelita*, 46–47. The infernal machine is usually on display in the Museo Histórico Nacional.

43. Di Meglio, *Mueran*.

44. Lynch, *Argentine Dictator*, 220.

45. For the three reports, see Lynch, 242–44. Lynch's best estimate is "in the region of 2,000 for the whole period 1829–52."

46. Rosas to Tomás de Anchorena, 6 May 1842, in Ternavasio, *Correspondencia*, 190–91.

47. Rosas to General Pacheco, 6 November 1840, in Ternavasio, 186.

48. For the harrowing account of Lavalle's end, see Pasquali, 355–61.

49. Sánchez to Florencia Lezica, 16 May 1841, in Vilaseca, *Cartas*, 63.

50. *Mercurio*, 19 April 1842, as found in Sarmiento, *Contra Rosas*, 4. Second reference from 23 December 1842, 25–26.

51. Myers, *Orden y virtud*, 52–57.

52. For more details of the complicated picture of river trade during this era, see Whigham, chap. 2 in *Politics of River Trade*.

53. "Pronunciamiento del gobierno de Corrientes contra el tirano Rosas," 7 October 1844, in Córdoba Province, *Compilación de leyes*, 242–44. The government of Corrientes also promised to protect the property of neutral parties.

54. 881/S 1321, FO.

55. As cited in Irazusta and Rosas, *Vida política*, 5:7–8.

56. Felipe Arana to governor of Córdoba, 22 August 1845, in Córdoba Province, *Compilación de leyes*, 248.

57. As quoted in Irazusta and Rosas, *Vida política*, 5:49.

58. Proclamation of Lucio Mansilla, 18 November 1845, in Irazusta and Rosas, *Vida política*, 5:54.

59. Colomb, *Astley Cooper Key*, 108–11.

60. Colomb, 110–12.

61. *Gaceta Mercantil*, November 1845.

62. José de San Martín to Fredrick Dickson, 28 December 1845, in Irazusta and Rosas, *Vida política*, 5:75–76.

63. San Martín to Rosas, 11 January 1846, in Irazusta and Rosas, *Vida política*, 5:108–9.

64. Peterson, *Argentina and the United States*, 138–42.

65. *Proceedings of the American Society of International Law*, 64–65.

66. *Proceedings*, 64–65.

67. Key to his mother, 14 May 1846, in Colomb, *Astley Cooper Key*, 113.

68. Vertanessian, *Retrato imposible*, 32–33. Pradere, writing just before 1914, argues that Rosas would never have allowed Monvoisin to paint him in gaucho attire, which, according to Pradere, would have been insulting. *Su Icconografía*, 227–29. Vertanessian disputes Pradere's version.

69. Howden to Aberdeen, 12 June 1847, add., MS 43, 124, BL. Lynch has Howden saying "American System," but a close look at the document shows that the phrase is "American question." *Argentine Dictator*, 294.

70. Sarmiento, "Significado de la intervención europea," *Progreso* (Chile), 18 August 1845, in *Contra Rosas*, 65–66. Sarmiento's cohort Bartolomé Mitre expressed similar ideas a few years later when France made its most ambitious Latin American gamble of the century by invading Mexico and installing the Austrian Prince, Maxi-

millian of Habsburg, as Emperor of Mexico. Mitre's newspaper, *La Nación*, justified French actions, arguing that "rudderless societies have throughout time been conquered or invaded because Providence always has people in reserve to occupy those lands possessed by flawed societies." As quoted in Nicolas Shumway, *Invention of Argentina*, 244.

CHAPTER ELEVEN

1. Sánchez to Florencia Lezica, 4 September 1847, in Vilaseca, *Cartas*, 164.

2. Sáenz Quesada, *Mariquita*, 231–32.

3. From letters written by Gutiérrez to Alberdi in December 1838 and January of 1839, as cited in Zavalía Lagos, *Mariquita*, 169.

4. The following taken from Echeverría, "Slaughterhouse," in *Argentina Reader*, 107–14.

5. Echeverría, "Slaughterhouse," 114.

6. Faustino Lezica to Sebastián Lezica, 14 October 1836, AL.

7. For an extensive discussion of Mariquita's financial woes, see Batticuore, chap. 6 in *Mariquita*.

8. Sánchez to Alberdi, in Mizraje, *Mariquita*, 337.

9. Notes from Sánchez to Alberdi, n.d., in Mizraje, 337–38. "Sweetened water" is a rough translation for "agua de goma," apparently a drink put together in the absence of quality alcoholic drinks.

10. Fouget to Sánchez, 14 March 1840 (copy of original difficult to distinguish), AL/AZL.

11. Fouget to Sánchez, 16 January 1846, AL/AZL.

12. Guido to Sánchez, 2 November 1848, AL/AZL.

13. See poem by Indarte in AZL.

14. Sánchez to Gutiérrez, n.d., in Mizraje, *Mariquita*, 333–34.

15. Alberdi, *Escritos póstumos*, 6:30, 111–13.

16. Obligado, *Tradiciones*, 262, 267.

17. Sánchez to Florencia Lezica, 14 July 1846, in Vilaseca, *Cartas*, 127.

18. Sánchez to Lezica, 12 September 1846, in Vilaseca, 128–30.

19. Sánchez to Lezica, 28 October 1846, in Vilaseca, 135.

20. Sánchez to Lezica, 12 September 1846, in Vilaseca, 128–30.

21. Sánchez to Lezica, 14 November 1846, in Vilaseca, 138–39.

22. Sánchez to Julio Mendeville, 28 October 1847, in Vilaseca, 167. Mariquita confessed to her son that her "mouth watered" when she saw the amount of the weekly lottery winnings.

23. Sánchez to Florencia Lezica, in Vilaseca, 139–41. Mariquita and her daughter spoke in coded language about this matter.

24. Eckartshausen, *God Is the Love Most Pure*, 27.

25. Sánchez to Florencia Lezica, 4 September 1847, in Vilaseca, *Cartas*, 162–63.

26. Sánchez to Lezica, 4 September 1847, in Vilaseca, 163.

27. As quoted in McCullough, *Greater Journey*, 31.

28. Alberdi, journal entry from 5 March 1844, in *Escritos póstumos*, 16:60.

29. As quoted in Fondebrider, *París*, 30–32. For more on Alberdi's shifting views on culture and politics, see Nicolas Shumway, chap. 7 in *Invention of Argentina*.

30. As cited in Sáenz Quesada, *Mariquita*, 201–2. Some names have been changed to common forms.

31. As quoted in Fondebrider, *París*, 63–64.

32. As quoted in Chávez, *Vuelta*, 103.

33. Sarmiento, *Contra Rosas*, 4.

34. Lynch, *Argentine Dictator*, 1.

35. *Muera Rosas!*, 23 December 1841.

36. Mármol, "25 de mayo de 1848," in *Manuela Rosas*, 170.

37. Mármol, *Amalia*.

38. Mármol, *Manuela Rosas*, 237–39.

39. Yerba mate culture has changed over the years, but a good introduction is Villanueva, *El mate*.

40. Hernández, *Martín Fierro*, 205. Juan Manuel de Rosas likely had various types of mates, from traditional gourds to ornate silver versions. Thanks to Daniel Gatica, who gave me my first mate, for pointing out the *Martín Fierro* reference. Martín Fierro is the quintessential gaucho character in the epic poem of the same name written by José Hernández in the late nineteenth century. The poem, for some, is the foundational piece of Argentine literature and identity.

41. See Sáenz Quesada, *Mujeres*, 183.

42. Fraser and Navarro, chap. 1 in *Evita*. Ernesto "Che" Guevara also habitually took advantage of the vulnerable position of domestic servants. Anderson, *Che Guevara*, 35.

43. Gotta et al., *Caserón de Rosas*, 27–30.

44. From a 1926 interview with his last surviving child, Nicanora, in Sáenz Quesada, *Mujeres*, 191. Sometimes when his children misbehaved, Rosas would order one of his lieutenants to give them five hundred lashes, which were only meted out symbolically.

45. Rosas to Urquiza, 18 July 1845, in Ternavasio, *Correspondencia*, 192–93.

46. Ibarguren, *Rosas*, 271.

47. Felipe Arana to Urquiza, 25 February 1847, in Córdoba Province, *Compilación de leyes*, 248–50.

48. García to Rosas, 22 December 1847, in Córdoba Province, 252.

49. García to Rosas, 22 December 1847, in Córdoba Province, 252.

50. Rosas to García, 17 January 1848, in Córdoba Province, 254–55.

51. Sáenz Quesada, *Mujeres*, 132.

52. Beruti, *Memorias curiosas*, 460.

53. As quoted in Sáenz Quesada, *Mariquita*, 194.

54. Note from Manuelita Rosas as found in Mariquita's papers in the Museo, Biblioteca y Archivo Histórico Municipal Dr. Horacio Beccar Varela. There is a high probability that this note was meant for Mariquita, but it also may have been meant for her daughter Florencia.

55. Sánchez to Florencia Lezica, 28 February 1847, in Vilaseca, *Cartas*, 145.

56. Sánchez to Lezica, 4 September 1847, in Vilaseca, 163.

CHAPTER TWELVE

1. Details taken from two notes from Mariquita Sánchez to Florencia Lezica, likely both on the day of the battle (3 February 1852). Vilaseca, *Cartas*, 186–87.

2. Ternavasio, *Revolución del voto*, 235.

3. See an example of the labeling of Urquiza in an invitation to a ball celebrating Manuelita in Vertanessian, *Retrato imposible*, 250.

4. Sánchez to Alberdi, 16 January 1851, in Vilaseca, *Cartas*, 345.

5. As quoted in Müller, *Burgess Farm*, 27.

6. As quoted in Müller, 79–81.

7. Sánchez to Florencia Lezica, 30 January 1852, in Vilaseca, *Cartas*, 185.

8. Sánchez to Lezica, February 1852, Montevideo, in Vilaseca, 186–87.

9. Sánchez to Lezica, February 1852, in Vilaseca, 188.

10. Sánchez to Lezica, February 1852, in Vilaseca, 188.

11. As quoted in Levene, *Lecturas históricas argentinas*, 271–72.

12. Sáenz Quesada, *Mujeres*, 190.

13. Lynch, *Argentine Dictator*, 334–37.

14. Alberdi, like Bolívar and others before him, saw Argentine society as not yet capable of functioning with full-fleged freedom. For more on this, see Adelman, "Between Order and Liberty," 98–103.

15. Urquiza to Alberdi, 22 July 1852.

16. Sánchez to Alberdi, 24 July 1852, in Vilaseca, *Cartas*, 346.

17. Urquiza to Alberdi, 22 July 1852.

18. Sánchez to Alberdi, 15 November 1852, in Vilaseca, *Cartas*, 347.

19. Thompson and Alberdi took turns snubbing each other in Madrid. See Sáenz Quesada, *Mariquita*, 280.

20. Sánchez to Enrique Lezica, 6 December 1854, in Vilaseca, *Cartas*, 299. Mariquita wrote numerous letters to Enrique from Montevideo, where she had returned to visit her son Julio.

21. Sánchez to Alberdi, Buenos Aires, 1 April 1856, in Vilaseca, 349–51.

22. Lynch *Argentine Dictator*, 337.

23. Müller, *Burgess Farm*, 72.

24. Müller, 63. Juan's letter from 8 April 1853, in Müller, 62–63. Rosas claimed that he needed 150 pounds sterling a month (while most in the middle class made 100–200 per year).

25. Müller, 68.

26. Müller, 88–89. Rosas started out renting about 500 acres but later reduced it to 140 acres.

27. Sáenz Quesada, *Mujeres*, 191.

28. Sáenz Quesada, 166–67.

29. Müller, *Burgess Farm*, 120, 123.

30. Rosas to Josefa Gómez, 7 August 1864, in Raed, *Cartas confidenciales*, 51.

31. Rosas to Gómez, 10 March 1869, in Raed, 112.

32. Rosas to Gómez, 10 March 1869, in Raed, 110–16.

33. Sáenz Quesada, *Mujeres*, 192.

34. Eugenia Castro to Rosas, 22 August 1859, in Sáenz Quesada, 231–32.

35. Angela Castro to Rosas, 21 May 1866, in Sáenz Quesada, 239.

36. Müller, *Burgess Farm*, 120, 123.

37. Pérez Rosales, *Times Gone By*, 368–69.

38. Pérez Rosales, 370–72.

39. Alberdi, journal entry from 18 October 1857, *Escritos póstumos*, 16:555.

40. Alberdi, journal entry from 18 October 1857, *Escritos póstumos*, 16:558–59. This sentiment was echoed a few years later by Bilbao in his biography of Rosas.

41. Vertanessian, *El retrato imposible*, 282.

42. Manuelita's letter to Josefa Gómez, and Alberdi's letter to Manuelita, as cited in Vertanessian, 282–83. Phrenology, the study of facial and head features as a way of analyzing a person, was popular in the early nineteenth century, but even though it was waning by the 1840s, it still had its adherents, including Domingo Sarmiento and Juan Bautista Alberdi.

43. *Proceso criminal contra Rosas*, 8–9.

44. Rosas to Gómez, 7 August 1864, in Raed, *Cartas confidenciales*, 51–52.

45. As quoted in Gallo, *Rivadavia*, 180.

46. As quoted in Gallo, 180–82.

47. Sáenz Quesada, *Mariquita*, 282.

48. Sánchez to Sarmiento, n.d., in Mizraje, *Mariquita*, 357–58.

49. Poem in footnote 4 of Vilaseca, *Cartas*, 364.

50. Sánchez to Alberdi, 16 January 1851 in Vilaseca, *Cartas*, 345.

51. Sánchez to Mendeville, 1 October 1853, in Vilaseca, 312.

52. Sánchez to Mendeville, 26 May 1860, in Vilaseca, 313.

53. Sánchez to Mendeville, 26 June 1860, in Vilaseca, 314–15.

54. Sánchez to Juan Bautista Mendeville, 13 March 1861, in Vilaseca, 316. See her list of recipes in AZL.

55. Sánchez to Alberdi, 13 March 1863, in Vilaseca, 356–57.

56. See note 43 in Vilaseca, 357.

57. Sánchez to Alberdi, 27 May 1863, in Vilaseca, 358.

58. Sánchez to Alberdi, 27 May 1863, in Vilaseca, 359. Argentina never resolved the issue of female identity in the case of marriage to a foreigner, at least in the nine-

teenth century. Civil codes did not address the issue. Instead, the Supreme Court decided that a married woman's domicile or nationality followed her husband's. See Augustine-Adams, "'She Consents Implicitly,'" 10.

59. Sánchez to Gutiérrez, 20 June 1868, in Vilaseca, *Cartas*, 340.

60. Zavalia Lagos, *Mariquita*, 276–79.

61. Rosas to Angela Castro, 3 December 1870, in Sáenz Quesada, *Mujeres*, 242–43.

62. As quoted in Anchorena, *Repatriación de Rosas*, 35.

63. From a poem Mármol wrote in exile in 1843, as cited in Vertanessian, *Retrato imposible*, 306–7.

EPILOGUE

1. Jeffrey Shumway, "Knowing How to Forget," 105–6.

2. Mariquita to Florencia Lezica, February 1852, in Vilaseca, *Cartas*, 188.

3. López, *Historia de República Argentina*, 135–38.

4. Obligado, *Tradiciones*, 225–29.

5. Batticuore, *Mariquita*, 85–87.

6. Subercaseaux, *Memorias*, 152–53. Subercaseaux likely used Obligado's writings as a source.

7. See Nicolas Shumway, preface of *Invention of Argentina*, for a profound discussion of the competing "guiding fictions" in Argentine history.

8. Buch, chap. 5 in *Juremos con gloria*.

9. Dellepiane, *Dos patricias ilustres*, 9–11.

10. Vilaseca, *Cartas*; Mizraje, *Mariquita*; Sánchez, *Recuerdos*; Sáenz Quesada, *Mariquita*; Batticuore, *Mariquita*.

11. Jeanmaire's *Montevideo* is a fictional portrayal, from Sarmiento's perspective, of his relationship with Mariquita during his time in Montevideo. Thanks to Ximena Espeche for referring this novel to me.

12. Batticuore places the main entrance to Mariquita's home between 268 and 272 Calle Florida. See her *Mariquita*, 110 (and all of chap. 3 for a discussion on the house).

13. As quoted in Lynch, *Argentine Dictator*, 154.

14. As quoted in Nicolas Shumway, *Invention of Argentina*, 191–92.

15. Anchorena, *Repatriación de Rosas*, 76–77.

16. For more on the continuing popularity of Rosas and other Federalist caudillos, see Fuente, *Children of Facundo*.

17. Pérez Rosales, *Times Gone By*, 366, 368–69.

18. Pérez Rosales, 362–70. Manuel Bilbao made similar statements. The full history of Rosas was yet to be told, according to Bilbao when he wrote *Historia de Rosas* in 1868. Rosas, he argued, was not to blame for the country's problems. He was part of a much deeper struggle between colonial traditions and revolutionary liberalism. Rival political groups, Bilbao argued, blamed individuals for a country's problems, but even after ousting numerous bad leaders, the same problem of disunity

remained. For Bilbao writing in 1868, the struggle between the colonial and the revolutionary mentality "still delays the triumph of democracy among us" (41–43).

19. As quoted in Chávez, *Vuelta*, 67.

20. All parties, Quesada pointed out, used those same methods. "Federalists and Unitarians, Rosistas and exiles, tyrants and the tyrannized: all were, in their turn and according to the circumstances, victims and executioners, executioners and victims." *Época de Rosas*, 122–23.

21. In the discipline of history, "revisionism" is applied to history that challenges and/or "revises" a previous view. In Argentina, however, the word "revisionism" usually points to history that looks at Rosas in a positive light. A group of academic scholars known as the New Historical School (Nueva Escuela Histórica) also emerged in the 1920s and 1930s; they pursued rigorous history but more often than not were critical of Rosas and his government. See Halperín-Donghi, *Revisionismo histórico argentino*, for a useful review of twentieth-century approaches to Rosas.

22. Anchorena, *Repatriación de Rosas*, 106.

23. Goebel, *Argentina's Partisan Past*, 90, 169. Perón sought to tap into the Nationalists' adoration of Rosas in order to build support while in exile.

24. Perón to Manuel de Anchorena, 8 January 1970, photocopy found in Anchorena, *Repatriación de Rosas*, 32–33.

25. British Archives, HO 282/84 and HO 282/84. As late as 22 January 1975, the British believed that Rosas's body would be exhumed and repatriated to Argentina. But then they received a notification from the Argentine government saying that the repatriation would be put on hold.

26. For a sampling, see Fisher, *Mothers of the Disappeared*; and Partnoy, *Tales of Disappearance*.

27. For the report on crimes of the dictatorship, see CONADEP, *Nunca más*. For military rebellions of the 1980s, see Norden, *Miltary Rebellion*.

28. Stevens, chap. 6 in *Based on a True Story*.

29. Menem, *Mensaje presidencial*.

30. Jeffrey Shumway, "Knowing How to Forget," 119–20.

31. Goebel found that most Argentine intellectuals were in favor of Rosas's repatriation. See his *Argentina's Partisan Past*, 206. For segments of interviews with intellectuals from the time, see Jeffrey Shumway, "Repatriación de Juan Manuel," 117–26.

32. Shumway, 116–17.

33. Mitre, "La repatriación de los restos de Rosas," *La Nación*, 10 September 1989.

34. Anchorena, *Repatriación de Rosas*, 27.

35. Menem, speech delivered at repatriation ceremony on 30 September 1989, Rosario, Argentina.

36. Menem, speech delivered at repatriation ceremony on 1 October 1989, Buenos Aires.

37. As quoted in Anchorena, *Repatriación de Rosas*, 112–14.

38. For a book on this phenomenon, see Castex, *Década de Rosas*.

39. Castex cites an article in *La Nación* trying to block the release of the twenty-peso bill with Rosas's image. *Década de Rosas*, 49.

40. Hernán Firp, "Rosas ya tiene su monumento," *El Clarín*, 11 September 1999.

41. "A Street Battle Rages," *New York Times*, 14 August 2003.

42. See, for example, Fradkin and Gelman, *Juan Manuel de Rosas*, especially chap. 10.

WORKS CITED

ARCHIVES

AGN: Archivo General de la Nación (Argentina)

AHPBA: Archivo Histórico de la Provincia de Buenos Aires, "Ricardo Levene"

AL: Archivo Lezica

AZL: Archivo Zavalía Lagos

BBA: Baring Brothers Archive, UK

BL: British Library

FO/HO: Archives of the Foreign Office / Home Office, UK

HSA: Hawai'i State Archives

NEWSPAPERS CITED

La Abeja Argentina

El Censor

El Clarín

The Evening Post

La Gaceta Mercantil

La Gazeta de Buenos Ayres

La Gazeta Ministerial

El Grito del Sud

El Lucero

Mercurio

La Moda

Muera Rosas!

La Nación

New York Times

El Observador American

Progreso

Telégrafo Mercantil: Rural, Político-Económico e Historiógrafo del Río de la Plata

PUBLISHED PRIMARY SOURCES

Alberdi, Juan Bautista. *Escritos póstumos de Juan Bautista Alberdi*. Vol. 6. Buenos Aires: Imprenta Alberto Monkes, 1898.

———. *Escritos póstumos de Juan Bautista Alberdi*. Vol. 16. Buenos Aires: Imprenta Juan Bautista Alberdi, 1901.

Artigas, José Gervasio. "Proclama de Mercedes, 11 April, 1811." In vol. 23 of *Pensamiento político de la emancipación*, edited by José Luis Romero and Luis Alberto Romero, 11. Caracas: Biblioteca Ayacucho, 1977.

Azamor y Ramírez, Manuel. *De matrimonio contrahendo insciis, inconsultis aut invitis parentibus*. Ca. 1795.

Barbará, Federico. *Con Rosas o contra Rosas*. Buenos Aires: Ediciones Federales, 1989.

Belgrano, Manuel. *Epistolario Belgraniano*. Buenos Aires: Taurus, 2001.

Beruti, Juan Manuel. *Memorias curiosas*. Buenos Aires: Emecé Editores, 2001.

Bolívar, Simón. *El Libertador: Writings of Simón Bolívar*. Edited by David Bushnell. Translated by Frederick H. Fornoff. New York: Oxford University Press, 2003.

Caldcleugh, Alexander. *Travels in South America, during the Years 1819–20–21, Containing an Account of the Present State of Brazil, Buenos Ayres, and Chile*. Vols. 1–2. London: John Murray, 1825.

Carranza, Neptali, ed. *Oratoria argentina*. Vol. 1, *Recopilación cronológica de las proclamas, discursos, manifiestos y documentos importantes, que llegaron a la historia de su patria, argentinos célebres, desde el año 1810 hasta 1904*. Buenos Aires: Sesé y Larrañaga, Editores, 1905.

Castañeda, Francisco de Paula. *Doña María Retazos*. Edited by Gregorio Weinberg. Buenos Aires: Coni, 1924.

Chelsea College Court Martial. *Trial of Lieutenant General John Whitelocke, Commander in Chief of the Expedition against Buenos Ayres*. London: B. Crosby and Co. Stationers, 1808.

Chesterfield, Lord, and David Roberts. *Lord Chesterfield's Letters*. London: Oxford University Press, 1992.

Colomb, P. H. *Memoirs of Admiral the Right Honble. Sir Astley Cooper Key, G.C.B., D.C.L.* London: Methuen, 1898.

CONADEP. *Nunca Más: The Report of the Argentine National Commission on the Disappeared*. New York: Farrar, Straus, Giroux. 1986.

Congress of Tucumán. *Acta de independencia en Sud-América*. Tucumán: 1816.

Córdoba Province. *Compilación de leyes, decretos, acuerdos de la Excma. Cámara de justicia y demás disposiciones de carácter público dictadas en la provincia de Córdoba. El año 1879*. Vol. 7. Córdoba: Imprenta Rivas, 1881.

Darwin, Charles. *The Voyage of the* Beagle. Vol. 29. Cambridge: Harvard Classics, 1909.

Eckarthausen, Karl von. *Dios es el amor más puro*. Barcelona: Ediciones Obelisco, 1988.

Ezcurra de Rosas, Encarnación. *Doña Encarnación Ezcurra de Rosas: Correspondencia inédita*. Buenos Aires: Talleres Gráficos, 1923.

Fitte, Ernesto J. *La agresión francesa a la escuadra argentina en 1829*. New York: G. P. Putnam's Sons, 1917.

Fondebrider, Jorge. *La París de los argentinos*. Buenos Aires: Bajo La Luna, 2010.

France, George Spence. *The Code Napoleon; or, The French Civil Code*. London: Bell-Yard, Lincoln's Inn, 1824.

Gaceta de Buenos Aires [*Gazeta de Buenos Ayres*]. Vol. 6. Argentina: Compañía Sud-Americana de Billetes de Banco, 1913.

Gillespie, Alexander. *Gleanings and Remarks Collected during Many Months of Residence at Buenos Ayres and within the Upper Country with a Preparatory Account of the Expedition from England and the Surrender of the Colony of the Cape of Good Hope, under the Joint Command of Sir D. Baird G.D.B.K.C. and Sir Home Popham K.C.B.* Leeds: B. Dewhirst, 1818.

Ginestá, Agustín. *El conservador de los niños*. Madrid: Imprenta Real, 1797.

Gutiérrez, Eduardo. *El Gaucho Juan Moreira*. Edited by William Acree. Translated by John Charles Chasteen. Indianapolis: Hackett Publishing, 2014.

Hernández, José. *Martín Fierro*. Edición especial. Buenos Aires: Distribuidora Quevedo de ediciones, 1997.

Hudson, William. H. *Far Away and Long Ago: A History of My Early Life*. New York: J. M. Dent and Sons, 1923.

Instituto Cultural de la Provincia de Buenos Aires, Comisión del Bicentenario de la Reconquista. *Las invasiones inglesas (1806–1807): Una aproximación documental*. La Plata: Instituto Cultural de la Provincia de Buenos Aires, 2006.

Irazusta, Julio, and Juan Manuel de Rosas. *Vida política de Juan Manuel de Rosas*. Buenos Aires: Editorial Albatros, 1961.

Iriarte, Tomás de. *Biografía del brigadier general D. José Miguel Carrera, dos veces primer magistrado de la República de Chile*. 1863.

———. *Memorias del general Tomás Iriarte: La nueva Troya*. With a prologue by Luis Iriarte Udaondo and an introduction by Enrique de Gandía. Buenos Aires: Editorial y Librería Goncourt, 1971.

Lamadrid, Gregorio Aráoz de. *Memorias del General Gregorio Aráoz de la Madrid*. Vol. 2. Buenos Aires: Campo de Mayo, 1948.

López y Planes, Vicente. "El triunfo argentino. Poema heroico en memoria de la gloriosa defensa de la capital de Buenos Aires contra el ejército de 12.000 hombres que atacaron los días 2 a 6 de julio de 1807." 1808.

Manning, Ray William, ed. *Diplomatic Correspondence*. Vol. 1. New York: Oxford University Press, 1925.

Mármol, José. *Amalia*. New York: Oxford University Press, 2001.

———. *Manuela Rosas y otros escritos políticos del exilio*. Edited by Gregorio Weinberg. Buenos Aires: Nueva Dimensión Argentina, 2001.

"Memoria sobre la necesidad de contener la demaciada y perjudicial licencia de las mujeres en hablar." B81 A692c, fols. 1–5, vol. 2. John Carter Brown Library.

Menem, Carlos Saúl. *Mensaje presidencial del Dr. Carlos Saúl Menem a la Honorable Asamblea Legislativa*. Buenos Aires: Secretaría de Prensa y Difusión Presidencia de la Nación República Argentina, 1989.

Mizraje, María Gabriela, ed. *Mariquita Sánchez de Thompson: Intimidad y política; Diario, cartas, y recuerdos*. Buenos Aires: A. Hidalgo, 2003.

Monteagudo, Bernardo de. "Observaciones didácticas." In *Horizontes políticos*. Buenos Aires: W. M. Jackson Inc. Editores, 1812.

Parish, Woodbine. *Buenos Ayres and the Provinces of the Rio de La Plata: From Their Discovery and Conquest by the Spaniards to the Establishment of Their Political Independence*. 2nd ed. London: W. Clowes and Sons, 1852.

Pérez Rosales, Vicente. *Times Gone By: Memoirs of a Man of Action*. Translated by John Polt and Brian Loveman. New York: Oxford University Press, 2000.

Popham, Sir Home Riggs. *A Full and Correct Account of the Trial of Sir Home Popham*. London: J. and J. Richardson, C. Chapple, 1807.

Proceedings of the American Society of International Law at its 8th Annual Meeting held at Washington D.C., April 22–25, 1914. Washington, DC: Adams, Byron S., 1914.

Proceso criminal contra Rosas ante los tribunales ordinarios de Buenos Aires. With a prologue by Juan Silva Riestra. Buenos Aires: Bases Editorial, 1955.

Raed, José. *Rosas: Cartas confidenciales a su embajadora Josefa Gómez, 1853–1875*. Buenos Aires: Humus Editorial, 1972.

Rivarola, Pantaleón. "Romance heroico." 1806. In Instituto Cultural de la Provincia de Buenos Aires, Comisión del Bicentenario de la Reconquista, *Las invasiones inglesas (1806–1807): Una aproximación documental*. La Plata: Instituto Cultural de la Provincia de Buenos Aires, 2006.

Robertson, John Parish, and William Parish Robertson. *Letters on South America; Comprising Travels on the Banks of the Paraná and Rio de la Plata*. Vol. 3. London: John Murray, Albemarle Street, 1843.

Rosas, Juan Manuel de. *Gramática y diccionario de la lengua pampa*. Edited by Oscar R. Suarez Caviglia and Enrique Stieben. Buenos Aires: Editorial Albatros, 1947.

Rousseau, Jean-Jacques. *The Social Contract*. Bk. 3, chap. 8. 1762.

Sánchez de Mendeville, Mariquita. *Recuerdos del Buenos Aires virreinal*. Buenos Aires: Ene Editorial, 1953.

Sarmiento, Domingo F. *Contra Rosas*. Buenos Aires: W. M. Jackson, n.d.

———. *Life in the Argentine Republic in the Days of the Tyrants; or, Civilization and Barbarism*. New York: Hurd and Houghton; Cambridge: Riverside Press, 1868.

Schmidt, Ulderico. "Going Wild." In *The Argentina Reader*. Durham, NC: Duke University Press, 2002.

Senado de la Nación. *Biblioteca de mayo: Colección de obras y documentos para la historia argentina*. 18 vols. Buenos Aires: Imprenta del Congreso de la Nación Argentina, 1960.

Subercaseaux, Pedro. *Memorias*. Vol. 2. Santiago: Editorial del Pacífico, 1962.

Sule, Jorge Oscar. *Rosas y sus relaciones con los indios*. Buenos Aires: Colección Estrella Federal, 2003.

Ternavasio, Marcela, ed. *Correspondencia de Juan Manuel de Rosas*. Buenos Aires: Eudeba, 2005.

———. *La revolución del voto: Política y elecciones en Buenos Aires, 1810–1852*. Buenos Aires: Siglo Veintiuno Editores Argentina, 2002.

Vilaseca, Clara, ed. *Cartas de Mariquita Sánchez: Biografía de una época*. Buenos Aires: Ediciones Peuser, 1952.

Warville, Jacques-Pierre Brissot de. *New Travels in the United States of America, Performed in MDCCLXXXVIII*. Vol. 1. 2nd ed. London, 1794.

Wilde, Antonio José. *Buenos Aires desde setenta años atrás*. Buenos Aires: W. M. Jackson, 1944.

SECONDARY SOURCES

Academia Nacional de la Historia. *Nueva historia de la nación argentina.* Vol. 4. Buenos Aires: Planeta, 2000.

Acree, William G. *Everyday Reading: Print Culture and Collective Identity in the Río de la Plata, 1780–1910.* Nashville: Vanderbilt University Press.

Adelman, Jeremy. "An Age of Imperial Revolutions." *American Historical Review* 113, no. 2 (2008): 320–21.

———. "Between Order and Liberty: Juan Bautista Alberdi and the Intellectual Origins of Argentine Constitutionalism." *Latin American Research Review* 42, no. 2 (June 2007): 86–110.

———. *Republic of Capital: Buenos Aires and the Legal Transormation of the Atlantic World.* Stanford: Stanford University Press, 1999.

———. *Sovereignty and Revolution in the Iberian Atlantic.* Princeton, NJ: Princeton University Press, 2006.

Alamán, Lucas. *Historia de México desde los primeros movimientos que prepararon su independencia en año 1808 hasta la época presente.* Vol. 2. Buenos Aires: Fondo de Cultura Económica, 1985.

Alencar, José. *Senhora: Profile of a Woman.* Translated by Catarina Feldmann Edinger. Austin, TX: University of Texas Press Austin, 1994.

Alonso, Paula, ed. *Construcciones impresas: Panfletos, diarios y revistas en la formación de los estados nacionales en América Latina, 1820–1920.* Buenos Aires: Fondo de Cultura Económica, 2004.

Anchorena, Manuel de. *La repatriación de Rosas.* Ediciones Nuestro Tiempo, 1990.

Anderson, John Lee. *Che Guevara, a Revolutionary Life.* New York: Grove Press, 1997.

Andrews, George Reid. *The Afro-Argentines of Buenos Aires, 1800–1900.* Madison: University of Wisconsin Press, 1980.

Arana, Enrique. *Juan Manuel de Rosas en la historia argentina: Creador y sostén de la unidad nacional.* Vols. 2–3. Argentina: Instituto Panamericano de Cultura, 1954.

Arana, Marie. *Bolívar: American Liberator.* New York: Simon and Schuster, 2013.

Assadourian, Carlos Sempat. *El sistema de la economía colonial: Mercado interno, regiones, y espacio económico.* Lima: Instituto de Estudios Peruanos, 1982.

Augustine-Adams, Kif. "'She Consents Implicitly': Women's Citizenship, Marriage and Liberal Political Theory in Late-Nineteenth and Early Twentieth-Century Argentina." *Journal of Women's History* 13, no. 4 (2002).

Barba, Enrique M. *Quiroga y Rosas.* Buenos Aires: Editorial Pleamar, 1974.

Barreneche, Osvaldo. *Crime and the Administration of Justice in Buenos Aires, 1785–1853.* Lincoln: University of Nebraska Press, 2006.

Barreneche, Osvaldo, and Andrés Bisso, eds. *Ayer, hoy y mañana son contemporáneos: Tradiciones, leyes y proyectos en América Latina,* eds. La Plata: Editorial Universidad Nacional de La Plata, 2010.

Batticuore, Graciela. *Mariquita Sánchez: Bajo el signo de la revolución.* Buenos Aires: Edhasa, 2011.

Beeman, Richard. *Plain, Honest Men: The Making of the American Constitution.* New York: Random House, 2010.

Bilbao, Manuel. *Historia de Rosas.* Buenos Aires: Casa Vaccaro, 1919.

Blanchard, Peter. "An Institution Defended: Slavery and the English Invasions of Buenos Aires of 1806–1807." *Slavery and Abolition,* vol. 35 (2014).

Blossom, Thomas. *Nariño: Hero of Colombian Independence.* Tucson: University of Arizona Press, 1967.

Borucki, Alex. *From Shipmates to Soldiers: Emerging Black Identities in the Río de la Plata.* Albuquerque: University of New Mexico Press, 2015.

Boyer, Richard. "Women, La Mala Vida, and the Politics of Marriage." In *Sexuality and Marriage in Colonial Latin America,* edited by Asunció Lavrin, 252–55. Lincoln: University of Nebraska Press, 1992.

Bragoni, Beatriz. *José Miguel Carrera: Un revolucionario chileno en el Río de la Plata.* Buenos Aires: Edhasa, 2012.

Brown, Jonathan. *A Brief History of Argentina.* New York City: Facts on File, 2011.

———. *A Socioeconomic History of Buenos Aires: 1776–1860.* Cambridge: Cambridge University Press, 1979.

Brown, Kendall W. *Bourbons and Brandy: Imperial Reform in Eighteenth-Century Arequipa.* Albuquerque: University of New Mexico Press, 1986.

Brown, Matthew, ed. *Informal Empire in Latin America: Culture, Commerce, and Capital.* New York: Cambridge University Press, 2008.

Buch, Esteban. *O juremos con gloria morir.* Buenos Aires: Sudamericana, 1994.

Burgin, Miron. *The Economic Aspects of Argentine Federalism, 1820–1852.* Cambridge, Massachusetts: Harvard University Press, 1941.

Bushnell, David. *Reform and Reaction in the Platine Provinces.* Gainesville: University of Florida Press, 1983.

Calvera, Leonor. "Revoluciones, minué y mujeres." In *Mujeres y culture en la Argentina del siglo XIX,* edited by Lea Fletcher. Buenos Aires: Editora Feminaria, 1994.

Carranza, Ambrosio Romero, Alberto Rodríguez Varela, and Eduardo Ventura. *Manual de historia política y constitucional Argentina, 1776–1976.* Buenos Aires: AZ Editora, 1977.

Castex, César María. *La década de Rosas.* Buenos Aires: Dunken, 2006.

Celesia, Ernesto. *Rosas: Aportes para su historia.* Buenos Aires: Peuser, 1954, 36–37.

Chambers, Sarah. *Families in War and Peace: Chile from Colony to Nation.* Durham, NC: Duke University Press, 2015.

———. "Letters and Salons: Women Reading and Writing the Nation." In *Beyond Imagined Communities: Reading and Writing the Nation in Nineteenth-Century Latin America,* edited by Sara Castro-Klarén and John Charles Chasteen. Baltimore: Johns Hopkins University Press, 2004.

Charlip, Julie A., and E. Bradford Burns. *Latin America: An Interpretive History.* 10th ed. New York: Pearson, 2017.

Chasteen, John Charles. *Americanos.* Oxford: Oxford University Press, 2008.

———. "Violence for Show: Knife Dueling on a Nineteenth-Century Cattle Frontier." In *The Problem of Order in Changing Societies: Essays on Crime and Policing in Argentina and Uruguay, 1750–1940,* edited by Lyman Johnson. Albuquerque: University of New Mexico Press, 1990.

Chávez, Fermín. *La vuelta de don Juan Manuel: Ciento diez autores y protagonistas hablan de Rosas.* Buenos Aires: Boletín Oficial de la Provincia, n.d.

Chiaramonte, José Carlos. "El federalismo argentino en la primera mitad del siglo XIX." In *Federalismos Latinoamericanos: México/Brasil/Argentina,* edited by Marcello Carmagnani. Mexico City: Fondo de Cultura Económica, 1993.

———. *La ilustración en Río de la Plata: Cultura eclesiástica y cultura laica durante el virreinato.* Buenos Aires: Puntosur Editores, 1989.

Cicerchia, Ricardo. *La historia de la vida privada.* Buenos Aires: Troquel, 1998.

Conniff, Michael L. *Populism in Latin America.* Tuscaloosa: University of Alabama Press, 1989.

Crosby, Alfred. *Ecological Imperialism: The Biological Expansion of Europe, 900–1900.* 2nd ed. Cambridge: Cambridge University Press, 2004.

Cutrera, María Laura. *Subordinarlos, someterlos, y sujetarlos al orden: Rosas y los indios amigos de Buenos Aires entre 1829 y 1855.* Buenos Aires: Teseo, 2013.

Dellepiane, Antonio. *Dos patricias ilustres: Una patricia de antaño: María Sánchez de Mendeville—La compañera de un estadista: Carmen Nobrega de Avellaneda.* Buenos Aires: Imprenta y Casa Editora "Coni," 1923.

———. *Rosas: Ordenamiento, notas y conclusión.* Buenos Aires: Editorial Oberón, 1956.

Di Meglio, Gabriel. *1816: La trama de la independencia.* Buenos Aires: Planeta, 2016.

———. *Manuel Dorrego: Vida y muerte de un líder popular.* Buenos Aires: Edhasa, 2014.

———. *¡Mueran los salvajes unitarios! La Mazorca y la política en tiempos de Rosas.* Buenos Aires: Editorial Sudamericana, 2007.

———. *¡Viva el bajo pueblo! La plebe urbana de Buenos Aires y la política entre la Revolución de Mayo y el Rosismo (1810–1829).* Buenos Aires: Prometeo Libros, 2006.

Dueñas-Vargas, Guiomar. *Of Love and Other Passions: Elites, Politics, and Family in Bogotá, Colombia.* Albuquerque: University of New Mexico Press, 2015.

Dusenberry, William. "Juan Manuel de Rosas as Viewed by Contemporary American Diplomats." *Hispanic American Historical Review* 41, no. 4 (1961): 495–514.

Echeverría, Esteban. "The Slaughterhouse." In *The Argentina Reader: History, Culture, Politics.* Durham, NC: Duke University Press, 2002.

Edwards, Erika. "Mestizaje, Córdoba's Patria Chica (Small Nation): Beyond the Disappearance of the Black Population." *African and Black Diaspora: An International Journal.* United Kingdom: Routledge, 2014.

Elena, Eduardo. "Steam-Age Eldorado: New Perspectives on British Informal Empire in Nineteenth-Century Argentina." Address given at Brigham Young University, November 2016.

Ellis, Joseph. *The American Creation: Triumphs and Tragedies at the Founding of the Republic.* New York: Vintage Books, 2008.

Etchepareborda, Roberto. *Rosas: Controvertida historiografía.* Buenos Aires: Pleamar, 1970.

Fernández Sebastián, Javier. "Toleration and Freedom of Expression in the Hispanic World between Enlightenment and Liberalism." *Past and Present* 211, no. 1 (May 2011): 159–97.

Fischer, David Hacket. *Paul Revere's Ride.* New York: Oxford University Press, 1995.

Fisher, Jo. *Mothers of the Disappeared.* Boston: South End Press, 1999.

Fitz, Caitlin. *Our Sister Republics: The United States in an Age of American Revolution.* New York: Norton, 2016.

Fletcher, Ian. *The Waters of Oblivion: The British Invasion of the Río de la Plata, 1806–1807.* England: Staplerhurst, 2006.

Fletcher, Lea, ed. *Mujeres y cultura en la Argentina del siglo XIX.* Buenos Aires: Editora Feminaria, 1994.

Fletcher, Richard A. *Moorish Spain.* New York: H. Holt, 1992.

Fowler, Will. *Santa Anna of Mexico.* Lincoln: University of Nebraska Press, 2009.

Fradkin, Raúl O. *Fusilaron a Dorrego.* Buenos Aires: Penguin Random House Grupo Editorial Argentina, 2012.

Fradkin, Raúl O., and Jorge Gelman. *Juan Manuel de Rosas: La construcción de un liderazgo político.* Buenos Aires: Edhasa 2015.

Francois, Marie. "Laundering Identities in the Americas: The Production of Individuals and Class in the Eighteenth and Nineteenth Centuries." Council on Latin American History and American Historical Association, San Diego, CA, 2010.

Fraser, Nicholas, and Marysa Navarro. *Evita: The Real Life of Eva Perón.* New York: Norton, 1996.

Fuente, Ariel de la. *Children of Facundo: Caudillo and Gaucho Insurgency during the Argentine State-Formation Process (La Rioja, 1853–1870).* Durham, NC: Duke University Press, 2000.

Furstenberg, Francois. *When the United States Spoke French: Five Refugees Who Shaped a Nation.* New York: Penguin / Random House, 2015.

Gallo, Klaus. *Bernardino Rivadavia: El primer president argentine.* Buenos Aires: Edhasa, 2012.

———. *Great Britain and Argentina: From Invasion to Recognition, 1806–26.* United Kingdom: Palgrave Macmillan, 2001.

———. *The Struggle for an Enlightened Republic: Buenos Aires and Rivadavia.* London: Institute for the Study of the Americas, 2006.

Gálvez, Manuel. *Vida de don Juan Manuel de Rosas*. 5th ed. Buenos Aires: Editorial Tor-S.R.L., 1949.

Garavaglia, Juan Carlos. "La apotéosis del Leviathán: El estado en Buenos Aires durante la primera mitad del siglo XIX." *Latin American Research Review* 38, no. 1 (2003): 135–68.

García Belsunce, Cesar et al. *Buenos Aires: 1810–1830*. Vol. 3, *Educación y asistencia social*. Buenos Aires: Ediciones del Banco Internacional y Banco Unido de Inversión, 1978.

Gatica, Daniel. *Yo quiero la paz: Mariano Rosas y los tratados de paz del pueblo Ranquel entre 1858 y 1880*. Buenos Aires: Editorial Dunken, 2015.

Gelman, Jorge. *Rosas bajo fuego: Los franceses, Lavalle, y la rebelión de los estancieros*. Buenos Aires: Sudamericana, 2009.

———. *Rosas, estanciero: Gobierno y expansión ganadera*. Buenos Aires: Capital Intelectual, 2005.

Goebel, Michael. *Argentina's Partisan Past: Nationalism and the Politics of History*. Liverpool: Liverpool University Press, 2011.

Goldberg, Marta. "La población negra y mulata de la ciudad de Buenos Aires, 1810–1840." *Desarrollo Económico* 16, no. 61 (1976).

Goldgel, Victor. *Cuando lo nuevo conquistó América: Prensa, moda y literatura en el siglo XIX*. Buenos Aires: Siglo Veintiuno Editores, 2014.

Goldman, Noemí. "Buenos Aires, 1810: La 'revolución' y el dilema de la legitimidad y de las representaciones de la soberanía del pueblo." *Historia y Política*, no. 24 (July–December 2010): 47–69.

———. "Los orígenes del federalismo rioplatense (1820–1831)." In *Revolución, República, Confederación (1806–1852)*, vol. 3 of *La nueva historia argentina*, edited by Noemí Goldman, 103–24. Buenos Aires: Editorial Sudamericana, 1998.

Goldman, Noemí, and Ricardo Salvatore, eds. *Caudillismos rioplatenses: Nuevas miradas a un viejo problema*. Buenos Aires: Eudeba, 1996.

Goñi Demarchi, Carlos A., José Nicolás Scala, and Germán W. Berraondo. *Rosas, Washington y Lincoln*. Buenos Aires: Ediciones Theoria, 1996.

González Lonzieme, Enrique. *Martín Jacobo Thompson: Ensayo para la biografía de un marino criollo*. Buenos Aires: Departamento de Estudios Históricos Navales de la Armada, 1969.

Goodman, Dena. *The Republic of Letters: A Cultural History of the French Enlightenment*. Ithaca and London: Cornell University Press, 1994.

Gotta, César, Bernardo González, Daniel Schávelzon, and Abel Alexander. *El Caserón de Rosas: Fotografías de la Escuela Naval Militar*. Buenos Aires: Olmo Ediciones, 2013.

Grieco, Viviana. "Family and Political Authority in Early Ninteenth-Century Buenos Aires: Rituals, Practices, and Texts, 1806–1816." *Colonial Latin American Historical Review* 17, no. 1 (Winter 2008): 63–96.

———. *The Politics of Giving in the Viceroyalty of the Río de la Plata: Donors, Lenders, Subjects, and Citizens*. Albuquerque: University of New Mexico Press, 2014.

Guerra, François-Xavier, ed. *Los espacios públicos en Iberoamérica: Ambigüedades y problemas; Siglos XVIII–XIX*. Mexico: Centro de Estudios Mexicanos y Centroamericanos, 2008.

Guy, Donna. *Sex and Danger in Buenos Aires: Prostitution, Family, and Nation in Argentina*. Lincoln: University of Nebraska Press, 1995.

———. *White Slavery and Mothers Alive and Dead: The Troubled Meeting of Sex, Gender, Public Health, and Progress in Latin America*. Lincoln: University of Nebraska Press, 2000.

———. *Women Build the Welfare State: Performing Charity and Creating Rights in Argentina, 1880–1955*. Durham, NC: Duke University Press, 2009.

Habermas, Jurgen. *The Structural Transformation of the Public Sphere*. Cambridge: MIT Press, 1989.

Halperín-Donghi, Tulio. *Politics, Economics, and Society in Argentina*. New York: Cambridge University Press, 1975.

———. *El revisionismo histórico argentino como visión decadentista de la historia nacional*. Buenos Aires: Siglo veintiuno, 2005.

———. *Revolución y guerra: Formación de una élite dirigente en la Argentina criolla*. Buenos Aires: Siglo XXI Editores Argentina, 1972.

Hamill, Hugh M., ed. *Caudillos: Dictators in Spanish America*. Norman: University of Oklahoma Press, 1992.

Higonnet, Patrice. *Paris: Capital of the World*. Cambridge: Harvard University Press, 2009.

Holloway, Thomas H. *A Companion to Latin American History*. Hoboken, NJ: Wiley-Blackwell, 2008.

Howe, Daniel Walker. *What Hath God Wrought: The Transformation of America, 1815–1848*. Oxford History of the United States. Oxford: Oxford University Press, 2009.

Ibarguren, Carlos. *Manuelita Rosas*. Buenos Aires: Librería y Editorial La Facultad de Juan Roldán, 1933.

———. *Rosas: Su vida, su drama, su tiempo*. 16th ed. Buenos Aires: Ediciones Theoria, 1972.

Jeanmaire, Federico. *Montevideo*. Barcelona: Seix Barral, 2009.

Johnson, John J. *A Hemisphere Apart: Foundations of United States Foreign Policy toward Latin America*. Baltimore: Johns Hopkins University Press, 1990.

Johnson, Lyman. *Workshop of Revolution: Plebian Buenos Aires and the Atlantic World, 1776–1810*. Durham, NC: Duke University Press, 2011.

Johnson, Lyman, and Sonia Lipsett Rivera, eds. *The Faces of Honor: Sex, Shame, and Violence in Colonial Latin America*. Albuquerque: University of New Mexico Press, 1998.

Jones, Kristine. "Calfucurá and Namuncurá: Nation Builders of the Pampas." In

The Human Tradition in Latin America: The Nineteenth Century, edited by Judith Ewell and William Beezley. Wilmington, NC: S&R Books, 1989.

Kale, Steven. *French Salons: High Society and Political Sociability from the Old Regime to the Revolution of 1848*. Baltimore: The Johns Hopkins University Press, 2004.

Knight, Alan. "Britain and Latin America." In *Oxford History of the British Empire*. Vol. 3, *The Nineteenth Century*. Oxford: Oxford University Press, 1999.

Langley, Lester D. *The Americas in the Age of Revolution, 1750–1850*. New Haven, CT: Yale University Press, 1996.

Lavrin, Asunción, ed. *Sexuality and Marriage in Colonial Latin America*. Lincoln: University of Nebraska Press, 1989.

———. *Women, Feminism and Social Change in Argentina, Chile, and Uruguay, 1890–1940*. Lincoln: University of Nebraska Press, 1995.

Levene, Ricardo. *Historia de la nación Argentina: Colonización y organización de hispano América. Adelantados y gobernadores del Río de la Plata*. Buenos Aires: Editorial el Ateneo, 1939.

———. *Lecturas históricas argentinas*. Vol. 2. Buenos Aires: Editorial de Belgrano, 1978.

López, Vicente Fidel. *Historia de República Argentina: Su origen, su revolución, y su desarrollo político*. Vol. 5. Buenos Aires: Imprenta de Mayo, 1886.

Lynch, John. *Argentine Caudillo: Juan Manuel de Rosas*. Wilmington, DE: Scholarly Resources, 2001.

———. *Argentine Dictator*. Oxford: Clarendon Press, 1982.

———. *Caudillos in Spanish America*. Oxford: Clarendon Press, 1992.

———. *San Martín: Argentine Soldier, American Hero*. New Haven, CT: Yale University Press, 2009.

———. *Simón Bolívar: A Life*. New Haven, CT: Yale University Press. 2006.

———. *The Spanish American Revolutions, 1808–1826*. 2nd ed. New York: Norton, 1986.

Mansilla, Lucio V. *Rozas: Ensayo histórico-psicológico*. Nabu Press, 2012.

Mayo, Carlos. "Landed But Not Powerful: The Colonial Estancieros of Buenos Aires (1750–1810)." *The Hispanic American Historical Review* 71, no. 4 (1991): 761–79.

———. *Porque la quiero tanto: Historia del amor en la sociedad rioplatense (1750–1860)*. Buenos Aires: Editorial Biblos, 2004.

McCullough, David. *The Greater Journey: Americans in Paris*. New York: Simon & Schuster, 2012.

Meyer Arana, Alberto. *Las primeras trece*. Buenos Aires: Imprenta de Gerónimo Pesce, 1923.

Myers, Jorge. "Identidades porteñas. El discurso ilustrado en torno a la nación y el rol de la prensa: *El Argos de Buenos Aires*, 1821–1825." In *Construcciones impresas: Panfletos, diarios y revistas en la formación de los estados nacionales en América Latina, 1820–1920*, edited by Paula Alonso, 39–63. Buenos Aires: Fondo de Cultura Económica, 2004.

———. *Orden y virtud: El discurso republicano en el régimen rosista*. Buenos Aires: Universidad Nacional de Quilmes, 1995.

———. "Una revolución de costumbres: Las formas de sociabilidad de la elite porteña, 1800–1860." In *Historia de la vida privada en la Argentina: País antiguo. De la colonia a 1870*, edited by Fernando Devoto and Marta Madero, 110–145. Buenos Aires: Taurus, 1999.

———. "La revolución en las ideas: La generación romántica de 1837 en la cultura y en la política argentinas." In *Revolución, República, Confederación (1806–1852)*, vol. 3 of *Nueva Historia Argentina*, edited by Noemí Goldman, 381–445. Buenos Aires: Editorial Sudamericana, 1998.

Müller, Roberto. *Notes from Burgess Farm: Vida de Rosas en el destierro*. Buenos Aires: Olmo Ediciones, 2010.

Nalle, Sara Tilgham. *Mad for God: Bartolomé Sánchez, the Secret Messiah of Cardenete*. Charlottesville: University Press of Virginia, 2001.

Obligado, Pastor. *Tradiciones argentinas*. Barcelona: Montaner y Simón Editores, 1903.

O'Donnell, Pacho. *Juan Manuel de Rosas: El maldito de la historia oficial*. Buenos Aires: Planeta, 2001.

Palermo, Miguel Ángel. "La compleja integración hispano-indígena del sur argentino y chileno durante el período colonial." *América Indígena* (Mexico) 51, no. 1 (1991).

Parker, Geoffrey. *Phillip II*. Chicago: Open Court, 2002.

Partnoy, Alicia. *The Little School: Tales of Disappearance and Survival*. Minneapolis: Cleis Press, 1998.

Pasquali, Patricia. *Juan Lavalle: Un guerrero en tiempos de revolución y dictadura*. Buenos Aires: Planeta, 1996.

———. *San Martín, confidencial: Correspondencia personal del Libertador con su amigo Tomás Guido (1816–1849)*. Buenos Aires: Planeta, 2000.

Peterson, Harold F. *Argentina and the United States*. New York: State University of New York, 1964.

Piccato, Pablo. "Public Sphere in Latin America: A Map of the Historiography." *Social History* 35 (2010), 165–92.

Piccirilli, Ricardo. *Juan Thompson: Su forja, su templo, su cuño*. Buenos Aires: Ediciones Peuser, 1949.

———. *Rivadavia*. Buenos Aires: Ediciones Peuser, 1952.

———. *Rivadavia y su tiempo*. Vol. 2. Buenos Aires: Ediciones Peuser, 1961.

Polasky, Janet. *Revolutions without Borders: The Call to Liberty in the Atlantic World*. New Haven, CT: Yale University Press, 2016.

Porro Girardi, Nelly Raquel. "Los juicios de disenso en el Río de la Plata. Nuevos aportes sobre la aplicación de la pragmática de hijos de familia." In vol. 5 of *Anuario Histórico Jurídico Ecuatoriano*. Quito, Ecuador: Corporación de Estudios y Publicaciones, 1980.

Pradere, Juan A. *Juan Manuel de Rosas: Su iconografía*. Buenos Aires: J. Mendesky & Son, 1914.

Prado, Fabricio. *A Colônia do Sacramento: O extremo sul da América portuguesa no século XVIII*. Porto Alegre, Brazil: Fumproarte, 2009.

———. *Edge of Empire: Atlantic Networks and Revolution in Bourbon Río de la Plata*. Oakland: University of California Press, 2015.

Premo, Bianca. *Children of the Father King: Youth, Authority, and Legal Minority in Colonial Lima*. Chapel Hill: University of North Carolina Press, 2005.

———. *The Enlightenment on Trial: Ordinary Litigants and Colonialism in the Spanish Empire*. New York: Oxford University Press, 2017.

Quesada, Ernesto. *La época de Rosas, su verdadero carácter histórico*. Buenos Aires, 1898.

Racine, Karen. *Francisco de Miranda: A Trans-Atlantic Life in the Age of Revolution*. Wilmington, DE: Scholarly Resources, 2002.

Ratto, Silvia. "Allá lejos y hace tiempo: El fuerte de Carmen de Patagones en la primera mitad del siglo XIX." *Revista Quinta del Sol* 12 (2008): 45–72.

———. "Caciques, autoridades fronterizas y lenguaraces: Intermediarios culturales e interlocutores válidos en Buenos Aires (primera mitad del siglo XIX)." *Mundo Agrario* 5, no. 10 (2005).

Rípodas Ardanaz, Daisy. *Matrimonio en Indias: Realidad social y regulación jurídica*. Buenos Aires: Fundación para la Educación, la Ciencia, y la Cultura, 1977.

Robertson, William Spence. *France and Latin-American Independence*. New York: Octagon Books, 1967.

Rock, David. *Argentina*. Oakland: University of California Press, 1985.

Root, Regina A. *Couture and Consensus: Fashion and Politics in Postcolonial Argentina*. Minneapolis: University of Minnesota Press, 2010.

Sáenz Quesada, María. *La Argentina: Historia del país y su gente*. Vol. 1. Buenos Aires: Editorial Sudamericanas, 2001.

———. *Mariquita Sánchez: Vida política y sentimental*. Buenos Aires: Editorial Sudamericana, 1995.

———. *Mujeres de Rosas*. Buenos Aires: Planeta, 2005.

Saldías, Adolfo. *Historia de la Confederación Argentina: Rozas y su época*. 4 vols. Buenos Aires: Editorial Universitaria, 1968.

Salvatore, Ricardo. "Expresiones Federales: Formas Políticas del Federalismo Rosista." In *Caudillismos rioplatenses: Nuevas miradas a un viejo problema*, edited by Noemí Goldman and Ricardo Salvatore, 189-222. Buenos Aires: Eudeba, 1998.

———. "Integral Outsiders: Afro-Argentines in the Era of Juan Manuel de Rosas and Beyond." In *Beyond Slavery: The Multilayered Legacy of Africans in Latin America*, edited by Darien J. Davis, 57-80. Lanham, Maryland: Roman and Littlefield, 2007.

———. *Wandering Paysanos: State Order and Subaltern Experience in Buenos Aires during the Rosas Era*. Durham, NC: University Press, 2003.

Sanders, James. *The Vanguard of the Atlantic World: Creating Modernity, Nation, and Democracy in Nineteenth-Century Latin America*. Durham, NC: Duke University Press, 2014.

Sarreal, Julia. *The Guaraní and Their Missions: A Socioeconomic History.* Stanford: Stanford University Press, 2014.

Scobie, James. *Buenos Aires: From Plaza to Suburb, 1870–1910.* New York: Oxford University Press, 1974.

Seed, Patricia. *To Love, Honor, and Obey in Colonial Mexico: Conflicts over Marriage Choice, 1574–1821.* Stanford: Stanford University Press, 1988.

Segreti, Carlos S. A. *Bernardino Rivadavia: Hombre de Buenos Aires, ciudadano argentino—Biografía.* Madrid: Planeta, 2000.

———. "Desacuerdos y enfrentamientos políticos (1810–1828)." In vol. 4 of *Nueva historia argentina,* 349–78. Buenos Aires: Planeta, 2000.

Segreti, Carlos S. A., Ana Inés Ferreyra, and Beatriz Moreira. "La hegemonía de Rosas: Orden y enfrentamientos políticos (1829–1852)." In Academica Nacional de la Historia, vol. 4 of *Nueva historia de la nación argentina,* 379–426. Buenos Aires: Planeta, 2000.

Shumway, Jeffrey M. "'A veces saber olvidar es también tener memoria': La repatriación de Juan Manuel de Rosas, el Menemismo, y las heridas de la memoria argentina." In *Ayer, hoy y mañana son contemporáneos: Tradiciones, leyes y proyectos en América Latina,* edited by Osvaldo Barreneche and Andrés Bisso, 93–132. La Plata: Editorial Universidad Nacional de La Plata, 2010.

———. *The Case of the Ugly Suitor and Other Histories of Love, Gender, and Nation in Buenos Aires.* Lincoln: University of Nebraska Press, 2005.

———. "The Purity of My Blood Cannot Put Food on My Table: Attitudes towards Interracial Marriage in Nineteenth-Century Buenos Aires." *Americas* 58, no. 1 (October 2001): 201–20.

———. "Sometimes Knowing How to Forget Is Also Having Memory." In *Death, Dismemberment, and Memory: Body Politics in Latin America,* edited by Lyman Johnson, 105–140. Albuquerque: University of New Mexico Press, 2004.

Shumway, Nicolas. *The Invention of Argentina.* Oakland: University of California Press, 1991.

Slatta, Richard. *Cowboys of the Americas.* New Haven, CT: Yale University Press, 1990.

———. *Gauchos and the Vanishing Frontier.* Lincoln: University of Nebraska Press, 1992.

Socolow, Susan M. "Acceptable Partners: Marriage Choice in Colonial Argentina, 1778–1810." In *Sexuality and Marriage in Colonial Latin America,* edited by Asunció Lavrin, 209–46. Lincoln: University of Nebraska Press, 1992.

———. *The Merchants of Buenos Aires, 1778–1810: Family and Commerce.* New York: Cambridge University Press, 1986.

———. "Spanish Captives in Indian Societies: Cultural Contact along the Argentine Frontier, 1600–1835." *Hispanic American Historical Review* 72, no. 1 (February 1992): 73–99.

———. *The Women of Colonial Latin America.* New York: Cambridge University Press, 2000.

Soriano, Cristina. *Tides of Revolution: Information, Insurgencies, and the Crisis of Colonial Rule in Venezuela*. Albuquerque: University of New Mexico Press, 2018.

Stevens, Donald Fithian. *Based on a True Story: Latin American History at the Movies*. Wilmington, DE: SR Books, 1997.

Street, John. *Artigas and the Emancipation of Uruguay*. Cambridge: Cambridge University Press, 1959.

Szuchman, Mark D. *Order, Family, and Community in Buenos Aires, 1810–1860*. Stanford: Stanford University Press, 1988.

Szurmuk, Mónica. *Women in Argentina: Early Travel Narratives*. Gainesville: University Press of Florida, 2000.

Taylor, Alan. *The Civil War of 1812: American Citizens, British Subjects, Irish Rebels, and Indian Allies*. New York: Random House, 2010.

Troisi Melean, Jorge. *Socios incómodos: Los franciscanos de Córdoba en una era de transformaciones (1767–1829)*. Rosario: Prohistoria, 2016.

Tueller, James B. *Good and Faithful Christians: Moriscos and Catholicism in Early Modern Spain*. Louisiana: University Press of the South, 2002.

Uribe-Uran, Victor M. "The Birth of a Public Sphere in Latin America during the Age of Revolution." *Comparative Studies in Society and History* 42, no. 2 (April 2000), 425–57.

Vera, Eugenia Roldán. *The British Book Trade and Spanish Independence*. Burlington, VT: Ashgate Publishing Limited, 2003.

Vertanessian, Carlos. *Juan Manuel de Rosas: El retrato imposible; Imagen y poder en el Río de la Plata*. Ediciones Reflejos del Plata. Buenos Aires: Academia Nacional de Bellas Artes, 2018.

Villanueva, Amaro. *El mate: Arte de Cebar*. Buenos Aires: Fabril Editora, 1960.

Weil, Patrick. *How to Be French: Nationality in the Making since 1789*. Translated by Catherine Porter. Durham, NC: Duke University Press, 2008.

Weinberg, Felix. *Esteban Echeverría: Ideólogo de la segunda revolución*. Buenos Aires: Aguilar, Altea, Taurus, Alfaguara, 2006.

Whigham, Thomas. *The Politics of River Trade: Tradition and Development in the Upper Plata, 1780–1870*. Albuquerque: University of New Mexico Press, 1991.

White, Ashli. *Encountering Revolution: Haiti and the Making of the Early Republic*. Baltimore, MD: Johns Hopkins University Press, 2010.

Wilentz, Sean. *The Rise of American Democracy: Jefferson to Lincoln*. New York: Norton, 2005.

Zavalía Lagos, Jorge A. *Mariquita Sánchez y su tiempo*. Buenos Aires: Plus Ultra, 1986.

INDEX

Page numbers in *italic* text indicate illustrations.

Ackermann, Rudolph, 127

African-descended peoples: and associations, 161; in Echeverría's "The Slaughterhouse," 212–14; in English invasions, 63–65; in militias, 65; roles debated in emerging nation, 84; roles in society, 10–11, 21–22

Age of Revolution, 2

Alberdi, Juan Bautista, 185, 214–15; and Constitution of 1853, 235–36; on Mariquita and Rosas, 227; in Paris, 220; shifting views of Rosas in England, 243–45; visits with Rosas in England, 240

Alfonsín, Raúl, 259–60

Algeria, 191, 194

Anchorena family, 31, 146

Anchorena, Manuel de, 258, 259, 261

Anchorena, Nicoás de, 161

Anchorena, Tomás de, 94, 146, 199

Andes, 12, 14, 79, 87, 101, 110, 222

Angelis, Pedro de, 170

Arana, Felipe, 146, 199, 202, 225–26

Argentina: Bolívar commenting on, 148; conquest and colonization, 9–12; constitutions, 235–36; dictatorship of 1976, 259–60; economic policy, 172–73; foreign interest in, 5, 8, 12–13; foreign intervention in, 189–93, 201–10; gradual and troubled emergence of, 8–9; nation of, 1, 2; 267; treaties, 105, 130, 137, 142, 199; and USA, 171–72; unification of, 236; women and, 118. *See also* constitutions; Indians

Artigas, José Gervasio: and May Revolution, 81; opposition to Buenos Aires, 93–94, 104; opposition to 1819 constitution, 104; progressive social reforms, 94

Astrada, Berón de: governor of Corrientes, 191

Asunción, Paraguay, 10

Atlantic World, 2, 32–33, 69, 84, 188

authoritarianism, 4

Balcarce, Juan Ramón (governor), 159, 160

Baltimore, Maryland: center of privateering in Americas, 97–98; exile of Manuel Dorrego, 136

Balzac, Honoré, 220

Banda Oriental (Eastern Shore), 267; as contested ground, 12; relations with Buenos Aires, 81; war between Argentina and Brazil, 131. *See also* Uruguay

Batticuore, Graciela, 255

Battle of Caseros, 230–31, 232–33

Battle of Cepeda, 105

Battle of Márquez Bridge, 141

Battle of San Lorenzo, 87

Battle of San Nicolás, 109

gauchos, 268; and Charles Darwin, 155,
    157–58; lifestyle, 22, 29–30; political/
    military role, 81, 105, 141; and Rosas,
    29–30, 108, 147, 154, 159, 172, 173, 242,
    253, 258, 262; in written word, 170,
    213. See also *Martín Fierro*
gender/gender roles, 8, 26, 27, 47, 179–
    80. *See also* patriarchy; women
Generation of 1837, 185–88. *See also*
    Young Argentine Generation
Gillespie, Alexander: on business
    potential in Buenos Aires, 66–67;
    and English invasions, 56–57, 61; on
    tertulias/salons of Buenos Aires, 72
Gómez, Josefa (Pepita), 238, 240, 245,
    279n24, 282n45
Great Britain. *See* England
Greece/Greek, 75, 240
Guarani Indians, 12
Guido, Tomás: friendship with
    Mariquita, 181, 216, 233; and San
    Martín, 140, 171
Gutiérrez, Juan María, 216, 217, 236
Gutiérrez, Ladislao, 226–27

Haiti, 55. *See also* Saint-Domingue
Hawai'i, 98
Hernández, José, 258, 277n43, 300n40
Holy Alliance: opposition to Hispanic
    American revolutions, 100–102
honor, 44
Howden, Lord, 207
Hugo, Victor, 7, 214–15, 220

Iberia/Iberian, 18, 19, 36, 75, 268
imperialism, 191–92, 203, 207
Indarte, José Rivera, 216, 222
independence: challenges to, 95–99;
    declaration of, 94–95; missions
    to secure recognition of, 96–99;
    recognition of, 98 (Hawai'i), 123
    (USA). *See also* Tucumán Congress

Indians, 30; Darwin's views of, 155–57;
    defending homelands, 15, 17, 132; in
    English invasions, 58, 63; friendly
    Indians, 14; frontier negotiations;
    language, 30; negotiations with
    Rosas, 131–32; political/military
    role, 105, 109, 110, 111–12, 130–32, 141;
    prejudice against, 37; reforms geared
    toward, 90, 94; and Rozas family,
    28–30; taking captives, 17–18, 224;
    territory, 79
indigenous groups. *See* Indians
Iriarte, Tomás de, 158

Jackson, Andrew, 3, 148
Jacobin, 32, 33, 82

Kamehameha I of Hawai'i, 98
Key, Astley Cooper, 204–5
Kirchner, Cristina Fernández de, 262–63

La Gaceta Mercantil, 202
La Gazeta de Buenos Ayres, 79, 80, 81, 82,
    83, 119
La Joven Generación Argentina, 187
Lamadrid, Gregorio, 109
La Moda, 186–87
Lancaster Method, 127
La Nación, 261, 298–99n70
Lavalle, Juan: Bolívar's views on, 148;
    coup versus Dorrego, 137–39; death,
    199–200; friendship with Rozas
    family, 137; invasion of Argentina,
    196, 199; Mariquita's view of,
    194–95
Lavalle, María González de, 25–26
Lezica, Florencia Thompson de. *See*
    Thompson, Florencia
Liniers, Santiago: and English
    invasions, 57, 61–63; execution, 81;
    and opposition to May Revolution,
    80–81; as viceroy, 61

loans: Baring Brothers loan, 123, 171
López, Estanislao: invasion of Buenos
    Aires, 105; opposition to 1819 consti-
    tution, 105–6; response to Dorrego
    execution, 139–40; relations with
    Rosas, 151
López de Osornio, Agustina: charity
    work, 27; early life, 18; education of
    children, 30–31; opposition to Juan
    Manuel's marriage, 42–44; person-
    ality, 26–29; relations with husband
    León, 26–29; relations with Lavalle
    family, 25–26, 137; in uprising of
    1829, 142
López de Osornio, Clemente, 15, 17
López, Vicente Fidel: on Mariquita's
    salon, 68, 73
López y Planes, Vicente: national
    anthem, 87–88, 90–91; poet in
    English invasions, 63–64
Lynch, John, 7

Mackau-Arana Treaty, 199
Macri, Mauricio, 263
Malvinas Islands/Falkland Islands, 144,
    171–72, 206, 210, 259, 262
Mansilla, Lucio, Jr., 134; and French in-
    fluence, 221; Mariquita's concern for,
    233; on Mariquita's influence, 227; on
    Rivadavia, 134; and Rosas, 221; and
    Rozas family, 25–26, 137
Mansilla, Lucio, sr., 202
Mapuche tribe: 14
Mármol, José: and anti-Rosas literature,
    222; and Generation of 1837, 183,
    187; on Manuelita, 222; prophecy of
    Rosas's remains, 252, 261; Rivadavia's
    repatriation, 246
marriage: and identity, 179–80; and legal
    rights, 249–50; Mariquita critiques
    of colonial practice of, 46; newspaper
    commentary, 47–48

marriage conflict cases: Mariquita and
    Martín Thompson, 39–42
Martín Fierro, 223, 258
masculinity, 3, 64; and dueling, 29–30,
    44, 277n43. *See also* gender
mate. *See* yerba mate
May Revolution: antecedents to, 74–76;
    challenges to, 79–81; donations to, 80;
    later development of, 94; Mariquita
    a symbol of, 212; May Revolution,
    77–78; spreading ideas of, 78–79; and
    relations with other provinces, 79–81
Maza, Manuel and Ramón, 195–96
Mazorca, 160–62, 196
Mendeville, Carlos, 121, 189
Mendeville, Enrique, 181, 189, 223, 230
    (Mariquita's grandson), 237
Mendeville, Jean Baptiste Washington:
    and crisis of 1829, 138, 142–44; and
    Mariquita, 120–21, 219; as French
    consul, 130, 135; relations with Rosas,
    143–44
Mendeville, Julio, 120, 121, 220, 250
Mendoza, Pedro de, 9
Menem, Carlos Saúl: curing and healing
    wounds of nation, 260; as president
    of Argentina, 253–54; repatriation
    of Rosas, 253, 253–54; speeches of
    repatriation, 261–62
Mercurio, 200
Mexican-American War, 5, 202–3
Mexico: and French intervention, 191;
    and Miguel Hidalgo revolt, 78; and
    Spanish intervention, 147; and USA,
    202–3
military dictatorship of 1976, 259
military uprisings of 1980s, 259
Miranda, Francisco de, 51, 74
Mitre, Bartolomé, 236, 246, 256
monarchism: debated in May Revolu-
    tion, 79, 93; Jeremy Bentham's views
    on, 101; San Martín's views on, 86–87

monopoly system, 12

Monroe Doctrine, 205–6

Monteagudo, Bernardo: in Mariquita's salon, 73; radical ideas in May Revolution,

Montesquieu, Baron de, 134; Rivadavia on, 122

Montevideo, Uruguay, 10, 33, 38, 52, 57, 61, 63, 80, 81, 93, 110, 137, 140, 143, 145, 151; 194; the "new Troy," 188. *See also* Sánchez, María (Mariquita); Montevideo

Monvoisin, Raymond Auguste Quinsac, *207, 209*

Moreno, Mariano: and English invasions, 54–55; and factions in May Revolution, 79; and free trade, 74; as secretary of May Revolution junta, 78–79; and views on the press, 79

moreno (racial term): use of term, 10; in English invasions, 63

Muera Rosas, 222

mulatto/*mulato*: and Artigas's reforms, 94; and English invasions, 65; and gauchos, 29; prejudice against, 37, 84, 214; roles in society, 24–25; relations with Rosas, 159, 174; servants in Mariquita's family, 20; servants in Rozas family, 20, 27, 28; in viceroyalty, 24–25; use of term, 10

Museo Histórico Nacional, 255

Napoleon. *See* Bonaparte, Napoleon

Napoleonic Code, 180

national anthem, 87–89, 90–91

nationalists, 257–59, 262

Nariño, Antonio, 70–71

newspapers: freedom of the press, 82; pro-Rosas, 170; and rise of Rosas, 159; role in in May Revolution, 79; shaping public opinion, 81, 140, 170; and social commentary in late-

colonial period, 46–48; and Urquiza, 237

Obligado, Pastor, 217, 254–55

O'Gorman, Camila, 226–27; movie about, 260

Oribe, Manuel, 188, 232

Pampas (plains), 270; abundance, 12, 30, 57, 66, 100, 206; Darwin and, 155, 156, 158; indigenous groups, 14, 18, 28, 30; interpretations of, 222; and Rosas, 29, 109, 136, 154; vastness, 109

Pampa tribe, 131; Rosas and language, 277n44

Panguitruz. *See* Rosas, Mariano

Paraguay: European settlement in Asunción; opposition to Buenos Aires, 81; war with Argentina, Uruguay, and Brazil, 250

Paraná: capital of country, 236

Paraná River, 9, 172, 201, 202, 206, 210, 231, 270

pardos: in English invasions, 63; in independence debate, 84; prejudice against, 128; use of term, 10

Paris. *See* France; Sánchez, María (Mariquita), France

Parish, Woodbine, 67

Pastry War, 191–92

patriarchy: definition, 37–38, 278n6; in marriage choice, 36–36; private and state patriarchy, 180; in Rozas family, 26–29

Payssac, Marquis de, 179–81

Paz, General José María: Rosas on Paz's memoirs, 240–41; Unitarian leader, 149, 151

Pellegrini, Carlos Enrique, 27

peninsular Spaniards, 19

Pérez Rosales, Vicente: and Mariquita, 241; on Rosas's legacy, 257; visit to Rosas in exile, 242–43

reform; on foreign intervention, 207–
10; Mariquita Sánchez, 185, 247–48;
Rivadavia's repatriation, 246

slavery: 14, 32, 55, 62–63; 107; free womb
law, 90

slaves: in English invasions, 61–62; in
Mariquita's home, 20; occupations in
Buenos Aires, 21–22; in Rozas home,
16, 25, 28; seeking recompense for
armed service, 64–65

slave trade, 20, 81, 174–75, 193

Smith, Adam, 74

smuggling, 12, 53

Sobremonte, Marquis de: and English
invasions, 53–54, 57, 61; as judge in
Mariquita and Martín's disenso case;
mocked by poets, 65

social classes: newspapers critique
mixing of, 47–48; in viceroyalty, 24

Sociedad de Beneficendia (Society of
Benificence): and education, 126–27;
founding, 118; 125–26; and race, 127–
28, 246–47; relations with Rosas, 149

Sociedad Popular Restauradora, 160–62

Solís, Juan de, 9

Southampton, England, 235, 238

Spain, 147; economic system in New
World, 12; Napoleon's invasion of,
75–76; political problems in empire,
74–75; reconquest versus Moors,
36–37; regionalism in, 10, 18. *See also*
Ferdinand VII

Stael, Germaine de (Madame de): as
inspiration for Mariquita, 3, 68, 70,
71–72, 124, 216–17

Subercaseaux, Pedro, *88, 254–55*

Talleyrand, 216–17

Telégrafo Mercantil, 46–48

Terrero, Máximo, 182, 224, 238, 239

The Terror, 198–99

tertulias. *See* salons

Thompson, Albina, 42, 185

Thompson, Clementina, 42, 43, 189

Thompson, Florencia (de Lezica), 200,
218, 228, 234

Thompson, Juan, 121, 185; and English
imperialism, 193–94

Thompson, Magdalena, 42, 43

Thompson, Martín: courtship with
Mariquita, 34, 37; diplomatic mission
to USA, 5, 92–93, 96–99; family
history, 35–36; marriage conflict case,
39–42; and May Revolution, 77;
return home, 119–20

Thompson, William (Guillermo), 35–36

Treaty of Madrid, 13

Treaty of Montevideo, 137

Treaty of Peace and Navigation
(Argentina and Great Britain), 130,
142

Treaty of Pilar, 105

Treaty of the Holy Alliance, 100–101

Trillo, Magdalena, 17, 20; marriage to
Cecilio Sánchez, 19; opposition to
Mariquita's marriage, 32, 35, 39–42

Tucumán Conference of 1816: debates
over type of government, 99–100;
proceedings, 94; Unitarian and
Federalist factions emerge, 100

unitarianism/unitarian, 104, 105, 113, 133,
149, 150–51, 166; emerge in Tucumán
conference debate, 100; overthrow
of Dorrego, 137–39; targeting of, 150,
161, 198–99, 212–14; in uprising of
1828–1829, 141–45

United States of America, 5; challenges
to its Independence, 99–100; and
Hispanic American rebellions, 96–
98, 101; imperialism, 202–3; as model
for independence debates in Argentina, 93–94; relations with Argentina,
171; relations with Rosas, 172